HUMAN RIGHTS IN A TIME OF POPULISM

The electoral successes of right-wing populists since 2016 have unsettled world politics. The spread of populism poses dangers for human rights within each country, and also threatens the international system for protecting human rights. *Human Rights in a Time of Populism* examines causes, consequences, and responses to populism in a global context from a human rights perspective. It combines legal analysis with insights from political science, international relations, and political philosophy. Authors make practical recommendations on how the human rights challenges caused by populism should be confronted. This book, with its global scope, international human rights framing, and inclusion of leading experts, will be of great interest to human rights lawyers, political scientists, international relations scholars, actors in the human rights system, and general readers concerned by recent developments.

GERALD L. NEUMAN is the J. Sinclair Armstrong Professor of International, Foreign, and Comparative Law and the Co-Director of the Human Rights Program at Harvard Law School. He teaches human rights, U.S. constitutional law, and immigration and nationality law. From 2011 to 2014, he was a member of the U.N. Human Rights Committee, the treaty body that monitors compliance with the International Covenant on Civil and Political Rights. Among others, he is the author of *Strangers to the Constitution: Immigrants, Borders and Fundamental Law* (1996) and co-editor of *Human Rights, Democracy, and Legitimacy in a World of Disorder* (2018).

Human Rights in a Time of Populism

CHALLENGES AND RESPONSES

Edited by

GERALD L. NEUMAN
Harvard Law School

CAMBRIDGE
UNIVERSITY PRESS

University Printing House, Cambridge CB2 8BS, United Kingdom

One Liberty Plaza, 20th Floor, New York, NY 10006, USA

477 Williamstown Road, Port Melbourne, VIC 3207, Australia

314–321, 3rd Floor, Plot 3, Splendor Forum, Jasola District Centre, New Delhi – 110025, India

79 Anson Road, #06–04/06, Singapore 079906

Cambridge University Press is part of the University of Cambridge.

It furthers the University's mission by disseminating knowledge in the pursuit of education, learning, and research at the highest international levels of excellence.

www.cambridge.org
Information on this title: www.cambridge.org/9781108485494
DOI: 10.1017/9781108751551

First published 2020

Printed in the United Kingdom by TJ International Ltd, Padstow Cornwall

A catalogue record for this publication is available from the British Library.

ISBN 978-1-108-48549-4 Hardback

Contents

Contributors

Helena Alviar García is Professor at Sciences-Po, Paris and was formerly professor and dean of the law school at the Universidad de Los Andes. She is an expert on feminist approaches to law and on the relationship between law and development, and has authored the book *Derecho, Desarrollo y Feminismo En América Latina: Propuesta Para Un Analisis Distributivo* (2008). In addition to her academic work, she is a founding member of Dejusticia, a Colombia-based research and advocacy organization dedicated to the strengthening of the rule of law and the promotion of social justice and human rights in Colombia and the Global South.

Laurence R. Helfer is the Harry R. Chadwick, Sr. Professor of Law at Duke University, the co-director of the Center for International and Comparative Law, and a senior fellow with Duke's Kenan Institute for Ethics. He also serves as a permanent visiting professor at the iCourts: Center of Excellence for International Courts at the University of Copenhagen, which awarded him an honorary doctorate in 2014. He has authored numerous publications, including, most recently, *Transplanting International Courts: The Law and Politics of the Andean Tribunal of Justice* (2017).

Richard Javad Heydarian is a Manila-based academic, having taught at De La Salle University and Ateneo De Manila University as a political science assistant professor, and is incoming research fellow at the National Chengchi University, Taiwan. He is currently a columnist for the *Philippine Daily Inquirer*, and a regular contributor to Center for Strategic and International Studies (CSIS) and Council on Foreign Relations (CFR), and has written for leading global publications. His latest book is *The Rise of Duterte: A Populist Revolt Against Elite Democracy* (2018).

Yee Mon Htun is a clinical instructor at the International Human Rights Clinic at Harvard Law School. Before joining the International Human Rights Clinic, she was the director of the Myanmar Program for Justice Trust. She was born in

Myanmar and left the country after the pro-democratic uprising in 1988, when she immigrated to Canada as a government-sponsored refugee. She is the recipient of the Robert A. Samek Award for excellence in General Jurisprudence and the David M. Jones Memorial Prize at Dalhousie University Faculty of Law.

Douglas A. Johnson is a lecturer in public policy and the former director of the Carr Center for Human Rights at Harvard Kennedy School. He has been a committed advocate of human rights since the 1970s, when he chaired the Infant Formula Action Coalition (INFACT), which launched a boycott against Nestlé to force it to change its marketing practices. Johnson has served as a consultant to human rights organizations in Latin America and as a consultant to UNICEF and the World Health Organization. He was also the first executive director of the Center for Victims of Torture from 1988 to 2012.

Daniel Levine-Spound received his J.D. degree in 2019 from Harvard Law School, where his research has focused on the intersections of international human rights law, international humanitarian law, and the protection of civilians in armed conflict. Prior to law school, he worked at the Euro-Mediterranean Human Rights Network and the Cairo Institute for Human Rights Studies in Tunis. Levine-Spound graduated from Brown University with honors in Comparative Literature in 2012. He recently coauthored a book, *A History of the Criminalization of Homosexuality in Tunisia* (2019), tracing the history and contemporary application of the Tunisian sodomy law.

Gerald L. Neuman is the J. Sinclair Armstrong Professor of International, Foreign, and Comparative Law and the co-director of the Human Rights Program at Harvard Law School. From 2011 to 2014, he was a member of the U.N. Human Rights Committee, the treaty body that monitors compliance with the International Covenant on Civil and Political Rights.

Jamie O'Connell is Lecturer in Residence at Stanford Law School. He teaches and writes on political and legal development, and has worked on human rights and development in more than a dozen countries in Africa, the Americas, Asia, and Europe, under the auspices of the United Nations, local and international nongovernmental organizations, and academic institutions. He is founding president of International Professional Partnerships for Sierra Leone, a nongovernmental organization that works with the government of Sierra Leone to enhance the performance of its agencies and civil servants.

Stephen Pomper served on the staff of the National Security Council as special assistant to President Obama and senior director for Multilateral Affairs and Human Rights. Prior to joining the staff of the National Security Council, he was the assistant legal adviser for Political-Military Affairs at the Department of State.

Wojciech Sadurski is the Challis Professor in Jurisprudence at the University of Sydney Law School, and a professor at the University of Warsaw, Centre for Europe. He was previously a professor of legal theory and philosophy of law and head of the department of law at the European University Institute in Florence. He has written extensively on philosophy of law, political philosophy, and comparative constitutional law. He was elected as a fellow of the Academy of the Social Sciences in Australia in 1990, and is a member of a number of supervisory or program boards in Poland.

Jeremy Waldron is University Professor at New York University School of Law. Until 2014 he held his NYU position conjointly with his position as Chichele Professor of Social and Political Theory at the University of Oxford (All Souls College). Waldron has written and published extensively in jurisprudence and political theory. He was elected a fellow of the British Academy in 2011 and a member of the American Academy of Arts and Sciences in 1998. In 2011, he was awarded the American Philosophical Society's prestigious Phillips Prize for lifetime achievement in jurisprudence.

Preface

The twin shocks of the Brexit referendum and then Donald Trump have added greater urgency to efforts to understand the effects and trajectory of populism. Although the consequences of these events may be far-reaching in many fields, one important inquiry concerns the impact of populism on human rights and on the international system for their protection. That topic, which has attracted less attention from political scientists, provides the focus for this book.

In March 2018, I convened for the Human Rights Program at Harvard Law School a multidisciplinary conference to explore the relationship between populism and human rights. The questions posed included the nature and causes of populism; whether populism conflicts with internationally recognized human rights or represents a legitimate exercise of such rights; the challenges populism creates for protection of human rights, and how advocates and institutions can respond to these challenges; whether the human rights system has contributed unintentionally to the rise of populism by provoking backlash, and what advocates and institutions should do in the face of backlash; and whether the spread of populism points in other ways to lessons that human rights advocates and institutions should learn. The conference was designed to discuss these questions both generally and in consideration of regional and national variations around the globe.

The chapters in this volume arise from the exchanges at that conference, and provide its main fruits. Not all the participants in the conference wrote for this volume, but their analyses deepened the discussion and are gratefully acknowledged.

Chapter 1, "Populist Threats to the International Human Rights System" (by the editor), frames the discussion that follows by examining the concept of populism, which is debated among political scientists, and the negative effects that populism may produce on internationally recognized human rights. It emphasizes, as several later chapters do, an understanding of populism as a form of politics that employs an exclusionary notion of the people – the "real people," as opposed to disfavored groups that are unworthy – and that purports to rule on behalf of the "real people," whose will should not be constrained. The chapter then describes both internal and external effects of such populists' rise to power. Domestically, populist governance not only threatens the human rights of the excluded group but also poses danger for members of the majority, as leaders seek to entrench themselves in power and undermine checks. Externally, the influence of populism on foreign policy reduces support for the international human rights regime, in a manner that has become increasingly problematic as populists gain power in more countries that previously played key roles in maintaining it.

The external effect of populism is further explored in Chapter 2, specifically with regard to the crucial example of the United States. In "US Human Rights Policy and the Trump Administration," Stephen Pomper and Daniel Levine-Spound explore the unfolding effects of the Trump presidency on human rights foreign policy. Taking into account the mixed character of US foreign policy in previous decades, they consider how the populist rhetoric of "America First" was translated into concrete actions, initially under Secretary of State Rex Tillerson and then increasingly under his successor Mike Pompeo and National Security Advisor John Bolton. The relative disorganization of the new administration left room for career officers to implement a relatively traditional human rights policy in some areas where they did not conflict with strong administration priorities. The Trump administration has departed most significantly from past practice by declining to embrace the core principles on which human rights policy is based, and by openly boosting the prospects of authoritarians, not out of a sense of strategic necessity but out of preference.

Chapter 3 examines some of the internal changes in human rights practice often sought by populists, and evaluates them from a normative perspective. In "Rule-of-Law Rights and Populist Impatience," Jeremy Waldron focuses on populist hostility toward the enforcement of "rule-of-law" rights, which protect procedural values and limit the imposition of swift and strong punishment. Reaction against these rights and their interpretation by "foreign" judges has featured strongly, for example, in attacks in the United Kingdom against the European Court of Human Rights and calls to replace the European Convention with a UK Bill of Rights. Waldron argues that reaffirmation of human rights values, and the principle that criminals do not forfeit all their human rights, may not provide sufficient answers to these objections. It is important also to consider how the structure of the system can adequately protect the rights and interests of ordinary citizens. At the same time, one should resist exaggeration of the need for cultural distinctiveness in the determination of basic procedural rights.

In Chapter 4, "Populism and Human Rights in Poland," Wojciech Sadurski offers a case study of how populism, understood as a form of anti-pluralist political organization that relies on popular support, undermines democracy and human rights. He demonstrates how the electoral victories of the populist Law and Justice Party were followed by legal changes that dismantled institutional checks on government and eroded a number of individual civil and political rights, including freedom of speech and assembly. This case study tends to show that there is a dynamic built into illiberal populism that eventually renders it antithetical to democratic rules of the game.

Chapter 5 shifts to Latin America, where observers have long recognized both left-wing and right-wing forms of populism. In "The Legal Architecture of Populism: Exploring Antagonists in Venezuela and Colombia," Helena Alviar García examines populism as a method of exercising power, rather than a specific set of substantive programs. She explores the commonalities between left-populism and right-populism as illustrated by two ideologically opposing figures, Hugo Chávez in Venezuela and Álvaro Uribe in Colombia. Despite their contrasting social and economic policies, there were more similarities than differences in the legal architecture they deployed. In both cases, the preferred tools included the resort to referenda to circumvent and control the legislature, delegitimation of the opposition, and activation of mechanisms allowing the Executive to legislate by decree. These shared methods illustrate how populist leaders use tools to produce arguments of legitimacy for their selection of winners and losers in society.

In Chapter 6, "Representation, Paternalism, and Exclusion: The Divergent Impacts of the AKP's Populism on Human Rights in Turkey," Jamie O'Connell shows how Turkish politics illustrates the complex relationships among populism, democracy, and human rights. Throughout the twentieth century, an urban, secularist elite largely monopolized government power and used it to modernize society against the will of much of the population. The Justice and Development Party (AKP) has reversed this pattern since it took power in 2002. Its leader, now-President Recep Tayyip Erdoğan, is a paradigmatic populist: a charismatic leader who portrays politics as a Manichean competition between the virtuous people and a domineering elite, and his policy agenda as embodying a homogeneous popular will. The AKP has neutered the Kemalist military, bureaucracy, and judiciary. It has implemented policies favored by its once-marginalized supporters, especially observant Sunnis. These changes exemplify the inclusionary potential of populism. But Erdoğan's successive purges of internal rivals have bolstered the critique that he – like many populists – merely uses citizen supporters to legitimate his rule and policy preferences, rather than genuinely representing them. Since 2013, his government has harshly repressed real and perceived opponents, jailing tens of thousands, while portraying them as enemies of the people – another classic antidemocratic populist habit. The AKP's record in other areas, including gender and minority rights, sheds further light on the ambiguous relationships among populism, democracy, and human rights.

Chapter 7 considers the different dynamics of populism in Asia, and particularly in the Philippines. In "Penal Populism in Emerging Markets: Human Rights and Democracy in the Age of Strongmen," Richard Javad Heydarian explores the mutually constitutive relationship between the rise of "penal populism" in fledgling democracies, on the one hand, and the erosion of democratic values and respect for human rights, on the other. Heydarian contextualizes this phenomenon within the broader landscape of democratic retreat across "emerging market democracies." In these rapidly growing economies with a relatively robust democratic tradition, dissatisfaction with unresponsive democratic institutions has gone hand in hand with the resurgence of so-called Asian values, which is gradually giving birth to illiberal democracies. He argues that the rise of Filipino strongman Rodrigo Duterte reflects a systemic deadlock within Philippine democracy as well as a more widespread backlash against enlightenment values. The way forward requires structural reforms in the penal system, so as to ensure the proper dispensation of justice and to revive public support for due process and human rights.

Chapter 8 considers how populist agitation can derail democracy at the outset. In "The Populist Threat to Democracy in Myanmar," Yee Mon Htun examines the causes and effects of current populist tensions in Myanmar. Despite the election of a civilian government in 2015, the transition from military rule to human-rights-respecting democratic governance is fragile. Persistent military offensives against ethnic and religious minorities, most acutely against the Muslim Rohingya population, are supported by a populist culture of intolerance, linked to radical Buddhist organizations, that not only threatens persecuted communities but places the future of democracy in Myanmar at risk. The chapter closes by examining how the international community and human rights systems can still contribute to developing an inclusive, human-rights-based culture in Myanmar.

The last three chapters return from the examination of specific situations to general reflection on the challenges for human rights adherents posed by current developments. In contrast to the primarily negative account of populism expressed in the preceding chapters, Chapter 9 by Douglas A. Johnson, "In Defense of Democratic Populism," questions the proposition that populism is antithetical to human rights. In a constitutional democracy with checks and balances, he argues, populism is a form of popular mobilization on moral grounds, and provides an arena for countering the status quo bias. There may indeed be dangers from authoritarian populists, perhaps better described as authoritarians masquerading as populists. But it is necessary to distinguish between liberal and illiberal populists. In either case, populism offers lessons that the human rights community should learn, including the importance of social movements, the need for clear narrative that encompasses both majorities and minorities, and the use of emotion as the language of values.

Chapter 10 discusses strategies that a broad range of international human rights institutions may adopt to address, or at least withstand, the current wave of populist governments. In "Populism and International Human Rights Law Institutions: A Survival Guide," Laurence R. Helfer assesses the distinctive challenges that populism poses to international human rights law institutions. Turning from diagnosis to prescription, he then reviews a range of legal and political tools that might be deployed to address those challenges and explores their potential efficacy and risks. The chapter's final section argues that international human rights law institutions should adopt four survival strategies in a period of populism – playing a long game, circumspection in interpretation, publicity and outreach, and creating windows of opportunity for supporters to mobilize.

Chapter 11 similarly offers the editor's own conclusions on how the human rights system – in this case, monitoring bodies such as courts and treaty bodies – should deal with the dilemmas presently posed by exclusionary populism. In "Human Rights Responses to the Populist Challenge," it is inferred from the varied accounts of populist governance that one size does not fit all. Human rights monitoring bodies should not address populism as such, but should rather continue to focus on the specific human rights violations that populism leads to, and on the violations that have contributed to the rise of populism. Meanwhile, monitoring bodies should also be attentive to the criticisms that populists have directed against the international human rights system, some of which (as examples show) may be meritorious even within a human rights analysis. These recommendations would not "solve" the problem that the spread of populism creates, but they would enable monitoring bodies to contribute positively toward particular solutions.

The title of this volume refers to a "Time of Populism," not an "Age of Populism." I do not expect the current wave of populism to last an Age. May the chapters here assist in making the duration of the wave shorter, and what follows, better.

Acknowledgments

I would like to express gratitude for the help of all the colleagues who made this book, and the conference that preceded it, possible – including my friends at the Human Rights Program, and especially Emily Nagisa Keehn and Dana Walters; the ever-patient and dedicated Ellen Keng; and the participants and commenters on various chapters. Deep thanks also to Rita and Gustave Hauser for sustaining the Human Rights Program's academic projects, and to the Asia Center at Harvard University for its support of the conference. And as always, to Carol.

1

Populist Threats to the International Human Rights System

Gerald L. Neuman

I INTRODUCTION

Since 2016, world politics has been unsettled by a series of electoral successes of right-wing populist parties, leaders, and movements. The Brexit vote in the United Kingdom was followed by such events as the election of Donald Trump in the United States of America, near-wins in the Netherlands and Austria, the rapid rise of Alternativ für Deutschland, the joint rule of two populist parties in Italy, and the victory of Jair Bolsonaro in Brazil. In France, Marine Le Pen outpolled both traditional candidates and was defeated as President only by the independent candidate Emmanuel Macron.

This unexpected series of developments adds greater urgency to the study of populism and its effect on human rights, already exemplified in countries such as Hungary, Poland, Turkey, and the Philippines, and in recurrent periods of both left-wing and right-wing populism in Latin America. The growing strength of populism in established democracies that have previously provided key support to the international human rights regime poses special concern: it not only endangers human rights within those countries' own borders, but also threatens to weaken the international system for protecting human rights abroad.

This chapter frames the discussion that follows by examining the concept of populism, which is debated among political scientists. While considering a range of definitions, the chapter favors the "ideational approach," which understands populism as employing an exclusionary notion of the people – the "real people," as opposed to disfavored groups that are unworthy – and that purports to rule on behalf of the "real people," whose will should not be constrained. The chapter then sketches the negative effects that populism may produce on internationally recognized human rights, both internally and through its influence on foreign policy.

II POPULISM IN THEORY

In this chapter, I will focus on one common framing of populism employed by political scientists, the ideational approach. In Jan-Werner Müller's phrasing, populism is a "a way of perceiving the political world that sets a morally pure and fully unified ... people against elites who are deemed corrupt or in some other way morally inferior."[1] Cas Mudde has defined populism in similar terms as "an ideology that considers society to be ultimately separated into two homogenous and antagonistic groups, 'the pure people' versus 'the corrupt elite', and which argues that politics should be an expression of the volonté générale (general will) of the people."[2] These efforts to capture the features of populism differ somewhat, but they share important common features: populists are anti-pluralist; populists have an exclusionary notion of the "real people" that they contrast with morally reprehensible elites; and populists claim to speak for the will of the "real people," which should not be constrained. This conception of populism is compatible with a range of policy orientations, depending on the values it attributes to "the people" and to the despised elites. It recognizes both left-wing and right-wing populists, and others who may be harder to place on a left/right spectrum. But not everyone who criticizes an elite or invokes "the people" is a populist.

Although these authors conceptualize populism in terms of antagonism to elites, they also make clear that there may be other segments of the population that populists exclude from the real "people." Müller has explained, "Right-wing populists also typically claim to discern a symbiotic relationship between an elite that does not truly belong and marginal groups that are also distinct from the people. In the twentieth-century United States, these groups were usually liberal elites on the one hand and racial minorities on the other."[3] Mudde's application of his definition to xenophobic parties shows that their populism rejects both mainstream politicians and non-native groups that these politicians are accused of unduly favoring.[4]

The ideational approach differs from other framings of populism, for example, as an opportunistic strategy pursued by particular leaders, or as a matter of performance or political style. Some political scientists define populism as the electoral strategy by which a personalistic leader asserts a direct, unmediated relationship with the people in order to achieve or exercise power.[5] This strategic approach considers

---

[1] Jan-Werner Müller, *What Is Populism?* (Philadelphia, PA: University of Pennsylvania Press, 2016), 19–20.

[2] Cas Mudde, "Populism: An Ideational Approach," in *The Oxford Handbook of Populism*, ed. Cristóbal Rovira Kaltwasser et al. (Oxford: Oxford University Press, 2017), 29.

[3] Müller, *Populism*, 23.

[4] Cas Mudde and Cristóbal Rovira Kaltwasser, "Exclusionary vs. Inclusionary Populism: Comparing Contemporary Europe and Latin America," *Government and Opposition* 48, no. 2 (2013): 166; Mudde, "Ideational Approach," 33.

[5] Kurt Weyland, "Populism: A Political-Strategic Approach," in *Oxford Handbook of Populism*, 48–72; Steven Levitsky and James Loxton, "Populism and Competitive Authoritarianism in the Andes," *Democratization* 20, no. 1 (2013): 110.

populism as a method employed by particular leaders, not as a characteristic of parties, unlike the ideational approach, which applies to both individuals and groups. Other authors define populism as a form of rhetoric, communicating an identification with the people, through symbolically freighted vocabulary or "low" cultural style or both. The rhetorical approach treats the populist character of a speaker as a matter of degree rather than as a binary attribute; most politicians in a democracy invoke the people and perform a "low" cultural style, at least some of the time.

A school of political thinkers on the left, following Ernesto Laclau and Chantal Mouffe, has theorized populist mobilization as a discursive method necessary for constructing a "people" unified in antagonism to the elites in power in order to bring about transformational change.[6] Whether such a transformation can develop into a stable, rights-protecting democracy, however, is disputed.[7] Nadia Urbinati has argued in critiquing Laclau that it is important to distinguish between social movements employing populist rhetoric, which may contribute to democratic debate, and populist movements seeking to exercise state power, which suppress pluralism once they succeed.[8]

The ideational approach also contrasts with other uses of the term populism. Some thinkers proudly claim the populist label for a pluralistic, participatory empowerment of the full electorate, consistent with equal rights for all.[9] Other authors, especially economists, refer to a category of economic populism, generally involving redistributive, protectionist, or fiscal policies that they consider unwise.[10] There have indeed been populists in the ideational sense who favor certain economic policies of that kind, but also pluralists who strongly respect existing

---

[6] See Ernesto Laclau, *On Populist Reason* (London: Verso, 2005); Yannis Stavrakakis, "Populism and Hegemony," in *Oxford Handbook of Populism*, 535–553.

[7] Compare Chantal Mouffe, *For a Left Populism* (London: Verso, 2018) (arguing that this kind of left populism can be consistent with pluralism and that it would reinterpret but not reject the ethico-political principles of liberal democracy), with Carlos de la Torre, "What Went Wrong? Leftwing Populist Democratic Promises and Autocratic Practices," *Comparative Politics Newsletter* 26, no. 2 (2016): 40–45.

[8] Nadia Urbinati, *Democracy Disfigured: Opinion, Truth, and the People* (Cambridge, MA: Harvard University Press, 2014), 130–132.

[9] See, e.g., Chapter 9 (in this volume); Peter Mair, "Populist Democracy vs Party Democracy," in Yves Mény and Yves Surel, *Democracies and the Populist Challenge* (Houndmills, Basingstoke: Palgrave, 2002), 81–98 (arguing in favor of "populist democracy" that deemphasizes parties but respects constitutionalism); Mark Tushnet, *Taking the Constitution Away from the Courts* (Princeton, NJ: Princeton University Press, 2000); Gregory P. Magarian, "The Pragmatic Populism of Justice Stevens's Free Speech Jurisprudence," *Fordham Law Review* 74, no. 4 (2006): 2201–2240.

[10] See, e.g., Jeffrey D. Sachs, *Social Conflict and Populist Policies in Latin America*, Cambridge, MA: National Bureau of Economic Research, Working Paper No. 2897 (1989); Weyland, "Political-Strategic Approach," 51; cf. Cristóbal Rovira Kaltwasser et al., "Populism: An Overview of the Concept and the State of the Art," in *Oxford Handbook of Populism*, 14 (excluding this category from the handbook).

institutional constraints. Indeed, leading institutions in the international human rights regime favor constraining economic policies by social rights in a manner that many economists would condemn as populist in their own professional sense.[11] Finally, some observers have criticized the term "populist" as a generalized term of opprobrium that members of the establishment apply too easily to disruptive rivals, rather than a word with determinate content.[12]

Taken together, these disagreements call for some caution in drawing conclusions from the literature on populism. Academics diverge on what populism consists in, and on who counts as a populist. I will argue in Chapter 11 that in the face of this uncertainty, human rights bodies should not treat populism as an operative legal concept, but should rather derive heuristic benefit from observations of populists' actions.

Without attempting to resolve disputes about which definition best captures the historical range of populists, or distinguishes current populists from nonpopulists, I will explain my own preference for the ideational approach in the context of this book. First, the ideational approach emphasizes that such populists consistently invoke the people in an anti-pluralist manner. Second, the ideational approach emphasizes the populists' claim to implement the people's will without legal or institutional constraint. Third, the ideational approach applies both to personalistic leaders and less tightly led parties. These features make the ideational understanding of populism particularly useful in understanding the human rights challenges of the present moment. If that means that I will be focusing on a subcategory of populism, then I accept the need for an appropriate caveat to that effect.

Perhaps the relevant category should be called "exclusionary populism." Professors Mudde and Rovira Kaltwasser, proponents of the ideational approach, have contrasted contemporary forms of populism in Europe and Latin America, and shown how European populists are often hostile to vulnerable ethnic groups and Latin American populists offer empowerment to vulnerable economic classes. Their study described the Europeans as exclusionary populists and the Latin Americans as inclusionary populists, while also observing that all populists are inclusive toward some and exclusionary toward others.[13] That duality is inherent in their ideational definition, under which populists divide society into two antagonistic groups, the real people and their enemies. For that reason, it may be worthwhile to call all populists under the ideational approach exclusionary populists, even if Mudde and

---

[11] See, e.g., Committee on Economic, Social and Cultural Rights, Public Debt, Austerity Measures and the International Covenant on Economic, Social and Cultural Rights, UN Doc. E/C.12/2016/1 (2016); Report of the United Nations High Commissioner for Human Rights, UN Doc. E/2013/82 (2013) (report on austerity measures and economic and social rights).

[12] See Kenneth M. Roberts, "Populism as Epithet and Identity: The Use and Misuse of a Contested Concept," *Comparative Politics Newsletter* 26, no. 2 (2016): 69–72; Roger Cohen, "It's Time to Depopularize 'Populist,'" *New York Times*, July 14, 2018.

[13] Mudde and Rovira Kaltwasser, "Exclusionary vs. Inclusionary Populism," 148.

Rovira Kaltwasser would consider that this usage renders the word "exclusionary" redundant.

Political scientists have made varied attempts to explore the causes of populism.[14] For that purpose it should be kept in mind that different factors may be operative in different countries and at different periods. Moreover, studies may presuppose different definitions or subcategories of populism. Some scholars see populist politics as appealing to voters whose identities have been destabilized by modernization or globalization. Other scholars also emphasize globalization but understand populism as a rational reaction by voters who suffer economic harm from globalization. Some authors explain populism as a consequence of failures of democratic governance, as in Latin American states where extreme corruption diverts the established parties from serving the basic needs of the citizenry, or in European states where convergence among parties offers too narrow a range of policy choices to voters. Pippa Norris and Ronald Inglehart argue that the current success of authoritarian populists reflects a cultural backlash produced by structural changes in economics, politics, and society.[15] Noam Gidron and Peter Hall provide evidence of social status anxiety among supporters of ideational populism in European democracies, where economic and cultural changes have decreased the subjective social status of less educated men.[16] Richard Heydarian emphasizes in Chapter 7 that different causes operate in emerging market democracies, where despite economic growth weak institutions have been unable to meet the rising expectations of the middle classes.[17]

It should be noted that some of the factors identified here involve governments that fail to serve the human rights of their population. Other factors, however, concern cultural backlash that includes the negative reaction of some citizens to improvements in the human rights of others, possibly racial minorities or women.[18] These types of causes may operate separately, or conjointly – as when majority group members whose economic and social rights are neglected resent attention to minority groups that may be even more disadvantaged.

---

[14] See Kirk A. Hawkins et al., "Populism and Its Causes," in *Oxford Handbook of Populism*, 267–286 (summarizing approaches).

[15] Pippa Norris and Ronald Inglehart, *Cultural Backlash: Trump, Brexit and Authoritarian Populism* (Cambridge: Cambridge University Press, 2019).

[16] Noam Gidron and Peter A. Hall, "The Politics of Social Status: Economic and Cultural Roots of the Populist Right," *British Journal of Sociology* 68, no. S1 (November 2017): S57–S84 (online special issue).

[17] See Chapter 7 (in this volume); see also Marcus Mietzner, "Movement Leaders, Oligarchs, Technocrats and Autocratic Mavericks: Populists in Contemporary Asia," in *Routledge Handbook of Global Populism*, ed. Carlos de la Torre (Abingdon: Routledge 2019), 381 ("rather than economic decline, it was the side effects of economic growth that facilitate the rise of third-generation populists in Asia").

[18] On the varying relationship between populism and women's roles, see Sahar Abi-Hassan, "Populism and Gender," in *Oxford Handbook of Populism*, 426–444.

The actual or perceived role of international human rights institutions in situations of backlash may vary. In some instances, populists recognize the institutions as responsible for a change in government policy, and object explicitly to their influence. In other cases, populist agitation focuses on the local change without attributing it to external institutions.

III HUMAN RIGHTS CONSEQUENCES OF EXCLUSIONARY POPULISM

This section describes and illustrates some of the dangers that exclusionary populism poses to human rights, and to the international system for protecting human rights. Two points deserve emphasis at the outset. First, I do not claim that these dangers are unique to populist governments. Racist governments need not be populist, for example, and fully authoritarian governments may attack freedom of expression more thoroughly than populist governments do. I would not characterize the present governments of China, North Korea, Saudi Arabia, or Russia as populist.[19] Some of the international risks that populism creates are intensified when populist governments make common cause with autocrats. Second, most of the facts mentioned in this section are not intended as evidence that particular leaders or governments are populist but rather assume that they have been correctly characterized as populist, and describe some of their actions.

The exclusionary aspects of populism threaten human rights in a variety of ways. Some of these risks already materialize before populists attain public office. Populist incitement may lead to private discrimination and violence. Once populist movements attract substantial electoral support, established parties may borrow versions of their policy proposals in order to lessen the competition.

The risks multiply once populists come to power and control governmental authority and resources. Most fundamentally, the combination of a narrowed definition of the people with the unconstrained implementation of what is claimed to be the will of the people poses dangers to the rights of those in the excluded group. The potential victims may belong to formerly powerful elites, or to vulnerable minorities who the populists think received better treatment than they deserve. The scope of the threat, to equality, economic rights, liberties, fair trial, or even life, will depend on the particular local situation.

The dangers are not limited, however, to the social groups initially targeted by the populists. Once in power, populism risks tipping over into authoritarianism. Political scientists have emphasized the tendency of populist leaders to claim that only they represent the popular will, and to deny the legitimacy of any opposition.

---

[19] See Luke March, "Populism in the Post-Soviet States," in *Oxford Handbook of Populism*, 221 (describing Vladimir Putin's later phase as anti-populist). But on China, see Elizabeth J. Perry, "The Populist Dream of Chinese Democracy," *Journal of Asian Studies* 74, no. 4 (2015): 903–915.

Thus the category of enemies of the people may expand to encompass former allies, dissenters, and critics, with resulting threats to their rights. Populists often try to entrench themselves in power, dismantling legal guarantees of fair electoral competition, and disrespecting the political rights of everyone, including their own constituency. They also express impatience with institutional checks and balances, and may seek to take over, replace or abolish independent components of government, such as the judiciary and other watchdog agencies. Meanwhile, populists may exploit their power to enrich themselves and their major supporters, neglecting the needs and rights of the people they purport to represent.

Nonetheless, populists sometimes employ the language of individual rights. Populists may sincerely believe that they are doing more than prior governments have done to vindicate rights of their voters – social rights of the poor, property rights of the middle class, free speech rights of the intolerant, or the religious rights of the majority, for example. And in some cases they may be correct. From a human rights perspective, however, the allegiance of populists to rights is generally selective and defeasible. The populist favors some rights of some people, and may cease to favor them when they interfere with the populist's other preferences. Moreover, rather than implementing genuine social rights, populist governments may distribute benefits to the poor on a discretionary basis, requiring personal political loyalty in return.[20]

When populists threaten the rights of those they govern, they put themselves in conflict with international human rights institutions. The contradiction between the populist understanding of the general will and the requirements of the human rights regime may itself provide a subject of populist agitation. Condemnation of the international regime may already have been an element of the populist program before they came to power, as with the Euroskeptics, or the conflict may begin later, after the international institutions criticize the populists' projects or their methods of governing, as when the International Criminal Court began to examine Rodrigo Duterte's sanguinary drug enforcement in The Philippines. The judges or personnel of the international institution, and human rights advocates relying on the institution, may then be identified as yet another corrupt elite.

Populists may reject international treaty obligations as inconsistent with national sovereignty, regardless of the fact that the treaties became binding through the consent of prior governments. They may dismiss the consent as coerced, or as a betrayal of the people by corrupt or disloyal politicians. They may portray the treaties as leading to government by foreigners, and thus objectionable in principle, or to government by a particularly despised category of foreigners. The populist strategy may then involve ad hoc defiance of particular rulings, or broader efforts to insulate

---

[20] See Carlos de la Torre, "Populism in Latin America," in *Oxford Handbook of Populism*, 202, 204; Asa K. Cusack, *Venezuela, ALBA, and the Limits of Postneoliberal Regionalism in Latin America and the Caribbean* (New York: Palgrave Macmillan, 2019), 10–11.

national policy from international interference. Using the United Kingdom as an example, opposition to implementing European Court of Human Rights judgments on prisoners' voting rights illustrates ad hoc defiance;[21] calls to repeal the UK Human Rights Act in order to prevent national judges from enforcing Strasbourg judgments embody one broader strategy, and proposals to denounce the European Convention on Human Rights altogether offer another.[22] Some populist governments have indeed withdrawn from treaties that authorize scrutiny by international bodies.[23] Venezuela under Hugo Chávez denounced the American Convention on Human Rights in 2012, thereby disabling future oversight by the Inter-American Court of Human Rights, and then his successor Nicolás Maduro resigned from the Organization of American States altogether in 2017, seeking to avoid the competence of both the Inter-American Commission on Human Rights and OAS political bodies.[24] The Philippines notified the International Criminal Court that it was denouncing the Rome Statute after the Prosecutor opened a preliminary examination regarding Duterte's extrajudicial killings.[25]

Nonetheless, populist regimes may be willing to use human rights mechanisms to serve their own goals, either as allies against domestic opponents or in support of their foreign policy positions. For example, Bolivia sought and received the help of the OAS under the Inter-American Democratic Charter in 2008 when Evo Morales faced resistance to his proposed constitutional reforms.[26] In 2016, Ecuador requested an advisory opinion from the Inter-American Court of Human Rights to support it in disputes with the United Kingdom and the United States over its effort to provide asylum for Julian Assange.[27] The right-populist Trump administration has repeatedly sought to invoke the Inter-American Democratic Charter against left-populist

---

[21] See, e.g., C.R.G. Murray, "Monstering Strasbourg over Prisoner Voting Rights," in *Human Rights in the Media: Fear and Fetish*, ed. Michelle Farrell, Eleanor Drywood, and Edel Hughes (Abingdon: Routledge, 2019), 101–126.

[22] See, e.g., "Brexit and the British Bill of Rights," ed. Tobias Lock and Tom Gerald Daly (2016), available at https://livrepository.liverpool.ac.uk/3006605/1/Brexit%20and%20Human%20Rights .pdf.

[23] Depending on the details of the particular treaty regime, withdrawal may have only prospective effect, and may leave the state subject to international obligations with regard to violations that have already occurred before the withdrawal takes effect. See, e.g., *Case of San Miguel Sosa v. Venezuela*, 348 Inter-Am. Ct. H.R., para. 12 (2018) (citing ACHR art. 78(2)). Moreover, withdrawal from one procedural forum may leave the state subject to other avenues of redress.

[24] See Antonio F. Perez, "Democracy Clauses in the Americas: The Challenge of Venezuela's Withdrawal from the OAS," *American University International Law Review* 33, no. 2 (2017): 391–476. During the two-year delay before the OAS withdrawal could take effect, its continuing validity became clouded by debate within the OAS over the legitimacy of Maduro's reelection.

[25] See Chapter 7 (in this volume); Office of the Prosecutor, International Criminal Court, *Report on Preliminary Examination Activities 2018* (2018), 15.

[26] Rubén M. Perina, *The Organization of American States as the Advocate and Guardian of Democracy* (Lanham, MD: University Press of America, 2015), 90–91.

[27] Advisory Opinion OC-25/18, The Institution of Asylum, and its Recognition as a Human Right under the Inter-American System of Protection (Interpretation and Scope of Articles 5, 22(7) and 22(8) in Relation to Article 1(1) of the American Convention on Human Rights),

Venezuela, and it promoted country-specific critical resolutions and mechanisms while it was a member of the Human Rights Council.

Populist governments also have effects on rights outside their borders. Some studies have concluded that there is no one typical populist foreign policy – populists may be inward-focused and pacifist, or assertive and interventionist, depending on their ideologies and situations.[28] In recent years, however, certain populist governments have contributed to the spread of populism by assisting like-minded populists in other countries. On the left, Hugo Chávez famously used Venezuela's oil wealth to assist populists in other Latin American countries.[29] On the right, Viktor Orbán of Hungary has openly campaigned for populist candidates in nearby countries such as Slovenia and North Macedonia,[30] and has reportedly channeled them financial support.[31]

Venezuela also created rival forms of regional cooperation to compete with those it rejected.[32] With Cuba, it founded the Bolivarian Alliance for the Peoples of Our America (ALBA) as a vehicle for economic cooperation and development, and the Union of South American Nations (UNASUR) as a substitute for the OAS from which the United States would be excluded. However, as mismanagement and

---

25 Inter-Am. Ct. H.R. (ser. A) (2018). The Court responded favorably to Ecuador's request by strictly defining its duties toward asylum-seekers in its embassies overseas. The Court declined Ecuador's invitation to spell out the obligations of non-OAS states such as the United Kingdom, but did address the duties of other OAS states. OC-25/18, paras. 32, 59, 199. However, by the time the Court issued its opinion in May 2018, Ecuador had a new President and its relationship with Assange had changed, and ultimately Ecuador withdrew his asylum. See Charlie Savage, Adam Goldman, and Elaine Sullivan, "Britain Arrests Assange, Ending 7-Year Standoff," *New York Times*, April 12, 2019.

28 Rosa Balfour et al., *Europe's Troublemakers: The Populist Challenge to Foreign Policy* (European Policy Center, 2016), 35–36, available at www.epc.eu/documents/uploads/pub_6377_europe_s_troublemakers.pdf?doc_id=1714; Bertjan Verbeek and Andrej Zaslove, "Populism and Foreign Policy," in *Oxford Handbook of Populism*, 393–395.

29 See Javier Corrales and Carlos A. Romero, *U.S.–Venezuela Relations Since the 1990s: Coping with Midlevel Security Threats* (New York: Routledge 2013), 24–26; Chávez's subsidies also extended to Cuba. Corrales and Romero at 26–28.

30 See Péter Krekó and Zsolt Enyedi, "Orbán's Laboratory of Illiberalism," *Journal of Democracy* 29, no. 3 (2018): 39–51. Orbán also joined with Russia in fueling populist opposition to the compromise name "Republic of North Macedonia" that enabled that country to resolve its dispute with Greece and become a member of NATO, and Hungary helped the populist former prime minister Nikola Gruevski evade a prison term for corruption. See Patrick Kingsley, "Did Hungary Help Spring a Fugitive Macedonian Leader?," *New York Times*, December 30, 2018.

31 Maja Jovanovska et al., "Right-Wing Hungarian Media Moves into the Balkans" (2018), available at www.occrp.org/en/spooksandspin/right-wing-hungarian-media-moves-into-the-balkans. Of course, right-wing populists in Europe have also received various forms of direct and indirect support from Russia. See Anton Shekhovtsov, *Russia and the Western Far Right: Tango Noir* (Abingdon: Routledge, 2018).

32 See Cusak, *ALBA*; Ximena Soley and Silvia Steininger, "Parting Ways or Lashing Back? Withdrawals, Backlash and the Inter-American Court of Human Rights," *International Journal of Law in Context* 14, no. 2 (2018): 251.

corruption and the fall in oil prices produced the collapse of the Venezuelan economy, these initiatives have withered.

Instead of withdrawing from a human rights mechanism in order to avoid its scrutiny, a populist government may remain in the system and make efforts to undermine or obstruct it. When successful, the government's effort has effects that impair human rights in other countries as well. A populist government may work actively to undermine the mechanism, alone or with allies, or it may passively fail to resist such efforts by other populist governments or fully autocratic states.

In Latin America, left-populist governments led by Venezuela, Bolivia, and Ecuador (under Rafael Correa) have protected each other from OAS sanctions for anti-democratic practices.[33] They have sought to impede the Inter-American Commission's Special Rapporteur on Freedom of Expression, and to constrict the funding of the Inter-American Commission and the Inter-American Court.[34] They have sought the return of Cuba to the OAS without any human rights conditionality. At the United Nations, Bolivia, Nicaragua, and Venezuela have joined with Russia and China in attempts to weaken the global treaty body system.[35]

The role of populist members who remain in the system has become increasingly problematic as populists gain power within key supporters of the international human rights regime. Prominent examples include the United States and the European Union.

Countries may decrease their financial support to international human rights institutions, either for the deliberate purpose of weakening them or merely because they prefer to reallocate the funds to other purposes. The budgets of human rights institutions often include portions that are collectively determined by a sponsoring organization, such as the United Nations, the Council of Europe, or the OAS, and portions that are funded by the voluntary contributions of individual states or organizations.[36] Populist governments may seek to reduce the collectively set budget, or may withhold their own legally owed dues or voluntary contributions.

---

[33] See Perina, *Organization of American States*. After Lenín Moreno Garces succeeded Rafael Correa as President, he made significant changes in domestic and foreign policy, and Ecuador withdrew from ALBA in August 2018. See Carlos de la Torre, "Ecuador after Correa," *Journal of Democracy* 29, no. 4 (2018): 77–88; "Ecuador Leaves Venezuela-Run Regional Alliance," Associated Press, August 23, 2018, available at www.apnews.com/6a7d8ed8738a475d8b6c276 ffa0b761e.

[34] See Mónica Pinto, "The Crisis of the Inter-American System," *American Society of International Law Proceedings* 107 (2018): 127–129 (2013); Katya Salazar, "Between Reality and Appearances," *Aportes DPLf* 19 (April 2014): 17–18.

[35] See Christen Broecker and Michael O'Flaherty, "The Outcome of the General Assembly's Treaty Body Strengthening Process: An Important Milestone on a Longer Journey" (2014), available at www.universal-rights.org/urg-policy-reports/the-outcome-of-the-general-assembly s-treaty-body-strengthening-process-an-important-milestone-on-a-longer-journey/ (discussing the efforts of the Cross-Regional Group to undermine the independence of the treaty bodies).

[36] See, e.g., Raísa Cetra and Jefferson Nascimento, "Counting Coins: Funding the Inter-American Human Rights System," in Camila Barretto Maia et al., *The Inter-American Human*

Countries may seek to change the outputs of international human rights institutions directly or indirectly. In political bodies where governments hold seats as such, like the General Assembly and the Human Rights Council, populist governments may join efforts to redefine human rights standards to decrease the level of protection. To the extent that the political body takes ad hoc positions on severe human rights situations in particular countries, populist governments may help block criticism, or to abandon the practice of adopting country-specific resolutions. Alternatively, they may weaken the enforcement of existing standards by modifying the procedures of the political body itself or of more independent expert bodies that it oversees. Some governments have also proposed forbidding human rights institutions to receive voluntary contributions, in order to limit their activities.

The European Union deserves separate attention here as a different kind of regional organization that maintains an active human rights policy outside its own region.[37] The EU engages in human rights promotion, monitoring, and diplomatic pressure. It participates in election observation; it grants development assistance, with varying forms of human rights conditionality attached; it provides financial support to human rights institutions at the global level and in other regions, while playing a supportive role within UN political bodies; and it supports particular human rights defenders. To be sure, EU foreign policy already weighs human rights considerations with other factors, but the increasing strength of exclusionary populists in EU member states threatens to change that balance.

The spread of populism in Europe has weakened the European Union's capacity for making its external contributions. The populist-fueled Brexit referendum has confronted the EU with the loss of an economically and diplomatically important member with a strong rule of law tradition. Although the terms of UK withdrawal are uncertain at this writing, and the character of post-Brexit cooperation between the UK and the EU is difficult to predict, Brexit is likely to damage both sides economically and to decrease their diplomatic leverage in other regions. The volume of EU assistance and the direction of its flow may change; the negotiation of a seven-year EU budget plan for 2021–2027 has included a restructuring of external assistance.[38] In the face of demands for more spending within EU borders,

Rights System: Changing Times Ongoing Challenges (Washington, DC: Due Process of Law Foundation, 2016), 53–94.

[37] See Annabel Egan and Laurent Pech, "Respect for Human Rights as a General Objective of the EU's External Action," in *Research Handbook on EU Law and Human Rights*, ed. Sionaidh Douglas-Scott and Nicholas Hatzis (Cheltenham: Edward Elgar, 2017), 243–266; EU, *Annual Report on Human Rights and Democracy in the World 2017* (2018), available at http://eeas.europa.eu/topics/human-rights-democracy/8437/eu-annual-reports-human-rights-and-democratisation_en.

[38] See Alexei Jones et al., *Aiming High or Falling Short? A Brief Analysis of the Proposed Future EU Budget for External Action*, European Centre for Development Policy Management Briefing Note No. 104 (2018), https://ecdpm.org/wp-content/uploads/ECDPM-2018-BN-104-Analysis-Proposed-Future-EU-Budget-External-Action.pdf.

and less external spending that does not benefit EU members, proposals would allocate a larger proportion of aid to discouraging migration from Eastern neighbors and Africa.

The ability of populist governments to achieve weakening effects within international organizations depends in part on the voting rules or conventions that control particular actions, and on the number of populist governments present and the other allies they can muster. (In some organizations with broad membership, collaboration between populists and governments of fully autocratic states becomes relevant.) When populists are in the minority, differences between simple majority voting, qualified majority (supermajority) voting, consensus practices and unanimity/veto rules influence the opportunity for the populists to block policies they oppose. The rules may enable a populist government to veto criticism or sanctions against itself, as the United States can in the UN Security Council,[39] and even when the government in question is ineligible to vote on its own case, as in some European Union procedures, a second populist government may wield the veto for its benefit.

Turning to the United States of America, the unprecedented ascension of the egregiously unqualified Donald Trump may have had many causes, but populist appeals formed a central feature of his campaign, and have continued on an essentially daily basis. As Ronald Inglehart and Pippa Norris observed, "Trump's rhetoric stimulated racial resentment, intolerance of multiculturalism, nationalistic isolationism and belligerence, nostalgia for past glories, mistrust of outsiders, sexism, the appeal of tough leadership, attack-dog politics, and racial and anti-Muslim animosity."[40] The threats that the Trump administration poses to human rights within the United States have received widespread attention, often expressed in terms of subversion of democracy and US constitutional principles.[41] Some of the danger signs are new – earlier Presidents have not condoned neo-Nazis – while others involve the deepening of prior trends of political polarization. This book, however, will not concentrate on the local effects, but on the impact of the Trump presidency on the broader human rights system.

As Stephen Pomper and Daniel Levine-Spound explain in Chapter 2, the current situation should not be contrasted with an imaginary golden age in which human rights norms provided the sole consideration in US foreign policy. Moreover, the United States has largely emphasized civil and political rights rather than the full range embraced by the international human rights system. Nonetheless, Trump's indifference to human rights and admiration for autocrats presents new dangers.

---

[39] See, e.g., Michael Schwirtz and Rick Gladstone, "U.S. Vetoes U.N. Resolution Condemning Move on Jerusalem," *New York Times*, December 19, 2017 (describing the veto of a Security Council resolution criticizing Trump's recognition of Jerusalem as the capital of Israel).

[40] Norris and Inglehart, *Cultural Backlash*, 76.

[41] E.g., Steven Levitzky and Daniel Ziblatt, *How Democracies Die* (New York: Crown, 2018).

Trump began his term with a populist speech, reportedly written by the white nationalist ideologue Stephen Bannon and his longtime collaborator Stephen Miller.[42] After thanking the former Presidents in attendance, he dismissed them with the typical populist claim that his inauguration, and only his, gave power back to the people. Prior administrations of whatever party benefitted a small political class, but he would protect the people. He announced a new vision: "From this day forward it's going to be America First – America First." Every decision in foreign policy would be made to benefit Americans. He would "bring back our borders," targeting both trade and immigration. The United States would seek friendship with other nations, but "with the understanding that it is the right of all nations to put their own interests first." The United States would "not seek to impose our way of life on anyone."

In May 2017 the new Secretary of State, former Exxon executive Rex Tillerson, gave a speech to his employees describing how an "America first" foreign policy should be conducted.[43] He explained that the priority was to advance US security interests and economic interests, but that there would sometimes be room for promoting "our values," where that did not impair security and economic goals. He referred to "our values," and contrasted them with values that other societies might hold – the speech exhibited no awareness that there might be universal values in international law, and never mentioned human rights, or even international law. As Stephen Pomper and Daniel Levine-Spound point out, a certain amount of low-level human rights diplomacy did continue in Tillerson's department, and the United States still deploys high profile human rights rhetoric against foreign governments that it has other reasons to oppose, such as Iran and (at times) North Korea.

Trump fired the pragmatic Tillerson in March 2018, replacing him with then-CIA director Mike Pompeo, and installed the notorious anti-internationalist John Bolton as National Security Adviser. Pompeo joined UN Ambassador Nikki Haley in announcing the United States's withdrawal from the UN Human Rights Council in June 2018.[44] The most salient reason for the withdrawal was probably the Council's refusal to end its disproportionate emphasis on Israel and the Occupied Palestinian Territories. But evidently the Trump administration did not care enough

---

[42] "The Inaugural Address," https://www.whitehouse.gov/briefings-statements/the-inaugural-address/; see Max Greenwood, "Miller and Bannon Wrote Trump Inaugural Address," *The Hill*, January 21, 2017, http://thehill.com. Bannon was pushed out of the White House after the neo-Nazi violence in Charlottesville in August 2017, but Miller remained. Bannon subsequently moved to Europe, where he has tried to become the leader of an international right-wing populist network. See Jason Horowitz, "Bannon Takes on Europe, with Populist Toolbox in Hand," *New York Times*, March 10, 2018.

[43] "Remarks to U.S. Department of State Employees," https://www.state.gov/remarks-to-u-s-department-of-state-employees/.

[44] See "Remarks by Mike Pompeo, Secretary of State and Nikki Haley, U.S. Permanent Representative to the United Nations," https://geneva.usmission.gov/2018/06/21/remarks-on-the-un-human-rights-council/. The United States has nonetheless continued to participate in the Universal Periodic Review as a nonmember of the Council.

about the positive contributions they could make by remaining on the Council, where the Obama administration had played an affirmative role. The US absence will strengthen the hand of Council members that prefer vague thematic resolutions and mandates and resist inquiries into severe violations in particular countries. It also makes the effectiveness of the Council even more dependent on the European Union at a time when the stability of the EU is itself in question. Of course, US absence or presence is not the sole concern; it is the loss of engaged and constructive US participation that matters.

In September 2018, Trump addressed the General Assembly for the second time, and once more emphasized that the United States would insist upon its own sovereignty and self-interest.[45] He encouraged other nations to do the same, praising India, Saudi Arabia, and Poland, and describing Benjamin Netanyahu's Israel as a thriving democracy. He condemned "global governance" in general, and particular organizations that did not sufficiently serve US interests. "America is governed by Americans. We reject the ideology of globalism, and we embrace the doctrine of patriotism." He expressed the intention to reduce US financial support for the United Nations, and to redirect more of it from the general budget to voluntary contributions for specific programs that the United States favors. A few weeks earlier, the United States had cut off all its funding for the United Nations Relief and Works Agency for Palestinian Refugees in the Near East (UNRWA).

The speech to the General Assembly also emphasized "threats to sovereignty from uncontrolled migration," and rebuffed the UN project to negotiate soft law principles on humane migration policy in a "global compact."[46] Xenophobic agitation has been one of Trump's signature methods, targeting nonwhite and Muslim immigrants especially. His administration has repeatedly tested the limits of its authority in measures against undocumented immigrants, Muslims, refugees and children, and has denounced legally required family reunification as destructive "chain migration." Trump's successive travel bans disrupted international efforts toward burden-sharing for Syrian refugees, and encouraged Eastern European populists who were defying the minimal quotas adopted by the European Union.

In international environmental law – not usually framed in human rights law terms, but with clear human rights consequences[47] – the United States now refuses

---

[45] See "Remarks by President Trump to the 73rd Session of the United Nations General Assembly, New York, NY," https://www.whitehouse.gov/briefings-statements/remarks-president-trump-73rd-session-united-nations-general-assembly-new-york-ny/ (2018).

[46] The United States pulled out of the negotiations for the Global Compact on Safe and Orderly Migration in December 2017, claiming that it would be incompatible with US sovereignty. Subsequent to Trump's September 2018 speech, his administration extended its opposition to the Global Compact on Refugees as well. Only the United States and Hungary voted against the latter in the General Assembly.

[47] See Advisory Opinion OC-23/17, The Environment and Human Rights (State obligations in relation to the environment in the context of the protection and guarantee of the rights to life and to personal integrity – interpretation and scope of Articles 4(1) and 5(1) of the American

to honor commitments to slow climate change. Trump formally announced the intention of withdrawing from the Paris Climate Change Agreement as soon as the terms of the agreement permit. In the meantime, federal agencies have been dismantling environmental regulations, suppressing discussion of climate change in government reports and websites, and degrading the government's capacity to analyze the issue scientifically.[48]

The accumulation of harm from US words and deeds goes beyond the specific injuries to individuals, and threatens systematic damage to the international system for protection of human rights. Some of the harms may persist only so long as Trump remains in office, while others may prove difficult or impossible for more enlightened successors to reverse.

IV CONCLUSION

Exclusionary forms of populism, such as those described by the ideational approach, present numerous dangers for human rights and the international human rights system. Within their own societies the narrow conception of the people, and the rejection of constraints on the enforcement of their will, threaten the rights of the excluded groups, and populists' hostility toward critics and competitors threatens the rights of their own supporters. Looking outward, these attitudes generate conflict with international bodies that seek to protect those rights.

Populists often disdain external obligations that would limit their freedom of action. They may contribute to like-minded populism in other countries, and ally themselves with autocracies in weakening international institutions that they regard as constraining.

These risks are reinforced as the number of populist governments increase, and especially when populists gain power in countries that have previously provided important support to the international human rights system. The populist shocks within the European Union and the extreme disorientation of US values brought by the 2016 election portend grave obstacles for the international protection of human rights.

Convention on Human Rights), 23 Inter-Am. Ct. H.R. (ser. A) (2017); Human Rights Committee, General Comment No. 36 (2018), on article 6 of the International Covenant on Civil and Political Rights, on the right to life, UN Doc. CCPR/C/GC/36 (2018) (advance unedited version), para. 62; Committee on Economic, Social and Cultural Rights, General Comment No. 15: The right to water (arts. 11 and 12 of the Covenant) (2002), in Compilation of General Comments and General Recommendations Adopted by Human Rights Treaty Bodies, UN Doc. HRI/GEN/1/Rev.9 (Vol. I) (2008), 97-113; Committee on the Elimination of Discrimination Against Women, General Recommendation No. 37 (2018), on the gender-related dimensions of disaster risk reduction in the context of climate change, UN Doc. CEDAW/C/GC/37 (2018).

[48] See, e.g., Union of Concerned Scientists, Science under Trump: Voices of Scientists across 16 Federal Agencies (2018), www.ucsusa.org/2018survey.

BIBLIOGRAPHY

Balfour, Rosa, Janis A. Emmanouilidis, Catherine Fieschi, Heather Grabbe, Christopher Hill, Timo Lochocki, Marie Mendras, Cas Mudde, Mari K. Niemi, Juliane Schmidt, and Corina Stratulat. "Europe's Troublemakers: The Populist Challenge to Foreign Policy." European Policy Center, 2016. Available at www.epc.eu/documents/uploads/pub_6377_europe_s_troublemakers.pdf?doc_id=1714.

Broecker, Christen, and Michael O'Flaherty. "The Outcome of the General Assembly's Treaty Body Strengthening Process: An Important Milestone on a Longer Journey." Universal Rights Group, 2014. Available at www.universal-rights.org/urg-policy-reports/the-outcome-of-the-general-assemblys-treaty-body-strengthening-process-an-important-milestone-on-a-longer-journey/.

Cetra, Raísa, and Jefferson Nascimento. "Counting Coins: Funding the Inter-American Human Rights System." In *The Inter-American Human Rights System: Changing Times Ongoing Challenges*, edited by Camila Barretto Maia et al., 53–94. Washington, DC: Due Process of Law Foundation, 2016.

Cohen, Roger. "It's Time to Depopularize 'Populist'." *New York Times*, July 14, 2018, p. A20.

Committee on Economic, Social and Cultural Rights. Public Debt, Austerity Measures and the International Covenant on Economic, Social and Cultural Rights, UN Doc. E/C.12/2016/1 (2016).

Corrales, Javier, and Carlos A. Romero. *U.S.–Venezuela Relations Since the 1990s: Coping with Midlevel Security Threats*. New York: Routledge, 2013.

Cusack, Asa K. *Venezuela, ALBA, and the Limits of Postneoliberal Regionalism in Latin America and the Caribbean*. New York: Palgrave Macmillan, 2019.

de la Torre, Carlos. "What Went Wrong? Leftwing Populist Democratic Promises and Autocratic Practices." *Comparative Politics Newsletter* 26, no. 2 (2016): 40–45.

    "Populism in Latin America." In *The Oxford Handbook of Populism*, edited by Cristóbal Rovira Kaltwasser, Paul Taggart, Paulina Ochoa Espejo, and Pierre Ostiguy, 195–213. Oxford: Oxford University Press, 2017.

    "Ecuador after Correa." *Journal of Democracy* 29, no. 4 (October 2018): 77–88.

"Ecuador Leaves Venezuela-Run Regional Alliance." *Associated Press*, August 23, 2018. www.apnews.com/6a7d8ed8738a475d8b6c276ffa0b761e.

Egan, Annabel, and Laurent Pech. "Respect for Human Rights as a General Objective of the EU's External Action." In *Research Handbook on EU Law and Human Rights*, edited by Sionaidh Douglas-Scott and Nicholas Hatzis, 243–266. Cheltenham: Edward Elgar, 2017.

[European Union]. *EU Annual Report on Human Rights and Democracy in the World 2017* (2018). Available at http://eeas.europa.eu/topics/human-rights-democracy/8437/eu-annual-reports-human-rights-and-democratisation_en.

Gidron, Noam, and Peter A. Hall. "The Politics of Social Status: Economic and Cultural Roots of the Populist Right." *British Journal of Sociology* 68, no. S1 (November 2017): S57–S84.

Greenwood, Max. "Miller and Bannon Wrote Trump Inaugural Address." *The Hill*, January 21, 2017, http://thehill.com.

Hawkins, Kirk A., Madeleine Read, and Teun Pauwels. "Populism and Its Causes." In *The Oxford Handbook of Populism*, edited by Cristóbal Rovira Kaltwasser, Paul Taggart, Paulina Ochoa Espejo, and Pierre Ostiguy, 267–286. Oxford: Oxford University Press, 2017.

Horowitz, Jason. "Bannon Takes on Europe, with Populist Toolbox in Hand." *New York Times*, March 10, 2018, at A5.

Jones, Alexei, Mariella Di Ciommo, Meritxell Sayós Monrás, Andrew Sherriff, and Jean Bossuyt. *Aiming High or Falling Short? A Brief Analysis of the Proposed Future EU Budget for External Action*. European Centre for Development Policy Management Briefing Note no. 104 (2018). https://ecdpm.org/wp-content/uploads/ECDPM-2018-B N-104-Analysis-Proposed-Future-EU-Budget-External-Action.pdf.

Jovanovska, Maja, Tamas Badoky, and Aubrey Belford. "Right-Wing Hungarian Media Moves into the Balkans" (2018). Available at www.occrp.org/en/spooksandspin/right-wing-hungarian-media-moves-into-the-balkans.

Kaltwasser, Cristóbal Rovira, Paul Taggart, Paulina Ochoa Espejo, and Pierre Ostiguy. "Populism: An Overview of the Concept and the State of the Art." In *The Oxford Handbook of Populism*, edited by Cristóbal Rovira Kaltwasser, Paul Taggart, Paulina Ochoa Espejo, and Pierre Ostiguy, 1–24. Oxford: Oxford University Press, 2017.

Kingsley, Patrick. "Did Hungary Help Spring a Fugitive Macedonian Leader?" *New York Times*, December 30, 2018, at A8.

Krekó, Péter, and Zsolt Enyedi, "Orbán's Laboratory of Illiberalism." *Journal of Democracy* 29, no. 3 (2018): 39–51.

Laclau, Ernesto. *On Populist Reason*. London: Verso, 2005.

Levitsky, Steven, and James Loxton. "Populism and Competitive Authoritarianism in the Andes." *Democratization* 20, no. 1 (2013): 107–136.

Levitzky, Steven, and Daniel Ziblatt. *How Democracies Die*. New York: Crown, 2018.

Lock, Tobias, and Tom Gerald Daly, eds., "Brexit and the British Bill of Rights" (2016). Available at https://livrepository.liverpool.ac.uk/3006605/1/Brexit%20and%20Human%20 Rights.pdf.

Magarian, Gregory P. "The Pragmatic Populism of Justice Stevens's Free Speech Jurisprudence." *Fordham Law Review* 74, no. 4 (2006): 2201–2240.

Mair, Peter. "Populist Democracy vs Party Democracy." In *Democracies and the Populist Challenge*, edited by Yves Mény and Yves Surel, 81–98. Houndmills, Basingstoke: Palgrave, 2002.

March, Luke. "Populism in the Post-Soviet States." In *The Oxford Handbook of Populism*, edited by Cristóbal Rovira Kaltwasser, Paul Taggart, Paulina Ochoa Espejo, and Pierre Ostiguy, 214–231. Oxford: Oxford University Press, 2017.

Mietzner, Marcus. "Movement Leaders, Oligarchs, Technocrats and Autocratic Mavericks: Populists in Contemporary Asia." In *Routledge Handbook of Global Populism*, edited by Carlos de la Torre, 370–384. Abingdon: Routledge, 2019.

Mouffe, Chantal. *For a Left Populism*. London: Verso, 2018.

Mudde, Cas. "Populism: An Ideational Approach." In *The Oxford Handbook of Populism*, edited by Cristóbal Rovira Kaltwasser, Paul Taggart, Paulina Ochoa Espejo, and Pierre Ostiguy, 27–47. Oxford: Oxford University Press, 2017.

Mudde, Cas, and Cristóbal Rovira Kaltwasser. "Exclusionary vs. Inclusionary Populism: Comparing Contemporary Europe and Latin America." *Government and Opposition* 48, no. 2 (2013): 147–174.

Müller, Jan-Werner. *What Is Populism?* Philadelphia, PA: University of Pennsylvania Press, 2016.

Murray, C.R.G. "Monstering Strasbourg over Prisoner Voting Rights." In *Human Rights in the Media: Fear and Fetish*, edited by Michelle Farrell, Eleanor Drywood, and Edel Hughes, 101–126. Abingdon: Routledge, 2019.

Norris, Pippa, and Ronald Inglehart. *Cultural Backlash: Trump, Brexit and Authoritarian Populism*. Cambridge: Cambridge University Press, 2019.

Office of the Prosecutor, International Criminal Court. *Report on Preliminary Examination Activities 2018* (2018), 15.

Perez, Antonio F. "Democracy Clauses in the Americas: The Challenge of Venezuela's Withdrawal from the OAS." *American University International Law Review* 33, no. 2 (2017): 391–476.

Perina, Rubén M. *The Organization of American States as the Advocate and Guardian of Democracy: An Insider's Critical Assessment of its Role in Promoting and Defending Democracy*. Lanham, MD: University Press of America, 2015.

Perry, Elizabeth J. "The Populist Dream of Chinese Democracy." *Journal of Asian Studies* 74, no. 4 (2015): 903–915.

Pinto, Mónica. "The Crisis of the Inter-American System." *American Society of International Law Proceedings* 107 (2013): 127–129.

Pompeo, Mike, and Nikki Haley. "Remarks on the UN Human Rights Council." Last modified June 19, 2018. https://geneva.usmission.gov/2018/06/21/remarks-on-the-un-human-rights-council/.

Roberts, Kenneth M. "Populism as Epithet and Identity: The Use and Misuse of a Contested Concept." *Comparative Politics Newsletter* 26, no. 2 (2016): 69–72.

Sachs, Jeffrey D. *Social Conflict and Populist Policies in Latin America*. National Bureau of Economic Research, Working Paper No. 2897, 1989.

Salazar, Katya, "Between Reality and Appearances." *Aportes DPLf* 19 (April 2014): 16–19.

Savage, Charlie, Adam Goldman, and Elaine Sullivan. "Britain Arrests Assange, Ending 7-Year Standoff." *New York Times*, April 12, 2019.

Schwirtz, Michael, and Rick Gladstone. "U.S. Vetoes U.N. Resolution Condemning Move on Jerusalem." *New York Times*, December 19, 2017.

Shekhovtsov, Anton. *Russia and the Western Far Right: Tango Noir*. Abingdon: Routledge 2018.

Soley, Ximena, and Silvia Steininger. "Parting Ways or Lashing Back? Withdrawals, Backlash and the Inter-American Court of Human Rights." *International Journal of Law in Context* 14, no. 2 (2018): 237–257.

Stavrakakis, Yannis. "Populism and Hegemony." In *The Oxford Handbook of Populism*, edited by Cristóbal Rovira Kaltwasser, Paul Taggart, Paulina Ochoa Espejo, and Pierre Ostiguy, 535–553. Oxford: Oxford University Press, 2017.

Tushnet, Mark. *Taking the Constitution Away from the Courts*. Princeton, NJ: Princeton University Press, 2000.

Union of Concerned Scientists. "Science under Trump: Voices of Scientists across 16 Federal Agencies." August 2018. www.ucsusa.org/2018survey.

[UN High Commissioner for Human Rights]. *Report of the United Nations High Commissioner for Human Rights*. UN Doc. E/2013/82 (2013).

Urbinati, Nadia. *Democracy Disfigured: Opinion, Truth and the People*. Cambridge, MA: Harvard University Press, 2014.

U.S. Department of State, "Remarks to U.S. Department of State Employees," 2017. www.state.gov/remarks-to-u-s-department-of-state-employees/.

  "Remarks by Mike Pompeo, Secretary of State and Nikki Haley, U.S. Permanent Representative to the United Nations," 2018. https://geneva.usmission.gov/2018/06/21/remarks-on-the-un-human-rights-council/.

U.S. White House, "The Inaugural Address," 2017. www.whitehouse.gov/briefings-statements/the-inaugural-address/.

"Remarks by President Trump to the 73rd Session of the United Nations General Assembly, New York, NY," 2018. www.whitehouse.gov/briefings-statements/remarks-president-trump-73rd-session-united-nations-general-assembly-new-york-ny/.

Verbeek, Bertjan, and Andrej Zaslove. "Populism and Foreign Policy." In *The Oxford Handbook of Populism*, edited by Cristóbal Rovira Kaltwasser, Paul Taggart, Paulina Ochoa Espejo, and Pierre Ostiguy, 384–405. Oxford: Oxford University Press, 2017.

Weyland, Kurt. "Populism: A Political-Strategic Approach." In *The Oxford Handbook of Populism*, edited by Cristóbal Rovira Kaltwasser, Paul Taggart, Paulina Ochoa Espejo, and Pierre Ostiguy, 48–72. Oxford: Oxford University Press, 2017.

2

US Human Rights Policy and the Trump Administration

Stephen Pomper and Daniel Levine-Spound

I INTRODUCTION

Human rights advocates could be forgiven for worrying in 2016 that a Donald Trump presidency might spell the end of human rights promotion as a focus of US foreign policy.

During the 2016 presidential campaign, then-candidate Trump professed his naked admiration for strongman regimes, defended the alleged extrajudicial killing of journalists by Vladimir Putin's government, and defended torture as a tactic in the fight against terrorism.[1] But perhaps the biggest sign that dramatic changes could be afoot was Trump's adoption of the slogan, "America First," as an organizing principle for his foreign policy. "From this moment on, it's going to be America First," announced Trump in his inaugural address. "Every decision on trade, on taxes, on immigration, on foreign affairs, will be made to benefit American workers and American families."[2] How precisely this rhetoric would translate into practice was unclear, but the populist and isolationist echoes were plain, and they raised serious – even, potentially, existential – questions about the role that human rights promotion would continue to play in US foreign policy.[3]

---

[1] Jenna Johnson, "Trump Says 'Torture Works,' Backs Waterboarding and 'Much Worse.'" *Washington Post*, February 17, 2016, www.washingtonpost.com/politics/trump-says-torture-works-backs-waterboarding-and-much-worse/2016/02/17/4c9277be-d59c-11e5-b195-2e29a4e13425_story.html; Philip Bump, "Donald Trump Isn't Fazed by Vladimir Putin's Journalist Murdering," *Washington Post*, December 18, 2015, www.washingtonpost.com/news/the-fix/wp/2015/12/18/donald-trump-glad-to-be-endorsed-by-russias-top-journalist-murderer/.

[2] Donald Trump, "Remarks of President Donald J. Trump – Inaugural Address," January 20, 2017, www.whitehouse.gov/briefings-statements/the-inaugural-address/.

[3] In discussing "populism" in this chapter we will follow the same "ideational" approach favored in Chapter 1 of this volume – i.e., a definition which understands populism as employing an exclusionary notion of the people (the "real people") whose will should not be constrained, deliberately excluding disfavored social groups and despised elites. For a discussion of the

This is not to argue that human rights promotion fails to serve American interests. Indeed, it is a standard trope among those who wish to see the United States play a leading role in pressing for the advancement of human rights around the world that doing so advances US interests by cultivating the emergence of rights-respecting democracies, which have traditionally been the United States' strongest and most stable partners.[4] But realist critics have scorned this logic as little more than wishful thinking, and though the critiques invariably go too far, they are not without some bite.[5] Certainly it is true that US efforts to support a rules-based order in the service of a more just and peaceful world – an idealist project generally traced back to President Woodrow Wilson – have a mixed record of success. And it is also the case that no administration has ever found it practicable to organize US foreign policy wholly around human rights principles. Even the most idealistic administrations have felt it necessary to work closely with authoritarian regimes to address the United States' security and economic interests.

Against this backdrop – and against the backdrop of candidate Trump's own statements – it seemed plausible that his administration would treat moral arguments for US investment in human rights promotion as insufficiently grounded in American interests, interest-based arguments as too speculative, and the entire enterprise of rights promotion as an elite project not worthy of US political or other capital. Put another way, there was a real question whether in appealing to sentiments that helped get it elected, the Trump administration might forge a determined path away from human rights promotion entirely – nominally implementing congressional mandates but doing little else, and breaking dramatically with US practice as it has evolved in the post-Vietnam period.

But for all the justified criticism of Trump's human rights record,[6] his administration's approach has in some ways constituted less of a departure from precedent than might have been expected. As this chapter will briefly explore, this is in some measure because a combination of inertia and the stewardship of career officials

---

"America First" movement in the pre-war period, and its ideological undertones, see Krishna-dev Calamur, "A Short History of 'America First,'" *The Atlantic*, January 21, 2017, www .theatlantic.com/politics/archive/2017/01/trump-america-first/514037/; Ron Elving, "Trump Vows Policy Vision of 'America First,' Recalling Phrase's Controversial Past," NPR, January 21, 2017, www.npr.org/2017/01/21/510877650/trump-vows-policy-vision-of-america-first-recalling-phrases-controversial-past.

4   Susan E. Rice, "Human Rights: Advancing American Interests and Values," Human Rights First Annual Summit, December 4, 2013, https://obamawhitehouse.archives.gov/the-press-office/2013/12/04/remarks-national-security-advisor-susan-e-rice-human-rights-advancing-am.

5   For recent long-form analysis along these lines, see Stephen M. Walt, *The Hell of Good Intentions: America's Foreign Policy Elite and the Decline of U.S. Primacy* (New York: Farrar, Straus and Giroux, 2018); John J. Mearsheimer, *The Great Delusion: Liberal Dreams and International Realities* (New Haven, CT: Yale University Press, 2018).

6   Sarah Margon, "Giving up the High Ground: America's Retreat on Human Rights," *Foreign Affairs* 97, no. 2 (2018): 39–45, www.foreignaffairs.com/articles/united-states/2018-02-13/giving-high-ground.

had – at least in the first year of the Trump administration – a somewhat sustaining effect on the rights promotion agenda. But it is also in large part because US efforts to promote human rights have always been laced with ambivalence and meaningfully blunted by a mix of sovereigntist realism and populism. Thus, while it is undoubtedly true that the Trump administration has worked closely with abusive regimes, engaged in activities that implicate the United States itself in abuses, and acted in a manner ranging from skeptical to contemptuous of international institutions that promote human rights, none of these actions set it categorically apart from its predecessors. Other administrations have done much the same.

Nonetheless, there is at least one significant way in which the Trump presidency – and the populist themes that ripple through its rhetoric and policies – have taken the United States into new territory when it comes to human rights. The novelty is that, while past administrations have supported strongmen, populists, and demagogues when it served other strategic and economic interests, this administration appears to embrace them because – not in spite – of their authoritarian qualities. It is in this new inclination to see virtue in models of governance that the US has stood long against that the administration may leave its most distinct (and damaging) human rights legacy.

II US HUMAN RIGHTS POLICY IN THE POST-WAR, PRE-TRUMP PERIOD

Since the earliest days of the post-war human rights system, US human rights policy has been pulled and shaped by the tensions between idealism, realism, and populism.

Charged with overseeing the formulation of the Universal Declaration of Human Rights, Eleanor Roosevelt both expressed her idealist designs (she wrote in *Foreign Affairs* that she hoped, "recognition of human rights might become one of the cornerstones on which peace could eventually be based"[7]) and an awareness of populist constraints on her ambition (she wrote to her aunt that, "(w)e will have trouble at home for it can't be a U.S. document & get by with 58 nations & at home that is hard to understand").[8]

While Roosevelt's idealist impulses won that tug of war – she successfully helped shepherd the Declaration into existence in 1948 – the next quarter century of US foreign policy was dominated by a Cold War realism that was largely uninterested in human rights promotion.[9] Stated broadly, US foreign policy was marked by alliances

---

[7]   Eleanor Roosevelt, "The Promise of Human Rights," *Foreign Affairs* 26, no. 3 (1948): 471, available at www.foreignaffairs.com/articles/1948-04-01/promise-human-rights.

[8]   Allida M. Black, "Eleanor Roosevelt and the Universal Declaration of Human Rights," *OAH Magazine of History* 22, no. 2 (2008): 36, www.jstor.org/stable/25162170.

[9]   Roberta Cohen, "Integrating Human Rights in U.S. Foreign Policy: The History, the Challenges, and the Criteria for an Effective Policy," *Brookings*, April 9, 2008, www.brookings.edu/on-the-record/integrating-human-rights-in-u-s-foreign-policy-the-history-the-challenges-and-the-criteria-for-an-effective-policy/.

with generally right-wing dictatorships forged in the ostensible service of fighting communism. Though US diplomats played leading roles in the negotiation of core human rights instruments, such as the International Covenant on Civil and Political Rights, Washington dragged its feet on formally joining them. Moreover, diplomats who strayed into human rights issues with their host governments risked a dressing down from their superiors, as one US ambassador famously learned when he was publicly rebuked for pressing Chilean strongman Augusto Pinochet on the arrest and torture of his political opponents.[10]

But the end of the Vietnam War brought dramatic changes in US policy toward human rights. As Roberta Cohen has written, "The human rights policy of the 1970s was . . . a reaction to a foreign policy largely devoid of ethical considerations."[11] In an effort to pry the executive branch away from the Kissingerian realpolitik that had become its default, Congress published reports calling for US leadership on human rights, legislated human rights reporting requirements with respect to US foreign aid recipients, and began pressing for the creation of a human rights office within the Department of State.[12] During the same period, President Jimmy Carter spoke in his January 1977 inaugural address of an absolute commitment to human rights, and several months later declared that this commitment was a "fundamental tenet" of US policy.[13] Then, in February 1978, President Carter issued a presidential directive declaring the promotion of human rights to be a "major objective" of US foreign policy.[14] Presidential Directive 30 instructed the government to use all diplomatic tools as well as positive and negative inducements in the pursuit of this objective, but left considerable flexibility in how it would be implemented.

From the post-Vietnam period on, the United States has consciously incorporated the promotion of human rights – by which it generally meant civil and political rather than economic, social, and cultural rights – as a component of its foreign policy.[15] To be sure, there were efforts to return to a pre-Carter posture. In 1979, Jeane Kirkpatrick, then a professor at Georgetown, wrote an influential article suggesting that human rights pressure should generally be reserved for left-wing totalitarians, rather than right-wing regimes more closely aligned with the United

[10] Cohen, "Integrating Human Rights."

[11] Cohen, "Integrating Human Rights."

[12] Robert McMahon, "Human Rights Reporting and U.S. Foreign Policy," *Council on Foreign Relations,* March 25, 2019, www.cfr.org/backgrounder/human-rights-reporting-and-us-foreign-policy.

[13] Jimmy Carter, "Inaugural Address," *The American Presidency Project,* January 20, 1977, www.presidency.ucsb.edu/documents/inaugural-address-0; "Jimmy Carter Reaffirms his Commitment to Human Rights," *History.com,* February 25, 2019, www.history.com/this-day-in-history/jimmy-carter-reaffirms-his-commitment-to-human-rights.

[14] President Jimmy Carter, "Presidential Directive/NSC 30," *The White House,* February 17, 1978, fas.org/irp/offdocs/pd/pd30.pdf.

[15] Samuel Moyn, "Economic Rights Are Human Rights," *Foreign Policy,* April 9, 2018, https://foreignpolicy.com/2018/04/09/the-freedom-america-forgot-populism-human-rights-united-nations/.

States.[16] And at the beginning of the Reagan presidency, officials signaled in word and deed that right-wing regimes that Carter had pressured and in some cases cut off from military assistance would find support in the new administration.[17] But Congress largely resisted the backsliding, including by blocking Reagan's preferred appointee to the top human rights post at the State Department.[18] And during his second term, Reagan himself committed – at least rhetorically – that the United States would "oppose tyranny in whatever form, whether of the left or the right."[19]

But although the US's broad commitment to promoting human rights has persisted, it has remained significantly constrained, both because of the limits of American influence abroad and because of the contradictions that characterize US foreign policy when it comes to human rights. In particular, abiding tensions between human rights advocates' idealist aspirations and the realist, sovereigntist, and populist currents present in US politics have consistently curbed or guided the pursuit of those idealist aspirations. Some of these tensions may have become especially visible during the Trump administration, or have manifested themselves in novel ways, but they have long been part of the US political landscape.

Consider, for example, the dissonance created when the United States violates or becomes complicit in a violation of the rules and principles that it presses other countries to follow. Often, the motive for this conduct is pragmatic (e.g., policy-makers claim that achieving a key security goal requires that certain human rights concerns temporarily take a back seat). But leaders also tend to frame these decisions in populist terms.

An especially damaging and enduring example is the Bush administration's abusive detention and interrogation program for alleged al Qaeda terrorists. If defenders of the program have argued from a realist/pragmatic perspective – insisting that the program's ostensible effectiveness should trump other considerations – they also tend to paint opponents as disconnected elitists, callously indifferent to the safety of ordinary Americans. Vice President Dick Cheney, who championed the program while in office during the Bush administration, wrote in his 2015 memoir that in labelling Bush-era abuses as torture and closing the interrogation program, President Obama "libel[led] the dedicated professionals who saved American lives" and acted in a way that was "misguided, unjust, and highly irresponsible."[20]

From an outside perspective, however, the picture is one of damaging hypocrisy. The US had, after all, helped fashion a global ban on torture under the Convention

---

[16] Tamar Jacoby, "The Reagan Turnaround on Human Rights," *Foreign Affairs* 64, no. 5 (1986): 1068, www.foreignaffairs.com/articles/1986-06-01/reagan-turnaround-human-rights.

[17] Jacoby, "Reagan Turnaround," 1069.

[18] Douglas Martin, "Ernest W. Lefever, Rejected as a Reagan Nominee, Dies at 89," *New York Times*, August 4, 2009, www.nytimes.com/2009/08/05/us/politics/05lefever.html.

[19] Jacoby, "Reagan Turnaround," 1067.

[20] Tom McCarthy, "Dick Cheney Defends America's Use of Torture, Again, in New Book," *The Guardian*, September 1, 2015, www.theguardian.com/us-news/2015/sep/01/dick-cheney-defends-america-torture-new-book.

Against Torture that was designed to be non-derogable, and that it pressed other governments to implement notwithstanding their arguments that it interfered with their security activities. And yet, when confronted with a security threat that overwhelmed senior policymakers' normative commitments to the treaty regime, Washington developed a web of later-discredited legal opinions and positions that created space for circumventing the ban. And although the Obama administration received deserved plaudits for ending the Bush administration's program and abrogating the legal theories that supported it, its self-described reluctance to pursue accountability – though motivated by an understandable desire to avoid the appearance of criminalizing political opponents – could only undermine the Convention Against Torture's requirement that states parties hold perpetrators to account.[21]

Another source of tensions that creates obstacles to US human rights promotion stems from the formal distance that the United States has maintained from the global human rights system that it ostensibly champions. Professor Louis Henkin alluded to this distant posture when he described the United States as preferring to play the role of a "flying buttress" to the international human rights "cathedral," rather than standing as a pillar within it.[22]

This distance is in part a function of US law. For American citizens, the US constitution provides the bulwark of safeguards protecting civil and political rights. International human rights treaties may bind the US government as a matter of international law, but unless they are explicitly specified to be "self-executing," these treaties create judicially enforceable rights only to the extent that they prompt the enactment of domestic implementing legislation. Nor – as the Supreme Court ruled in its *Medellin* v. *Texas* decision (2008) – do the pronouncements of the International Court of Justice automatically translate into domestic law.[23]

Relatedly, the US stands arguably alone among the western democracies in its squeamishness about committing to international human rights obligations. Echoing populist themes, politicians and other public figures have tended to characterize

[21] Convention against Torture and Other Cruel, Inhuman or Degrading Treatment or Punishment (Convention against Torture), adopted December 10, 1984, G.A. res. 39/46, annex, 39 U.N. GAOR Supp. (No. 51) at 197, U.N. Doc. A/39/51 (1984), entered into force June 26, 1987, arts. 4–7, www.ohchr.org/Documents/ProfessionalInterest/cat.pdf.

[22] Louis Henkin, "Human Rights and United States Foreign Policy," in *The Age of Rights* (New York: Columbia University Press, 1996), 76; Anne-Marie Slaughter and Catherine Powell, "Louis Henkin (1917–2010): The Power of His Ideas Live On," *Opinio Juris*, October 10, 2010, http://opiniojuris.org/2010/10/22/louis-henkin-1917-2010-the-power-of-his-ideas-live-on/.

[23] *Medellin* v. *Texas*, 552 U.S. 491 (2008). It is also worth noting that the reach of US obligations under human rights instruments is further circumscribed by other legal doctrines. With limited exceptions, the United States does not regard its human rights treaty obligations as applying extraterritorially, and has developed a broadly defined *lex specialis* doctrine according to which the law of armed conflict alone governs the conduct of hostilities in armed conflict. Beth Van Schaack, "United States Report to the UN Human Rights Committee: Lex Specialis and Extraterritoriality," *Just Security*, October 16, 2013, www.justsecurity.org/1761/united-states-lex-specialis-extraterritoriality/.

human rights treaties as infringing on US sovereignty and ceding authority over the day-to-day lives of American citizens to treaty bodies staffed by elite foreign bureaucrats. The Obama administration sought to coopt populist arguments in seeking Senate advice and consent for the ratification of the UN Convention on the Rights of Persons with Disabilities, arguing that the treaty was closely patterned on US antidiscrimination law and that joining it would help the US press other countries to provide disabled veterans and other Americans abroad with the same level of accessibility that they enjoy at home.[24] But the treaty hit familiar shoals, with members of the homeschool community taking the lead in arguing (tendentiously at best) that the treaty would interfere with the rights of US parents to educate their children with disabilities.[25]

In addition, administrations of both parties have wrestled with the question of how much support to give the multilateral institutions that serve as dedicated fora for defending and promoting human rights. The United States' on-again-off-again relationship with the UN Human Rights Council – it declined to join upon the Council's formation in 2006 under Bush, then joined for two successive terms under Obama, then left under Trump – is in part related to its concerns about the Council's standing agenda item that focuses on the "human rights situation in Palestine and other occupied Arab territories." (No other regional situation is afforded a standing agenda item.) But the United States' rocky relationship with the Council likely reflects a broader sovereigntist discomfort with a multilateral institution passing morally inflected judgments on the United States and its allies. And whatever the motivation, separating the US from the Council weakens both US human rights promotion and the efforts of Council.[26] Similar observations apply to the United States' still more distant and intermittently adversarial posture toward the International Criminal Court.[27]

Finally, US efforts at human rights promotion have been hobbled over the decades by the non-uniform application of human rights principles understood to

[24] Committee on Foreign Relations, U.S. Senate, "Convention on the Rights of Persons with Disabilities: Report," 113th Congress: Senate Executive Report 113-12, July 28, 2014 ("If we join, we will help ensure that our wounded warriors from Afghanistan and Iraq – vets like Dan Berschinski – have the same opportunities abroad as other Americans. That's why the American Legion – the Nation's largest wartime veterans service organization – the VFW, and many other veterans groups support ratification."), www.congress.gov/congressional-report/113th-con gress/executive-report/12.

[25] Joshua Keating, "Homeschoolers Help Torpedo Disability Rights Treaty in Senate," *Foreign Policy*, December 4, 2012, https://foreignpolicy.com/2012/12/04/homeschoolers-help-torpedo-dis ability-rights-treaty-in-senate/.

[26] Keith M. Harper and Stephen Pomper, "On the U.N. Human Rights Council, Quitters are Losers," *Foreign Policy*, January 29, 2018, https://foreignpolicy.com/2018/01/29/on-the-u-n-human-rights-council-quitters-are-losers/.

[27] Stephen Pomper, "USG Statement on International Criminal Court Probe Is Missing Some Things," *Just Security*, December 14, 2017, www.justsecurity.org/49360/usg-statement-intl-crim inal-court-probe-alleged-u-s-war-crimes-missing-2/.

be universal. It is commonplace for the US government to acknowledge – as, for example, President Obama did on several occasions – that the US government's economic and security interests require doing business with governments that do not share the United States' democratic form of governance.[28] And certainly, US diplomatic history is rife with examples – both in the deep and recent past – of the US government materially supporting regimes with egregious human rights records and quietly looking the other way at their transgressions. Often, the beneficiaries are resource-rich or strategically situated countries in the Middle East. While the pragmatic (realist) logic of this selective approach is relatively straightforward, it comes at an undeniable cost to rights promotion, allowing leaders of countries faced with US pressure to argue, not unreasonably, that they are being subjected to double standards and unfair treatment.

III US HUMAN RIGHTS POLICY UNDER THE TRUMP ADMINISTRATION

As referenced above, the Trump administration's rhetoric and actions regarding human rights have often echoed and sometimes amplified the traditional tensions that have shaped the work of prior administrations. But President Trump has also created new challenges for those committed to human rights in US foreign policy. Stated simply, the Trump administration has consistently appeared to embrace authoritarian regimes due to ideological affinity, rather than out of strategic necessity or political convenience.

A *Old Habits*

Despite a number of deeply troubling actions taken domestically, the Trump administration's first year marked less of a radical departure from previous international human rights promotion policies than might have been expected. As *The Economist* observed in 2017, the somewhat surprising level of policy continuity – notwithstanding the distorting effects of "America First" – probably owed something to longstanding congressional support for human rights promotion, long-term budgets that guarantee continued funding of human rights programming, and deep institutional knowledge and commitment within the civil and foreign service.[29] It likely could also be partially attributed to the absence of ideologically committed

---

[28] Ben Wolfgang, "Obama: Despite Human Rights Troubles, We Must Work with Saudi Arabia," *The Washington Times*, January 27, 2015, www.washingtontimes.com/news/2015/jan/27/obama-saudi-arabia-human-rights-troubles/; Rice, "Human Rights: Advancing American Interests and Values."

[29] "Donald Trump's Administration is Promoting Democracy and Human Rights," *The Economist*, December 6, 2017, www.economist.com/united-states/2017/12/06/donald-trumps-administration-is-promoting-democracy-and-human-rights.

sovereigntists and realists with firm commitments to upending the status quo in the top ranks of the administration during its first year.

Whatever the reason, at least some pockets of the US government continued to engage in a wide range of traditional promotion activities during the beginning of Trump's presidency, even if they were sometimes nearly overshadowed by countervailing messages. For example, several months after President Trump hosted Egyptian President al-Sisi in the Oval Office and praised him for doing a "fantastic job," the State Department slashed $100 million of military and economic assistance to Egypt, specifically citing human rights concerns. In Hungary, US diplomats pressed the increasingly illiberal Orbán government to back off efforts to drive the Central European University out of the country, and announced $700,000 in funding to promote independent media in rural Hungary.[30] And at the United Nations, Ambassador Nikki Haley used her platform to shed light on civilian protection and governance crises in the Democratic Republic of Congo and South Sudan.

It was particularly striking that, during the Trump administration's first year, the US government did not immediately turn its fire on the multilateral institutions for which a Republican administration with more traditional realist/sovereigntist leanings would have shown little patience. As of the Spring of 2018, the administration had not left the UN Human Rights Council – which the Obama administration had come to see as a useful forum for cultivating human rights norms – nor had it attacked the legitimacy of the International Criminal Court– both institutions had been singled out for derision by John Bolton during his time in the Bush administration and in private life.[31] Indeed, a US delegation even appeared at the 2017 annual meeting of the ICC Assembly of States parties as an observer and gave a short presentation, something it never did during the Bush administration.

Moreover, during its first year, the Trump administration undertook some potentially important initiatives to develop new tools and revitalize old ones for the purposes of human rights promotion. For example, in crafting an executive order to implement the Global Magnitsky Act, the administration created a powerful new global sanctions authority that can be used against non-US human rights abusers

---

[30] "U.S. Launches Media Fund for Hungary to Aid Press Freedom," *Reuters*, November 13, 2017, www.reuters.com/article/us-hungary-us-media/u-s-launches-media-fund-for-hungary-to-aid-press-freedom-idUSKBN1DD21C; Patrick Kingsley, "Hungary's Leader was Shunned by Obama, but Has a Friend in Trump," *New York Times*, August 15, 2018, www.nytimes.com/2018/08/15/world/europe/hungary-us-orban-trump.html.

[31] Kenneth Hanner, "Bolton: US Should Resign from 'Clown Convention' at UN," *Newsmax*, April 30, 2013, www.newsmax.com/newsfront/bolton-un-human-rights/2013/04/30/id/502008/; John Bolton, "The Hague Aims for U.S. Soldiers," *Wall Street Journal*, November 2017, www.wsj.com/articles/the-hague-tiptoes-toward-u-s-soldiers-1511217136; Nahal Toosi, "Bolton Returns to a U.N. He Made a Career of Blasting," *Politico*, September 23, 2018, www.politico.com/story/2018/09/23/john-bolton-united-nations-iran-836454/.

wherever they reside.[32] The State Department also commissioned an in-depth study – reminiscent of a study commissioned by the Bush administration to determine whether genocide had been perpetrated in Darfur – to help it assess the extent to which atrocity crimes had been committed by Myanmar government authorities against the minority Rohingya population in Rakhine State.[33]

If the Trump administration's first year showed continuity with certain affirmative aspects of traditional US human rights, there were also worrying signals of the direction US human rights policy would ultimately take under Trump. Just months into the new administration, Secretary of State Tillerson appeared to advocate for the demotion of human rights as a policy priority in remarks to State Department officials, generating a wave of public criticism.[34] A leaked memo from one of his top aides subsequently made the case that "badgering" US allies about human rights would diminish US alliances and – recalling Kirkpatrick's 1979 article – suggested that human rights pressure should generally be reserved for US adversaries.[35] Still, it was not until the Spring of 2018, when John Bolton became the National Security Adviser and Mike Pompeo replaced Tillerson as Secretary of State, that there were senior officials in place with both the ideological motivation and the influence to pivot more visibly and forcefully away from the idealist instincts that had continued to govern aspects of human rights policy during the administration's first year.

B *The Second Year Pivot*

Soon after Bolton joined the Trump administration, his influence became immediately apparent in the hard turn US policy took regarding the UN Human Rights

---

[32] Robert Berschinski, "Trump Administration Notches Human Rights Win. No, Really," *Just Security*, January 10, 2018, www.justsecurity.org/50846/trump-administration-notches-human-rights-win-no-really/. The Obama administration had deliberated over issuing a less far-reaching iteration of such an executive order but ultimately declined to do so, partially due to concerns expressed by the Treasury Department. Namely, the Treasury Department worried that "creating a new global authority would crank expectations unrealistically high for a constant stream of high-impact designations and place an unsustainable burden on scarce Treasury Department personnel." Stephen Pomper, "Atrocity Prevention Under the Obama Administration: What We Learned and the Path Ahead," *United States Holocaust Memorial Museum*, February 2018, pp. 8–9, 24, www.ushmm.org/m/pdfs/Stephen_Pomper_Report_02-2018.pdf.

[33] U.S. Department of State, "Documentation of Atrocities in Northern Rakhine State," *Reliefweb*, September 24, 2018, https://reliefweb.int/report/myanmar/documentation-atrocities-northern-rakhine-state.

[34] Nahal Toosi, "Leaked Memo Schooled Tillerson on Human Rights," *Politico*, December 19, 2017, www.politico.com/story/2017/12/19/tillerson-state-human-rights-304118.

[35] Commentators noted the inverse correlation between this sort of selectivity and US credibility as an advocate for universal rights. For example, Tom Malinowski, a former assistant secretary of state for democracy, human rights, and labor in the Obama administration, argued that Hook's memo, "tells Tillerson that we should do exactly what Russian and Chinese propaganda says we do – use human rights as a weapon to beat up our adversaries while letting ourselves and our allies off the hook." Malinowski also noted that Hook's memo, "utterly misses the elemental fact that America's moral authority is one of our main advantages in the world, and that it would disappear if we apply it as selectively as he advises." Toosi, "Leaked Memo."

Council and the International Criminal Court. Prior to Bolton's arrival in government, Ambassador Nikki Haley's team in New York had led an effort pushing the Human Rights Council to abandon its standing agenda item focused on human rights abuses committed by Israel, but the US retained its seat in Geneva. But if there was a chance that the Trump administration might make its peace with the Council, such an opportunity quickly disappeared once Bolton had taken his seat. In June 2018, Haley announced that the United States would pull out of the Council altogether, characterizing the institution as a "cesspool of political bias" and a "protector of human rights abusers."[36]

The Trump administration's break with the Human Rights Council was mild compared to Bolton's subsequent attack on the International Criminal Court. In a September 2018 speech that responded ferociously to a possible ICC investigation of alleged war crimes committed by US forces in Afghanistan, Bolton threatened to prosecute and sanction ICC personnel involved in the investigation, asserting that the court was "for all intents and purposes ... already dead to us."[37] The speech borrowed sovereigntist themes that prior administrations had emphasized in criticizing the court for intruding on US prerogatives, while applying an unmistakably Trumpian populist gloss that quixotically characterized the court as simultaneously feckless and an unacceptable fetter on the defense of US interests. Bolton argued that "the hard men of history are not deterred by fantasies of international law such as the ICC," and that "history has proven that the only deterrent to evil and atrocity is what Franklin Roosevelt once called 'the righteous might' of the United States and its allies[.]"[38] And he closed his speech with a fiery promise that the administration would "fight back to protect American constitutionalism, our sovereignty, and our citizens," and would "put the interests of the American People FIRST."[39]

While Bolton focused on undercutting multilateral institutions, Secretary Pompeo made his mark on human rights policy with a different project, announcing in July 2019 the creation of a "Commission on Unalienable Rights" to reexamine fundamental questions about human rights, including through the lens of natural law.[40] The Commission appeared to have no meaningful relationship to the State

---

[36] Nikki Haley, "Remarks on the U.N. Human Rights Council," *The United States Mission at the United Nations*, June 19, 2019, https://usun.state.gov/remarks/8486.

[37] John Bolton, "Full Text of John Bolton's Speech to the Federalist Society," *Al Jazeera*, September 10, 2018, www.aljazeera.com/news/2018/09/full-text-john-bolton-speech-federalist-society-180910172828633.html.
   The United States did, in fact, announce visa sanctions against court personnel in early 2019. Lesley Wroughton, "U.S. Imposes Visa Bans on International Criminal Court Investigators – Pompeo," *Reuters*, March 15, 2019, www.reuters.com/article/uk-usa-icc/u-s-imposes-visa-bans-on-international-criminal-court-investigators-pompeo-idUSKCN1QW1ZH.

[38] Bolton, "Speech to Federalist Society."

[39] Bolton, "Speech to Federalist Society."

[40] Christina Ruffini, "Pompeo Unveils New 'Unalienable Rights' Commission amid Concerns over Progressive Rollbacks," CBS News, July 8, 2019, www.cbsnews.com/news/mike-pompeo-unveils-new-unalienable-rights-commission-amid-concerns-over-progressive-rollbacks/.

Department's human rights bureau and featured a number of prominent right-leaning academics and other critics of the US approach to human rights in recent years (many with a conservative religious background). Advocates and human rights officials from prior administrations expressed alarm that the Commission might seek to narrow the United States' conception of human rights in a way that would work to the detriment of certain groups – women, LGBTQ individuals, and Muslims among them.[41]

Over the course of the second and third years of the Trump presidency, the administration also began to struggle more visibly with its response to increasingly pointed allegations regarding the United States' own complicity in international human rights and humanitarian law violations, particularly in relation to US support for the Saudi-led coalition's military campaign in Yemen. Because of widespread allegations of war crimes and other atrocities committed by the coalition, the United States received pointed criticism for the ongoing support – which has at various times included refueling, logistical support, and intelligence sharing – and its ongoing arms sales to coalition partners.[42]

To be sure, responsibility for US complicity in the Yemen campaign did not fall wholly on the Trump administration. Indeed, it was the Obama administration that made the initial decision to back the Saudi-led coalition in 2015, and that maintained its support even after reports of the campaign's devastating impact on civilians had begun to surface.[43] But while the Obama administration began, toward the end of its tenure, to signal that its support was not a blank check, and to hold back on arms transfers, the Trump administration was for the most part reluctant to distance itself from the coalition. Secretary Pompeo drew strong criticism when, in September 2018, he certified the sufficiency of coalition efforts to protect civilians from the effects of the military campaign just weeks after an errant Saudi strike killed 51 people, including 40 school children, in a bus on the way to a field trip.[44] And when both chambers of Congress passed a law directing the president to withdraw US forces from hostilities in Yemen, President Trump issued a veto along with a statement that detailed a long list of US interests

---

[41] Christopher White, "Former U.S. Envoy to Vatican Opposes New Commission Headed by Predecessor," *Crux*, July 23, 2019, https://cruxnow.com/church-in-the-usa/2019/07/23/former-u-s-envoy-to-vatican-opposes-new-commission-headed-by-predecessor/.

[42] International Crisis Group, "Ending the Yemen Quagmire: Lessons from Washington from Four Years of War," *International Crisis Group*, April 15, 2019, www.crisisgroup.org/united-states/003-ending-yemen-quagmire-lessons-washington-four-years-war.

[43] International Crisis Group, "Yemen Quagmire."

[44] Nina Elbagir et al., "The Schoolboys on a Field Trip in Yemen were Chatting and Laughing. Then came the Airstrike," *CNN*, February 27, 2019, www.cnn.com/2018/08/13/middleeast/yemen-children-school-bus-strike-intl/index.html; Larry Lewis, "Grading the Pompeo Certification on the Yemen War and Civilian Protection: Time for Serious Reconsideration," *Just Security*, September 18, 2018, www.justsecurity.org/60766/grading-pompeo-certification-yemen-war-civilian-protection-time-reconsideration/.

(including the need to stand by allies in the Gulf region) that he viewed as militating against it.[45]

Separately, President Trump took steps that, intentionally or not, could only undermine the legal protections for civilians caught in the crossfire of armed conflict. After Secretary Mattis resisted ideas floated during the campaign that the military reintroduce unlawful detention and interrogation techniques, and other operators made clear their dismay at suggestions – made directly by the president – that they were being too discriminating in their targeting, Trump explored another way to attack the United States' civilian protection framework.[46] As Memorial Day approached in 2019, word leaked that the president was preparing to pardon a group of individuals accused or convicted of war crimes.[47] The measure seemed calculated to appeal to Trump's political base, and indeed conservative talk show hosts sounded populist themes in arguing that those under consideration for pardons were "the good guys," and suggesting that the elite voices opposed to the pardons were disconnected from public sentiment.[48] Although he did not issue the pardons, Trump appeared to take partial credit when several weeks later one of the accused was acquitted of the most serious charges against him.[49]

But perhaps the most striking evolution in the administration's foreign policy actions and rhetoric has been its increasingly unapologetic embrace of double standards in human rights policy along the lines that Tillerson's staff had endorsed in 2017. In confronting US adversaries, the administration has layered bitter criticism with soaring language evoking the country's commitment to democratic governance. After pulling the United States out of the Iran nuclear deal and shifting to a "maximum pressure" strategy, for example, Secretary Pompeo boasted that the United States "proudly amplif[ies] the voices of those in Iran longing to have those inalienable and universal rights," and is "unafraid to expose human rights violations and support those who are being silenced."[50] The administration also

[45] Donald Trump, "Presidential Veto Message to the Senate to Accompany S.J. Res. 7," *White House Presidential Memoranda*, www.whitehouse.gov/presidential-actions/presidential-veto-message-senate-accompany-s-j-res-7/.

[46] Sheri Fink and Helene Cooper, "Inside Trump Defense Secretary Pick's Efforts to Halt Torture," *New York Times*, January 2, 2017, www.nytimes.com/2017/01/02/us/politics/james-mattis-defense-secretary-trump.html; https://thehill.com/homenews/administration/381925-trump-asked-cia-official-why-drone-strike-didnt-also-kill-targets.

[47] Dave Phillips, "Trump May Be Preparing Pardons for Servicemen Accused of War Crimes," *New York Times*, May 18, 2019, www.nytimes.com/2019/05/18/us/trump-pardons-war-crimes.html?smtyp=cur&smid=tw-nytimesatwar.

[48] Aidan Mclaughlin, "*Fox and Friends Backs SEAL Accused of Shooting Little Girl: 'These Are the Good Guys,'*" *Mediaite*, May 19, 2019, www.mediaite.com/tv/fox-friends-backs-seal-accused-of-shooting-little-girl-these-are-the-good-guys/.

[49] Paul Szoldra, "Trump Says 'Glad I Could Help!' in Congratulatory Tweet to Navy SEAL Eddie Gallagher," *Task & Purpose*, July 3, 2019, https://taskandpurpose.com/trump-congrats-eddie-gallagher.

[50] Michael Pompeo, "Supporting Iranian Voices," *Remarks*, U.S. Department of State, July 22, 2018, www.state.gov/supporting-iranian-voices/.

placed human rights front and center in its Venezuela policy as it sought to pressure the Maduro government out of office: President Trump received opposition activist Lilian Tintori in the Oval Office in February 2017, and nearly two years later the White House expressly invoked human rights (a rare occurrence during the Trump administration) in a January 2019 statement affirming that the President "stands with the people of Venezuela as they demand democracy, human rights, and prosperity denied to them by Maduro."[51] The Trump administration similarly attacked other left-leaning hemispheric neighbors on human rights grounds, including in November 2018 when Bolton referred to a "troika of tyranny … stretching from Havana to Caracas to Managua," and announced that the administration is defending "the rule of law, liberty, and basic human decency in our region."[52]

In striking contrast, the Trump administration tended to be effusive in its public embrace of strongman governments in countries where it deemed the US to have strategic interests. During the first half of his presidency, Trump spoke of his "great relationship" with Philippine President Rodrigo Duterte and of his "great friend" Egyptian President al-Sisi (to whom suspended aid was restored after Pompeo took over as Secretary of State).[53] Through flattering tweets and a warm reception at the White House, Trump broadcast his approval of far-right Brazilian President Jair Bolsonaro[54] – with whom he has partnered in pressuring Venezuelan President Maduro – in spite of Bolsonaro's history of bigoted comments about LGBTQ individuals, his outspoken fondness for Brazil's former military

---

[51] Abby Phillip, "Trump Calls on Venezuela to Release Political Prisoner after Meeting with Rubio," *Washington Post*, February 15, 2017, www.washingtonpost.com/news/post-politics/wp/2017/02/15/trump-calls-on-venezuela-to-release-political-prisoner-after-meeting-with-rubio/; Donald Trump, "President Donald J. Trump Supports the Venezuelan People's Efforts to Restore Democracy in their Country," *White House Factsheets*, January 29, 2019, www.white house.gov/briefings-statements/president-donald-j-trump-supports-venezuelan-peoples-efforts-restore-democracy-country/. The January 2019 statement was notable in large part because of the president's sparse use of the term "human rights."

[52] John R. Bolton, "Remarks by National Security Advisor Ambassador John R. Bolton on the Administration's Policies in Latin America," *White House Remarks*, November 2, 2018, www .whitehouse.gov/briefings-statements/remarks-national-security-advisor-ambassador-john-r-bolton-administrations-policies-latin-america/.

[53] Donald Trump and Rodrigo Duterte, "Remarks by President Trump and President Duterte of the Philippines before Bilateral Meeting," *White House Remarks*, November 13, 2017, www .whitehouse.gov/briefings-statements/remarks-president-trump-president-duterte-philippines-bilateral-meeting-manila-philippines/; Donald Trump and Abdel Fattah al-Sisi, "Remarks by President Trump and President Al-Sisi of the Arab Republic of Egypt before Bilateral Meeting," *White House Remarks*, September 24, 2018, www.whitehouse.gov/briefings-statements/remarks-president-trump-president-al-sisi-arab-republic-egypt-bilateral-meeting/.

[54] Jonathan Watts, "Trump Joy over Bolsonaro Suggests New Rightwing Axis in Americas and Beyond," *The Guardian*, October 29, 2018, www.theguardian.com/world/2018/oct/29/jair-bolso naro-brazil-trump-rightwing-axis; "Trump Praises Brazil's New President Bolsonaro after He Vowed to 'Strengthen Democracy,'" *CNBC*, January 1, 2019, www.cnbc.com/2019/01/01/trump-praises-brazils-new-president-bolsonaro-after-he-vowed-to-strengthen-democracy-.html.

junta, and steps he has taken as president that threaten the ability of NGOs to operate independently.[55]

Trump has also singled out right-wing populist governments in Eastern Europe for positive attention, even as they presided over the dismantling of democratic governance in their countries. Hungarian President Viktor Orbán, a leader who has called for "illiberal democracy" and worked assiduously to narrow political and expressive space in Hungary, has been particularly well received – including in the Oval Office, where Trump hailed him as "respected all over Europe."[56] The administration has similarly embraced the far-right Polish government, which has also narrowed space for political opposition and dissent. Following a February 2019 White House meeting, Trump and Polish President Duda called for a greatly enhanced U.S–Polish partnership.[57]

But perhaps the greatest beneficiary of the Trump administration's selective approach to human rights has been Saudi Arabia. Beyond its continued support for the Saudi-led military campaign in Yemen, and its public insistence that responsibility for the civil war in Yemen lies with Iran,[58] the administration has gone to great lengths to avoid assigning responsibility to senior Saudi officials – and in particular Crown Prince Mohamed bin Salman – for the murder of *Washington Post* journalist and US resident Jamal Khashoggi at the Saudi Consulate in Turkey.[59] In explaining the US approach to the Saudi murder, Trump offered a nakedly realist rationale, noting among other things that his administration was relying on Saudi Arabia to compensate for diminished oil production by the Iranian government following the US withdrawal from the Iran nuclear deal and reimposition of sanctions on Tehran.[60]

[55] Philip Reeves, "Dictatorship Was a 'Very Good' Period, Says Brazil's Aspiring President," *NPR*, July 30, 2018, www.npr.org/2018/07/30/631952886/dictatorship-was-a-very-good-period-says-brazil-s-aspiring-president; Gimena Sánchez-Gimoli, "Bolsonaro Acts on Promises to Dismantle Human Rights Protections in Brazil," *WOLA*, January 1, 2019, www.wola.org/analysis/bolsonaro-acts-promises-dismantle-human-rights-protections-brazil/.

[56] Kingsley, "Hungary's Leader"; Donald Trump and Viktor Orbán, "Remarks by President Trump and Prime Minister Orbán of Hungary before Bilateral Meeting," *White House Statements & Releases*, May 13, 2019, www.whitehouse.gov/briefings-statements/remarks-president-trump-prime-minister-orban-hungary-bilateral-meeting/.

[57] Donald Trump and Andrzej Duda, "Joint Statement by President Donald J. Trump and President Andrzej Duda of the Republic of Poland," *White House Statements & Releases*, September 18, 2019, www.whitehouse.gov/briefings-statements/joint-statement-president-donald-j-trump-president-andrzej-duda-republic-poland/.

[58] Umar Farooq, "US: Pompeo Blames Iran for Yemen's Civil War," *Anadolu Agency*, April 29, 2019, www.aa.com.tr/en/americas/us-pompeo-blames-iran-for-yemens-civil-war/1465422.

[59] Aaron Blake, "Trump Won't Believe His Own Intelligence Community – Again," *Washington Post*, November 17, 2018, www.washingtonpost.com/politics/2018/11/15/trump-administration-is-trying-hard-not-blame-saudi-crown-prince-khashoggis-death/; Tamara Cofman Wittes, "Sanctions on Saudi Arabia Aren't Enough," *Brookings*, December 5, 2018, www.brookings.edu/blog/order-from-chaos/2018/12/05/sanctions-on-saudi-arabia-arent-enough/.

[60] Donald Trump, "Statement from President Donald J. Trump on Standing with Saudi Arabia," *White House Statements & Releases*, November 20, 2018 ("After the United States, Saudi Arabia is the largest oil producing nation in the world. They have worked closely with us and have

C *Sowing a Populist Backlash against Human Rights*

While John Bolton helped steer the Trump administration's human rights policy in a sharply realist and sovereigntist direction, with sometimes jarring results, President Trump has gone a step further, creating a different and more novel imprint on US policy. Trump has gone beyond the traditional "realist" approach of working with authoritarian regimes to advance perceived US interests and knocking down multilateral institutions that, from a sovereigntist's perspective, seem threatening to US assertions of power. His unique legacy will be the extent to which he has appeared to join these authoritarians in purposefully attacking or diminishing the institutional foundations of human rights and democratic governance.

Perhaps most notably, he has adopted the rhetoric of an oppressive government that is seeking to discredit the checks and balances that are essential to a functional democracy. Trump has often used terms like "fake news" and described the press as the "enemy of the people" in order to discredit his own media critics. But in so doing, he has also given cover to authoritarian leaders around the world seeking to mute or muzzle critical journalists.[61] This should be no mystery to the administration. Relatively soon into his presidency, it became clear that governments around the world with troubling human rights records relied on the US President's words to validate their actions.[62] Despite this troubling development, Trump's rhetoric has remained consistent. Noting that the president had made over 1,300 negative tweets about the media (i.e., tweets that criticized the media or were threatening, condemning, or insinuating) as of January 2019, the Committee to Protect Journalists observed that:

> The president's tweets can have an impact and consequences for the press both at home and abroad. His rhetoric has given cover to autocratic regimes: world leaders from Cambodia to the Philippines have echoed terms like "fake news" in the midst of crackdowns on press freedom. And the rhetoric has sometimes resulted in harassment of individual journalists in the U.S., where CPJ is aware of several journalists who say they were harassed or threatened online after being singled out on Twitter by Trump.[63]

been very responsive to my requests to keeping oil prices at reasonable levels – so important for the world. As President of the United States I intend to ensure that, in a very dangerous world, America is pursuing its national interests and vigorously contesting countries that wish to do us harm. Very simply it is called America First."), www.whitehouse.gov/briefings-statements/statement-president-donald-j-trump-standing-saudi-arabia/.

[61] Andrew Boyle, "The Free Press Aren't 'Enemies of the People,'" *Brennan Center for Justice*, August 24, 2018, www.brennancenter.org/blog/free-press-arent-enemies-people; Steven Erlanger, "'Fake News,' Trump's Obsession, Is Now a Cudgel for Strongmen," *New York Times*, December 12, 2017, www.nytimes.com/2017/12/12/world/europe/trump-fake-news-dictators.html.

[62] Jason Schwartz, "Trump's 'Fake News' Rhetoric Crops up Around the Globe," July 30, 2018, *Politico*, www.politico.com/story/2018/07/30/trump-media-fake-news-750536.

[63] Stephanie Sugars, "From Fake News to Enemy of the People: An Anatomy of Trump's Tweets," *Committee to Project Journalists*, January 30, 2019, https://cpj.org/blog/2019/01/trump-twitter-press-fake-news-enemy-people.php.

And Trump went further than simply serving as a rhetorical role model. He also appeared at various times to lend political support to authoritarian regimes, specifically for the purposes of striking a blow against traditional US values or weakening historic allies. Even as the European Union struggled with how to handle increasingly repressive Polish and Hungarian member states, particularly in light of the EU's strong human rights commitments, the Trump administration appeared to go out of its way to support those governments politically. Appearing to suggest that Trump longed for the powers of an authoritarian, the US ambassador to Hungary, David Cornstein, suggested in an interview that Trump "would love to have the situation that Viktor Orbán has, but he doesn't."[64] As noted above, Trump also gave Orbán a public relations coup by meeting him in the Oval Office – and praising him for "doing a tremendous job in so many ways" – shortly before a consequential European Parliament election in which hard right parties sought to make significant gains.[65] It was a new twist on the United States' Cold War-era practice of siding with authoritarians in order to make common cause against communism – this time, the Trump administration sided with authoritarians in order to make common cause against rights-respecting democracies.

It was also meaningful that, in defending the strongman states with which the administration hoped to build bonds, Trump encouraged unflattering equivalencies between these countries and the United States. This rhetorical choice appeared prominently during the campaign, when Trump defended allegations that the Russian government was responsible for initiating wars of conquest and murdering journalists, arguing that "at least he's a leader, unlike what we have in this country," and that "our country does plenty of killing too."[66] Following his election, Trump continued in the same vein. Objecting to the idea that Russian President Vladimir Putin's brutality should be an impediment to a warm and respectful bilateral relationship, Trump struck a note of moral relativity: "There are a lot of killers. We have a lot of killers ... Well, you think our country is so innocent?"[67]

[64] Chris Riotta, "Trump 'Would Love to Have Orban's Situation in Hungary' US Ambassador Says," *The Independent*, May 9, 2019, www.independent.co.uk/news/world/americas/us-politics/trump-viktor-orban-hungary-david-cornstein-fidesz-illiberal-democracy-a8907246.html.

[65] Peter Baker, "Viktor Orban, Hungary's Far-Right Leader, Gets Warm Welcome from Trump," *New York Times*, May 13, 2019, www.nytimes.com/2019/05/13/us/politics/trump-viktor-orban-oval-office.html.

[66] Bump, "Donald Trump Isn't Fazed by Vladimir Putin's Journalist Murdering," www.washingtonpost.com/news/the-fix/wp/2015/12/18/donald-trump-glad-to-be-endorsed-by-russias-top-journalist-murderer/.

[67] Abby Phillip, "O'Reilly Told Trump that Putin Is a Killer. Trump's Reply: 'You Think our Country Is so Innocent?," *Washington Post*, February 4, 2017, www.washingtonpost.com/news/post-politics/wp/2017/02/04/oreilly-told-trump-that-putin-is-a-killer-trumps-reply-you-think-our-countrys-so-innocent/.

IV CONCLUSION

For as long as it has had a human rights policy, the United States has been pulled by competing ideological currents, and has consistently fallen short of its stated aspirations. As we have explained, it is therefore not in the Trump administration's often unprincipled approach to human rights where it is most dramatically breaking with precedent and threatening to do the greatest damage to US human rights policy.

The place where it is threatening to do the greatest damage is here: At a moment when populist strongmen are threatening to roll back democratic progress across the globe, the Trump administration has turned away from the rights-respecting democracies with which the United States has traditionally made common cause, and openly worked to boost the prospects of authoritarians. From Poland to Hungary to Brazil, it has embraced governments as they have moved away from the principles that the United States has for decades espoused as fundamental to good governance. And unlike in the past, it has done so not out of a sense of strategic necessity, but out of preference.

It is still too early to tell how significant the damage will be. As Professor Henkin suggested four decades ago, the US has long struggled to define its place in the global human rights system. But the metaphors that Henkin chose – pillar and buttress in the cathedral of human rights – also presupposed that for all the contradictions in the US posture toward human rights, its leadership generally aspired to be supportive of a system that in important ways mirrored its own values and system of government. The Trump administration's words and actions make clear that this aspiration should not be taken for granted. Perhaps the US will someday become the pillar of human rights that advocates have called for it to be. But first it must pass through the current political moment without becoming a wrecking ball.

BIBLIOGRAPHY

"Donald Trump's Administration is Promoting Democracy and Human Rights." *The Economist*, December 6, 2017.

"Jimmy Carter Reaffirms his Commitment to Human Rights." *History.com*, February 25, 2019. www.history.com/this-day-in-history/jimmy-carter-reaffirms-his-commitment-to-human-rights.

"Trump Praises Brazil's New President Bolsonaro after He Vowed to 'Strengthen Democracy.'" *CNBC*, January 1, 2019. www.cnbc.com/2019/01/01/trump-praises-brazils-new-president-bolsonaro-after-he-vowed-to-strengthen-democracy-.html.

"U.S. Launches Media Fund for Hungary to Aid Press Freedom." *Reuters*, November 13, 2017. www.reuters.com/article/us-hungary-us-media/u-s-launches-media-fund-for-hungary-to-aid-press-freedom-idUSKBN1DD21C.

Baker, Peter. "Viktor Orban, Hungary's Far-Right Leader, Gets Warm Welcome from Trump." *New York Times*, May 13, 2019. www.nytimes.com/2019/05/13/us/politics/trump-viktor-orban-oval-office.html.

Berschinski, Robert. "Trump Administration Notches Human Rights Win. No, Really." *Just Security*, January 10, 2018. www.justsecurity.org/50846/trump-administration-notches-human-rights-win-no-really/.

Black, Allida M. "Eleanor Roosevelt and the Universal Declaration of Human Rights." *OAH Magazine of History* 22, no. 2 (2008): 34–37. www.jstor.org/stable/25162170.

Blake, Aaron. "Trump Won't Believe His Own Intelligence Community – Again." *Washington Post*, November 17, 2018. www.washingtonpost.com/politics/2018/11/15/trump-adminis tration-is-trying-hard-not-blame-saudi-crown-prince-khashoggis-death/.

Bolton, John. "Full Text of John Bolton's Speech to the Federalist Society." *Al Jazeera*, September 10, 2018. www.aljazeera.com/news/2018/09/full-text-john-bolton-speech-feder alist-society-180910172828633.html.

"Remarks by National Security Advisor Ambassador John R. Bolton on the Administration's Policies in Latin America." *White House Remarks*, November 2, 2018. www.whitehouse .gov/briefings-statements/remarks-national-security-advisor-ambassador-john-r-bolton-administrations-policies-latin-america/.

"The Hague Aims for U.S. Soldiers." *Wall Street Journal*, November 2017. www.wsj.com/ articles/the-hague-tiptoes-toward-u-s-soldiers-1511217136.

Boyle, Andrew. "The Free Press Aren't 'Enemies of the People.'" *Brennan Center for Justice*, August 24, 2018. www.brennancenter.org/blog/free-press-arent-enemies-people.

Bump, Philip. "Donald Trump Isn't Fazed by Vladimir Putin's Journalist Murdering." *Washington Post*, December 18, 2015. www.washingtonpost.com/news/the-fix/wp/2015/ 12/18/donald-trump-glad-to-be-endorsed-by-russias-top-journalist-murderer/.

Calamur, Krishnadev. "A Short History of America First." *The Atlantic*, January 21, 2017. www .theatlantic.com/politics/archive/2017/01/trump-america-first/514037/.

Carter, Jimmy. "Inaugural Address." *The American Presidency Project*, January 20, 1977. www .presidency.ucsb.edu/documents/inaugural-address-0.

"Presidential Directive/NSC 30." *The White House*, February 17, 1978, https://fas.org/irp/ offdocs/pd/pd30.pdf.

Cofman Wittes, Tamara. "Sanctions on Saudi Arabia Aren't Enough." *Brookings*, December 5, 2018. www.brookings.edu/blog/order-from-chaos/2018/12/05/sanctions-on-saudi-arabia-arent-enough/.

Cohen, Roberta. "Integrating Human Rights in U.S. Foreign Policy: The History, the Challenges, and the Criteria for an Effective Policy." *Brookings*, April 9, 2008. www .brookings.edu/on-the-record/integrating-human-rights-in-u-s-foreign-policy-the-history-the-challenges-and-the-criteria-for-an-effective-policy/.

Committee on Foreign Relations, U.S. Senate, "Convention on the Rights of Persons with Disabilities: Report." 113th Congress: Senate Executive Report 113-12, July 28, 2014. www .congress.gov/congressional-report/113th-congress/executive-report/12.

Elbagir, Nina et al. "The Schoolboys on a Field Trip in Yemen were Chatting and Laughing. Then came the Airstrike." *CNN*, February 27, 2019. www.cnn.com/2018/08/13/mid dleeast/yemen-children-school-bus-strike-intl/index.html.

Elving, Ron. "Trump Vows Policy Vision of 'America First,' Recalling Phrase's Controversial Past." *The Atlantic*, January 21, 2017. www.npr.org/2017/01/21/510877650/trump-vows-policy-vision-of-america-first-recalling-phrases-controversial-past.

Erlanger, Steven. "'Fake News,' Trump's Obsession, Is Now a Cudgel for Strongmen." *New York Times*, December 12, 2017. www.nytimes.com/2017/12/12/world/europe/trump-fake-news-dictators.html.

Farooq, Umar. "US: Pompeo Blames Iran for Yemen's Civil War." *Anadolu Agency*, April 29, 2019. www.aa.com.tr/en/americas/us-pompeo-blames-iran-for-yemens-civil-war/1465422.

Fink, Sheri and Helene Cooper. "Inside Trump Defense Secretary Pick's Efforts to Halt Torture." *New York Times,* January 2, 2017. www.nytimes.com/2017/01/02/us/politics/james-mattis-defense-secretary-trump.html.

Haley, Nikki. "Remarks on the U.N. Human Rights Council." *The United States Mission at the United Nations,* June 19, 2019. https://usun.state.gov/remarks/8486.

Hanner, Kenneth. "Bolton: US Should Resign from 'Clown Convention' at UN." *Newsmax,* April 30, 2013. www.newsmax.com/newsfront/bolton-un-human-rights/2013/04/30/id/502008/.

Harper, Keith M. and Stephen Pomper. "On the U.N. Human Rights Council, Quitters are Losers." *Foreign Policy,* January 29, 2018. https://foreignpolicy.com/2018/01/29/on-the-u-n-human-rights-council-quitters-are-losers/.

Henkin, Louis. "Human Rights and United States Foreign Policy." In *The Age of Rights,* 65–80. New York: Columbia University Press, 1996.

International Crisis Group. "Ending the Yemen Quagmire: Lessons from Washington from Four Years of War." *International Crisis Group,* April 15, 2019. www.crisisgroup.org/united-states/003-ending-yemen-quagmire-lessons-washington-four-years-war.

Jacoby, Tamar. "The Reagan Turnaround on Human Rights." *Foreign Affairs* 64, no. 5 (1986): 1066–1086. www.foreignaffairs.com/articles/1986-06-01/reagan-turnaround-human-rights.

Johnson, Jenna. "Trump Says 'Torture Works,' Backs Waterboarding and 'Much Worse.'" *Washington Post,* February 17, 2016. www.washingtonpost.com/politics/trump-says-torture-works-backs-wa;terboarding-and-much-worse/2016/02/17/4c9277be-d59c-11e5-b195-2e29a4e13425_story.html.

Keating, Joshua. "Homeschoolers Help Torpedo Disability Rights Treaty in Senate." *Foreign Policy,* December 4, 2012. https://foreignpolicy.com/2012/12/04/homeschoolers-help-torpedo-disability-rights-treaty-in-senate/.

Kingsley, Patrick. "Hungary's Leader was Shunned by Obama, but Has a Friend in Trump." *New York Times,* August 15, 2018. www.nytimes.com/2018/08/15/world/europe/hungary-us-orban-trump.html.

Lewis, Larry. "Grading the Pompeo Certification on the Yemen War and Civilian Protection: Time for Serious Reconsideration." *Just Security,* September 18, 2018. www.justsecurity.org/60766/grading-pompeo-certification-yemen-war-civilian-protection-time-reconsideration/.

Margon, Sarah. "Giving up the High Ground: America's Retreat on Human Rights." *Foreign Affairs* 97, no. 2 (2018): 39–45. www.foreignaffairs.com/articles/united-states/2018-02-13/giving-high-ground.

Martin, Douglas. "Ernest W. Lefever, Rejected as a Reagan Nominee, Dies at 89." *New York Times,* August 4, 2009. www.nytimes.com/2009/08/05/us/politics/05lefever.html.

McCarthy, Tom. "Dick Cheney Defends America's Use of Torture, Again, in New Book." *The Guardian,* September 1, 2015. www.theguardian.com/us-news/2015/sep/01/dick-cheney-defends-america-torture-new-book.

Mclaughlin, Aidan. *"Fox and Friends Backs SEAL Accused of Shooting Little Girl: 'These Are the Good Guys.'" Mediaite,* May 19, 2019. www.mediaite.com/tv/fox-friends-backs-seal-accused-of-shooting-little-girl-these-are-the-good-guys/.

McMahon, Robert. "Human Rights Reporting and U.S. Foreign Policy." *Council on Foreign Relations,* March 25, 2019. www.cfr.org/backgrounder/human-rights-reporting-and-us-foreign-policy.

Mearsheimer, John J. *The Great Delusion: Liberal Dreams and International Realities.* New Haven, London: Yale University Press, 2018.

Moyn, Samuel. "Economic Rights Are Human Rights." *Foreign Policy*, April 9, 2018. https:// foreignpolicy.com/2018/04/09/the-freedom-america-forgot-populism-human-rights-united-nations/.

Phillip, Abby. "O'Reilly Told Trump that Putin Is a Killer. Trump's Reply: 'You Think our Country Is so Innocent?'" *Washington Post*, February 4, 2017. www.washingtonpost.com/ news/post-politics/wp/2017/02/04/oreilly-told-trump-that-putin-is-a-killer-trumps-reply-you-think-our-countrys-so-innocent/.

"Trump Calls on Venezuela to Release Political Prisoner after Meeting with Rubio." *Washington Post*, February 15, 2017. www.washingtonpost.com/news/post-politics/ wp/2017/02/15/trump-calls-on-venezuela-to-release-political-prisoner-after-meeting-with-rubio/.

Phillips, Dave. "Trump May Be Preparing Pardons for Servicemen Accused of War Crimes." *New York Times*, May 18, 2019. www.nytimes.com/2019/05/18/us/trump-pardons-war-crimes.html?smtyp=cur&smid=tw-nytimesatwar.

Pompeo, Michael R. "Supporting Iranian Voices." *Remarks*, U.S. Department of State, July 22, 2018. www.state.gov/supporting-iranian-voices/.

Pomper, Stephen. "Atrocity Prevention under the Obama Administration: What We Learned and the Path Ahead." *United States Holocaust Memorial Museum*, February 2018. www .ushmm.org/m/pdfs/Stephen_Pomper_Report_02-2018.pdf.

"USG Statement on International Criminal Court Probe Is Missing Some Things." *Just Security*, December 14, 2017. www.justsecurity.org/49360/usg-statement-intl-criminal-court-probe-alleged-u-s-war-crimes-missing-2/.

Reeves, Philip. "Dictatorship Was A 'Very Good' Period, Says Brazil's Aspiring President." *NPR*, July 30, 2018. www.npr.org/2018/07/30/631952886/dictatorship-was-a-very-good-period-says-brazil-s-aspiring-president.

Rice, Susan E. "Human Rights: Advancing American Interests and Values." Human Rights First Annual Summit, December 4, 2013. https://obamawhitehouse.archives.gov/the-press-office/2013/12/04/remarks-national-security-advisor-susan-e-rice-human-rights-advan cing-am.

Riotta, Chris. "Trump 'Would Love to Have Orban's Situation in Hungary' US Ambassador Says," *The Independent*, May 9, 2019. www.independent.co.uk/news/world/americas/us-politics/trump-viktor-orban-hungary-david-cornstein-fidesz-illiberal-democracy-a8907246 .html.

Roosevelt, Eleanor. "The Promise of Human Rights." *Foreign Affairs* 26, no. 3 (1948): 470–477. www.foreignaffairs.com/articles/1948-04-01/promise-human-rights.

Ruffini, Christina. "Mike Pompeo Unveils New 'Unalienable Rights' Commission Amid Concerns over Progressive Rollbacks." *CBS News*, July 8, 2019. www.cbsnews.com/ news/mike-pompeo-unveils-new-unalienable-rights-commission-amid-concerns-over-pro gressive-rollbacks/

Sánchez-Gimoli, Gimena. "Bolsonaro Acts on Promises to Dismantle Human Rights Protec-tions in Brazil." *WOLA* January 1, 2019. www.wola.org/analysis/bolsonaro-acts-promises-dismantle-human-rights-protections-brazil/.

Schwartz, Jason. "Trump's 'Fake News' Rhetoric Crops up Around the Globe." *Politico*, July 30, 2018. www.politico.com/story/2018/07/30/trump-media-fake-news-750536.

Slaughter, Anne-Marie and Catherine Powell. "Louis Henkin (1917–2010): The Power of His Ideas Live On." *Opinio Juris*, October 10, 2010. http://opiniojuris.org/2010/10/22/louis-henkin-1917-2010-the-power-of-his-ideas-live-on/.

Sugars, Stephanie. "From Fake News to Enemy of the People: An Anatomy of Trump's Tweets." *Committee to Project Journalists*, January 30, 2019. https://cpj.org/blog/2019/01/ trump-twitter-press-fake-news-enemy-people.php.

Szoldra, Paul. "Trump Says 'Glad I Could Help!' in Congratulatory Tweet to Navy SEAL Eddie Gallagher." *Task & Purpose*, July 3, 2019. https://taskandpurpose.com/trump-congrats-eddie-gallagher.

Toosi, Nahal. "Bolton Returns to a U.N. He Made a Career of Blasting." *Politico*, September 23, 2018. https://www.politico.com/story/2018/09/23/john-bolton-united-nations-iran-836454/.

———. "Leaked Memo Schooled Tillerson on Human Rights." *Politico*, December 19, 2017. www.politico.com/story/2017/12/19/tillerson-state-human-rights-304118.

Trump, Donald. "President Donald J. Trump Supports the Venezuelan People's Efforts to Restore Democracy in their Country." *White House Factsheets*, January 29, 2019. www.whitehouse.gov/briefings-statements/president-donald-j-trump-supports-venezuelan-peoples-efforts-restore-democracy-country/.

———. "Presidential Veto Message to the Senate to Accompany S.J. Res. 7." *White House Presidential Memoranda*. www.whitehouse.gov/presidential-actions/presidential-veto-message-senate-accompany-s-j-res-7/.

———. "Remarks of President Donald J. Trump – Inaugural Address." *White House Remarks*, January 20, 2017. www.whitehouse.gov/briefings-statements/the-inaugural-address/.

———. "Statement from President Donald J. Trump on Standing with Saudi Arabia." *White House Statements & Releases*, November 20, 2018. www.whitehouse.gov/briefings-statements/statement-president-donald-j-trump-standing-saudi-arabia/.

Trump, Donald, and Abdel Fattah al-Sisi. "Remarks by President Trump and President Al-Sisi of the Arab Republic of Egypt before Bilateral Meeting." *White House Remarks*, September 24, 2018. www.whitehouse.gov/briefings-statements/remarks-president-trump-president-al-sisi-arab-republic-egypt-bilateral-meeting/.

Trump, Donald, and Andrzej Duda. "Joint Statement by President Donald J. Trump and President Andrzej Duda of the Republic of Poland." *White House Statements & Releases*, September 18, 2019. www.whitehouse.gov/briefings-statements/joint-statement-president-donald-j-trump-president-andrzej-duda-republic-poland/.

Trump, Donald, and Rodrigo Duterte, "Remarks by President Trump and President Duterte of the Philippines before Bilateral Meeting." *White House Remarks*, November 13, 2017. www.whitehouse.gov/briefings-statements/remarks-president-trump-president-duterte-philippines-bilateral-meeting-manila-philippines/

Trump, Donald, and Viktor Orbán. "Remarks by President Trump and Prime Minister Orbán of Hungary before Bilateral Meeting." *White House Statements & Releases*, May 13, 2019. www.whitehouse.gov/briefings-statements/remarks-president-trump-prime-minister-orban-hungary-bilateral-meeting/.

U.S. Department of State, "Documentation of Atrocities in Northern Rakhine State." *Reliefweb*, September 24, 2018. https://reliefweb.int/report/myanmar/documentation-atrocities-northern-rakhine-state.

Van Schaack, Beth. "United States Report to the UN Human Rights Committee: Lex Specialis and Extraterritoriality." *Just Security*, October 16, 2013. www.justsecurity.org/1761/united-states-lex-specialis-extraterritoriality/.

Walt, Stephen M. *The Hell of Good Intentions: America's Foreign Policy Elite and the Decline of U.S. Primacy*. New York: Farrar, Straus and Giroux, 2018.

Watts, Jonathan. "Trump Joy over Bolsonaro Suggests New Rightwing Axis in Americas and Beyond." *The Guardian*, October 29, 2018. www.theguardian.com/world/2018/oct/29/jair-bolsonaro-brazil-trump-rightwing-axis.

White, Christopher. "Former U.S. Envoy to Vatican Opposes New Commission Headed by Predecessor." *Crux*, July 23, 2019. https://cruxnow.com/church-in-the-usa/2019/07/23/former-u-s-envoy-to-vatican-opposes-new-commission-headed-by-predecessor/.

Wolfgang, Ben. "Obama: Despite Human Rights Troubles, We Must Work with Saudi Arabia." *The Washington Times*, January 27, 2015. www.washingtontimes.com/news/2015/jan/27/obama-saudi-arabia-human-rights-troubles/.

Wroughton, Lesley. "U.S. Imposes Visa Bans on International Criminal Court Investigators – Pompeo." *Reuters*, March 15, 2019. www.reuters.com/article/uk-usa-icc/u-s-imposes-visa-bans-on-international-criminal-court-investigators-pompeo-idUSKCN1QW1ZH.

3

Rule-of-Law Rights and Populist Impatience

Jeremy Waldron

I RULE-OF-LAW RIGHTS

Human rights are a mixed bag, and populist antipathy towards human rights is not spread evenly across its contents. The idea of a human right *as such* is too abstract to be sustained as an object of political suspicion. Usually it is some subset of human rights or some particular aspect of human rights practice that excites critical attention from populist politicians and the citizens who support them. The subset of rights that I want to concentrate on I will call "Rule-of-Law rights." By that I mean the cluster of rights in each of the main human rights instruments that protect Rule-of-Law values, particularly procedural values.

In the International Covenant on Civil and Political Rights (ICCPR), these are the rights referred to in Articles 9 and 14–16. They prohibit arbitrary arrest and detention, they require persons arrested to be informed of the charges against them and brought quickly before a judicial officer, they empower detained persons to challenge their detention, they entitle those charged with criminal offenses to trial within a reasonable time, with detailed procedural guarantees such as the presumption of innocence, a right to the assistance of counsel, a right to compel and examine witnesses, a right to appellate opportunities, and the benefit of protection against double jeopardy. They also comprise rules against retrospective laws, and rules governing pre-trial custody and release. There is a similar list of Rule-of-Law rights in Articles 5–7 of the European Convention on Human Rights (ECHR). National constitutions and Bills of Rights include these measures too: the UK Human Rights Act, obviously (because it is a domestication of the ECHR), and – from a much earlier era – the various due process (or procedural due process) guarantees of the Constitution of the United States (such as the Fifth and Sixth Amendments). I call these "Rule-of-Law rights" ("ROL rights," for short) to indicate that their function is to convey, in rights-form, the burden of certain principles of the political ideal we call "the Rule of Law." This characterization calls for a brief digression.

Among those who are interested in the Rule of Law there is a debate about whether that ideal should be understood to comprise substantive commitments to human rights or whether it should be treated as a "thin" formal/procedural ideal.[1] It should be noted that the existence of human rights like those just mentioned does not affect this dispute. Rights such as Articles 5–7 of the ECHR and articles 9–10 and 14–16 of the ICCPR are not what defenders of a "thick" conception of the Rule of Law have in mind. They think it comprises rights like free speech, freedom of religion, and other civil liberties. It is true that "thin" conceptions of the Rule of Law haven't given as much attention to procedural principles as they ought to have: following Lon Fuller, they have focused more on formal principles, like generality, clarity, prospectivity, publicity, stability, and so on.[2] But the procedural principles mentioned in the second paragraph of this chapter are usually taken to be part of a "thin" conception of the Rule of Law.

One other point: that some human rights provisions convey the importance of certain Rule-of-Law requirements doesn't mean that human rights documents embody the full panoply of Rule-of-Law ideas (even on a "thin" conception). Of the formal principles just mentioned, only the principle of prospectivity figures explicitly in the human rights materials;[3] human rights documents do not enact other aspects of Lon Fuller's inner morality of law,[4] though aspects of Fuller's conception have figured in doctrine concerning what counts as "prescribed by law" or "provided by law" for the purposes of the exception provisos for freedom of thought, conscience and religion, free speech, and freedom of association.[5]

Though human rights present themselves as a simple list, no subset of rights can be considered in isolation, particularly so far as the attitudes they elicit in the community are concerned. As we shall see, populist (and, actually, even elite) reactions to the rights I have identified are affected by some other principles that govern their operation. Some of these are rights in their own right, like the ECHR's Article 8 (the right to protection of family life). Others are interpretations of rights or doctrines that have grown up around ROL rights, such as principles restricting whole-life sentences and forbidding the disenfranchisement of prisoners. In what follows, we will consider the possibility that the entanglement of these principles

---

[1] Compare the "thin" conception in Joseph Raz, "The Rule of Law and Its Virtue," in his collection *The Authority of Law: Essays on Law and Morality* (Oxford: Clarendon Press, 1979), 211–229, with the "thicker" account in Tom Bingham, *The Rule of Law* (London: Allen Lane, 2010), 66–67.

[2] Lon Fuller, *The Morality of Law* (New Haven, CT: Yale University Press, 1964). See also Jeremy Waldron, "The Rule of Law and the Importance of Procedure," in *Getting to the Rule of Law*, ed. James E. Fleming (New York: New York University Press, 2011) (Nomos 50), 3–31, for an attempt to correct this.

[3] International Covenant on Civil and Political Rights (ICCPR), Article 15; [European] Convention on Human Rights and Fundamental Freedoms (ECHR), Article 7.

[4] Fuller, *Morality of Law*, ch. 2.

[5] ICCPR, Articles 18 (3), 19 (3) and 22 (2).

with ROL rights has undermined respect for the latter, so that disentanglement might be seen as a way of offsetting populist resentment.

II POPULISM

In this chapter I consider recent expressions of populist antipathy towards human rights, with special reference to the subset of rights I have mentioned. I am interested in hostility towards these rights, but I am interested also in the central place they are likely to occupy in any conception of human rights that can be retrieved from populist hostility. I am aware that just as the category of *human rights* is wide and variegated – with different clusters of rights worth distinguishing and studying for various purposes – so too the category of *populism* is also wide and variegated. It is not easy to define, especially across different political communities. I will not spend too much time trying to pin down exactly the populists whose expressed antipathy towards ROL rights interests me. My account is mainly impressionistic.

Much of my focus will be on the United Kingdom, though I will move back and forth a bit between British and American populism. So far as the UK is concerned, I am especially interested in the views of those who in the recent past have described the European Convention on Human Rights and its statutory embodiment in the UK's Human Rights Act as "a charter for criminals," those who associate human rights in general with foreign imposition, and those who have demanded the establishment of what they call "a British Bill of Rights." (Examples of all these characterizations will be given shortly.)

Some will associate the demand for a British Bill of Rights with the national mood that led to the Brexit decision – the 2016 referendum decision in the UK to leave the European Union (EU). In principle, of course, the two areas of populist concern – rage against the ECHR and rage against the EU – are distinct. By itself Brexit will not affect Britain's participation in or obligations under the ECHR system (in respect of its membership of and obligations to the Council of Europe). But the distinction is not widely understood, and in the popular – and populist? – mind they are often blurred together. There are obvious resonances between Brexit and the demand for a British Bill of Rights to replace the ECHR; indeed, many ECHR doctrines that people find objectionable have counterparts in EU law as well.[6]

In an excellent discussion, Jan-Werner Müller associates populism with opposition to internal pluralism and with the emergence of a politics that is appropriate to a perceived or wished-for social homogeneity, whether in fact such homogeneity is likely ever to exist or not.[7] But it is not just denial of internal pluralism; modern populism also involves an attempt to defend a given community from outside

---

[6] Charter of Fundamental Rights of the European Union, 2000 O.J. (C 364), 1.
[7] Jan-Werner Müller, *What Is Populism?* (Philadelphia, PA: University of Pennsylvania Press, 2016).

influences that threaten to compromise the flourishing of its native values and
ideals. It involves strident nationalism and antipathy to universalist, globalist, and
cosmopolitan modes of thought. Both these dimensions of populism – and the
interplay between them – will be important in what follows.

Populism is sometimes understood as a specifically non-elite or anti-elite phenomenon. I shall not assume that. Some of the rhetoric attacking ROL rights comes
from politicians in office, and not just erstwhile outsiders like Donald Trump in the
US, but also establishment figures like former Prime Minister David Cameron in
the UK. Such figures can be seen as responding to populist campaigns but also as
fueling them and taking advantage of them. Also some of the antipathy towards
human rights culture in Britain has come from respected scholars and judges.[8]
These too I will mention, if only because they resonate to a certain extent with more
low-brow populist critiques.

III POPULIST COMPLAINTS AGAINST ROL RIGHTS

A miscellany of populist and quasi-populist complaints will illustrate the kind of
resentment against ROL rights that I have in mind.

In the UK, one hears the Human Rights Act condemned as a "Criminals'
Charter." In 2012, *The Mail on Sunday* opined:

> [I]t is time the convention was made to work as originally intended, rather than as a
> charter for criminals and parasites ... And above all, the 'human rights' of the
> indigenous population must be considered. Do these rights not safeguard them
> from having dangerous rapists placed in their midst? If they do not, then they are
> not worth having, and we would be better off without them.[9]

We are told that "[t]he Human Rights culture is creating an increasingly dangerous Britain, where the bullies are guarded by the state, where common sense has
disappeared and where anarchy triumphs over order ... [E]ven Jack Straw, the
Labour minister who piloted the Act through Parliament, said: 'there is a sense that
it's a villains' charter.'"[10]

A few years later, in submissions to the House of Lords committee considering the
possibility of a British Bill of Rights, a government spokesman said that, to the

---

[8] See, for example, Noel Malcolm, *Human Rights and Political Wrongs: A New Approach to
Human Rights* (London: Policy Exchange, 2017). This work is available at https://policyex
change.org.uk/wp-content/uploads/2017/12/Human-Rights-and-Political-Wrongs.pdf.

[9] Comment, "Human Rights Is a Charter for Criminals and Parasites: Our Anger Is No Longer
Enough," *Mail on Sunday*, July 14, 2012, www.dailymail.co.uk/debate/article-2173666/Human-
rights-charter-criminals-parasites-anger-longer-enough.html.

[10] Leo McKinstry, "Human Right's [sic] Act Has Become the Villain's Charter: The Human
Rights Act Continues to Exert Its Malign Influence," *Daily Express*, October 3, 2011, www
.express.co.uk/comment/columnists/leo-mckinstry/275220/Human-right-s-act-has-become-the-
villain-s-charter.

Government's regret "human rights … have a bad name in the public square." Human rights had become associated with "unmeritorious individuals pursuing through the courts claims that do not command public support or sympathy."[11] People have the sense that criminals (and their attorneys) are taking wrongful advantage of human rights provisions that protect various aspects of the criminal law process. ROL rights provide ample opportunities for smart-ass lawyers to exploit technicalities and loopholes, either to avoid their clients' conviction or to diminish or delay punishment.

One thing that ROL rights seek to do is to maintain procedural Rule-of-Law values in the face of pressure brought by an impatient public for quick action on law-and-order issues and swift punishment for those accused of offenses. This is true in the US as it is in the UK. Consider, for example, President Trump's 2017 comments about our "disgraceful" justice system. Responding to various terrorist incidents, he said that the country must "come up with punishment that's far quicker and far greater than the punishment these animals are getting now." He said that "[t]hey'll go through court for years … We need quick justice and we need strong justice, much quicker and much stronger than we have right now. Because what we have right now is a joke and it's a laughingstock."[12] The expression of impatience here is important, because as we shall see patience and long-drawn-out procedures are exactly what the procedural aspect of the Rule of Law seems to require.

Trumpian impatience is matched by a sense that criminals and their unscrupulous counsel are taking serial advantage of loophole after loophole, technicality after technicality, appeal after appeal, to drag things out in criminal proceedings. And there is incredulity and outrage when those who have dragged things out to this extent then make claims that are supposed to derive from the protraction of the proceedings against them, for example, under the auspices of the so-called death row syndrome.[13] When the issue was raised in American proceedings, Justice Thomas wrote angrily that he was "unaware of any support in the American constitutional tradition or in this Court's precedent for the proposition that a defendant can avail himself of the panoply of appellate and collateral procedures and then complain when his execution is delayed."[14]

---

[11] Secretary of State for Justice, quoted in House of Lords, European Union Committee, *The UK, the EU, and a British Bill of Rights*, HL 139 (2016), 13.

[12] President Trump, as quoted in Ruth Marcus, "Our Criminal Justice System Is Not a 'Joke.' Yet," *Washington Post*, November 3, 2017, www.washingtonpost.com/opinions/our-criminal-justice-system-is-not-a-joke-yet/2017/11/03/8aeb386c-c0d6-11e7-97d9-bdab5a0ab381_story.html.

[13] For the death row syndrome (or death row "phenomenon"), see the Privy Council decision in *Pratt* v. *Attorney-General for Jamaica*, [1993] UKPC 1, and the decision of the European Court of Human Rights in *Soering* v. *United Kingdom* 161 Eur. Ct. H.R. (ser. A) (1989).

[14] These comments were made by Justice Thomas in *Knight* v. *Florida*, 528 U.S. 990 (1999), concurring in the denial of certiorari.

Some of the discontent with the Rule-of-Law rights has to do with the way that certain other rights interact with them. In the ECHR context, this is particularly true of the interaction of ROL rights with Article 8, which holds that "everyone has the right to respect for his private and family life, his home and his correspondence." It is widely believed that Article 8 prevents or delays the deportation of non-British individuals convicted of serious offenses on account of the fact that this this will separate the criminals in question from their wives, parents, children, or pets. Even if one accepts that in principle Article 8 offers valid protection for family values, there is anger at the way in which it supervenes on the criminal process. The problem is partly that this application of the principle is unexpected and shocking, perhaps counter-intuitive. People's expectations that the law will protect them from offenders are shocked by the offenders' use of this safeguard. It seems like an affront to common sense.

Both in the UK and in the US there is a sense that doctrines like these – death row syndrome and respect for family life precluding deportation – represent alien innovations in the regular (English or American) criminal process. In another case where the death row syndrome argument was raised, Justice Thomas complained about the imposition of "foreign moods, fads, or fashions on Americans."[15] A report of the House of Lords committee considering the case for a "British Bill of Rights" recorded a government submission to the effect that "troublingly, human rights are seen as something that are done to British courts and the British people as a result of foreign intervention, rather than something that we originally championed and created and seek to uphold."[16] These complaints do not represent a direct attack on the Rule of Law. That ideal is still seen as quintessentially British. But there is a widespread view that a Diceyan world of Anglo-Saxon common sense (British and American)[17] in these matters being besieged by funny and ill-thought-out foreign ideas.

This resentment of what seems like foreign imposition is also evident in the debate over prisoner voting that erupted in the wake of the decision of the European Court of Human Rights (ECtHR) in *Hirst* (No. 2), upholding a complaint that Britain was in violation of the First Protocol to the ECHR (regarding elections) in peremptorily denying all convicted prisoners the right to vote.[18] ECtHR decisions are often not popular in the UK, often resented; but by and large the UK abides by its treaty obligation to implement them. The case of *Hirst* is a rare exception. Contemplating the possibility that *Hirst* might lead to voting by violent offenders while serving their sentence in the UK, then Prime Minister David Cameron said

---

[15] *Foster v. Florida*, 537 U.S. 990 (2002).
[16] House of Lords, *UK, EU, and a British Bill of Rights*, 13.
[17] Consider Dicey's rather gauche and patronizing enlistment of American constitutional ideas in his account of English Rule-of-Law constitutionalism in A.V. Dicey, *Introduction to the Study of the Law of the Constitution* (Indianapolis: Liberty Fund, 1982) (reprint of 8th edition, 1915), 118–19.
[18] *Hirst v. United Kingdom* (No. 2), [2005] ECHR 681 [GC].

the prospect made him physically ill, and the House of Commons rejected the idea of legislation to enable prisoner voting.[19] More recently there seems to have been a compromise: prisoners on temporary release and at home under curfew – a few hundred at most – will gain the right to vote. Apparently this can be done administratively without the need for formal legislation.[20]

Less prominent than concern about foreign imposition in these complaints, but certainly present, is resentment of policy-making by judges in areas like criminal procedure, where it is felt that the will of the people as represented in Parliament ought to prevail. This complaint can respond as much to decisions by British judges under the auspices of the Human Rights Act as it does to "foreign" decisions by the ECtHR. (It is usually through judicial pronouncements focused on particular cases that the public first becomes aware of the counter-intuitive doctrines.) It is worth noting, on the other hand, that some of the support for a British Bill of Rights is based on the proposition that it is better to have rights imposed by British courts, and by British courts acting independently of European jurisprudence, if they are to be judicially imposed at all. The case that was made for a British Bill of Rights in the 2015 Conservative Party manifesto was (in part) that it would "break the formal link between the British courts and the European Court of Human Rights" and make the Supreme Court "the ultimate arbiter of human rights matters in the UK."[21] In doing so, it would actually enhance the legitimacy of judicial incursions into politics. Or so it was thought.

In the United States, too, there is a chronic debate about judicial activism and a tendency towards judicial supremacy in matters of criminal procedure.[22] It is aggravated by the sense that some elements in the Supreme Court of the United States have become overly susceptible to foreign ideas.[23] But populist resentment of

---

[19] Matthew Holehouse, "David Cameron: I Will Ignore Europe's Top Court on Prisoner Voting," *Daily Telegraph*, October 4, 2015, www.telegraph.co.uk/news/uknews/law-and-order/11911057/David-Cameron-I-will-ignore-Europes-top-court-on-prisoner-voting.html. For the 2011 parliamentary vote on the matter (which was not legislative), see "MPs Reject Prisoner Votes Plan," *BBC News*, February 10, 2011, www.bbc.com/news/uk-politics-12409426.

[20] Owen Bowcott, "Council of Europe Accepts UK Compromise on Prisoner Voting Rights," *The Guardian*, December 7, 2017, www.theguardian.com/politics/2017/dec/07/council-of-europe-accepts-uk-compromise-on-prisoner-voting-rights: "The compromise should remove one of the main sources of resentment felt by Conservative rightwingers over the Strasbourg court's role. Prisoners on temporary release and at home under curfew will gain the right to vote."

[21] *Strong Leadership, a Clear Economic Plan, a Brighter, More Secure Future: The Conservative Party Manifesto 2015*, www.conservatives.com/manifesto2015, 73.

[22] See, for example, the discussion in Jennelle London Joset, "May It Please the Constitution: Judicial Activism and Its Effect on Criminal Procedure," *Marquette Law Review* 79, no. 4 (1996): 1021–1040.

[23] See Robert Barnes, "Breyer Says Understanding Foreign Law Is Critical to Supreme Court's Work," *Washington Post*, September 12, 2015, www.washingtonpost.com/politics/courts_law/breyer-says-understanding-foreign-law-is-critical-to-supreme-courts-work/2015/09/12/36a38212-57e9-11e5-8bb1-b488d231bba2_story.html (discussing Stephen Breyer, *The Court and the World: American Law and the New Global Realities* [New York: Alfred A. Knopf, 2015]).

judiciary on these matters would exist even if there had been no appeal to foreign law in cases like *Roper* v. *Simmons*,[24] and resentment of judicial imposition in the area of criminal justice antedates the controversy about foreign law by decades.[25] The British debate about judicial power is underdeveloped by comparison and not fully separated from concern about the influence of the ECtHR.

IV ABSTRACT THEMES

Some more abstract themes also emerge from populist statements about ROL rights. Some of these are more articulate in the public debate than others. I set them out here, not only to fill out our understanding of these concerns but also to begin the process of considering how populist complaints might be answered.

I believe that, in many of these areas, more theoretical work is needed, so that defenders of ROL rights can set out more clearly why we should continue to uphold them or what concessions should be made to their critics. I am not suggesting that populist criticism represents a demand for more philosophy. But one or two of the populist criticisms are telling at a political level because rights-scholars have, for whatever reason, avoided dealing with some of the difficulties that current ideas about rights give rise to.[26]

For example, a complaint is sometimes heard from respected scholars about the proliferation of human rights. Rights advocates, it is said, appear to have abandoned the idea that rights are moral minima and that they are not supposed to cover the whole domain of political and social morality but only the most basic requirements necessary for decent treatment of people by their governments.[27]

There is some justice to this complaint, but we have to be careful how we understand moral *minima*. From one point of view, we list the worst horrors – "barbarous acts which have outraged the conscience of mankind,"[28] such as torture and slavery – that people are subject to, and we say that the function of human rights is to protect people from *these*. We do this simply by mentioning the horrors and associating them with an absolute prohibition, such as the prohibitions in Article 7 of the ICCPR.[29] In other areas, however, including the area of ROL rights, rights

---

[24] *Roper* v. *Simmons*, 543 U.S. 551 (2005). See the discussion in Jeremy Waldron, *"Partly Laws Common to All Mankind": Foreign Law in American Courts* (New Haven, CT: Yale University Press, 2012), 1–3.

[25] There is an excellent overview of the history of complaints about judicial activism in Keenan D. Kmiec, "The Origin and Current Meanings of Judicial Activism," *California Law Review* 92, no. 5 (2004): 1441–1477.

[26] See, for example, the issues raised in Malcolm, *Human Rights and Political Wrongs*.

[27] Malcolm, *Human Rights and Political Wrongs*.

[28] Universal Declaration of Human Rights, Preamble.

[29] ICCPR, Article 7: "No one shall be subjected to torture or to cruel, inhuman or degrading treatment or punishment. In particular, no one shall be subjected without his free consent to medical or scientific experimentation."

operate in a slightly different way. Items in the array of ROL rights may not be moral *minima* or represent recoil from past horrors; but they work together as a system, which is calculated to make social and political life fair and bearable in regard to the coercive exercise of state power. That "[a]nyone arrested or detained on a criminal charge shall be brought promptly before a judge"[30] is not exactly on a par with Article 7 so far as the avoidance of moral horror is concerned. It is nevertheless a constitutive part of a system whose absence (the system's absence) would represent a horrific vulnerability to power in the lives of ordinary people.

On a different front, there is a worry that human rights – and this may apply specifically to ROL rights – are being treated just as something to be exploited for selfish or anti-social purposes by those endowed with them. Perhaps we need to cultivate the idea that abuse of rights (taking wrongful advantage of one's rights) should have consequences.[31] But if they ever had doctrines to this effect, philosophers who study human rights have long since abandoned them.

This is connected with a sense that we need to cultivate a stronger connection between rights and responsibilities. Now, the call for an equal emphasis on responsibilities can mean a number of things: it can mean (i) responsibility as the content of a right (e.g., parental rights);[32] (ii) responsibility in the way one exercises one's rights; (iii) responsibility in regard to the rights of others; (iv) responsibility for the integrity of the whole system of rights; and (v) the responsibilities – whether associated with rights or not – that make the life of a community possible and bearable.

A similar complaint is that some human rights charters uphold a skewed balance between the rights of criminals or criminal suspects and the duties that they have violated (sometimes presented as duties correlative to the rights of society or the rights of victims). It is difficult to know what to make of this at a general level, as opposed to addressing particular allegations of skewed balance. One general point is to insist that we have to develop our normative sense of appropriate and inappropriate ways of dealing with (say) suspects and convicts as a matter of right that stands relatively independent of concerns that we might have about the interests of victims or possible beneficiaries of deterrence. It is my view that we do not and should not begin the process of rights-thinking with a balancing calculation (which then we somehow get wrong). The safeguards set out in the criminal justice system are partly to ensure the dignity of the defendant and partly to ensure that there is a proper inquiry into the defendant's guilt or innocence. These are imperatives that are not to

---

[30] ICCPR, Article 9 (3).

[31] But see ICCPR, Article 5 (1): "Nothing in the present Covenant may be interpreted as implying for any State, group or person any right to engage in any activity or perform any act aimed at the destruction of any of the rights and freedoms recognised herein or at their limitation to a greater extent than is provided for in the present Covenant."

[32] See the discussion in Jeremy Waldron, "Dignity, Rights and Responsibilities," *Arizona State Law Journal* 43, no. 4 (2011): 1107–1136.

be balanced or traded off against the rights of actual or potential victims – assuming that these latter can be articulated in the criminal justice system at all.

Nevertheless, even if rights-thinking is not a matter of balance *ab initio*, issues of balance cannot be ruled out in subsequent discussions. Defenders of ROL rights posit a certain kind of dystopia in which suspects and convicts are treated in a more severe and less careful way than they are at present (with many more innocents being convicted and many more cruel punishments imposed). We uphold ROL rights, it is said, to avoid this dystopia. But that presentation can be answered with a dystopia of a different kind, set out by those who are skeptical about such rights. They imagine a society in which ROL rights are fully respected, but in which bullies and thugs roam unpunished, terrorizing our communities. It may seem like a question of balance which of these dystopias we have greater reason to fear and how adjustments to the law might mitigate one or other of them. Whether this is an appropriate methodology for fine-tuning our sense of people's rights is another matter.

Some of these criticisms veer dangerously close to the view that human rights can be forfeited for criminal wrong-doing. That seems to be behind the resistance to the enfranchisement of prisoners, for example. The view that human rights can be forfeited is of course a dangerous one. But it is not enough simply to denounce it. There has not been nearly enough theoretical work done to reconcile the idea of liability to punishment (which inevitably involves loss of some rights) with the idea that rights, being based on human dignity, are inalienable, and to distinguish this from the more draconian implications of a full-fledged forfeiture theory.

V POSSIBLE RESPONSES

In these last few paragraphs, we have already tiptoed around some possible responses to the populist critique or at least around some work that needs to be done in response. Let us consider other responses more directly.

So first: is it true (as Kenneth Roth of Human Rights Watch says) that "[t]he best way to counter populist trends is by vigorous reaffirmation of human rights"?[33] Roth believes that we should continue to defend ROL rights in the way they have always been defended – by highlighting the system they define, the interests they protect, and the victims of their violation. Or is it true, as Philip Alston says, that as a result of populism, "the challenges the human rights movement now faces are fundamentally different from much of what has gone before,"[34] and that "human rights proponents need to rethink many of their assumptions, re-evaluate their strategies, and broaden their outreach, while not giving up on the basic principles."[35]

---

[33] Kenneth Roth, "The Dangerous Rise of Populism: Global Attacks on Human Rights Values," *Journal of International Affairs*, 2017 (Special 70th Anniversary issue): 79–84.

[34] Philip Alston, "The Populist Challenge to Human Rights," *Journal of Human Rights Practice* 9, no. 1 (2017): 2.

[35] Alston, "Populist Challenge," 2.

One might respond, in a traditional way, to impatient demands for more expedited forms of justice, by illustrating what a system of peremptory justice would look like. (I mean the first kind of dystopia imagined above.) I can't resist offering a venerable example of this kind of defense of ROL rights. In Book VI of *The Spirit of the Laws*, Montesquieu observed that "[i]t is constantly said that justice should be rendered everywhere as it is in Turkey."[36] Apparently this was constantly said by people who were irritated by the elaborate technicality and legalism of French society, where there were innumerable rules, privileges and jurisdictions, and interminable procedures for securing any sort of relief. Each claim was broken down into its detailed parts and assessed legalistically against the relevant standards and the repository of judicial decisions. And many good-hearted people apparently protested against this elaborate legalism, imagining that it would be better to be ruled by a sort of Solomonic cadi-figure, able to cut through all the legalism and see through to the moral essentials of the matter.

When he heard this, Montesquieu could hardly believe his ears: complex legal structures, he insisted, are all that stand between monarchy and despotism. You don't get wise King Solomon, if you take the Turkish option; you get lazy, unthinking, undifferentiated exercises of power:

> In Turkey, where one pays very little attention to the fortune, life, or honor of the subjects, all disputes are speedily concluded in one way or another. The manner of ending them is not important, provided they are ended. The pasha is no sooner informed than he has the pleaders bastinadoed according to his fancy and sends them back home.[37]

By contrast, he said: "[I]n moderate governments, where the life of the meanest subject is deemed precious, no man is stripped of his honour or property until after a long inquiry."

So one possibility is to drive home to populist critics that ROL rights protect them too, in the event of their falling under the suspicion of the authorities. It has been well said that if a conservative is a liberal who has been mugged, so a liberal may be described as a conservative who has been arrested.[38] Those who criticize long-drawn-out criminal processes, procedural guarantees, and the availability of technical defenses may feel differently when it is their interests that are at stake. Montesquieu's response to the Turkish justice demand was oriented not just to abstract rights-sensibilities but to men of honor who might worry about the detail of their situation – their side of the story, considerations that seem to them to go to the heart of the matter even though others see them as technicalities – not being

---

[36] Montesquieu, *The Spirit of the Laws*, trans. and ed. Anne M. Cohler, Basia Carolyn Miller, and Harold Samuel Stone (Cambridge: Cambridge University Press, 1989), 74 (Bk. VI, ch. 2).

[37] Montesquieu, *Spirit of the Laws*, 74.

[38] This *bon mot* is commonly attributed to Tom Wolfe.

properly taken into account in the peremptory system that the eighteenth-century critics were demanding.

But this response is unlikely to convince the populist. For even if a populist critic can imagine that he may at some time need to claim the benefit of ROL rights, he also believes here and now that such rights sell short the interests of ordinary law-abiding people. In a passage quoted earlier, a British newspaper, *The Mail on Sunday*, insisted that "the 'human rights' of the indigenous population must be considered. Do these rights not safeguard them from having dangerous rapists placed in their midst? If they do not, then they are not worth having, and we would be better off without them."[39] (The phrase "indigenous population" refers, I think, to the white majority, as opposed to the aliens and terrorists who are supposedly protected by ROL rights.) The populists complain that rights like the ones we are interested in misconceive the balance that needs to be struck between the interests of those who fall foul of the law and the interests of ordinary law-abiding citizens.

How might a system of rights better protect the latter? It might do so by matching ROL rights with a clearer statement of responsibilities that people have to the communities in which they reside (along lines already intimated). I suppose it might also incorporate strong reference to victims' rights – their rights to be heard at various stages in the criminal process, e.g., at sentencing. (Such claims may not seem to be the most urgent rights that can be imagined, but what we said earlier about criminal justice as a system may be relevant here too.) And taking this one step further, one might represent certain law-and-order demands – for better street-level policing, for example – as rights held by ordinary citizens. I am not sure how such rights would be made justiciable, though populists in a spirit of irony might invoke so-called third generation rights – rights protecting people's interests in certain collective goods (like peace or the environment) – as a model.

I said at the outset (in section IV) that ROL rights do some of the work of the Rule-of-Law ideal itself. It may be worth considering whether that ideal should be defended simply as such, rather than as the content of rights. In a Diceyan sense, the Rule of Law as a principle of political morality may seem more "British" than the human rights that have been formulated to embody its requirements. No doubt this is a specious distinction, but let us not pretend that issues of rhetoric and semantics are absent from this debate.

VI NATIONALIZATION OF HUMAN RIGHTS?

Should defenders of human rights in the UK support or connive at populist demands for what is called "a British Bill of Rights"? In 2015, the Conservative manifesto promised to "scrap the Human Rights Act and introduce a British Bill of Rights." It was said that this would

---

[39] "Charter for Criminals and Parasites," *Mail on Sunday*. See above, text accompanying note 9.

restore common sense to the application of human rights in the UK. The Bill will remain faithful to the basic principles of human rights, which we signed up to in the original European Convention on Human Rights. It will protect basic rights, like the right to a fair trial, and the right to life, which are an essential part of a modern democratic society ... [I]t will reverse the mission creep that has meant human rights law being used for more and more purposes, and often with little regard for the rights of wider society. Among other things the Bill will stop terrorists and other serious foreign criminals who pose a threat to our society from using spurious human rights arguments to prevent deportation.[40]

According to the House of Lords Committee considering this proposal, the Secretary of State said that the Government's two main objectives in introducing a British Bill of Rights were "to restore national faith in human rights, and to give human rights greater national identity."[41]

Since then, the matter has been discreetly dropped by the Conservative government, faced as it is already with the momentous constitutional changes and dilemmas that Brexit involves. A minister said it was "important for us to sort out the EU side of matters, and the exit from the EU, before we return to that subject."[42] The then justice secretary, Lynn Truss, said the government wants to only "do one constitutional reform at a time."[43] All the same, since this idea has come and gone and come back again over the past decades, it is worth some further consideration.

The idea of a British Bill of Rights should not be confused with the old English Bill of Rights of 1689, source of the "cruel and unusual" formulation in the 1791 American Bill of Rights. But the modern proposal for a British Bill of Rights is seen by its defenders as a way of capitalizing on some sort of immemorial Anglo-Saxon heritage that stretches back through the 1689 Bill all the way to Magna Carta. Nor should it be confused with the existing Human Rights Act (dating from 1998). That statute is already a British Bill of Rights, but its status as such is demeaned in the eyes of populist critics by the fact that it just reproduces the content of the ECHR and subjects British courts to the doctrines of the European Court of Human Rights. What is demanded is something more deliberately and resiliently "British" than that.

Sometimes, as in the Manifesto quotation mentioned above, there is a sense that a British Bill of Rights will distinguish between what the UK is supposed to have originally signed up for in the ECHR in 1950 and all the unfortunate doctrines that have accreted around it ever since. There is a sort of originalism in the proposal.

---

[40] *Conservative Party Manifesto 2015*, 73.

[41] House of Lords, *UK, EU, and a British Bill of Rights*, 15.

[42] Sir Oliver Heald, quoted in Stephen Swinford, "Theresa May Is Preparing to Abandon Plans for a British Bill of Rights, Sources Suggest," *Daily Telegraph*, January 26, 2017, www.telegraph .co.uk/news/2017/01/26/theresa-may-preparing-abandon-plans-british-bill-rights-sources/.

[43] Jon Stone, "British Bill of Rights Plan Shelved again for Several More Years," *The Independent*, February 23, 2017, www.independent.co.uk/news/uk/politics/scrap-human-rights-act-british-bill-of-rights-brexit-liz-truss-theresa-may-a7595336.html.

There is also a sort of minimalism. Part of the purpose of a British Bill of Rights "is to affirm the fact that things like a prohibition on torture or a right to due process and an appropriate trial before a properly constituted tribunal . . . are fundamental British rights." The Secretary of State said to the Lords committee: "I do think that we can make changes that ensure that people recognize that these rights spring from our traditions, these rights are our patrimony and these rights can be given effect to in the courts in a better way and a more British way."[44]

In principle there is nothing wrong with the idea of a national legal system setting out its own understanding of fundamental rights, independently of what is done in other legal systems or under regional umbrellas like the Council of Europe. Some sort of legal autarchy on human rights is not in itself offensive, not something to oppose in principle. It was appropriate for South Africa in the 1990s to respond to its own history and experience with its own Bill of Rights. It was appropriate for Canada to formulate its own Charter of Fundamental Right and Freedoms and to develop a jurisprudence that evinced some caution about following US doctrinal developments. And the United States developed a Bill of Rights for itself in 1791 which has not been affected in major ways by twentieth-century conventions.

That said, however, it is worth recognizing that national Bills of Rights will inevitably and quite properly draw on each other's experiences in regard to contents, formulations, and even doctrine. The "cruel and unusual punishment" formulation was adopted by the US framers from the English Bill of Rights of 1689, and by the Canadian framers from their American counterparts. Even if national Bills of Rights are seen as responses to local values and experiences, they should also be understood as positivizations of the same normative ideas represented in the texts of international covenants.[45] National differences cannot be ruled out, nor can differences between the national and the international level. But on a matter like human rights, it might be a mistake to make a positive virtue of such differences, as though distinctiveness were everything in this realm.

Or is it?[46] In 1998 at the time of the passage of Britain's Human Rights Act, Lord Hoffmann, a Lord of Appeal in the House of Lords, delivered an address to the Common Law Bar Association in which he attempted to resist the "Europeanization" of British rights jurisprudence.[47] Lord Hoffmann said, "We . . . have our own hierarchy of moral values, our own culturally-determined sense of what is fair and unfair, and I think it would be wrong to submerge this under a pan-European jurisprudence of human rights." He didn't mean that we believe in different rights.

---

[44] House of Lords, *UK, EU, and a British Bill of Rights*, 13.

[45] Cf. Gerald L. Neuman, "Human Rights and Constitutional Rights: Harmony and Dissonance," *Stanford Law Review* 55, no. 5 (2003): 1863–1900.

[46] I have adapted much in this section from Chapter 8 of Jeremy Waldron, *Partly Laws Common to All Mankind*, 219ff.

[47] Leonard Hoffmann, "Human Rights and the House of Lords," *Modern Law Review* 62, no. 2 (1999): 159–166.

He agreed there was an "irreducible minimum" of rights we all share. But beyond that, he said, each country was on its own: "Voltaire said that morality was the same in all civilised nations. This is a half-truth; of course we share a common humanity and there are some forms of behaviour such as torture which we all either reject or are unwilling to acknowledge." And he went on: "Of course, I applaud the patient efforts of the human rights movement since the Second World War to promote the acceptance of basic human rights throughout the world ... Nevertheless, I say that Voltaire's remark was only half true and that in a confident democracy such as the United Kingdom the other half is important." Lord Hoffmann's position seems to have been that even if our basic beliefs about rights are the same, difficult questions of balance have to be determined according to the cultural predilections of each society:

> The problem about the hierarchy of rights is not the conflict between good and evil but the conflict between good and good. Free speech is a good thing; justice is a good thing, but there are cases in which free speech and justice come into conflict with each other. For example, the law that preserves the anonymity of rape victims is an infringement of the freedom of the press, but it assists justice by encouraging women to make complaints against rapists. How then are these two desirable objectives – free speech and justice – to be reconciled with each other? There is no right answer to that question; any choice involves some degree of sacrifice. But in my view, the specific answers, the degree to which weight is given to one desirable objective rather than another, will be culturally determined. Different communities will, through their legislatures and judges, adopt the answers which they think suit them.

The implication seems to be that allowing British courts to be influenced in these delicate judgments by what Justice Scalia would call "the disapproving views of foreigners"[48] is to unacceptably pollute what are essentially the contingent cultural judgments of one community with those of another.

I am reluctant to accept such a view. I don't think these cases involve different cultures simply yielding different answers or judges casting around to find which answers suit the native ethos of their people. They may think it appropriate to do their own reasoning on this issue, and no doubt reasoners of good faith can differ. But that doesn't mean they are asking different questions like "What is the British way of dealing with this right?" or "What best suits the Canadian mentality?" We should not confuse the difficulty and likely disagreement on a given issue, on the one hand, with any form of cultural relativism, on the other.

I guess the final thing to say about the British Bill of Rights proposal is that it is one thing for a nation to develop a Bill of Rights for itself, it is another thing for it to set about dismantling a regional effort to foster a shared sense of human rights in

---

[48] *Sosa v. Alvarez-Machain* 542 U.S. 692, 750 (2004) (Scalia, J., concurring in part and concurring in the judgment).

many countries. The United Kingdom has been a key player in the Council of Europe system, and it would be a pity if that system now had to solve its undoubted problems without the participation of the UK. However, whether that is a consideration that will, ultimately, weigh against the enthusiasm for a British Bill of Rights in populist circles remains to be seen.

BIBLIOGRAPHY

Comment, "Human Rights Is a Charter for Criminals and Parasites: Our Anger Is No Longer Enough." *Mail on Sunday*, July 14, 2012, www.dailymail.co.uk/debate/article-2173666/Human-rights-charter-criminals-parasites-anger-longer-enough.html.

"MPs Reject Prisoner Votes Plan." *BBC News*, February 10, 2011, www.bbc.com/news/uk-politics-12409426.

"Strong Leadership, a Clear Economic Plan, a Brighter, More Secure Future: The Conservative Party Manifesto 2015." www.conservatives.com/manifesto2015.

Alston, Philip. "The Populist Challenge to Human Rights." *Journal of Human Rights Practice* 9, no. 1 (2017): 1–15.

Barnes, Robert. "Breyer Says Understanding Foreign Law Is Critical to Supreme Court's Work." *Washington Post*, September 12, 2015, www.washingtonpost.com/politics/courts_law/breyer-says-understanding-foreign-law-is-critical-to-supreme-courts-work/2015/09/12/36a38212-57e9-11e5-8bb1-b488d231bba2_story.html.

Bingham, Tom. *The Rule of Law*. London: Allen Lane, 2010.

Bowcott, Owen. "Council of Europe Accepts UK Compromise on Prisoner Voting Rights." *The Guardian*, December 7, 2017, www.theguardian.com/politics/2017/dec/07/council-of-europe-accepts-uk-compromise-on-prisoner-voting-rights.

Dicey, A.V. *Introduction to the Study of the Law of the Constitution*. Indianapolis: Liberty Fund, 1982.

Fuller, Lon. *The Morality of Law*. New Haven, CT: Yale University Press, 1964.

Hoffmann, Leonard. "Human Rights and the House of Lords." *Modern Law Review* 62, no. 2 (1999): 159–166.

Holehouse, Matthew. "David Cameron: I Will Ignore Europe's Top Court on Prisoner Voting." *Daily Telegraph*, October 4, 2015, www.telegraph.co.uk/news/uknews/law-and-order/11911057/David-Cameron-I-will-ignore-Europes-top-court-on-prisoner-voting.html.

House of Lords, European Union Committee, *The UK, the EU, and a British Bill of Rights*, HL 139 (2016).

Joset, Jennelle London. "May It Please the Constitution: Judicial Activism and Its Effect on Criminal Procedure." *Marquette Law Review* 79, no. 4 (1996): 1021–1040.

Kmiec, Keenan D. "The Origin and Current Meanings of Judicial Activism." *California Law Review* 92, no. 5 (2004): 1441–1477.

Malcolm, Noel. *Human Rights and Political Wrongs: A New Approach to Human Rights*. London: Policy Exchange, 2017. Available at https://policyexchange.org.uk/wp-content/uploads/2017/12/Human-Rights-and-Political-Wrongs.pdf.

Marcus, Ruth. "Our Criminal Justice System Is Not a 'Joke.' Yet." *Washington Post*, November 3, 2017, www.washingtonpost.com/opinions/our-criminal-justice-system-is-not-a-joke-yet/2017/11/03/8aeb386c-c0d6-11e7-97d9-bdab5a0ab381_story.html.

McKinstry, Leo. "Human Right's [sic] Act Has Become the Villain's Charter: The Human Rights Act Continues to Exert Its Malign Influence." *Daily Express*, October 3, 2011, www.express.co.uk/comment/columnists/leo-mckinstry/275220/Human-right-s-act-has-become-the-villain-s-charter.

Montesquieu, *The Spirit of the Laws*, translated and edited by Anne M. Cohler, Basia Carolyn Miller, and Harold Samuel Stone. Cambridge: Cambridge University Press, 1989.

Müller, Jan-Werner. *What Is Populism?* Philadelphia, PA: University of Pennsylvania Press, 2016.

Neuman, Gerald L. "Human Rights and Constitutional Rights: Harmony and Dissonance." *Stanford Law Review* 55, no. 5 (2003): 1863–1900.

Raz, Joseph. "The Rule of Law and Its Virtue," in *The Authority of Law: Essays on Law and Morality*. Oxford: Clarendon Press, 1979.

Roth, Kenneth. "The Dangerous Rise of Populism: Global Attacks on Human Rights Values." *Journal of International Affairs*, 2017 (Special 70th Anniversary issue): 79–84.

Stone, Jon. "British Bill of Rights Plan Shelved again for Several More Years." *The Independent*, February 23, 2017, www.independent.co.uk/news/uk/politics/scrap-human-rights-act-british-bill-of-rights-brexit-liz-truss-theresa-may-a7595336.html.

Swinford, Stephen. "Theresa May Is Preparing to Abandon Plans for a British Bill of Rights, Sources Suggest." *Daily Telegraph*, January 26, 2017, www.telegraph.co.uk/news/2017/01/26/theresa-may-preparing-abandon-plans-british-bill-rights-sources/.

Waldron, Jeremy. "Dignity, Rights and Responsibilities." *Arizona State Law Journal* 43, no. 4 (2011): 1107–1136.

"The Rule of Law and the Importance of Procedure." In *Getting to the Rule of Law*, edited by James E. Fleming (Nomos 50). New York: New York University Press, 2011.

"Partly Laws Common to All Mankind": Foreign Law in American Courts. New Haven, CT: Yale University Press, 2012.

4

Populism and Human Rights in Poland

Wojciech Sadurski

As Polish Ombudsman Dr Adam Bodnar noted recently, "the legal environment [in Poland] is becoming more and more difficult to exercise political rights."[1] This observation is at the same time prudent and realistic. It is prudent, because it does not assert that human rights themselves are under direct attack (at least, under a particularly massive attack) in Poland. But it notes, realistically, that "the legal environment" important for the protection of human rights is being eroded. This observation encapsulates the situation regarding human rights in Poland since the election of the populist Law and Justice Party (Polish acronym: PiS) in 2015: its main target has so far been the steady erosion and weakening of institutions that are considered vital for human rights, and in particular the judiciary (including the constitutional judiciary, which in all post-communist states has been elevated as the main pillar in rights-protection institutional structure). The real power is centred in one person, Jarosław Kaczyński, the founder and leader of PiS, and ex-Prime Minister (in 2006–2007, in the first iteration of PiS rule), who is commanding the country without constitutional responsibility and accountability: his only state function is being a member of parliament. While statutory changes regarding the protection of constitutional rights have not been enormous so far, the institutional infrastructure for protecting and enforcing those rights has been largely dismantled, with the legislature (in fact, the non-constitutional power concentrated in the hands of the PiS leadership) having the final say on the rights of citizens. With the effective paralysis of the Constitutional Tribunal (CT) and the conversion of this rights-protective body into a branch of the legislature invariably taking the side of the dominant party, the interpretation of the legitimacy of statutory restrictions on constitutional rights has become the prerogative of the political leadership.

---

[1] Adam Bodnar, "Protection of Human Rights after the Constitutional Crisis in Poland," *Jahrbuch des öffentlichen Rechts der Gegenwart* 66 (2018): 657.

Therefore, the developments in Poland since mid-2015 corroborate an assertion by Gerald Neuman that once in power, populists "often try to entrench themselves in power, dismantling legal guarantees of fair electoral competition … They also express impatience with institutional checks and balances, and may seek to take over, replace or abolish independent components of government, such as the judiciary and other watchdog agencies."[2] All this has happened in Poland – and more. When observing that the populist assault on liberal democracy in Poland has so far proceeded by the erosion of institutional infrastructure and not by restricting rights themselves, I do not want to overstate this point. As this chapter will note, a number of important political rights have been systematically breached, by legislative changes and/or in the process of enforcement, and the PiS approach to rights has been highly "selective and defeasible."[3] The PiS government has also been openly hostile towards rights-oriented non-governmental organizations (with the exception of pro-governmental and faith-based NGOs) as well as EU "intervention" in the Polish legislative process. To its credit, it has not taken any spectacular actions towards the European Court of Human Rights, even though the Court has already had several occasions to pronounce on certain, isolated aspects of the Polish politics of rights after 2015.[4]

In the background to PiS's assault on the institutional prerequisites for human rights in Poland is the active, deliberate, ideological and cultural "counter-revolution," which is not only displayed in official declarations but also in actual governmental acts. While it does not amount to any comprehensive ideological platform for PiS rule, it is nevertheless quite clear that elected authoritarians have an agenda that is anti-modernist, anti-progressivist and anti-liberal, carrying with it a dislike of many individual rights and rights-enhancing policies, in particular those targeting inequalities. A number of offices and programmes to combat discrimination were discontinued as soon as PiS came to power. For instance, in June 2016, just over six months after its electoral victory, PiS extinguished the governmental Council for Counteracting Racial Discrimination, Xenophobia and Intolerance. Significantly, this happened at a time when there had been a clear rise in acts of violence – verbal and physical – against non-whites in Poland. Furthermore, public schools ceased to accept visitors from NGOs running workshops against intolerance and xenophobia while also opening their doors to radical nationalistic groups such as the openly neo-Nazi ONR (The National-Radical Front). The government stopped subsidies for civil society activities such as the so-called Blue Line, a phone-in for young people in desperate psychological situations, often on the verge of committing suicide. In turn, governmental subsidies were generously conferred upon faith-based and right-wing groups, such as the network of organizations connected with

---

[2] Chapter 1 (in this volume).
[3] Chapter 1 (in this volume).
[4] Section VI of this chapter.

Catholic-fundamentalist Radio Maryja. In their official public statements, leading PiS politicians appealed to traditional and conservative values while distancing themselves from liberal and progressive ideologies.

In this chapter, I will begin by explaining my own use of the term "populism" driven by my interpretation of populism Polish-style, as it may be somewhat different from the concept adopted by many other scholars employing this word (Section I). I will then provide a brief, bird's-eye view of Polish populist rule since 2015. In Section II, I will describe an assault on the main institutional safeguard for constitutional rights in Poland, namely on the Constitutional Tribunal. Next, I will survey PiS actions intruding upon the main political rights: of assembly (Section III) and freedom of speech (Section IV). I will then sketch violations of privacy rights (Section V), and the cases in which post-2015 Poland has been taken to the European Court of Human Rights (Section VI). A concluding remark will close the chapter.

I WHAT IS POPULISM?

Populism is a vague and contested concept but, however understood, it is a crucial part of my description of Polish anti-democratic backsliding post-2015. The notion of "populism" emphasizes that what is going on in Poland is not "authoritarianism" as such, but that it is an illiberal condition whereby the rulers *care* about popular support. The notion of authoritarianism per se may apply to regimes that are totally insensitive to the level of societal support of their rule, and govern through the massive use of violence, but this is not the case for Poland post-2015. We need a language to distinguish between authoritarianisms that govern by resort to bare force and where a degree of societal support for the rule is not important for the rulers because they know that they can, and they do, rely on oppression and coercion, and, on the other hand, illiberal regimes that want to be liked or even loved, at least by a significant segment of the electorate. This does not necessarily render them democratic (once they begin dismantling separation of powers, constitutional checks and democratic rights, they undermine democracy itself), but it makes them qualitatively different from authoritarian regimes where public opinion does not count. In contrast, populists care a great deal about societal support, obsessively follow opinion polls to check their popularity rankings, and have a special weakness for mass rallies as a method of mobilizing "the people."[5]

In recent years, the most influential understanding of populism has been offered by Jan-Werner Müller, who identifies populism with anti-pluralism, and more specifically, with making the "claim to *exclusive* moral representation of the real

---

[5] See Kurt Weyland, "Populism: A Political–Strategic Approach," in *The Oxford Handbook of Populism*, ed. Cristóbal Rovira Kaltwasser, et al. (Oxford: Oxford University Press, 2017), 56–58.

or authentic people."[6] It is this type of definition that has been largely adopted by Gerald Neuman in Chapter 1 of this volume: Neuman dubs it (consistently with the other endorsers of this approach) "the ideational approach."[7] As Müller explains, not all anti-pluralists are necessarily populist, but all populists make such claim to exclusive representation. Populists, Müller adds, attempt "to speak in the name of the people as a whole" and "to morally de-legitimate all those who in turn contest that claim (which is to say: those who contest their involuntary inclusion in a 'We the People'; such resisters to populism are effectively saying: 'not in our name')."[8]

While Müller is certainly correct that this type of rhetoric can *often* be found in populist manifestos and public statements, I doubt whether Müller's criterion of populism is sufficiently stable and determinate enough to distinguish populist from non-populist politicians and governments: it focuses too much on what populists *say* as opposed to what they *do*. This is not to deny the importance of a specific *discourse* for populist politics. Discourse matters a great deal and carries distinctive characteristics, with its own style of demagoguery, easy simplifications, enemy targeting and unattainable promises. But to hinge a characterization fully on rhetoric, a narrative, or discourse is always risky: politicians often use their language in strategic or deceptive ways, and in particular do not always reveal the deep understandings (such as that about the exclusive representation of real people) that motivate them to action.

As a result, this definition is both over-inclusive and under-inclusive. It is over-inclusive because Müller's criterion is unlikely to provide a good distinction between populists and perfectly unimpeachable democrats who, in a pluralist democracy, often (though not always) claim that they have actually better grasped the true *common* interest than their opponents; they claim to find a better amalgamation between different ingredients of public good, and more rational trade-offs between incompatible preferences, than their opponents. On the other hand, the definition is under-inclusive: populists such as Kaczyński or Orbàn do not necessarily say: "We and only we are the people,"[9] and that those who disagree with them are beyond the pale of the nation: they are not "real" Poles, Hungarians etc. Rather, they may characterize, and try to delegitimize, their opponents by presenting them as corrupt, mistaken, treacherous, serving foreign powers etc.

My own understanding of populism identifies it with *actions*, which usually speak louder than words: in this sense, it is different from Müller's because it views populism not as an ideology but rather as a form of political organization and action. But it overlaps with Müller's understanding in that it is, inter alia, connected with

---

[6] Jan-Werner Müller, "Populism and Constitutionalism," in *The Oxford Handbook of Populism*, ed. Cristóbal Rovira Kaltwasser, et al. (Oxford: Oxford University Press, 2017), 593 (emphasis in original).
[7] Chapter 1 (in this volume).
[8] Müller, "Populism and Constitutionalism," 601.
[9] Müller, "Populism and Constitutionalism," 601.

anti-pluralism, or more specifically, with hostility to *institutional* pluralism. Populists typically try to build bridges to the "real" people above the heads of intermediary institutions that in a constitutional democracy mediate between people and the exercise of power. They dislike and disparage these institutions even if, as Kaczyński does, they pay lip service to them, but in the process erode them of the reasons that underlie the creation of these institutions in the first place. Their political action is usually of a plebiscitary character, aimed at translating the will of the mythical, pre-political people into political action; they "bypass all forms of intermediation" and "rely on unmediated, quasi-direct appeals."[10] Society as a complex web of diverse preferences, interests and identities, which triggers a pluralistic structure aimed at aggregating those diversities in a compromise-based polity, is displaced by a homogenous entity, the interests of which are best grasped by populists: that is, the ultimate leader. This admittedly vague and under-theorized understanding of populism will be adopted in this chapter: I find it more stable and better suited to discuss the advances of populism in Poland.

II TRANSFORMATION OF THE CONSTITUTIONAL TRIBUNAL

When a problematic change is introduced in a largely liberal-democratic structure, the larger constitutional environment cushions its potentially anti-liberal function, and the system produces protections for individual liberties and checks and balances. In Poland, however, the situation is the opposite: a broad assault upon liberal-democratic constitutionalism produces a cumulative effect, and the sum is greater than the totality of its parts. For example, the disempowering of the Constitutional Tribunal [CT], to be discussed in this section, should not be seen as a phenomenon in itself, lamentable but confined in its nefarious effects, but rather as mainly aimed at disabling the constitutional review of liberal rights such as freedom of assembly.

Jarosław Kaczyński candidly admitted that the so-called reforms of the CT were needed in order to ensure there were no legal blocks on government policies. At the height of the struggle by PiS to capture the CT in December 2016, Kaczyński said – using a pre-eminently populist argument – that "the reforms to the constitutional court" were needed "to ensure there are no legal blocks on government policies aimed at creating a fairer economy."[11] As Polish constitutional scholar Tomasz Tadeusz Koncewicz correctly noted: "The Constitutional Court was targeted first because that would ensure that next phases would sail through without any scrutiny from its side. Who cares that the new legislation flies in the face of the constitution

---

[10] Weyland, "Political–Strategic Approach," 58.
[11] "Poland's Kaczynski Calls EU Democracy Inquiry an 'Absolute Comedy,'" *Reuters Online*, 23 December 2016, www.reuters.com/article/us-poland-politics-kaczynski-democracy/polands-kaczynski-calls-eu-democracy-inquiry-an-absolute-comedy-idUSKBN14B1U5 (accessed 7 November 2017).

since there is no procedural and institutional avenue to enforce constitutional rules?"[12] This explains why PiS's most immediate and spectacular anti-constitutional action was addressed against the Constitutional Tribunal.

Prior to 2015, the Tribunal had established itself as a strong protector of democratic processes and of rights-based limits upon legislative and executive powers. This is not to say that its entire case law is unimpeachable from the point of view of a strong liberty-protective ideal. Many of its judgments were controversial and lacked the necessary vigour, as many observers have pointed out. For instance, the Tribunal was almost always feeble when it came to insisting on the constitutionally entrenched separation of church and state, and the principle of the secularity of the republic: it was all too willing to give in to various Church demands for its active and ideologically slanted interference in the shape of law, whether it came to the place of religion in public schools, the presence of religious symbols in the public sphere, or general conceptions about the privileged role of religious freedom vis-à-vis other individual liberties.[13] What matters is that, on balance, the Tribunal had established itself as a constructive and valuable actor defending human rights. For example: it pronounced on the unconstitutionality of a provision of an Aviation Law that gave the authorities the right to permit shooting down a passenger aircraft in the event of a special risk to national security.[14] It established the strongly libertarian constitutional status of spontaneous[15] and other assemblies, finding unconstitutionality in a provision of the Road Traffic Act that required permission for a public road assembly, and took the opportunity to pronounce several general propositions about the freedom of assembly, the most important of which is that lawmakers and administrative authorities may not sit in judgment on which substantive messages pronounced by the participants of assemblies are contrary to "public morality."[16] It strengthened the rights of criminal defendants, pronouncing for instance on the unconstitutionality of a provision of the Code of Civil Procedure that excluded legally incapacitated persons from the circle of subjects entitled to put forward a motion to revoke the declaration of, or change the scope of legal incapacitation.[17]

More specifically, PiS had good reasons (from *its* point of view) to dislike the CT as it had frustrated some of PiS's legislative proposals during the party's first episode

---

[12] Tomasz Tadeusz Koncewicz, "Farewell to the Separation of Powers – On the Judicial Purge and the Capture in the Heart of Europe," *VerfassungsBlog*, 19 July 2017, verfassungsblog.de/farewell-to-the-separation-of-powers-on-the-judicial-purge-and-the-capture-in-the-heart-of-europe (accessed 2 January 2019).

[13] See Wojciech Sadurski, *Rights before Courts: A Study of Constitutional Courts in Postcommunist States of Central and Eastern Europe*, 2nd edn (Dordrecht: Springer, 2014), 188–193; Aleksandra Gliszczyńska-Grabias and Wojciech Sadurski, "Freedom of Religion versus Humane Treatment of Animals: Polish Constitutional Tribunal's Judgment on Permissibility of Religious Slaughter," *European Constitutional Law Review* 11, no. 3 (2015): 596–608.

[14] Judgment K 44/07 of 30 September 2008.

[15] Judgment P 15/08 of 15 July 2008.

[16] Judgment K 21/05 of 18 January 2006.

[17] Judgment K 28/05 of 7 March 2007.

of rule in 2005–07, on "lustration" (or purge of "unreliable" personnel in public service) in particular, but also on freedom of assembly, entry to the legal profession, or the broadcasting council. The memory of these collisions between the PiS government and the CT in 2005–2007 certainly coloured PiS's attitude to constitutional review when it returned to power in 2015. But its antipathy was more generalized, not limited to specific judgments. The very existence of a body that may invalidate laws adopted by the majority seemed anathema to the institutional design in which the "sovereign" embodied in the parliamentary majority could implement all its political wishes. The element of contingency, instability and revocability of "reforms" inherent in any robust system of judicial review, uncontrollable by the executive and/or parliamentary majority, is something that an illiberal authority can hardly tolerate. The example of Poland provides strong confirmation of this general proposition.

The capture of the CT by the ruling party after 2015 took place in two main stages. The first stage was paralysis, which mainly consisted of several actions aimed at rendering the CT powerless to curb arbitrary power. Once this aim was achieved at the end of 2016, the second stage began, which has continued to this day: that of the actual positive use of the CT against the opposition and in support of the ruling party. In contrast to the traditionally anti-majoritarian mission of constitutional courts, the Tribunal became an active helper of the parliamentary majority. While the first stage gave reason to believe that the very existence of the CT was at stake, and that a purely cosmetic body was all that PiS wanted, the second iteration of the Tribunal – as an active collaborator in anti-constitutional assault by PiS – showed that, perhaps contrary to initial attempts at destroying the CT as such, the rulers had identified a function for the CT in their design for democratic backsliding.

Immediately after coming to power, PiS engaged in energetic court-packing that after one year resulted (in combination with natural attrition) in gaining a majority on the Tribunal. PiS-appointed judges and "quasi-judges" (the term to be explained shortly) effectively paralyzed the Tribunal, rendering it unable to subject new laws to effective constitutional scrutiny.

The most important step by the new ruling majority was to fail to recognize three properly appointed judges, elected to their positions at the end of the previous term of the Parliament, and to elect into those seats three new "quasi-judges," who were fully loyal to PiS. The story of this step is quite complex, and I will not go into detail here.[18] What is important to stress is that the gambit of "electing" three judges to the already-filled seats, and of not recognizing the three judges properly elected before PiS gained a parliamentary majority, would not have succeeded except for the active collaboration of President Andrzej Duda. The President swore in five PiS-elected judges

---

[18] See Wojciech Sadurski, "Polish Constitutional Tribunal under PiS: From an Activist Court, to a Paralysed Tribunal, to a Governmental Enabler," *Hague Journal on the Rule of Law* 11, no. 1 (2019): 63–84, DOI:10.1007/s40803-018-0078-1.

including three "quasi-judges"[19] elected to the already-occupied judicial posts hours after the election, in the middle of the night of 2/3 December 2015, thus earning them the film-noir sounding name of "midnight judges."[20] The swearing-in took place literally hours before the CT determined that the grounds for the election of the three judges by the *former* term of Sejm were constitutional, which was equivalent to saying that three (out of five) judges elected in October 2015 were "proper" judges, while the three persons elected in their place by the new Sejm ("quasi-judges") were not elected correctly, despite the swearing-in ceremony in the President's office.[21]

The process of court-packing was successful owing to collusion between the parliamentary majority, the President, and the newly elected judges (including quasi-judges) supported by the PiS majority. And it achieved its purpose: all of the new judges and quasi-judges elected by the PiS parliamentary majority, with a single exception,[22] have so far behaved predictably and voted in lockstep for government positions in all cases considered by the Tribunal. It was greatly assisted by the fact that the new President (Chief Justice) of the Tribunal, Ms Julia Przyłębska, thoroughly changed the composition of panels in pending cases, including the judges-rapporteurs, by removing "older" (pre-December 2015) judges from the responsibilities of being rapporteurs in many panels in which they had already been working on a draft judgment for some time. As a result, in *all* politically sensitive issues, the panels have had a majority of PiS-elected and/or "quasi-judges."

Court-packing was not the only process employed by PiS to disable the Tribunal from scrutinizing PiS legislation. Throughout 2016 (or to be exact, between November 2015 and December 2016), the Parliament adopted no fewer than six statutes on the CT, some of which abrogated parts of the older laws, and replaced them with new provisions. Bombarded by these new laws, the CT was compelled to deal mainly with laws about itself rather than substantive laws adopted at the same time.

Looking at the totality of provisions contained in the laws of late 2015 and 2016, one can divide them into three categories (with a caveat that there is clearly an overlap between categories (1) and (2)): (1) provisions exempting current PiS legislation from constitutional scrutiny, such as the requirement of strictly respecting the sequence of judgments according to the time the motion reaches the CT;[23]

---

[19] A term used in Polish journalistic language (by those who believe that the election of the three "judges" to the already filled places was improper) is *"dubler"* (which corresponds, roughly, to a "double," as in "body double" in a film, or to an understudy in a theatre production). I will be using here the word "quasi-judges" as a rough, but in my view most adequate, translation of the Polish word *"dubler."*

[20] See Anna Śledzińska-Simon, "Midnight Judges: Poland's Constitutional Tribunal Caught between Political Fronts," *VerfassungsBlog*, 23 November 2015, http://verfassungsblog.de/mid night-judges-polands-constitutional-tribunal-caught-between-political-fronts (accessed 9 January 2018).

[21] Judgment K 34/15.

[22] Judge Piotr Pszczółkowski.

[23] Article 1(10) of the statute of 22 December 2015; Article 38 (3–6) of the statute on the CT of 22 July 2016.

(2) provisions paralyzing decision-making by the CT, such as the requirement of a difficult-to-achieve qualified two-thirds majority for judgments of the CT;[24] and (3) provisions enhancing the powers of the executive and legislature towards the CT, such as the new powers of the President of the Republic and Minister of Justice to move a motion for a disciplinary process against a judge of the CT,[25] and of the Sejm to decide on the disciplinary removal of a judge.[26]

Most of these provisions were eventually found to be unconstitutional by the CT,[27] but in the process, the CT became effectively paralyzed by having to mainly consider laws on itself ("existential jurisprudence").[28] The government for its part tried to disable the Tribunal from invalidating these provisions by claiming that the procedure for scrutinizing them must be based *on the very laws under scrutiny* (this, on the basis of the doctrine of the presumption of constitutionality of statutes and the principle that a law is immediately binding unless it contains a *vacatio legis* provision, which these laws as a rule did not). This created a Catch-22 situation for the CT: in assessing constitutionality of a statute, it was expected to use the rules provided by that very statute! The Tribunal refused to fall into this trap and found that it could not, in its judgments, use the very provisions that it scrutinizes for unconstitutionality, and that the only proper approach is to apply the Constitution directly.

After the pro-PiS judges obtained a majority on the court, in late 2016, PiS transformed the CT from a powerless institution paralyzed by consecutive bills rendering it unable to review new PiS laws into a positive supporter of enhanced majoritarian powers. In a fundamental reversal of the traditional role of a constitutional court, it is now being used to protect the government from laws enacted long before PiS rule. Whatever else constitutional courts around the world are expected to do, there is no doubt that their first and primary function is "to ensure adherence to a ... constitution and its protection against legislative majorities."[29] In Poland, the Tribunal became a defender and protector of the legislative majority.[30] This changed role, combined with a general distrust of the CT and concerns about the legitimacy of its judgments, explains the extraordinary drop in the number of

---

[24] Article 1(3) of the statute of 22 December 2015.

[25] Article 1 (5) of the statute of 22 December 2015.

[26] Article 31 (3) of the statute of 22 December 2015.

[27] In particular by the judgments of 9 December 2015 (K 35/15), 9 March 2016 (K 47/15) and of 11 August 2016 (K 39/16).

[28] For this term, see Tomasz Tadeusz Koncewicz, "The Court is Dead, Long Live the Courts? On Judicial Review in Poland 2017 and 'Judicial Space' Beyond," *Verfassungsblog*, 8 March 2018, verfassungsblog.de/the-court-is-dead-long-live-the-courts-on-judicial-review-in-poland-in-2017-and-judicial-space-beyond/ (accessed 9 November 2018).

[29] Andrew Harding, Peter Leyland and Tania Groppi, "Constitutional Courts: Forms, Functions and Practice in Comparative Perspective," *Journal of Comparative Law* 3, no. 2 (2008): 4.

[30] I discuss the examples of CT decisions that match this pattern in Sadurski, "Polish Constitutional Tribunal under PiS."

judgments issued.[31] For all practical purposes, the CT as a mechanism of consti-tutional review has ceased to exist: a reliable aide of the government and parliamen-tary majority has been born.

III FREEDOM OF ASSEMBLY

When populists come to power, they characteristically attempt to tilt the political playing field in their favour, and to disadvantage the opposition in forthcoming elections, thus perpetuating their own status as rulers of the country. They do so in various ways: by their social policies, by propaganda and, most importantly, by disabling institutional checks on their power. But they also use legislation affecting civil rights to this effect, and it is obvious that the two most fundamental rights that they redesign and recalibrate for this purpose are those related to the political democratic process, namely the rights of assembly and political speech. In this and the following sections, I will discuss the PiS assault upon these rights, in turn.

The new statute of 13 December 2016 (amending the Peaceful Assembly Statute of 24 July 2015) established priority for so-called cyclical assemblies and demonstra-tions. An assembly is recognized as cyclical when (a) it has the same organizer, and occurs at least four times a year or once a year if it falls on an important national day; (b) has its own history (i.e., it has taken place at least for three years); and (c) is aimed at celebrating events of significance in Polish history. In this way, the law created a hierarchy of peaceful assemblies, and set a priority for preferred ones. It is now legally impossible to organize a demonstration in the same location where a recognized "cyclical assembly" organized by public authorities or churches is to take place. To dot the i's and cross the t's, the statute expressly prohibits counter-demonstrations against periodic assemblies (counter-demonstrators must be dis-tanced from the principal assembly by at least 100 metres). The purpose of the law was clear from the beginning: it was to prevent anti-government activists from registering their assemblies prior to PiS-sponsored assemblies, thus reserving for themselves the space and time for an assembly.

The effect of this new regulation is to ensure a privileged position for assemblies devoted to "patriotic," religious and historic events, which in Poland de facto singles out governmental or government-supported assemblies in particular, such as the monthly events held until 10 April 2018 to commemorate the crash of an aircraft carrying 96 leading Polish politicians, military commanders and religious and civic

---

[31] In 2017, 284 motions (including constitutional complaints, concrete reviews initiated by courts, and abstract reviews) were lodged in the CT, while in 2014, 2015 and 2016, the annual numbers were, respectively, 530, 623 and 360. In 2017, the CT handed down 36 judgments while in 2014, 2015 and 2016, 71, 63 and 39, respectively. In other words, in 2016, the first full year of the process of capturing the Tribunal, the Tribunal received 42 percent fewer motions than in the previous year (2015), while in 2017, 22 percent fewer than in 2016, which already had noted a record decline. In comparison with 2015, the number of motions in 2017 fell by 55 percent.

leaders, including President Lech Kaczyński (Jarosław's twin brother) and his wife, on 10 April 2010 on its descent towards the airport in Smolensk, Russia. The visit was fraught with deep symbolism: it was meant to commemorate the memory of over 21,000 Polish officers and soldiers murdered at Stalin's orders by KGB in the five killing fields – one of them the forest of Katyń, not far from Smolensk, in April 1940. It was generally understood that Lech Kaczyński intended this visit to be the inauguration of his presidential election campaign, less than three months before the election, and at a time when his ratings were at an all-time low. After his tragic death, these monthly manifestations, held in the centre of Warsaw and always culminating with a speech by Jarosław Kaczyński in front of the Presidential Palace, became hate rallies against the opposition, and understandably enough, provoked peaceful counter-assemblies. The effect of the new law made it illegal for counter-assemblies to take place within the direct vicinity of these PiS regular assemblies.

This hierarchy of assemblies formally endorsed by the new law is in direct contradiction to the established, strongly libertarian regime for the law of assembly in Poland, based mainly on the CT judgment of 18 January 2006[32] (on the unconstitutionality of a provision of the Road Traffic Act that required permission for a public road assembly) and the judgment of 10 July 2008[33] (on the constitutional status of spontaneous assemblies). The former judgment was of especially great significance; the "old" CT had relied on three main premises: first, a right to "counter-demonstration" cannot go so far as to undermine the citizens' rights to peaceful assembly; second, public authorities are obliged to ensure the protection of peaceful assemblies regardless of the substance of the messages of these assemblies (as long as they are not illegal); third, "public morality" as a constitutional basis for restricting a right to assembly must not be equated with the moral beliefs of public officials.[34] As a result, provisions of the Road Traffic Act 1997, insofar as they restricted those assemblies that could create hindrances or changes in road traffic upon obtaining permission, were struck down.

The new law on "cyclical assemblies" found its way to the "new" CT,[35] and the Tribunal gladly affirmed the constitutionality of the new statutory provisions. According to the judgment, assemblies of a cyclical nature have a constitutionally legitimate aim connected with the protection of national values proclaimed in the Preamble of the Constitution. The Tribunal stressed that owing to "the connection with the Nation's values and history," precedence over other assemblies should be guaranteed for this newly established type of assembly.

After the new law's entry into force, it became settled practice for local authorities to routinely ban counter-assemblies, usually at the last moment or even at the

---

[32] K 21/05.
[33] P 15/08.
[34] The Constitutional Tribunal ruled on the unconstitutionality of such regulations; for a discussion, see Sadurski, *Rights before Courts*, 220–221.
[35] Judgment KP 1/17 of 16 March 2017.

beginning of such demonstrations, making it impossible for the activists to challenge the bans in courts. Participants of counter-assemblies (relegated by the new law to the status of inferior assemblies) became subject to increasingly harsh persecutions and intimidation, with hundreds of people interrogated by police, and often treated brutally by the police and voluntary security teams of the PiS-sponsored assemblies. As a result, it is not only the content of the law but also its actual enforcement that breaches the right of assembly. As Ombudsman Dr Bodnar recognized in his 2018 report, during the last few years "all over Poland during the preparation and running of . . . assemblies, there have been many violations of the constitutional freedom of assembly by public institutions."[36] For instance, in the so-called Independence March of 11 November 2017, police protected the organizers and activists of the principal march (even though several participants carried banners with clearly racist and neo-fascist slogans, directly banned under Polish law) while persecuting counter-assemblies, as well as turning a blind eye to the aggressive actions of marchers towards passive, peaceful protesters.[37] Many of the participants in anti-government rallies have been formally indicted: at the time of the writing, some 180 such cases are pending. But the number of persons harassed and persecuted in various other ways is much higher: the NGO Obywatele RP (Citizens of the Republic of Poland) has documented over 560 cases in its files in which participants of various demonstrations and marches have been fined for their participation in anti-government or anti-fascist assemblies, usually on the basis of an offence against public order.[38] Many were fined for damage to public property, for instance for slogans sprayed on pavements. Some were even fined for acting as an aid to those summonsed to the prosecutor's office for hearings.[39]

IV FREEDOM OF SPEECH

Immediately after coming to power, the PiS government fully seized the public media, sacking over 200 journalists, and transforming public TV and radio into vehicles of primitive propaganda. In addition, there have also been attempts to silence independent journalists and writers, and to produce a chilling effect by threats of legal action, often disproportionate to alleged "offences." Perhaps the best-known attempt was the case of investigative journalist and writer Tomasz Piątek, who published a book[40] that was the product of his investigation into the allegedly

---

[36] *Wolność zgromadzeń w Polsce w latach 2016–2018: Raport Rzecznika Praw Obywatelskich* (Warsaw: Biuro Rzecznika Praw Obywatelskich, September 2018), 8.

[37] For example, a group of twelve women sitting at the footpath with a banner "Stop Fascism!" were beaten up and spat upon by some marchers – with no reaction from the police.

[38] Magdalena Kursa, "Obywatele ścigani za protesty," *Czarna Księga, Gazeta Wyborcza*, 17 October 2018, 14.

[39] Kursa, "Obywatele ścigani za protesty," 14.

[40] Tomasz Piątek, *Macierewicz i jego tajemnice* (Warsaw: Arbitror, 2017).

suspicious contacts and professional relationships of the Minister of Defence Antoni Macierewicz[41] – a top politician in PiS (a Vice President of PiS, he is generally considered to be the leader of its hard-line faction). After Macierewicz lost his position as minister at the beginning of 2018, the investigation was probably discontinued – there have been no official announcements about its progress – but the very threat surely had, or at least could have had, a strong chilling effect.

In a separate development at the end of January 2018, the parliament enacted a law amending the statute on the Institute of National Remembrance (Polish acronym: IPN). The new law established the offence of publicly and falsely attributing responsibility or co-responsibility to the Polish nation or the state for crimes against humanity committed by the Nazis during the Second World War, punishable by up to three years in jail. The same law also provides civil sanctions for statements violating the reputation of Poland or the Polish nation. According to the law, the Institute of National Remembrance as well as NGOs would be empowered to bring civil law actions in order to protect the good name of the Republic of Poland or the Polish nation. In the case of a judgment finding that there had been a violation, the State Treasury shall be entitled to compensation.

The chilling effect of such penal and civil sanctions upon scholarly or journalistic debates regarding the darker sides of Polish history is obvious, and the law clearly resonates with nationalistic governmental rhetoric, under which Polish history is comprised exclusively of heroic acts and undeserved victimhood, and never of criminal deeds. The proposed law is sometimes referred to as "lex Gross," referring to Professor Jan T. Gross of Princeton whose books and articles depicting Polish crimes against Jews on German-occupied territories during the Second World War have provoked heated public debates in Poland over recent decades.

The government's publicly avowed motive for proposing this law was to counteract the admittedly unfortunate use of the concept of "Polish concentration (or death) camps." This rationale, however, is manifestly insufficient to carry the burden of defending the law: while no one ever uses these words in Poland, the law would be utterly toothless with regard to foreigners committing this "crime" in non-Polish media. In fact, both the further justification and plain meaning of the text of the law suggest that its intended reach was much broader: it covered statements other than "Polish concentration camps," but also those which can be seen as "attributing responsibility or co-responsibility" to the Polish nation for, inter alia, the crimes of the Holocaust.

The defenders of the law pointed at two types of exceptions that were allegedly speech-protective. First, the punishment would be meted out only for the statements "contrary to facts." But the "facts" are often disputed – including about the pogrom and massacre in Jedwabne in Eastern Poland on 10 July 1941, when over three

---

[41] Macierewicz ceased to be minister as a result of a governmental reshuffle on 8 January 2018, but maintained his position as Vice President of PiS.

hundred (perhaps many more) Jews were burned alive in a barn by their Polish neighbours. While a group of "old" IPN experts pointed to the active agency of Polish neighbours in murdering the Jedwabne Jews, the new Chairman of the Institute, Dr Jarosław Szarek (appointed by the PiS majority in the parliament), claimed that Poles acted under coercion by the Germans. This has never been demonstrated but is kept as an article of faith by the Polish nationalist right. The practical outcome is that prosecutors and judges will have to determine historical facts about which there is an ongoing dispute among historians. Second, "scholarly and artistic" works will be exempt from liability. But this does not include journalism and the popularization of scholarship. Will a historian appearing in the media attract criminal responsibility, while lecturing in a classroom will be exempt? All this shows how dangerous and malleable the new law is. In addition, rather than protecting the pride and "good name" of Poland, the fact of enacting criminal sanctions for making "improper" statements about Poland's past suggested to many that there must be ulterior reasons – a sense of guilt? – for such an unusual, restrictive response to certain statements made in the course of public debate. As Tomasz Koncewicz observed, the law "is the most recent proof that in Poland the past continues to be seen as a collection of indisputable truths, not open to divergent interpretations and historical debate."[42]

The law quickly became a matter of major international embarrassment for the government, with both the US and Israeli governments reacting angrily. The former protested, on the basis of the general violation of freedom of speech and academic inquiry. The latter objected that the law may silence the testimonies of many Holocaust survivors who remember the inhospitable (to put it mildly) attitude of their Polish neighbours during the German occupation. Oddly enough, President Duda signed the law *and* sent it to the CT for a post-factum scrutiny: an arguably internally contradictory action. If the President has doubts about the constitutionality of the law, constitutional convention requires him to send the law to the CT for an ex-ante review, but if the President signs the law, this would signify the absence of constitutional doubts on his part. The President, being formally a "guardian of the Constitution," must not promulgate a law that is putatively unconstitutional. The real reason for this incoherent action was an attempt to reconcile an appeal to nationalistic pressures within Poland with an attempt to placate observers abroad. Political opportunism once again produced a constitutionally scandalous action.

---

[42] Tomasz Tadeusz Koncewicz, "On the Politics of Resentment, Mis-memory, and Constitutional Fidelity: The Demise of the Polish Overlapping Consensus?," in *Law and Memory: Towards Legal Governance of History*, ed. Uladzislau Belavusau and Aleksandra Gliszczyńska-Grabias (Cambridge: Cambridge University Press, 2017), 271. Note that the observations by Professor Koncewicz refer to an earlier iteration of the same law but the differences between the two versions of the law are insignificant.

In the end, the CT did not get an occasion to pronounce on the law because the government neutered the statute on 27 June 2018. The most controversial provisions, namely criminal punishment for an act described in the statute and also a proviso that it also applies to acts committed abroad, were withdrawn. The possibility of claiming civil-law damages remains intact. In any event, major damage to the image of Poland was already done, even though the government tried to present a short-lived law as a great success. One ironic and unintended by-product of the law, ostensibly aimed at protecting 'the good name' of Poland, was to draw the attention of domestic and international public opinion to those who really do damage to the Polish reputation – namely the racists, neo-Nazis and anti-Semites in Poland. Since Poland found it necessary to punish accusations against Poland being, inter alia, anti-Semitic, there must be a reason for it, the argument went, and the reason must have something to do with the embarrassing aspects of the Polish past and present. Countries that have 'nothing to hide' do not need to resort to criminal punishment to protect their reputation. This train of thought led to an inquiry into persistent extremist streams in Polish life – and they were, alas, not too difficult to find. A serious recent study has shown that one of the side effects of the statute on responsibility for the Holocaust was that it triggered a huge increase in violently anti-Semitic themes in public discourse (as an example, one of the leading MPs of the parliamentary party Kukiz-15 said that "Israel wants to appropriate to itself all the suffering which occurred during the Second World War"),[43] and especially on social media. The report, having studied the use frequency of certain derogatory anti-Semitic descriptions and words, concluded: "While before the debate about the law on IPN Internet conversations about 'Jews' and 'Israel' did not necessarily have anti-Semitic character, after the commencement of the debate about the new law posts about Jews and their state used [predominantly] anti-Semitic phrases and hashtags."[44]

V PRIVACY RIGHTS VERSUS COUNTER-TERRORISM MEASURES AND POLICE ACT

Two laws adopted in 2016 increased the discretionary powers of the special services and police: the statute of 10 June 2016 on counter-terrorist activities and the statute of 15 January 2016 on the police.

The statute of 10 June 2016 established a vast and vaguely defined scope of powers for the Internal Security Agency (Polish acronym: ABW) in order to protect the state against terrorism, as well as to control citizens and collect personal data without

---

[43] Maria Babińska et al., *Stosunek do Żydów i ich historii po wprowadzeniu ustawy o IPN* (Warsaw: Centrum Badań nad Uprzedzeniami, 2018), 8 (translation); the words are those of Mr Marek Jakubiak. The report was commissioned by the Ombudsman.

[44] Babińska et al., *Stosunek do Żydów i ich historii po wprowadzeniu ustawy o IPN*, 20.

following regular statutory procedures. The Ombudsman questioned the constitutionality of a significant part of the statute before the Constitutional Tribunal just after the statute entered into force.[45] The motion of unconstitutionality was supported by the following arguments. First, there is no clear definition of the term "terrorist act," even though the new law uses it as one of the most important statutory criteria for intervention by anti-terrorist services. This term is also a part of another crucial statutory definition: "anti-terrorist activities."[46] Under the new law, the Internal Security Agency would create a new database in order to control persons associated with terrorist acts. There is, however, no clear statutory purpose, nor principles or limits for such a database. The provisions do not guarantee any efficient judicial control over it, nor do they allow any interested party to demand, correct and delete false or incomplete data. The Internal Security Agency may demand and shall have unlimited access to data and information collected by all public agencies or bodies at the central as well as the local level.[47] A mere threat or attempt to commit a terrorist act shall be a sufficient premise to apply for pre-trial detention.[48] Moreover, under the new statutory provisions, the Internal Security Agency may make orders to block Internet services in order to prevent (undefined) terrorist acts.[49] Judicial review of the Agency's acts is strictly limited.

The second of the two laws (amending the Police Act) gives the police and its agencies access to Internet data, including the communication's content, under court orders (up to three months but without a requirement of necessity or proportionality)[50] or to metadata without the need for court orders.[51] The latter provision is especially cause for serious concern: metadata may be obtained without the prior consent of a court, and the only requirement is for an ex-post court review of a *generalized* (i.e., basically limited to statistics) report by the police on metadata collection. While metadata is theoretically not content-related, a combined analysis of various types of metadata (something that is not excluded by the law), collected secretly by law enforcement agencies, and which may be used against a person unaware of the fact of the collection of those data, may significantly intrude into a person's privacy and give insight into intimate aspects of a person's private life. As the Venice Commission noted, the law regarding collection of this information contains no "probability test" (no need for the police to have a specific reason to believe that criminal activity is going on or being prepared), and no "subsidiarity test" (a requirement that metadata collection be a subsidiary means of obtaining

---

[45] See case no. K 35/16, now discontinued owing to the improper composition of the panel of judges to consider the case.

[46] Article 2 (1) of the statute of 10 June 2016.

[47] Article 11 of the statute of 10 June 2016.

[48] Article 26 (2) of the statute of 10 June 2016.

[49] Article 38 subpara 6 of the statute of 10 June 2016.

[50] Article 19 of the statute of 6 April 1990 on the Police as amended.

[51] Article 20c of the statute of 6 April 1990 on the Police as amended.

information).[52] In combination with no effective oversight of such activities, the law allows for a very deep intrusion into a person's private life, without him or her even being aware of such surveillance.

Eventually, the Ombudsman withdrew his constitutional challenge, on the basis that the new Court President, Ms Przyłębska, had unlawfully tampered with the composition of the panels after she took over the leadership of the CT. This compelled the CT to discontinue the case.

The last legal innovation worth mentioning in this context, though strictly speaking made as an amendment to the Code of Criminal Proceedings, concerned the doctrine of the "fruits of poisonous tree." On 11 March 2016, an amendment to the Code was enacted allowing such evidence to be admissible in a criminal trial even though it was collected illegally – for example, as a result of an illegal search or seizure or illegal surveillance.[53] This reversed a major achievement of Polish criminal procedure and brought back incentives for police and prosecutors to take shortcuts with the law of criminal evidence.

VI POLAND BEFORE THE EUROPEAN COURT OF HUMAN RIGHTS

Over the past few years especially, Poland has systematically violated the rights of asylum-seekers, particularly from Chechnya, Armenia and Tajikistan, who, in violation of international law and also Polish Constitution itself (Art. 56 (2)), have been denied the right to enter upon Polish territory to seek asylum, or once they had, were in most cases deported in an inhumane manner, without the right to judicial review of their deportation, and to places where their lives and security are endangered. This has led to a string of cases before the ECtHR (none of which have resulted in a judgment at the time of writing of this chapter) concerning the horrific treatment of refugees by Polish border guards.

Complaints to the ECtHR were made by refugees who were not allowed into, or immediately deported from, the territory of Poland, without having an effective opportunity to lodge applications for refugee status, in violation of Article 3 of the ECHR (prohibition of degrading and inhuman treatment), Article 34 (admissibility of individual applications to the ECtHR) and Article 4 of Protocol 4 (prohibition against the collective expulsion of aliens). Representative of the cases concerning this matter[54] is *M.A. and Others* v. *Poland*,[55] lodged by a family of refugees from the

---

[52] European Commission for Democracy through Law (Venice Commission), Opinion on the Act of 15 January 2016 amending the Police Act and Certain Other Acts, adopted by the Venice Commission at its 10th Plenary Session, Venice, 10–11 June 2016, Opinion No 839/2016, CDL-AD (2016)012, paras 55–59.

[53] Act of 11 March 2016 on amending the Code of Criminal Proceedings and selected other acts.

[54] *MA* v. *Poland* (App. no 42902/17), *MK* v. *Poland* (App no 40503/17), and *DA* v. *Poland* (App no 51246/17).

[55] App no 42902/17, lodged on 16 June 2017, communicated on 3 August 2017.

Chechen war, depicting a truly disturbing story of a man who had been cruelly tortured back in Chechnya, and who was, while accompanied by his wife and children, turned away several times from the border crossing in Terespol (at the border of Poland with Belarus), despite a Polish judge having made an order, as an interim measure, to allow the family to stay in Poland until their asylum requests were properly considered. In its questions communicated to the government, the European Court queried, among other things, whether "the denial to review the applicants' motion for international protection" was in breach of Article 3 ECHR,[56] whether the applicants were expelled "as part of a collective measure" in breach of Article 4 of Protocol 4,[57] and whether there had been any "hindrance by the State ... with the effective exercise of the applicants' right of application," in breach of Article 34 of the Convention.[58] The facts summarized earlier by the Court suggest that the answers to these questions are all affirmative, and that the judgment will find Poland in breach of the Convention. The case (as with the other related cases) is still pending, and at the time of writing, the government's answer is still awaited.

While the cases related to the treatment of refugees raised relatively little reaction in Poland, both because judgments have not yet been handed down and because of the overall insensitivity of general public opinion to the fate of refugees, the judgment in Strasbourg of 20 September 2018 produced a huge wave of reactions from both proponents and critics, as it directly touched on an issue of great symbolic and political value to PiS, namely the aftermath of the Smolensk air crash of 10 April 2010. In *Solska and Rybicka* v. *Poland*,[59] the First Section of the Court unanimously found Poland in breach of the Article 8 rights of the relatives of some victims who disagreed with the exhumation of the dead bodies of those victims, as ordered by public prosecutors. The exhumation process was part of PiS's paranoia-ridden policy, under which it has continuously maintained a conspiracy theory about the crash and used it to mobilize its hard-core electorate in its hatred against political opponents. Some relatives – including the complainants in this case – strongly opposed the exhumations, maintaining that they were pointless and contributed to their mental anguish, but their objections were not recognized, and they found themselves with no means of seeking judicial review of the prosecutors' decisions, which were clearly politically motivated.

But the judgment was also important for reasons exceeding its directly relevant subject-matter, specifically having to do with the extreme insensitivity of the actions of public prosecutors employed to carry on a partisan, political campaign, and also concerned, albeit indirectly, with issues regarding the condition of the rule of law in

---

[56] Communication of 3 August 2017, Question 1.
[57] Question 4.
[58] Question 6.
[59] App no 30491/17 and 31083/17, ECHR (20 September 2018).

today's Poland. One such matter arose with regard to the status of the CT as allegedly providing a domestic remedy, the exhaustion of which is a prerequisite for taking the matter to Strasbourg. Or so the government argued, while the complainants pointed at the unconstitutional staffing of the Tribunal, as a result of which it "could no longer be regarded as an effective and impartial judicial body able to fulfil its constitutional duties."[60] The European Court opted for a Solomonic solution. On the one hand, it said that in this concrete case, the CT procedure of constitutional complaint was not relevant because of the specificity of the exhumation issue: whatever the CT decided, it would not have stopped the exhumation proceedings. For this reason, there was no need to consider "the alleged lack of effectiveness and independence of the Constitutional Court."[61] On the other hand, the Court itself left the door open to reconsider the status of the CT in some future case; it just "does not consider it necessary to examine" this issue in the present case.[62] In this way, the issue of the Polish CT's disabling made its way to a judgment of the ECtHR for the first time.

But perhaps the most striking aspect of the judgment is that it was based on a categorical statement of illegality (a government action done not 'in accordance with the law') rather than coming about as the result of employing a proportionality analysis, which the Court did not even embark upon. As one knows, in order to proceed to a proportionality analysis, the ECtHR must first be satisfied as to the certain early stages of scrutiny, the failure with regard to which pre-empts the need of "proportionality." One of these is scrutiny into whether the action was "in accordance with the law." Failure under this test is much more invidious than failure under proportionality, on the conduct of which reasonable lawyers may disagree. The Court foreclosed the road to conducting a proportionality test by categorically condemning Poland at an earlier stage. Polish prosecutorial practice based on Polish code of criminal procedure was found to be lacking in "adequate legal protection against arbitrariness,"[63] and failed "to ensure that the discretion left to the executive is exercised in accordance with the law and without abuse of powers."[64] The Court found that *some* prosecutorial decisions *are* subject to judicial review – but decisions on exhumations are not reviewable.[65] This led the Court to conclude that "Polish law did not provide sufficient safeguards against arbitrariness with regard to a prosecutorial decision ordering exhumation."[66] This was a harsh condemnation of the law, but also of the barbaric practice of Polish prosecutors under PiS rule.

---

[60] *Solska*, para 61.
[61] *Solska*, para 70.
[62] *Solska*, para 70.
[63] *Solska*, para 112.
[64] *Solska*, para 113.
[65] *Solska*, paras 123–125.
[66] *Solska*, para 126.

VII CONCLUSION

As this chapter has shown, there have been some very troubling developments in Poland in the field of human rights, especially those with direct implications for the political process, such as freedom of assembly. Political rights have also been adversely affected by many other statutory and political developments discussed in the previous chapter: for instance, voting rights – the most critical political right of them all – have been drastically diminished by institutional changes which pack electoral system institutions with ruling party nominees, and which diminish standards of the impartiality of electoral officials.

Without therefore denying the seriousness of the developments discussed in this chapter, in terms of infractions of fundamental rights, it would be fair to say that Poland's constitutional breakdown proceeds via, to use Dimitry Kochenov's words (not in the context of discussing Poland), "a well-executed dismantlement of the Rule of Law and the constitutional checks and balances … [and] without bald violations of human rights."[67] This combination, of course, is not something to be applauded. By dismantling the institutional protections of individual rights and liberties, the ruling party has paved the way for future assaults on rights – and if they happen, the institutions that would be normally expected to prevent this state of affairs from occurring, will not be there.

BIBLIOGRAPHY

Babińska, Maria, Michał Bilewicz, Dominika Bulska, Agnieszka Haska, and Mikołaj Winiewski. *Stosunek do Żydów i ich historii po wprowadzeniu ustawy o IPN*. Warsaw: Centrum Badań nad Uprzedzeniami, 2018.

Bodnar, Adam. "Protection of Human Rights after the Constitutional Crisis in Poland." *Jahrbuch des öffentlichen Rechts der Gegenwart* 66 (2018): 639–657.

European Commission for Democracy through Law (Venice Commission). Opinion on the Act of 15 January 2016 amending the Police Act and Certain Other Acts, adopted by the Venice Commission at its 10th Plenary Session, Venice, 10–11 June 2016, Opinion No 839/2016, CDL-AD(2016)012.

Gliszczyńska-Grabias, Aleksandra, and Wojciech Sadurski. "Freedom of Religion versus Humane Treatment of Animals: Polish Constitutional Tribunal's Judgment on Permissibility of Religious Slaughter." *European Constitutional Law Review* 11, no. 3 (2015): 596–608.

Harding, Andrew, Peter Leyland, and Tania Groppi. "Constitutional Courts: Forms, Functions and Practice in Comparative Perspective." *Journal of Comparative Law* 3, no. 2 (2008): 1–21.

---

[67] Dimitry Kochenov, "The Acquis and Its Principles: The Enforcement of the 'Law' versus the Enforcement of 'Values' in the EU," in *The Enforcement of EU Law and Values: Ensuring Member States' Compliance*, ed. András Jakab and Dimitry Kochenov (Oxford: Oxford University Press, 2017), 22.

Kochenov, Dimitry. "The Acquis and Its Principles: The Enforcement of the 'Law' versus the Enforcement of 'Values' in the EU." In *The Enforcement of EU Law and Values: Ensuring Member States' Compliance*, edited by András Jakab and Dimitry Kochenov, 9–27. Oxford: Oxford University Press, 2017.

Koncewicz, Tomasz Tadeusz. "Farewell to the Separation of Powers – On the Judicial Purge and the Capture in the Heart of Europe." *VerfassungsBlog*, 19 July 2017, verfassungsblog .de/farewell-to-the-separation-of-powers-on-the-judicial-purge-and-the-capture-in-the-heart-of-europe (accessed 2 January 2019).

"On the Politics of Resentment, Mis-memory, and Constitutional Fidelity: The Demise of the Polish Overlapping Consensus?" In *Law and Memory: Towards Legal Governance of History*, edited by Uladzislau Belavusau and Aleksandra Gliszczyńska-Grabias, 263–290. Cambridge: Cambridge University Press, 2017.

"The Court is Dead, Long Live the Courts? On Judicial Review in Poland 2017 and 'Judicial Space' Beyond." *Verfassungsblog*, 8 March 2018, https://verfassungsblog.de/ the-court-is-dead-long-live-the-courts-on-judicial-review-in-poland-in-2017-and-judicial-space-beyond/ (accessed 9 November 2018).

Kursa, Magdalena. "Obywatele ścigani za protesty." *Czarna Księga, Gazeta Wyborcza*, 17 October 2018, 14.

Müller, Jan-Werner. "Populism and Constitutionalism." In *The Oxford Handbook of Populism*, edited by Cristóbal Rovira Kaltwasser, Paul Taggart, Paulina Ochoa-Espejo and Pierre Ostiguy, 593–602. Oxford: Oxford University Press, 2017.

Piątek, Tomasz. *Macierewicz i jego tajemnice*. Warsaw: Arbitror, 2017.

"Poland's Kaczynski Calls EU Democracy Inquiry an 'Absolute Comedy.'" *Reuters Online*, 23 December 2016, (accessed 7 November 2017).

[Rzecznika Praw Obywatelskich]. *Wolność zgromadzeń w Polsce w latach 2016–2018: Raport Rzecznika Praw Obywatelskich*. Warsaw: Biuro Rzecznika Praw Obywatelskich, September 2018.

Sadurski, Wojciech. "Polish Constitutional Tribunal under PiS: From an Activist Court, to a Paralysed Tribunal, to a Governmental Enabler." *Hague Journal on the Rule of Law* 11, no. 1 (2019): 63–84, DOI:10.1007/s40803-018-0078-1.

Rights before Courts: A Study of Constitutional Courts in Postcommunist States of Central and Eastern Europe, 2nd edn Dordrecht: Springer, 2014.

Śledzińska-Simon, Anna. "Midnight Judges: Poland's Constitutional Tribunal Caught between Political Fronts." *VerfassungsBlog*, 23 November 2015, http://verfassungsblog .de/midnight-judges-polands-constitutional-tribunal-caught-between-political-fronts (accessed 9 January 2018).

Weyland, Kurt. "Populism: A Political–Strategic Approach." In *The Oxford Handbook of Populism*, edited by Cristóbal Rovira Kaltwasser, Paul Taggart, Paulina Ochoa-Espejo and Pierre Ostiguy, 48–72. Oxford: Oxford University Press, 2017.

5

The Legal Architecture of Populism

Exploring Antagonists in Venezuela and Colombia

Helena Alviar García

I INTRODUCTION

There are many ways to dissect the term populism. It can be embodied in economic policies, political institutions as well as practices, or performed as an aesthetic manifestation. These characteristics can be contained in a single figure and regime, or some aspects of it can be found within liberal democratic systems.

The expression has been linked to reckless public spending, to a strategy to downplay representative democracy and govern through direct participation, and to a way to perform politics that includes a personality cult and a call to nationalism. It can be seen as an exceptional – albeit long-lasting – event or it can be interpreted as a continuum where many countries, including liberal democracies, could fall into place. Populism can be of the left or right, and for this reason it can be depicted as more a form of exercising power than a specific set of substantive provisions.

This chapter engages with the ideational approach to populism emphasized by Gerald Neuman, the editor of this volume. This ideational approach is described in the following terms: "First, the ideational approach emphasizes that such populists consistently invoke the people in an anti-pluralist manner. Second, the ideational approach emphasizes the populists' claim to implement the people's will without legal or institutional constraint. Third, the ideational approach applies both to personalistic leaders and less tightly led parties."[1]

Both Hugo Chávez Frias, the President of Venezuela from 1999 until his death in 2013, and Álvaro Uribe Vélez, the President of Colombia from 2002 through 2010,[2] fit

---

[1] Chapter 1 (in this volume).

[2] The only fact that prevented Uribe from staying longer was a Constitutional Court ruling that rejected a second reelection. With a seven to two vote, the Colombian Constitutional Court ruled that the law that allowed a referendum to modify the constitution and permit President Uribe to run for a third term was unconstitutional. The arguments covered both formal issues related to the way in which the law was passed by Congress and a substantive analysis of the

squarely into the ideational approach, as this chapter will demonstrate. They invoked a monolithic understanding of "el pueblo"; both of them used direct democracy (with varying levels of success) in order to circumvent limitations imposed by separation of powers as well as constitutional arrangements; and both of them created movements based on their persona, namely Chavismo and Uribismo.[3]

Nevertheless, there are also important differences. Populism in Latin America has been characterized as inclusionary populism. Neuman describes this idea in the following terms:

> Professors Mudde and Rovira Kaltwasser, proponents of the ideational approach, have contrasted contemporary forms of populism in Europe and Latin America, and shown how European populists are often hostile to vulnerable ethnic groups and Latin American populists often offer empowerment to vulnerable economic classes. Their study described the Europeans as exclusionary populists and the Latin Americans as inclusionary populists, while also observing that all populists are inclusive toward some and exclusionary toward others. That duality is inherent in their ideational definition, under which populists divide society into two antagonistic groups, the real people and their enemies.[4]

As Uribe's case in Colombia will show, he belongs more to the exclusionary form of populism and possibly set the stage for this style in the region. On the other hand, Chávez embodies the characteristics of an inclusionary populist.

The aim in this chapter will therefore be to argue, that at least in the case of two ideologically opposing figures in Latin America – Hugo Chávez and Álvaro Uribe – there were more similarities than differences in relation to the legal architecture they deployed. Populism is not lawless: law is necessary in order to provide a structure to interact and exchange; solve conflicts; adjudicate public resources; distribute entitlements; settle disputes over property and provide social services, among many others.

The content of the laws in the two systems was ideologically opposite, but the legal instruments used to develop specific economic, political, and social transformations were very similar. In both cases, the preferred tools included calling for a

---

content of the reform. The ruling established that the violation of procedural congressional rules meant that important electoral principles were being violated, among them: transparency; respect for the political pluralism of voters; and the tenets of a participatory democracy. In addition, the Court found that allowing a second reelection would be tantamount to a new constitution. This was a consequence of transforming structural elements of the 1991 Charter (separation of powers, checks and balances as well as the legislative process in Congress). Colombian Constitutional Court, STC C-141/10, February 26, 2010 (Humberto Sierra Porto, reporting judge).

3   Gregory J. Lobo, "Colombia, from Failing State to a Second Independence: The Politics and the Price," *International Journal of Cultural Studies* 16, no. 4 (2012): 351–366.

4   Chapter 1 (in this volume) (citing Cas Mudde and Cristóbal Rovira Kaltwasser, "Exclusionary vs. Inclusionary Populism: Comparing Contemporary Europe and Latin America," *Government and Opposition* 48, no. 2 [2013]: 147–174).

referendum, changing or attempting to transform constitutional provisions in order to increase the power of the presidency, and a marked preference for legislation by executive decree.

It is here, in the legal architecture, where the greatest risks occur of the undermining of democracy and the authoritarian turn. Populism per se is not necessarily bad. After all, if the measures are geared towards aiding marginal classes at the cost of experimentation or departures from orthodox economic thinking, they should be welcome. The problem is when democratic institutions are undermined and an authoritarian figure emerges, is strengthened and ends up being impossible to dislodge.

Despite their striking similarities, the analysis of both cases sheds light on an important difference. Hugo Chávez was able to effectively concentrate power in the executive branch and intervene in a wide range of economic, social, and political matters. As a consequence he was able to undermine judicial independence, weaken central bank autonomy, and take a firm grip on freedom of speech. Álvaro Uribe, on the other hand and despite his desire to do so, was less able to achieve these things. The Colombian Constitutional Court consistently blocked many of his initiatives, both constitutional and legal.

In order to present my argument, this chapter will have three sections. In the first, I will paint a broad picture of both leaders. It will describe how they both represented themselves as men of the people, "el pueblo." In addition, it will lay out in what terms they justified the dichotomy of *us versus them* discourse or, in what Gerald Neuman, quoting Cas Mudde, defines as "an ideology that considers society to be ultimately separated into two homogenous and antagonistic groups, 'the pure people' versus 'the corrupt elite.'"[5] This antagonism is relevant for the objectives of this chapter because it lays the ground for the turn to authoritarianism, using the power of the state to persecute enemies, and along the way engage in violations of human rights including free speech, due process, and formal equality. Then, the next section will analyze the similar legal architecture in both cases that structured and made possible the authoritarian turn. These tools include the use of referendums and the strengthening of executive power. Finally, I will propose some concluding observations.

II MEN OF THE PEOPLE, IDEOLOGICAL ADVERSARIES

Álvaro Uribe and Hugo Chávez shared many similarities. Both liked to present and represent themselves as men of the people: *el pueblo.* But what the term *pueblo* meant for each of them was quite different. In this section I will describe how each one's personal history marked their understanding of whom they represented and whom they were up against. It will also sketch out their ideological influences and

---

[5] Chapter 1 (in this volume).

corresponding outlook on democracy, the rule of law, management of the economy, and social transformation. It will finish by laying out the similarities in terms of performance and style as well as their deep ideological differences.

Where Chávez's accent was on the popular classes, Uribe appealed to the middle class and the aspiring middle class.[6] In addition, their discourse contained the classical antagonist rhetoric of "us versus them." Again, who was the "us" and who was the "them" were divergent concepts.

For Chávez, the "us" was the Venezuelan nation represented by the popular classes, the "them" was the oligarchy. There are many references to this, including the slogan: *Con Chávez manda el pueblo!* (with Chávez the people rule!), and the language and style of his speeches.

Uribe's distinction cut differently, with for him, "us" consistently representing those who opposed FARC and its sympathizers, "them." In his own words: "The country has to choose now if we are going to continue the path to peace of our Democratic Security Policy or we are going to move back so that disguised communism takes over our homeland."[7]

Both men used the media – mostly TV – to reach out, and famously spent intoxicating amounts of time in front of the cameras. Thus, an important tool was their direct contact with citizens through televised town meetings: *Aló Presidente* in the case of Chávez and *Consejos Comunitarios* in the case of Uribe. In both cases they decided public spending, granted social services, fired and accused both state officials and enemies, in a show of power transmitted by TV. By 2012, Chávez had spent the equivalent of one year of nonstop broadcasting.[8] In the case of Uribe, during his first two years in office, he spent 2240 hours onscreen, a striking average of almost three hours per day.[9]

Chávez came from a family that had a long tradition of connections to Left politics in Venezuela. He grew up in a province, Barinas, where the citizens have long fought for regional autonomy, opposing the fact that many decisions were taken by elites in the capital. He identified himself as a "mestizo" who critiqued the excessive political, economic, and social power of the white, Spanish-descendant Caracas upper class. Being part of the military placed him in a privileged position not only to view firsthand the problems of poor Venezuelans but also because the military was exceptionally egalitarian, promoting social mobility and access to

---

[6] Álvaro Uribe Vélez, "Manifiesto Democrático 100 Puntos," *Asociación Primero Colombia*, February 24, 2015, www.primerocolombia.com/content/manifiesto-democratico-100-puntos (last accessed January 27, 2019).

[7] "Dilema es Seguridad o Comunismo: Uribe," *Diario El Tiempo*, May 6, 2006, www.eltiempo .com/archivo/documento/MAM-2012895.

[8] Rachel Nolan, "The Realest Reality Show in the World: Hugo Chávez's Totally Bizarre Talk Show," *New York Times*, May 4, 2012, www.nytimes.com/2012/05/06/magazine/hugo-chavezs-totally-bizarre-talk-show.html (last accessed April 8, 2019).

[9] Cristina de la Torre, *Álvaro Uribe: El Neopopulismo en Colombia* (Medellín: La Carreta, 2005), 101.

higher education. Chávez himself started but never finished a graduate degree in political science. Against this personal background, he described himself as the people, *el pueblo* – not as a representative, more as an extension. His triumphant electoral speech on being elected in 1998, for example, stated:

> All of me belongs to you, the Venezuelan people. This power you have granted me is your power. You will guide the government that will not be Chávez's government because *Chávez is the people*. The government of the majorities, the government of dignity, the Bolivarian government, the Venezuelan government, a patriotic government. You are the owners of this government. I will simply fulfill your mandate.[10]

There are of course many, many other speeches where he equated himself to the people. For the purpose of this chapter it is also interesting to note the ethnic, class, and gender choices he made when he described *el pueblo*:

> We are one of the liberating peoples of the world, we are a people of creators, poets, of fighters, of warriors, of workers, there's history to prove it, let's honor it, let's honor the spirit of our aborigines, our liberators, of our women, of our youth … all of that we have in our veins and in the clay from which we are made, let us show it, it is the moment to show it.[11]

Chávez, at least initially, thought that leadership was a way to channel the desires of the people. He believed that once they became involved, citizens would start to participate and engage more politically. Given Venezuela's high levels of inequality and legal limits on the creation of parties outside the two traditional groupings,[12] once they became aware of these injustices, people would mobilize against the traditional political, economic, and social elite.[13] This decentering of his importance

---

[10] One of Chávez's leading followers, Diosdado Cabello, hosts a TV program and corresponding website, *Con El Mazo Dando*, dedicated to defending Chávez's legacy. This quote comes from an article published on the website in 2018 commemorating five years since Chávez's death. See "La importancia y el amor de Chávez por el pueblo en sus propias palabras," *Con El Mazo Dando*, March 4, 2018, www.conelmazodando.com.ve/la-importancia-y-el-amor-de-chavez-por-el-pueblo-en-sus-propias-palabras/ (last accessed January 30, 2019), author's translation, emphasis added.

[11] Barry Cannon, *Hugo Chávez and the Bolivarian Revolution: Populism and Democracy in a Globalised Age* (Manchester: Manchester University Press, 2009), 57.

[12] In an article published shortly after his election, *The New York Times* described the 1961 Venezuelan Constitution in the following terms: "For Mr. Chavez and his supporters, the 1961 Constitution is a symbol of a corrupt political system that has fed popular resentment and apathy. It was written by leaders of the two traditional parties, Acción Democrática and Copei, to keep Marxist groups then aligned with Cuban-backed guerrillas out of the political process." Clifford Krauss, "New President in Venezuela Proposes to Rewrite the Constitution," *The New York Times*, February 4, 1999, www.nytimes.com/1999/02/04/world/new-president-in-venezuela-proposes-to-rewrite-the-constitution.html.

[13] Cannon, transcribing parts of his discourse, illustrates this faith in popular mobilization: "The people are an 'unleashed force, equal to rivers' being channeled by leaders such as Chávez, because either 'we provide a course for that force, or that force will pass over us.' Chávez was

was obviously disingenuous, changed over time, and did not prevent the development of authoritarian measures that increased his power.

In Uribe's case, from the beginning he unapologetically embraced the centrality of his own person. Álvaro Uribe's background and upbringing were completely different. He was born in Medellín, the second city of Colombia. He came from an upper middle-class family who owned large landed estates and a private helicopter. His father was killed in a failed attempt to kidnap him in 1983.[14] Uribe has always argued that the assassins were FARC members, and this fact explains his obsession with fiercely battling this guerrilla group. In his memoir published in 2012, *No hay causa perdida* (No Lost Causes), he describes his father as saying: "I prefer to be dead than kidnapped."[15] His father's murder is narrated in the following terms: "My father was assassinated on June 14, 1983 in the afternoon. He was shot twice ... According to the accounts of witnesses the crime was committed by more than 12 FARC members."[16] Further on he tells his family that this fact was determinant in his political thinking: "The pain we are feeling is also suffered by half of the Colombian population. Ours is a personal tragedy and also a national problem. We must face this problem in some way."[17]

Uribe has been accused of using his personal hatred for FARC to design a range of policies that included legalizing paramilitary groups when he was the governor of Antioquia,[18] and his description of FARC as terrorists and not a guerrilla group with a leftist ideological agenda. In addition, he argued that there was no internal conflict in Colombia because the country had a longstanding democracy, not a dictatorship or an oppressive regime. Thus, there was no reason to oppose the state. He made this point in many speeches and interventions. In 2003, during the installation of one of his town meetings, *consejos comunales*, the day after a bomb exploded in a social club frequented by the conservative elite, he said:

> The terrorist guerrilla has only come up with bad excuses for their existence. Colombia has presented evidence of it being a democratic country and the goal of this government is to reestablish law and order has left them with no justification for their terrorist acts. [. . .]

not a 'cause but a consequence' and an 'instrument of the collective.' Leadership, he believed, is multiple and is part of a greater movement, in which 'there is a leadership which has been extending on a number of levels, there is a popular force, there are some very strong parties, there are institutions; it would be a sad revolutionary or political process which depended on one man.'" Cannon, *Hugo Chávez*, 57.

14. "El Estremecedor Relato de la Muerte del papá de Uribe," *Revista Semana*, September 18, 2014, www.semana.com/nacion/articulo/el-estremecedor-relato-de-la-muerte-del-papa-de-uribe/403223-3.

15. Álvaro Uribe Vélez, *No hay causa perdida* (New York: Penguin Random House, 2012), 20, author's translation.

16. Uribe, *No hay causa perdida*, 30, author's translation.

17. Uribe, *No hay causa perdida*, 30, author's translation.

18. "Así nacieron las Convivir," *El Tiempo*, July 14, 1997, www.eltiempo.com/archivo/documento/MAM-605402.

What we have in Colombia, which hit Bogota last night, and has equally hit other parts of our country, isn't a guerrilla with ideals but a terrorist guerrilla. This mix of terrorist guerrilla and drug trafficking is a horrible combination that entails only one path: defeating them. [...]

The world must know that there are no democratic restrictions in Colombia.[19]

In addition, Uribe famously stated that since the end of the Cold War, guerrilla groups could have no political ideal to fight for: they were only acting as a form of organized crime for drug trafficking and extorting rents from oil, coca, and gold production. Therefore, they were not revolutionaries but criminals.[20]

In his early political career Uribe did not appeal to the people in the same way as Chávez did, but he did structure his discourse towards the half of the Colombian population that had suffered directly from the acts of guerrilla groups. As a consequence, he divided the country between "us," those who were FARC victims and "them," those who opposed his government. Despite his less classical approach to populism during his first presidential campaign and initial couple of years in office, slowly but surely Uribe structured a term that was not only populist but consolidated his authoritarian trend. This term was Rule of Opinion – *Estado de Opinión* in Spanish – which he described as a state above the rule of law. In his own words: "I would say that Colombia is in a superior stage to the Rule of Law, which is the Rule of Opinion, where laws are not determined by the current President or majorities in Congress, all laws are rigorously scrutinized by the people."[21]

An essential element of both leaders' political discourse was corruption, a term that has been so central to populist and authoritarian rulers that it deserves a book on its own. In the case of Chávez, the traditional, white, corrupt Venezuelan elite had held on to power for centuries and therefore was the culprit of all evils. An article published in 2003 about the rise of populism in Venezuela describes how Chávez reiterated over and over again this antagonism in the following terms:

If Chávez and his movement represent the popular will, those who oppose them are the corrupt elites, the *cogollos* and the *cupulas del poder* (the cabals and chambers of power), the *escualidos* (the filthy ones), the elites and leaders of the traditional parties. [...]

During a speech before election day in 1998, he declared, "The rotten elites of the parties are boxed in, and they will soon be consigned to the trash bin of history ... In 8 days we make the final assault to remove the corrupt elites from power ...

---

[19] "Que perdamos todas las elecciones, pero que no perdamos la lucha contra el terrorismo," *Archivo General Presidencia de la República*, November 16, 2003, http://historico.presidencia .gov.co/prensa_new/discursos/cc45bquilla.htm (last accessed January 27, 2019).

[20] "Si Hay Guerra Señor Presidente," *Revista Semana*, February 6, 2005, www.semana.com/ portada/articulo/si-guerra-senor-presidente/70763-3.

[21] Álvaro Uribe Vélez, speech given during a Presidential visit to the Prince of Asturias, May 27, 2009, quoted in Laura Jaramillo, "Uribe: 'El Estado de Opinión es la Fase Superior del Estado de Derecho,'" *La Silla Vacía*, June 5, 2009, https://lasillavacia.com/historia/2296, author's translation.

Participants in the recent national strike were called *golpistas* (coup plotters) and 'saboteurs' (while his own attempted coup was a 'movement' or 'rebellion')."[22]

In Uribe's case the antagonists against "us" included not only anybody who failed to believe FARC should be militarily defeated but also what he defined as corrupt state officials and politicians. In the document that structured his campaign promises, the attack on the corrupt bureaucracy read: "I dream of a State that serves the people, not a State that allows corruption to profit or manipulation of politicians for their personal gain. Today the state is permissive toward corruption as well as toward political manipulation and stingy with social investment."[23]

In sum, although they came from starkly different backgrounds (which in turn had consequences on how they defined the desires of the people, *el pueblo*), both leaders claimed to embody the desires of the people. This messianic vision led to a slow but sure attempt at undermining classical democratic institutions in order to centralize their person as leader, as embodied in Chavismo and Uribismo. In both cases the authoritarian turn was designed on several fronts. The rest of this chapter text is dedicated to analyzing the legal architecture they deployed in order to structure this authoritarian turn.

Despite sharing a legal architecture, their ideological differences have been well documented. Hugo Chávez was decidedly anti-neoliberal. He strongly believed in a state-led economy that included not only the public provision of social services and state ownership of key sectors, even if this meant expropriation. His government promoted a cooperative style for enterprise management as well as an increase in worker participation. In addition, he pursued land redistribution and a range of state-run initiatives (*Misiones*), designed to attack poverty; provided pre-school, primary, secondary, and college education; promoted access to health and housing, and a wide scope of cultural, scientific and environmental initiatives. All of this was translated into high levels of public spending.[24]

Álvaro Uribe was his complete opposite in economic terms. He was a staunch neoliberal, who opposed state intervention and was obsessed with reducing the size of the state[25] and privatizing the few existing state-owned enterprises.[26] Uribe was a

---

[22] Kirk Hawkins, "Populism in Venezuela: The Rise of Chavismo," *Third World Quarterly* 24, no. 6 (2003): 1137–1160, www.jstor.org/stable/3993447.

[23] Álvaro Uribe Vélez, "Manifiesto Democrático 100 Puntos," *Asociación Primero Colombia*, February 24, 2015, www.primerocolombia.com/content/manifiesto-democratico-100-puntos (last accessed January 27, 2019), author's translation.

[24] Cannon, *Hugo Chávez*, 77–111.

[25] He merged the ministries of the Interior with Justice; Health and Environment with Labor; Housing and Economic Development. This created such an administrative and institutional disaster that most of the ministries were reinstated in 2011. For more on this, see "Era de Uribe, con menos ministerios," *Portafolio*, November 27, 2007, www.portafolio.co/economia/finanzas/uribe-ministerios-470420.

[26] "Los $13 Billones en Empresas Públicas que vendió Uribe," *Las 2 Orillas*, January 13, 2016, www.las2orillas.co/los-13-billones-en-empresas-publicas-que-vendio-uribe/.

conservative who dismantled and fragmented the institution in control of providing access to land for poor peasants,[27] and tried, unsuccessfully, to exclude the Constitutional Court from adjudicating social and economic rights.

III THE LEGAL ARCHITECTURE THEY SHARED

The aim to concentrate power was present in both leaders. Nevertheless, context provided more opportunities than obstacles for Chávez. Both men had large congressional majorities initially, which allowed them to pass many of their reforms without appearing as totally authoritarian. A major difference, as I referred to in the introduction, was that in the Colombian case the Constitutional Court was able to overturn many of Uribe's proposals.[28]

A *Direct Democracy*

The two leaders tried, with varying degrees of success, to change the constitution through referendums. Both of them started their mandate with calls for a referendum and further along unsuccessfully used this mechanism at least once again. In the first part of this subsection I will address two initiatives of the Chávez government. The second part will be dedicated to the description of Uribe's use of this tool.

1 Hugo Chávez

The first announcement that Chávez made upon assuming power was to propose not one, but two referendums: the first one on whether to rewrite the Constitution, a second one to ratify it.[29] When he inaugurated the sessions of the assembly, he promised the Venezuelan people a radical break from the past. The new foundational document relied heavily on popular participation, assuming that the solutions for social and economic difficulties would come from the bottom up. Barry Cannon, in his fascinating book about Chávez, summarizes his words (shown inside quotation marks) in relation to these two topics (rebirth of the nation and direct political participation) in the following terms:

> The new constitution would instead place the people of Venezuela as the true sovereign of the Nation "a universal and elemental principle." An Enabling Law and the Constituent Assembly rather than being a panacea, however, would have a

[27] For more on this initiative, see Helena Alviar García, "The Unending Quest for Land: The Tale of Broken Constitutional Promises," *Texas Law Review* 89, no. 7 (2011): 1895–1914.

[28] Among them not authorizing an extension of the state of exception in 2003, and not allowing a second reelection in 2010.

[29] Clifford Krauss, "New President in Venezuela Proposes to Rewrite the Constitution," *New York Times*, February 4, 1999, www.nytimes.com/1999/02/04/world/new-president-in-venezuela-pro poses-to-rewrite-the-constitution.html.

"fundamental objective which is the transformation of the State and the creation of a new Republic, the re-founding of the Republic, the re-legitimation of democracy... It's political, it's macro political but it is not economic or social in the immediate term." However, in the end the process of the *Constituyente* would lead to the return of the "collective mentality," to a "return [of] the idea of utopia to the national mind that is to say, of a country which begins to exist in the collective imagination."[30]

The final product was not as radical as Chávez announced, and many elements of the previous constitution remained. Nevertheless, there were important changes that undermined the neoliberal economic model: a longer list of social and economic rights that could be directly adjudicated; the prohibition of selling of shares in the state oil company, PdVSA; the establishment of governmental control over pensions.[31] Paradoxically, and despite creating mechanisms for direct political participation – which could bring as a consequence the diffusion of political power – it also strengthened the executive by increasing the presidential term from five to six years and including the possibility of reelection more than once. It was approved by 71 percent of the vote in a referendum, with a 50 percent abstention.[32]

Seven years later, Chávez sought to reform the constitution once again in order, in his own words, to consolidate the socialist state. The themes drafted in 69 articles included expanding presidential power by augmenting the presidential term to seven years; eliminating limits on reelection; allowing the president to design special military and development zones; and curtailing Central Bank autonomy by giving the president direct access to the country's international financial reserves.[33] In relation to the management of the economy it included the strengthening of collective and social property and proposed the elimination of state protection of privately owned corporations.[34] The amendment would also recognize and grant special rights for Venezuelan afro-descendants and ban discrimination on the grounds of sexual orientation.[35] Despite the fact that Chávez announced that whoever voted "no" was voting in favor of his enemy George W. Bush,[36] the referendum was rejected by a slim margin of 50.65 percent against and 49.34 percent in favor.[37]

---

[30] Cannon, *Hugo Chávez*, 62.

[31] Diego González Cadenas, *El único proceso constituyente democratico en Venezuela: la constituyente de 1999*, forthcoming, Ediciones Uniandes, on file with the author.

[32] Cannon, *Hugo Chávez*, 62.

[33] Enrique Krauze, "Hell of a Fiesta," *The New York Review of Books*, March 8, 2018, www.nybooks.com/articles/2018/03/08/venezuela-hell-fiesta/.

[34] "Chávez presenta la reforma constitucional que le permitirá gobernar indefinidamente," *El País*, August 17, 2007, www.nytimes.com/2007/12/03/world/americas/03venezuela.html.

[35] Cannon, *Hugo Chávez*, 64.

[36] "Chávez: el que vote por el NO lo hace por George W. Bush," *Agencia Bolivariana de Noticias*, November 30, 2007, www.aporrea.org/actualidad/n105636.html.

[37] Cannon, *Hugo Chávez*, 64.

2 Álvaro Uribe

In the case of Uribe, one of his first acts in government was a referendum aimed at attacking what he considered bad political practices – *politiquería* – and corruption, in 2003. It had 19 questions, which covered a range of topics from a lifelong ban on the possibility of running for office for citizens found guilty of corruption; reducing the size of Congress; diminishing legislators' wages; placing a cap on pensions and salaries of Congress members and a range of former government officials, as well as freezing public spending for two years. It also included some odd provisions: the elimination of mandatory military service and the prohibition to cultivate, produce, distribute, carry or sell drugs that led to addiction such as cocaine, heroin, marihuana, Ecstasy, and similar substances.[38] The law established that citizens had to vote for all the questions as a block. The Constitutional Court struck down this possibility, arguing that it limited the rights of voters.[39] Although he was very popular at the time, Uribe could not persuade citizens to cast their vote. At the end, only one of the 15 questions (namely that regarding the ban on running for office for those found guilty of corruption) was approved.[40]

In 2010, at the same time that Chávez was pursuing his socialist transformation of the constitution, Uribe and his supporters were proposing a referendum to amend the Colombian Constitution in order to eliminate the prohibition against running for a third term. In the words of the leader of Uribe's political party at the time, "no army changes its general at the precise moment they are winning the battle."[41] According to Uribe and his supporters, the referendum proposed only a marginal reform of the constitution, including the phrase: "Anyone who has been elected to the Presidency for two constitutional periods, can be elected for an additional period."[42] Obviously, this was hardly a minor constitutional reform – if passed it would effectively distort the power equilibrium typical of a system of checks and balances, and unduly concentrate power in the executive.[43] Voting on the proposal

---

[38] Republic of Colombia, Law 796 of 2003, January 21, 2003. By which a referendum is summoned and plans for people's consideration a Constitutional Reform. Diario Oficial No. 45.070.

[39] "Aprobadas 15 de las 19 preguntas del Referendo," *Revista Semana*, July 7, 2003, www.semana .com/noticias/articulo/aprobadas-15-19-preguntas-del-referendo/59216-3.

[40] "Uribe habla sobre resultados del referendo y plantea propuestas al respecto," *Revista Semana*, October 27, 2003, www.semana.com/noticias/articulo/uribe-habla-sobre-resultados-del-refer endo-plantea-propuestas-respecto/61590-3.

[41] "Referendo: historia de una causa perdida," *Revista Semana*, February 26, 2010, www.semana .com/politica/articulo/referendo-historia-causa-perdida/113678-3.

[42] "Referendo: historia de una causa perdida."

[43] According to Dejusticia, the reelection would entail an extreme concentration of power, which would restrict separation of powers principles; it was a reform that was intended to benefit a single individual, Álvaro Uribe, therefore it was not designed to promote institutional improvement; political candidates would start their political campaigns at a disadvantage toward the person in office. "Intervención ciudadana en el proceso No. CRF-003," *Intervención Referendo Final*, December 4, 2009, https://cdn.dejusticia.org/wp-content/uploads/2017/04/fi_name_ recurso_169.pdf (last accessed January 27, 2019).

never took place because the Constitutional Court struck down the referendum law on procedural grounds.[44]

As this subsection has demonstrated, both leaders attempted to use referendums as a way to effectively concentrate power in their own hands, and in this way nail down the authoritarian turn. Nevertheless, the road was not a smooth one in either case. In the case of Chávez's second referendum, he clearly overestimated his popular support. After all, this was the first time he had been electorally defeated in nine years.[45] In Uribe's case he faced institutional constraints (in the form of checks from the Constitutional Court), and he also assumed his popularity would lead to unwavering approval and a shift in voting habits.

B *Exercise of Executive Power: Pushing the Limits*

The use of executive power is another characteristic of both regimes. Both leaders exercised or tried to exercise executive power extensively, either by the use of existing constitutional mechanisms such as *leyes habilitantes* in the case of Venezuela or by declaring states of exception in the case of Colombia. Both of these methods allowed the executive to adopt decrees that were equivalent to statute. When this option was not possible they retreated to regulatory power through administrative law. Again, there are many examples, but I will concentrate on enabling laws, *leyes habilitantes* in the case of Venezuela and the states of exception in the case of Colombia.

1 Enabling Laws – *Leyes Habilitantes*

The possibility of legislating by delegation to the executive branch is not a new or exotic provision designed by Chávez. In fact, the 1961 Venezuelan Constitution included this possibility, and it had been used six times to regulate economic matters before the election of Chávez in 1998. The Bolivarian Constitution of 1999 established a procedure for an enabling law, *ley habilitante*, which allowed the National Assembly to delegate to the president its law-making power. Article 203 reads as follows: "Enabling laws have to be approved by three fifths of the National Assembly members. The National Assembly must establish the directives, goals and frame of the themes to be delegated to the President or Presidency. Enabling laws have to include a determined period of time during which they can be exercised."[46]

---

[44] Colombian Constitutional Court, STC C-141/10, February 26, 2010 (Humberto Sierra Porto, reporting judge).

[45] Cannon refers to this fact in the following terms: "This was the first electoral loss by President Chávez out of thirteen electoral contests held since first being elected in 1998." Cannon, *Hugo Chávez*, 64.

[46] Carlos Reverón Boulton, "Sobre la Ley Habilitante Antiimperialista para La Paz," *Boletín Electrónico de Derecho Administrativo de la Universidad Católica Andrés Bello* no. 1 (2016):

During his presidency, Chávez secured four enabling laws (in 1999, 2000, 2007, and 2010).[47] It is interesting to observe how this delegation evolved in terms of scope and length of time. The first one in 1999 established very narrow subjects and a term of six months. In 2000, the themes were broader and the period for which it was granted covered a year. In 2007 and 2010 the themes were all-encompassing and the period was extended to 18 months.[48] This trend has only increased subsequently. Since he took office in 2013, President Nicolás Maduro has been granted 53 months to regulate under enabling laws.[49]

The first law of this type used by Chávez was employed to reform the taxing system, reducing VAT, and increasing or imposing new duties. This use was neither unusual nor did it aim to regulate a broad range of themes. In 2001 the National Assembly delegated legislative powers to him for a second time. This time, the power was used to significantly increase state intervention in various sectors. Among them was an agrarian reform, *Ley de Tierras y Desarrollo Agrario*, in which Chávez declared land of essential social interest as well as of public utility; greatly limited the maximum area of large landed estates, *latifundio*; enshrined the ability to intervene in the use of public and private land; and established a publicly owned coastal zone of 260 feet bordering beaches, rivers, and lakes. In addition he regulated fishing, providing special protection for artisanal fishermen; engaged in the promotion of small/midsize enterprises; and adopted an organic law regulating the oil sector that increased public participation in its ownership and redesigned its structure.[50]

By 2007, after the defeat of the referendum, the scope and breadth of this power was greatly increased. In that year the enabling law approved by the assembly included: the transformation of state agencies; the strengthening of popular power; social and economic matters; taxing and financial issues; citizen safety; science and technology; geographical and territorial organization; national security and defense; infrastructure, transport and services, and the energy sector.[51] It is difficult to

---

93–106, http://w2.ucab.edu.ve/tl_files/POSTGRADO/BEDA/Numero%201%20(2016)/BEDA%201%20010%20-%20Sobre%20la%20Ley%20CR.pdf.

[47] Tomás A. Arias Castillo, "A manera de reflexión final: las cuatro delegaciones legislativas hechas al Presidente de la República (1999–2012)," *Revista de Derecho Público, Upliano-Academia de Ciencias Políticas y Sociales* 130 (2012): 393–399, www.ulpiano.org.ve/revistas/bases/artic/texto/RDPUB/130/rdpub_2012_130_393-399.pdf.

[48] Arias, "Reflexión final."

[49] "Venezuela, Maduro ha gobernado 53 meses con habilitantes y decretos de emergencia," *Econométrica*, February 7, 2018, www.econometrica.com.ve/blog/maduro-ha-gobernado-53-meses-con-habilitantes-y-decretos-de-emergencia.

[50] "Camino Hacia el Socialismo," *El Universal*, December 2, 2013, www.venezuelaawareness.com/?s=modelo+socialista+se+estructur%C3%B3+con+leyes+habilitantes.

[51] Juan Domingo Alfonzo Paradisi, "Decretos Leyes Dictados en 2008 conforme a la Ley Habilitante de 2007 y su relación con la reforma constitucional improbada el 2 de diciembre de 2007," *Revista de Derecho Público, Ulpiano-Academia de Ciencias Políticas y Sociales* 125 (2011): 98–105, www.ulpiano.org.ve/revistas/bases/artic/texto/RDPUB/125/rdpub_2011_125_98-105.pdf.

imagine what could be outside the scope of this law. All in all, these enabling laws in turn produced an extensive array of presidentially adopted laws, 215 in total.[52]

2 States of Exception

The Colombian Constitution also allows for the President to be invested with exceptional legislative power when facing war with a foreign country,[53] internal conflict[54] or when there is an economic, social or ecological emergency.[55] Uribe tried four times,[56] with very little success, to use this special instrument. Here I will present two attempts at concentrating power.

a INTERNAL TURMOIL – *ESTADO DE CONMOCIÓN INTERIOR*

Colombia has a long tradition of legislating through executive power. As a matter of fact, in seventeen of the twenty years preceding the 1991 Constitution, presidents were enabled to legislate through this constitutional instrument,[57] making it hardly an exceptional measure. The length of these enabling powers meant that the president was effectively the main legislator during this period and that many civil and political rights were easily curtailed.

Given this background, it is not surprising the 1991 Constitution increased procedural requirements and established important limitations on this instrument. The first part of article 213 stated:

> In the case of a serious internal upheaval, imminently threatening institutional stability and State security or the peaceful coexistence among citizens – which cannot be otherwise faced with the use of existing policy authority – the President of the Republic, with the approval of all ministers, may declare a state of internal turmoil (*estado de conmoción interior*) throughout the Republic or part of it, for a period no longer than ninety (90) days, which can be prolonged for two (2)

---

52 Carlos Ramírez López, "El Crimen con las Leyes Habilitantes," *El Universal*, November 20, 2017, http://webcache.googleusercontent.com/search?q=cache:NLsEZZbaJVgJ:www.el-nacio nal.com/noticias/columnista/crimen-con-las-leyes-habilitantes_213483+&cd=5&hl=es&ct=clnk& gl=us.

53 Colombian Political Constitution, July 20, 1991, Official Constitutional Gazette No. 116, art. 212.

54 Colombian Political Constitution, art. 213.

55 Colombian Political Constitution, art. 215.

56 The first was in 2002, through Decree 1837 of 2002, declaring internal turmoil; the Court ended the authorization through ruling C-327/03. The second declaration of internal turmoil came in 2008, through Decree 3929 of 2008 in order to deal with a strike of workers (including some judges) of the judiciary branch. The Court struck down the declaration through ruling C-070 of 2009. Also in 2008 Uribe declared a state of economic emergency in face of a financial crisis. Finally, in 2009 he declared a state of social emergency to avert a healthcare system crisis. The Constitutional Court struck down the declaration in 2010 through ruling C-252/10.

57 Mauricio García Villegas, "Un País de Estados de Excepción," *El Espectador*, October 11, 2008, www.elespectador.com/impreso/politica/articuloimpreso43317-un-pais-de-estados-de-excepcion.

additional terms, the second of which requires prior and favorable vote of the Senate of the Republic.

The government will be strictly limited to confront the causes of this declaration and to prevent further effects.[58]

Article 214 established additional limitations, including the obligation to send the declaration as well as the legislative decrees adopted by the government to the Constitutional Court for judicial review.[59] Therefore, there were important restrictions in terms of both form and substance. The Constitution established that no declaration could surpass 270 days (the last term requiring Senate study and approval). The substance of legislative decrees was strictly limited to the facts narrated in the declaration. The Constitutional Court had the power to verify the constitutionality of the decrees.

Uribe declared a "state of internal turmoil" four days into his term.[60] The issues he regulated while invested with exceptional powers included a new tax on the assets of wealthy Colombians;[61] the design of special "Rehabilitation and Consolidation Zones" in which military commanders were granted powers to search, arrest, and intercept communications without judicial order; the identification of the people who inhabited these areas; and the requirement that foreign journalists request permission to enter these areas.[62]

The Constitutional Court analyzed both the declaration and the legislative decree that was set forth to deal with the "state of internal turmoil." In terms of the causes for the declaration, which included many general descriptions and included the phrase "Colombia has the highest rate of criminality in the world,"[63] the Court reprimanded the government for using language that was too general and not justifying appropriately the imminent causes. In addition, most of the provisions allowing military commanders to search, arrest, and intercept communications were struck down. The Court argued that the state of exception had as its limits the Constitution; existing laws that had not been expressly suspended; and human rights and humanitarian law treaties and conventions by which Colombia was bound.[64] Later, when the government tried to extend the state of exception for a third time,

---

[58] Colombian Political Constitution, art. 213.

[59] Colombian Political Constitution, art. 214.

[60] Republic of Colombia, Decree 1837/02, August 11, 2002. By which the President declared a state of internal turmoil. Official Journal No. 44.877.

[61] Republic of Colombia, Decree, 1838/02, August 11, 2002. By which a new tax is created in order to ensure democratic security policy – Seguridad democratica. Official Journal No. 44.897.

[62] Republic of Colombia, Decree 2002/02, September 9, 2002. By which specific measures relating to public order are adopted and special "Rehabilitation and Consolidation Zones" are designed. Official Journal No. 44.930.

[63] Colombian Constitutional Court, STC C-802/02, October 2, 2002 (Jaime Córdoba Triviño, reporting justice).

[64] Colombian Constitutional Court, STC C-1024/02, November 26, 2002 (Alfredo Beltrán Sierra, reporting justice).

the Court opposed it, arguing that the Senate had not fulfilled the previous steps required to authorize the final 90 days.[65]

In response to the constraints imposed by judicial review, Uribe unsuccessfully tried to reform the Constitution in 2004 in order to weaken the Constitutional Court, which had managed to curtail Uribe's regulatory excesses. Among the proposed changes were to limit judicial review in the cases of states of exception only to formal requirements; to shift judicial finances from an independent entity to the executive branch; to eliminate judicial adjudication of social and economic rights; and to bar the Court from making decisions that had macroeconomic impact.[66] This constitutional amendment never received the necessary votes to be approved by Congress.

b ECONOMIC OR SOCIAL EMERGENCY, *ESTADO DE EMERGENCIA SOCIAL*

In 2009 the Uribe government declared a state of social emergency in order to confront a healthcare system crisis.[67] According to the executive, this exceptional move was required because there had been an abrupt and accelerated increase in demand for healthcare services and drugs, not included in the mandatory national health care program, *plan obligatorio de salud*. This increase was translated into a stark lack of public resources. The government developed a set of legislative decrees including a tax increase on alcohol, beer, and gambling; imposing penalties on doctors who demanded treatments that were not covered by the mandatory national healthcare program; and creating surveillance mechanisms for medical practices.

Once again the Constitutional Court in its judicial review struck down the declaration of a social emergency. For the court, the circumstances that led to the declaration were not extraordinary or exceptional. To the contrary, and according to the Court, the healthcare system crisis had been developing for several years and therefore it was a structural problem. In addition, there was no clear relationship between the facts that the declaration described and the proposed solutions.[68]

As this section shows, both leaders attempted to be invested with exceptional legislative power in order to design and redesign economic and social policy. In this method specifically, Chávez was much more successful than Uribe. The possibility to legislate was effectively translated into an acute concentration of power in Venezuela. In Colombia, Uribe had to leave office in 2010 without being able to fully redesign economic and social topics with the breadth and scope he would have wanted.

---

[65] "Corte tumba Estado de Conmoción Interior," *Revista Semana*, April 28, 2003, www.semana .com/noticias/articulo/corte-tumba-estado-conmocion-interior/57876-3.

[66] Javier Revelo Rebolledo, "La Independencia Judicial en Tiempos de Uribe," *Papel Político* 13, no. 1 (2008): 80, https://works.bepress.com/javier_revelo-rebolledo/4/.

[67] Republic of Colombia, Decree 4975/09, December 23, 2009. By which the President declared a social state of emergency. Official Journal No. 47.572.

[68] Colombian Constitutional Court, STC C-252/10, April 16, 2010 (Jorge Ivan Palacio, reporting judge).

IV FINAL THOUGHTS

Despite their huge ideological differences and the fact that each one of them used the other to embody their most hated enemy, Hugo Chávez and Álvaro Uribe were very similar leaders. They both argued that they represented the desires and needs of the people. Both had more faith in a direct democracy than in a representative one. The fact that they were so convinced of their aura and infallibility led them to move towards authoritarianism. Notwithstanding their similarities, the most striking difference is a strong and independent Constitutional Court in Colombia, which was able to block Uribe's many attempts to concentrate power.

In the end, this chapter proposes that as academics and citizens, we should be alert to the uses and abuses of direct democracy and the granting of exceptional legislative powers to the executive.

BIBLIOGRAPHY

"Aprobadas 15 de las 19 preguntas del Referendo." *Revista Semana*, July 7, 2003. www.semana .com/noticias/articulo/aprobadas-15-19-preguntas-del-referendo/59216-3.

"Así nacieron las Convivir." *El Tiempo*, July 14, 1997. www.eltiempo.com/archivo/docu mento/MAM-605402.

"Camino Hacia el Socialismo." *El Universal*, December 2, 2013. www.venezuelaawareness .com/?s=modelo+socialista+se+estructur%C3%B3+con+leyes+habilitantes.

"Chávez presenta la reforma constitucional que le permitirá gobernar indefinidamente." *El País*, August 17, 2007. www.nytimes.com/2007/12/03/world/americas/03venezuela.html.

"Chávez: el que vote por el NO lo hace por George W. Bush." *Agencia Bolivariana de Noticias*, November 30, 2007. www.aporrea.org/actualidad/n105636.html.

"Corte tumba Estado de Conmoción Interior." *Revista Semana*, April 28, 2003. www.semana .com/noticias/articulo/corte-tumba-estado-conmocion-interior/57876-3.

"Dilema es Seguridad o Comunismo: Uribe." *Diario El Tiempo*, May 6, 2006. www.eltiempo .com/archivo/documento/MAM-2012895.

"El Estremecedor Relato de la Muerte del papá de Uribe." *Revista Semana*, September 18, 2014. www.semana.com/nacion/articulo/el-estremecedor-relato-de-la-muerte-del-papa-de-uribe/403223-3.

"Era de Uribe con menos ministerios." *Portafolio*, November 27, 2007. www.portafolio.co/ economia/finanzas/uribe-ministerios-470420.

"Intervención ciudadana en el proceso No. CRF-003." *Intervención Referendo Final*, December 4, 2009. https://cdn.dejusticia.org/wp-content/uploads/2017/04/fi_name_recurso_169 .pdf.

"La importancia y el amor de Chávez por el Pueblo en sus propias palabras." *Con El Mazo Dando*, March 4, 2018. www.conelmazodando.com.ve/la-importancia-y-el-amor-de-chavez-por-el-pueblo-en-sus-propias-palabras/.

"Los $13 Billones en Empresas Públicas que vendió Uribe." *Las 2 Orillas*, January 13, 2016. www.las2orillas.co/los-13-billones-en-empresas-publicas-que-vendio-uribe/.

"Que perdamos todas las elecciones, pero que no perdamos la lucha contra el terrorismo." *Archivo General*, Presidencia de la República, November 16, 2003. http://historico .presidencia.gov.co/prensa_new/discursos/cc45bquilla.htm.

"Referendo: historia de una causa perdida." *Revista Semana*, February 26, 2010. www.semana .com/politica/articulo/referendo-historia-causa-perdida/113678-3.

"Si Hay Guerra Señor Presidente." *Revista Semana*, February 6, 2005. www.semana.com/ portada/articulo/si-guerra-senor-presidente/70763-3.

"Uribe habla sobre resultados del referendo y plantea propuestas al respect." *Revista Semana*, October 27, 2003. www.semana.com/noticias/articulo/uribe-habla-sobre-resultados-del-referendo-plantea-propuestas-respecto/61590-3.

"Venezuela, Maduro ha gobernado 53 meses con habilitantes y decretos de emergencia." *Econométrica*, February 7, 2018. www.econometrica.com.ve/blog/maduro-ha-gobernado-53-meses-con-habilitantes-y-decretos-de-emergencia.

Alfonzo Paradisi, Juan Domingo. "Decretos Leyes Dictados en 2008 conforme a la Ley Habilitante de 2007 y su relación con la reforma constitucional improbada el 2 de diciembre de 2007." *Revista de Derecho Público, Ulpiano-Academia de Ciencias Políticas y Sociales* 125 (2011): 98–105. www.ulpiano.org.ve/revistas/bases/artic/texto/RDPUB/125/ rdpub_2011_125_98-105.pdf.

Alviar García, Helena. "The Unending Quest for Land: The Tale of Broken Constitutional Promises." *Texas Law Review* 89, no. 7 (2011): 1895–1914.

Arias Castillo, Tomás A. "A manera de reflexión final: las cuatro delegaciones legislativas hechas al Presidente de la República (1999–2012)." *Revista de Derecho Público, Upliano-Academia de Ciencias Políticas y Sociales* 130 (2012): 393–399. www.ulpiano.org.ve/ revistas/bases/artic/texto/RDPUB/130/rdpub_2012_130_393-399.pdf.

Cannon, Barry. *Hugo Chávez and the Bolivarian Revolution: Populism and Democracy in a Globalised Age.* Manchester: Manchester University Press, 2009.

De la Torre, Cristina. *Álvaro Uribe: El Neopopulismo en Colombia.* Medellín: La Carreta, 2005.

García Villegas, Mauricio. "Un País de Estados de Excepción." *El Espectador*, October 11, 2008. www.elespectador.com/impreso/politica/articuloimpreso43317-un-pais-de-estados-de-excepcion.

González Cadenas, Diego. *El único proceso constituyente democratico en Venezuela: la constituyente de 1999,* forthcoming, Ediciones Uniandes, on file with the author.

Hawkins, Kirk. "Populism in Venezuela: The Rise of Chavismo." *Third World Quarterly* 24, no. 6 (2003): 1137–1160. www.jstor.org/stable/3993447.

Jaramillo, Laura. "Uribe: El Estado de Opinión es la Fase Superior del Estado de Derecho." *La Silla Vacía*, June 5, 2009. lasillavacia.com/historia/2296.

Krauss, Clifford. "New President in Venezuela Proposes to Rewrite the Constitution." *The New York Times*, February 4, 1999. www.nytimes.com/1999/02/04/world/new-president-in-venezuela-proposes-to-rewrite-the-constitution.html.

Krauze, Enrique. "Hell of a Fiesta." *The New York Review of Books*, March 8, 2018. www .nybooks.com/articles/2018/03/08/venezuela-hell-fiesta/.

Lobo, Gregory J. "Colombia, from Failing State to a Second Independence: The Politics and the Price." *International Journal of Cultural Studies* 16, no. 4 (2012): 351–366.

Nolan, Rachel. "The Realest Reality Show in the World: Hugo Chávez's Totally Bizarre Talk Show." *New York Times*, May 4, 2012. www.nytimes.com/2012/05/06/magazine/hugo-chavezs-totally-bizarre-talk-show.html.

Ramírez López, Carlos. "El Crimen con las Leyes Habilitantes." *El Universal*, November 20, 2017. http://webcache.googleusercontent.com/search?q=cache:NLsEZZbaJVgJ:www.el-nacional.com/noticias/columnista/crimen-con-las-leyes-habilitantes_213483+&cd=5&hl= es&ct=clnk&gl=us.

Revelo Rebolledo, Javier. "La Independencia Judicial en Tiempos de Uribe." *Papel Político* 13, no. 1 (2008). works.bepress.com/javier_revelo-rebolledo/4/.

Reverón Boulton, Carlos. "Sobre la Ley Habilitante Antiimperialista para La Paz." *Boletín Electrónico de Derecho Administrativo de la Universidad Católica Andrés Bello* no. 1 (2016): 93–106. http://w2.ucab.edu.ve/tl_files/POSTGRADO/BEDA/Numero%201%20 (2016)/BEDA%201%20010%20-%20Sobre%20la%20Ley%20CR.pdf.

Uribe Vélez, Álvaro. "Manifiesto Democrático 100 Puntos." *Asociación Primero Colombia*, February 24, 2015. www.primerocolombia.com/content/manifiesto-democratico-100-puntos

No hay causa perdida. New York: Penguin Random House, 2012.

6

Representation, Paternalism, and Exclusion

The Divergent Impacts of the AKP's Populism on Human Rights in Turkey

Jamie O'Connell[1]

Turkey provides an unusual opportunity to observe how populists affect human rights when they govern a large electoral democracy for a prolonged period. In the first years after it took office in 2002, the ruling Justice and Development Party ("AKP" in Turkish), led by now-President Recep Tayyip Erdoğan, initially appeared to be enhancing democracy. In the mid-2000s, however, Erdoğan and his colleagues increasingly employed populist rhetoric as they took on power centers that had traditionally constrained democratic politics, such as the military. Since then, the AKP politicians' rhetoric and actions have suggested a conviction that they alone are entitled to rule, unchecked by others inside or outside government – a characteristically populist belief. That view may have contributed to the AKP government's systematic and successful assault on democratic institutions and norms, which has involved large-scale violations of civil and political rights and brought the country to the brink of dictatorship. Although the AKP's populism may have increased its motivation to deliver economic and social benefits to much of the population and reduce discrimination against religious Turks, especially women, those positive effects on human rights pale next to its devastating impact on democracy and civil and political freedoms.

This chapter uses the Turkish case to analyze the influence of specific aspects of populism on human rights, organizing the effects into three categories.[2] *Representation* involves expanding the role of previously marginalized groups in politics and

[1] I thank Eva Anduiza Perea, Anne Joseph O'Connell, Murat Somer, and the participants in the Harvard Law School Human Rights Program conference "Human Rights in a Time of Populism" for invaluable comments on this chapter. They bear no responsibility for its interpretations or factual accuracy.
[2] Conceptualizing the AKP's politics as "polarizing" rather than "populist" also yields valuable insights on the party's impact on Turkish democracy. See Murat Somer, "Turkey: The Slippery Slope from Reformist to Revolutionary Polarization and Democratic Breakdown," *Annals of the American Academy of Political and Social Science* no. 681 (January 2019): 42–61.

their influence on public policy. *Paternalism* describes populists' arrogation of the right to identify the interests of "the people" for whom they claim to speak, rather than listen to the views of real citizens about their preferences. *Exclusion* refers to populists' marginalization from politics, and often broader repression, of groups they define as enemies of the people.

The AKP's record casts some doubt on Rovira's characterization of populism's relationship to democracy as "ambivalent," potentially benefitting and threatening democracy.[3] In Turkey, the AKP rebalanced the political system, recognized traditionally marginalized groups, and changed public policy according to those groups' preferences, exemplifying representation. Those changes could have strengthened democracy – but they have been overwhelmed by the two dynamics that undermine democracy, paternalism and especially exclusion. The paternalist tendencies of the AKP, and especially of Erdoğan himself, limited popular empowerment. Over time, exclusionary tendencies in the populist worldview seem to have contributed to the AKP's drive to destroy all checks on its power, leaving Turkey's democratic system in shambles.

This case study generates causal hypotheses about populism's impact on human rights that could be tested elsewhere. I argue that in Turkey representation, paternalism, and exclusion are driven significantly by core aspects of populism that the AKP shares with populists in many other countries. Systematic comparative research could establish whether populism generally has some or all of these effects.

Populist politics may appear viable only outside government: once populists take power, how can they portray themselves as struggling against an oppressive ruling elite on behalf of a virtuous people? The AKP has maintained a populist posture while leading the executive and legislative branches of government, neutering the once-dominant military and judiciary in the late 2000s, and achieving supremacy over all branches and agencies of government by about 2014. This case adds another layer to this paradox: the AKP used populist rhetoric only sparingly before it took power and has shifted to a strongly populist stance only in the mid-2000s, several years after taking office.

Turkey's history of military coups and judicial intervention in democratic politics, as well as top-down management of state and society, may partly explain why the AKP's constituents seem to have taken seriously its claim to be fighting a domineering elite even while it was leading the government. By 2002, many scholars of Turkish politics and ordinary citizens believed that since the founding of the Turkish Republic in 1923, the military, bureaucracy, and judiciary, sometimes supported by business and intellectual elites, had constrained popularly elected leaders and enforced socially and culturally liberal policies, including secularism, against the wishes of much of the population. (Those policies are often described as

---

[3] Cristóbal Rovira Kaltwasser, "The Ambivalence of Populism: Threat and Corrective for Democracy," *Democratization* 19, no. 2 (April 2012): 196–199.

"Kemalist," because they reflect principles set out by the Republic's founder, Mustafa Kemal Atatürk.) Many felt that repeated military coups, judicial dissolution of popular political parties, and imprisonment of politicians and activists for violating vague restrictions on speech, such as a ban on "insulting Turkishness," constituted important flaws in Turkish democracy.

Beginning in the mid-2000s, Erdoğan and his AKP colleagues shifted away from the moderate, inclusive rhetoric that had won them office in 2002, in favor of a populist version of history that described a nefarious, unified elite consistently marginalizing a virtuous, homogeneous mass, in political, economic, and cultural terms. This fable abstracted out numerous important patterns that complicated the populist narrative. For example, it omitted the military's support for Islamist politics in the 1980s and the Kemalist state's repression of Kurds and leftists, which was more consistent and brutal than its actions against Islamists. Yet the AKP's populist narrative appealed to many Turks, who seem to have seen the missing nuances as irrelevant. Erdoğan and his colleagues interpreted new developments through the populist lens, taking advantage of instances in which a broader portion of the elite or citizenry agreed with some part of it. For example, in 2007, the secularist elite blocked the AKP's preferred presidential candidate, even though he commanded sufficient votes in the parliament. They also tried to persuade the courts to dissolve the AKP itself. The AKP eventually prevailed in both contests. Leading constitutionalists and other scholars agreed that the AKP's opponents had pushed democratic limits, and the AKP used the conflict to bolster its claim to represent the people against an elite bent on thwarting them.[4]

I begin, in Section I, by clarifying the key concepts used in my analysis: human rights, democracy, and populism. Section II summarizes the key developments in Turkish politics from 1923 to the 2000s that the AKP fashioned into a compelling populist narrative. Section III describes the populist approach to politics that the party adopted starting in the mid-2000s, and that can be glimpsed in its earlier rhetoric. It summarizes the AKP's populist version of history and elaborates on its omissions. Section IV, the chapter's heart, analyzes the relationship between the AKP's populism and its human rights record, using the rubric of representation, paternalism, and exclusion.

I CONCEPTS: POPULISM, HUMAN RIGHTS, AND DEMOCRACY

Tracing populism's impact on human rights, including democracy, in Turkey requires clarity about what I mean by those terms. "Human rights" is the most straightforward, having been operationalized in a discrete set of international

---

[4] See Ergun Özbudun, "Democracy, Tutelarism, and the Search for a New Constitution," in *Turkey's Democratization Process*, ed. Carmen Rodríguez, Antonio Ávalos, Hakan Yılmaz, and Ana I. Planet (New York: Routledge, 2014), 299–306.

treaties. This chapter does not comprehensively assess the AKP's complex, varied, and disputed human rights record over its seventeen years in power. Instead, it concentrates on the areas of human rights that have been most clearly affected by populism as practiced by the AKP: democracy, related civil and political rights, certain economic and social rights, and non-discrimination based on religion and gender.[5]

"Democracy" takes on a wide range of meanings in the work of political theorists, political scientists, legal scholars, and human rights practitioners. The analysis below does not depend on a specific definition of democracy, but is informed by a functionalist conception: a more democratic system is one in which institutional structures, cultural norms, and patterns of elite and popular behavior combine to disperse, among individual citizens, influence over the decisions that their society makes collectively.[6] A perfect democracy – which of course is unattainable – thus would be one in which all citizens had equal influence over these decisions.

International human rights treaties contain provisions that effectively create a human right to democracy, even though they do not use that word.[7] Turkey is a party to the International Covenant on Civil and Political Rights (ICCPR), Article 25 of which provides that all citizens have the right to "take part in the conduct of public affairs, directly or through freely chosen representatives."[8] As I have argued elsewhere, based on the compelling analysis by the UN Human Rights Committee, which oversees compliance with the ICCPR, Article 25 "amounts to a right to democracy."[9] The ICCPR and the European Convention for the Protection of Human Rights and Fundamental Freedoms also guarantee rights that support democracy, including freedoms of thought, expression, association, and assembly.[10]

I employ an ideational conception of populism, articulated particularly cogently by Mudde and Rovira.[11] They define populism as "a thin-centered ideology that

---

[5] I consider here only the AKP's impact within Turkey, because I do not see its populism as having clearly shaped its extraterritorial influence on human rights.

[6] Brad R. Roth, "Evaluating Democratic Progress," in *Democratic Governance and International Law*, ed. Gregory H. Fox and Brad R. Roth (Cambridge: Cambridge University Press, 2000), 497.

[7] Jamie O'Connell, "Common Interests, Closer Allies: How Democracy in Arab States Can Benefit the West," *Stanford Journal of International Law* 48, no. 2 (2012): 352–354. Some scholars have also argued that customary international law provides a right to democracy. O'Connell, 352 n.46.

[8] International Covenant on Civil and Political Rights (ICCPR), December 16, 1966, 999 U.N.T.S. 171, art. 25(a).

[9] O'Connell, "Common Interests, Closer Allies," 353.

[10] ICCPR, arts. 18, 19, 21, 22; Convention for the Protection of Human Rights and Fundamental Freedoms, November 4, 1950, 213 U.N.T.S. 221, arts. 9–11.

[11] See Cas Mudde and Cristóbal Rovira Kaltwasser, "Populism," in *The Oxford Handbook of Political Ideologies*, ed. Michael Freeden and Marc Stears (New York: Oxford University Press, 2013); Cas Mudde, "Populism: An Ideational Approach," in *The Oxford Handbook of Populism*, ed. Cristóbal Rovira Kaltwasser, Paul Taggart, Paulina Ochoa Espejo, and Pierre Ostiguy (New York: Oxford University Press, 2017).

considers society to be ultimately separated into two homogeneous and antagonistic camps, 'the pure people' versus 'the corrupt elite,' and which argues that politics should be an expression of the volonté générale (general will) of the people."[12] Rather than a fully fledged political ideology, this view sees populism as "a mental map through which individuals analyze and comprehend political reality."[13] This thin definition encompasses politicians and movements with a range of programs, for example economic policies from socialistic to market-oriented.[14]

Populists understand "the people" to possess homogeneous interests and preferences, which constitute a Rousseauvian "general will," or as Erdoğan prefers, "national will." (I use those terms, as well as "popular will," interchangeably.) Populist leaders believe they infallibly perceive the content of this general will. If some of the people disagree, populists dismiss them as confused or perverse – or decide they are no longer, or never were, members of "the people," but instead belong to the hated elite and its allies. Populists abhor any limitation on the people's will as illegitimate. In power, they chafe at constitutional and other constraints on their power, such as protections of individual rights and countervailing power centers, and often work to limit or eliminate them.

Fervent anger and grievance distinguish populist politicians and their followers from many of their non-populist counterparts. Viewing politics as defined by conflict between an oppressive elite and virtuous people seems almost inevitably to produce passionate hatred toward those citizens labeled as part of the elite or its supporters. In Turkey, this aspect of populism may have fed vicious repression.

II ELITISM AND EXCLUSION IN TURKISH POLITICS, 1923–2002

Understanding the elitist, exclusionary strain in Turkish politics and governance is necessary to appreciate both the appeal and potential human rights impact of the AKP's populism.[15] The Republic was founded in 1923 on top-down governance. A central theme in the country's politics since then has been struggle between democratically elected politicians and unelected, Kemalist-dominated institutions – the military, judiciary, and bureaucracy, often supported by big business and intellectuals. Atatürk was an authoritarian by temperament and dominated policy and politics from before 1923 to his death in 1938. He attempted to "modernize" Turkey's politics, economy, and society by mandating sweeping changes and using expansive state power to implement them. These reforms included subordinating

---

[12] Mudde and Rovira, "Populism," 498.

[13] Mudde and Rovira, "Populism," 498–499.

[14] My understanding of populism is also consistent with the approaches of many other scholars of the phenomenon, including Jan-Werner Müller. See Jan-Werner Müller, *What Is Populism?* (Philadelphia, PA: University of Pennsylvania Press, 2016).

[15] For greater depth on Turkish political history since 1923, see Alpaslan Özerdem and Matthew Whiting, eds., *The Routledge Handbook of Turkish Politics* (New York: Routledge, 2019).

religion to secular authorities, banning religious appeals in politics, industrializing the economy, and increasing women's involvement in public life, along with more superficial changes, such as promoting Western music and clothing.

Atatürk viewed the largely conservative, religious, and modestly educated Turkish masses as backward, uncivilized, and unqualified to rule. (Most of the population then lived in rural areas and small towns, reflecting the economy's agricultural orientation.) He understood modernization to require a democratic political system, so the 1924 constitution created one – vesting all "legislative and executive powers" in an elected parliament – but only in a nominal sense.[16] In practice, Atatürk and his successor İsmet İnönü dominated the parliament until 1950. Atatürk "seemed to have reasoned that unless a modern, secular, and national culture [was] solidly established, a modern political system, potentially hosting some form of democracy, could not have any chance of survival."[17] Political parties were effectively banned until 1946, with the exception of the Republican People's Party (CHP), founded by Atatürk and led after his death by İnönü. Any religious expression connected to politics was harshly repressed. The urban elite – bureaucrats, intellectuals, judges, and soldiers – implemented Atatürk's modernization program without regard for popular preferences.

The advent of multiparty politics in the late 1940s somewhat democratized governance and public life. Competition for mass support led İnönü to restore optional religious instruction in public schools. In 1950, the CHP lost the country's first free elections to the Democrat Party (DP) led by Adnan Menderes. As prime minister, Menderes directed development resources toward rural areas, which Atatürk and İnönü had neglected, including by extending the national electricity grid. Menderes maintained the secular state, but was less hostile to religion: mosque construction boomed, and the DP used religious symbols to appeal to conservative voters.

From the 1960s through the 1980s, Turkish politics turned on struggles between civilians and the military for control of the state, between left- and right-wing ideologies, and between a rising Kurdish ethnic consciousness and an assimilationist Turkish identity. The military used violence and coercion to constrain civilian politicians' conduct of politics and choice of public policies. Coups in 1960, 1971, and 1980 followed breakdowns in elite civilian politics and public order, including widespread violence between left and right on university campuses. The 1960 coup-makers executed Prime Minister Menderes and two other ministers. After the 1980 coup, imprisonment and torture of trade union and other leftist activists dramatically reduced political mobilization for the rest of the decade. Meanwhile, Kurds who attempted to assert an ethnic identity, rather than identify entirely as Turks, faced

---

[16] Turkey Const. (1924), arts. 5, 10.
[17] Ersin Kalaycıoğlu, *Turkish Dynamics: Bridge Across Troubled Lands* (New York: Palgrave Macmillan, 2005), 46.

repression from the civilian state, which barred using Kurdish in public institutions and giving children Kurdish names. When the separatist Kurdistan Workers Party (PKK) launched an insurgency in southeastern Turkey, the Turkish military responded with a brutal counterinsurgency campaign, imprisoning, torturing, and killing thousands of civilians as well as PKK fighters.[18]

The military and judiciary continued to enforce Kemalist orthodoxies in the 1990s and early 2000s. After the reestablishment of constitutional rule in 1983, the military initially promoted Islamist politics.[19] It hoped that religion-based political mobilization would be more orderly than the often-violent ideological conflict between left and right in the 1960s and 1970s. In the 1991 parliamentary elections, the Welfare Party, led by pioneering Islamist politician Necmettin Erbakan, garnered 17 percent of a fragmented popular vote. This established the party as a force in national politics, and it came in first in the 1995 election with 21 percent.[20] Erbakan had aggressively pushed the boundaries of the establishment's tolerance for years, presiding over a rally just before the 1980 coup at which supporters called for the imposition of *sharia* law, an idea as shocking to the Kemalist establishment as it would be to the U.S. Republican Party today.[21] His parties' electoral success in the 1990s secured him the leadership of a coalition government from 1995 to 1997.

By the late 1990s, military leaders and their allies were alarmed by Islamists' popularity and reined them in through intimidation and legal action. In 1997, the army forced Erbakan to resign as prime minister. The following year, the Constitutional Court dissolved his Welfare Party for violating the constitutional principle of secularism. Erbakan formed the Virtue Party, which came in second in the 1999 election before the Constitutional Court shut it down in 2001. The campaign against Islamist politics employed criminal sanctions, too, most notoriously against future President Recep Tayyip Erdoğan. In 1999, Erdoğan, at that time the Welfare Party mayor of Istanbul, was forced from office and jailed for religious incitement for reciting a poem at a political rally. These were only the most dramatic examples of repression of popular Islamist politicians, which many secular Turks supported.

III THE AKP'S POPULISM

The AKP was formed in 2001 by Erdoğan and other Erbakan protégés who advocated pragmatic politics that avoided confrontation, especially with the military and

---

[18] See Doğu Ergil, "The Kurdish Question in Turkey," *Journal of Democracy* 11, no. 3 (July 2000): 123–128.

[19] See Özlem Denli, "Freedom of Religion: Secularist Policies and Islamic Challenges," in *Human Rights in Turkey*, ed. Zehra F. Kabasakal Arat (Philadelphia, PA: University of Pennsylvania Press, 2007), 93–94.

[20] Kalaycıoğlu, *Turkish Dynamics*, 126.

[21] Nicole Pope and Hugh Pope, *Turkey Unveiled: A History of Modern Turkey* (New York: Overlook Duckworth, 2011), 137.

judiciary. Populist tropes have been part of their political arsenal from the beginning, but they preferred more inclusive rhetoric and policies during the 2002 election campaign and early years in power. Their use of populist rhetoric has grown dramatically since the mid-to-late 2000s.[22]

Erdoğan and the AKP have fashioned the events described in the previous section into a compelling populist story of a unified elite that for decades excluded the "real" Turkish people from power and marginalized their religion, while pretending that Turkey was a democracy. They point to the Kemalists' top-down political, economic, and social engineering during the early years of the Republic, the military's "tutelage" of elected civilian politicians from 1960 through the 1980s, and the repression of popular Islamist politicians in the 1990s and early 2000s.

This version of history leaves out important patterns that weaken the populist interpretation, however. While governments from 1923 to 2002 aimed to reduce the influence of religion in society and politics, they also used Islam as a key tool for constructing the Turkish nation, legitimating the state, and securing their rule.[23] Since 1923, Turkey's elites have looked more divided than unified, fracturing along numerous axes, including social values (progressive secular versus religious conservative), political ideology (left versus right), and ethnic identity (Turkish nationalist versus multiculturalist or Kurdish nationalist). The military has clashed repeatedly with the secular left, and repressed it brutally after the 1980 coup. Kurdish activists, peaceful as well as militant, have been marginalized and repressed more consistently and thoroughly than religious conservatives. The military favored Islamist politicians in the 1980s before suppressing them in the 1990s. The AKP has had ambivalent relations with leftists and Kurds since 2002, so those groups' conflicts with the Kemalist state fit awkwardly with the party's picture of a single oppressed population fighting a monolithic oppressor. The success of politicians representing rural conservatives, such as Menderes and Süleyman Demirel, complicates the AKP's claim

---

[22] A recent academic study of political leaders' speeches, sponsored by and reported in *The Guardian*, found that Erdoğan's deployment of populist ideas rose sharply from the 2003–2007 period to 2007–2014, and again in 2014–2018. See Paul Lewis, Caelainn Barr, Seán Clarke, Antonio Voce, Cath Levett, and Pablo Gutiérrez, "Revealed: The Rise and Rise of Populist Rhetoric," *The Guardian*, March 6, 2019, www.theguardian.com/world/ng-interactive/2019/mar/06/revealed-the-rise-and-rise-of-populist-rhetoric. Erdoğan's level of populism in 2003–2007 matched UK Prime Minister Tony Blair's very low level throughout his administration. In 2007–2014 Erdoğan was similar to Hungary's Viktor Orbán since 2010. Since 2014 he has used populist rhetoric as much or more than Bolivia's Evo Morales and Ecuador's Raphael Correa during their most populist phases. See Bethan McKernan, "From Reformer to 'New Sultan': Erdoğan's Populist Evolution," *The Guardian*, March 11, 2019, www.theguardian.com/world/2019/mar/11/from-reformer-to-new-sultan-erdogans-populist-evolution; Kirk A Hawkins, Rosario Aguilar, Erin Jenne, Bojana Kocijan, Cristóbal Rovira Kaltwasser, and Bruno Castanho Silva, Global Populism Database: Populism Dataset for Leaders 1.0, 2019, https://populism.byu.edu/Pages/Data.

[23] See, for example, Pınar Kemerli, "Religious Militarism and Islamist Conscientious Objection in Turkey," *International Journal of Middle East Studies* 47 (2015): 282–283; Denli, "Freedom of Religion," 89–94.

that its core constituency has always been marginalized in politics. While the two were overthrown by the military three times (in 1960, 1971, and 1980), Menderes dominated Turkish politics in the 1950s and Demirel served as prime minister five times from 1965 to 1993 and as president from 1993 to 2000.

Erdoğan and other AKP politicians have ignored those complexities as they have gradually shifted the theme of struggle between the virtuous people and an exclusionary elite to the center of their political messaging. Since his campaign for the mayoralty of Istanbul, Erdoğan has highlighted his "Black Turk" origins: his large, religious family moved from a small Anatolian town to a working-class neighborhood of Istanbul when he was a child. By using a label for the conservative, rural masses that draws a sharp metaphoric contrast with urban, secular "White Turks," Erdoğan suggests that Turkish society is fundamentally divided. Occasionally in the early years, but now constantly, he has identified his supporters as "the people" and their opponents as a small elite. For example, he told an October 2002 rally: "My story is the story of this people. Either the people will win and come to power, or the pretentious and oppressive minority estranged from the reality of Anatolia and looking over it with disdain will remain in power. The authority to decide on this belongs to the people."[24]

Erdoğan and other AKP politicians now frequently contrast their respect for the people with the dismissive attitude of the Kemalist elite, often invoking their history of imposing secularism. For example, in 2012 Erdoğan told another rally: "These people look down their noses at the people, at the sweat and blood of the people, the culture and choices of the people. ... For years they have belittled the true servants of this nation – its clergymen."[25]

AKP leaders also refer to a unified, homogeneous "national will," another pillar of populist thought. In May 2007, Erdoğan argued that Kemalist opposition to the election of Gül as president showed that "they could not put up with the national will."[26] In June 2013, mass protests against AKP policies began in Istanbul's Gezi Park, then spread to many other cities, drawing hundreds of thousands. Erdoğan responded by mustering supporters in a series of "Respect the National Will" rallies. The slogan of his 2014 presidential campaign was "National Will, National Power." At a 2017 rally, he was introduced as "the guardian of our democracy, the strong voice of the national will."[27]

---

[24] Quoted in Bilge Yabanci, "Populism as the Problem Child of Democracy: The AKP's Enduring Appeal and the Use of Meso-Level Actors," *Southeast European and Black Sea Studies* 16, no. 4 (2016): 599.

[25] Quoted in William Eichler, "The Making of a Demagogue: How Erdoğan Became Turkey's Strongman," *Open Democracy*, April 18, 2017, www.opendemocracy.net/william-eichler/making-of-demagogue-how-erdo.

[26] Quoted in Şakir Dinçşahin, "A Symptomatic Analysis of the Justice and Development Party's Populism in Turkey, 2007–2010," *Government and Opposition* 47, no. 4 (2012): 634.

[27] Quoted in Orçun Selçuk, "Strong Presidents and Weak Institutions: Populism in Turkey, Venezuela, and Ecuador," *Southeast European and Black Sea Studies* 16, no. 4 (2016): 577.

As they have consolidated power, Erdoğan and other AKP spokespeople have increasingly argued that their electoral victories anoint them as the sole authoritative exponents of the national will. As elaborated in Subsection IVB, below, the AKP decides the content of this will, allowing ordinary citizens little voice in the party's and government's policymaking and other decisions. The AKP's conception of the national will has authoritarian aspects, as Mustafa Akyol explains: "The winners of the ballots represent the 'national will' in this discourse, which is a kind of metaphysical truth that cannot be limited by any law, tradition, international norm, or universal value. Moreover, those who oppose the 'national will' are illegitimate."[28]

Even as the AKP has consolidated power and marginalized actual and potential adversaries in the judiciary, military, bureaucracy, news media, and other political parties, it has lost the support it initially received from liberals. As Subsection IVC, below, discusses, the party has defined each wave of its opponents as foes of "the people," denied the legitimacy of their disagreement, and harshly repressed many of them.

A 2019 study of public opinion confirmed that the AKP's constituents have significantly more populist views than supporters of other Turkish political parties. (The study does not make clear whether this was true when the party took power, using little populist rhetoric, or has increased over time.) AKP partisans are more likely to hold a Manichean view of politics, seeing it as "ultimately a struggle between good and evil." They share the party's anti-elitism, believing that "[t]he power of a few special interests prevents our country from making progress." Their ideas about the proper allocation of power track the idea of national will: they are more likely than other parties' supporters to agree that "the people, not politicians, should make our most important policy decisions," and that political leaders should not be checked by rules or institutions.[29]

IV AKP POPULISM: IMPACT ON HUMAN RIGHTS

After its creation in 2001, the AKP quickly gained support from a wide swath of the Turkish electorate. The following year it swept to victory in the first general election it contested. Its 34.3 percent share of the national vote yielded nearly two-thirds of the seats in the parliament, owing to political fragmentation and an electoral rule that denies parliamentary seats to small parties. (The AKP has received between 40.9 percent and 49.8 percent of the vote in the five general elections since 2002 and maintained its parliamentary majority except during a few months in 2015.) The AKP's core constituency included what many scholars call Turkey's political

---

[28] Mustafa Akyol, "Erdoganism [Noun]: From 'National Will' to 'Man of the Nation,' an Abridged Dictionary for the Post-Secular Turkish State," *Foreign Policy*, June 21, 2016, foreign policy.com/2016/06/21/erdoganism-noun-erdogan-turkey-islam-akp/.

[29] S. Erdem Aytaç and Ezgi Elçi, "Populism in Turkey," in *Populism Around the World*, ed. Daniel Stockemer (Cham, Switzerland: Springer, 2019), 101–105.

"periphery" – conservative, religious people of all economic classes. These citizens once were concentrated in small towns and rural areas across Anatolia, but now are also heavily represented in large cities after mass urbanization from 1950 to 2000. The AKP also received wide support from less conservative and religious segments of the working class and poor, building on Erdoğan's record as mayor of effectively administering Istanbul and improving public services. Initially, the AKP marketed itself as a mainstream, center-right party and played down religion. For example, it stated that relaxing restrictions on women wearing headscarves was not a party priority. In 2002, this combination of competence and centrism also secured the support of many liberals, who blamed squabbling and incompetence by the established parties for repeated economic crises in the preceding decade.

Since taking power in 2002, the AKP has partially ruptured, partially continued, and partially mirrored and deepened the elitist, anti-democratic patterns in Turkish politics since 1923. It began cautiously, but since the mid-2000s has challenged the status quo ever more openly and aggressively. Its increasingly populist rhetoric has paralleled increasingly vigorous action. AKP politicians' populist understanding of politics, and framing of political and social relations in populist terms, have had significant effects on a wide range of human rights, most negative but some positive. I elaborate these below, using the rubric of representation, paternalism, and exclusion.[30]

A *Representation*

The AKP has represented, in various senses, a large group of Turks, amounting in some cases to a majority of the population. Each aspect of representation emanates from the party's populism and has had particular effects on the human rights of the whole group or part of it. All three aspects have benefitted rural and urban Turks of the conservative, religious "periphery," from all economic classes.[31] Since 1923,

---

[30] This chapter does not attempt a comprehensive description of the AKP's impact on human rights, but instead examines only those impacts that are connected to the party's populism. For example, the treatment of ethnic Kurds by the Turkish government and private actors is one of the country's most important human rights issues. The AKP government shifted its predecessors' policies in significant ways – for example, by recognizing Kurdish identity and launching peace talks with the PKK. However, it also has repressed Kurdish politicians and in 2015 launched a brutal military assault on PKK-affiliated armed groups that also killed at least 400 civilians and displaced over 350,000 people. See Berkay Mandiraci, "Turkey's PKK Conflict Kills Almost 3,000 in Two Years," July 20, 2017, www.crisisgroup.org/europe-central-asia/western-europeme diterranean/turkey/turkeys-pkk-conflict-kills-almost-3000-two-years. However, I do not focus on the AKP's approach to the "Kurdish question" because I do not see clear links between it and the party's populism.

[31] The center–periphery distinction simplifies Turkish politics significantly, as would any binary rubric for analyzing a country of 80 million people. Nonetheless, it facilitates understanding of the human rights impacts of AKP populism. In the text, I refer more often to "marginalized" groups to cover the poor and working class (regardless of religious and political views) as well as

those citizens have had little influence over public policy and received a less-than-proportionate share of government funds and attention. Those who had less money or education, or who lived outside the urban areas, were especially neglected – as such groups are in many countries. Politicians supported by the periphery, such as Menderes, Demirel, and Erbakan, have been the targets of many of the military and judicial interventions in politics, through coups, prosecutions, and party dissolutions – although, as noted above, Kurds have been more consistent targets and the political left was also repressed, particularly after 1980. The secularist limits enforced by the Kemalist elite have precluded some policies supported by religious conservatives in particular, and constrained their political expression.

By the early 2000s, more liberal, less religious Turks who were working class or poor may also have felt marginalized from politics. They had supported some of the civilian governments overthrown by the military. They suffered from its repression of civil society, including trade unionists, after 1980. Few of the state resources that flowed to huge family-owned conglomerates trickled down to them, while the economic crises of the 1990s and 2000s devastated their standards of living.

The AKP has "represented" both of these groups more effectively than its predecessors, in three distinct senses.[32] First, the AKP has dramatically changed the balance of political power in Turkey, ending Kemalists' control over institutions that had given them disproportionate influence over state policy and public life. By doing so, it may have increased the power of those traditionally marginalized – although the AKP's paternalism and exclusion, explained in the following two subsections, have largely undermined that potential benefit. Second, the AKP has symbolically placed conservative, religious, working-class, and poor Turks at the center of the political community and connected with them at the grassroots level, unlike any previous ruling party. Third, representation has had a substantive dimension. The AKP has delivered extensive benefits to these constituents through services, government jobs, and policies that advantaged them directly. It also has represented religious conservatives substantively by shaping other state policies according to their preferences.

1 Structural Reform

When the AKP took power in 2002, both scholars and many ordinary Turks had long seen the country as a flawed democracy, because the military, judiciary, and other

the conservative, religious "periphery," but some points apply more to the latter. For political analysis using the center–periphery dichotomy, see, for example, Şerif Mardin, "Center–Periphery Relations: A Key to Turkish Politics," *Daedalus* 102, no. 1 (Winter 1973); Kalaycıoğlu, *Turkish Dynamics*, 50–53; Aytaç and Elçi, "Populism in Turkey," 90–93. On the limitations of the dichotomy, see Onur Bakinur, "A Key to Turkish Politics? The Center–Periphery Framework Revisited," *Turkish Studies* 19, no. 4 (2018).

[32] The generalizations are, of course, imperfect: the tens of millions of people who constitute these groups are not homogeneous and the impact of these representation dynamics varies within each group.

unelected actors significantly constrained citizens' choice of political leaders and those leaders' ability to implement popular policies. The countermajoritarian forces' concern for secularism meant their oversight especially reduced the influence of conservative, religious Turks. For nearly a decade after 2002, the AKP appeared to be an ally for those who had long hoped to improve Turkish democracy. With varying support from other political parties, Turkish NGOs, and the European Union, the democratically elected AKP government gradually increased its control over the bureaucracy, military, and judiciary. It eventually ended their role in enforcing Kemalist orthodoxy and restricting democratic politics. The AKP has fit this long, complex, and risky struggle into the simple populist trope of conflict between the oppressive elite and a virtuous people (or its representatives). A 2013 retrospective by Erdoğan's office described its purpose as "eliminat[ing] a system of government shaped by bureaucratic oligarchy and special power groups and replac[ing] it with a system of democratic government ruled by the will of the people."[33]

Some of the methods used to achieve this dramatic shift in political power respected both the letter of Turkish law and a liberal democratic spirit. Statutory and constitutional changes increased civilian control over the military. Curtailing discrimination against religious people – perhaps coupled with political influence over the hiring processes – has shifted the composition of the civil service, judiciary, and military to include many religious conservatives. Voters resolved the constitutional crisis of 2007 and 2008, in which secularist politicians and judges used a dubious interpretation of the constitution to block the AKP from electing Abdullah Gül as president.[34]

Other AKP tactics for redressing the tutelary state's democratic deficits have been more dubious, and some have straightforwardly violated human rights. The prosecution of hundreds of military officers for involvement in alleged coup plots – the so-called Ergenekon and Balyoz affairs – undermined public support for the military and convinced much of the officer corps that intervention in politics was too risky. The trials relied on shaky – and in some cases fabricated – evidence, however, and unjustly victimized many officers. The prosecutors and judges are widely believed to have been affiliated with the shadowy Gülen religious movement, which allied with the AKP until 2013 and systematically infiltrated the state bureaucracy, judiciary, and military.[35] Since 2010, the entire judiciary, including both judges and prosecutors,

---

[33] Republic of Turkey, Prime Ministry, Undersecretariat of Public Order and Security, *The Silent Revolution: Turkey's Democratic Change and Transformation Inventory, 2002–2012* (Ankara: Republic of Turkey Prime Ministry, 2013), 17.

[34] The parliamentary deadlock led to new elections, and the AKP's resounding victory was widely seen as an endorsement of Gül. A small party then reversed its stance and allowed the parliament to vote Gül into office. For a critique of the secularists' actions and legal positions by one of Turkey's leading constitutional scholars, see Özbudun, "Democracy, Tutelarism, and the Search for a New Constitution," 299–306.

[35] Beginning in the 1970s, Turkish Muslim cleric Fethullah Gülen amassed a covert international network of followers that initially focused on religious practice, mutual support in business, and

has been almost completely subordinated to the AKP-led executive branch, through the Gülenist infiltration and a series of reforms to judicial oversight and management processes that followed constitutional procedures. After a bitter split between the AKP and Gülen movement in 2013, the AKP government used its new powers to transfer or fire thousands of prosecutors and judges who were connected to the movement or who merely declined to follow the executive's dictates. Since then, judicial decisions in politically tinged cases have generally matched the AKP government's preferences.

This rebalancing of political power – through both legitimate and dubious means – empowered democratically elected politicians, which initially enhanced Turkish democracy because it dispersed political power. Changes in the constitution, statutes, personnel, political culture, and the country's political economy continued to weaken checks on the power of the executive branch, however.

Around 2010 the balance began tipping in the wrong direction, toward a reconcentration of power, this time in the hands of Erdoğan and his government.[36] By 2011, the AKP had won three straight national elections, a record for any party since the 1960 coup. It had enough seats in the parliament to enact any law unilaterally, and nearly enough to call referenda to amend the constitution. The military, judiciary, and bureaucracy were unable or unwilling to resist Erdoğan and his AKP subordinates. Since the late 2000s, the AKP government had been pressuring media outlets to cut back criticism. Party supporters took over major news outlets and turned them into party organs. The government facilitated this process, in one case levying a $2.5 billion tax fine that forced the sale of two leading newspapers. In early 2014, Erdoğan crushed investigations into AKP corruption by allegedly Gülenist prosecutors, showing that he could vanquish even that once-feared network. The government proceeded to liquidate or take over scores of large, Gülen-linked media outlets, businesses, and educational institutions. President Abdullah Gül was nominally independent of Erdoğan and his government, having resigned from the AKP as the constitution required, but in practice he deferred to them. After a

---

the creation of a network of schools and universities. Professor Hakan Yavuz describes the movement as "a massive web of formal and informal connections tasked with constantly recruiting new members and strengthening their loyalty." M. Hakan Yavuz, "The Three Stages of the Gülen Movement: From Pietistic Weeping Movement to Power-Obsessed Structure," in *Turkey's July 15th Coup: What Happened and Why*, ed. M. Hakan Yavuz and Bayram Balcı (Salt Lake City, UT: University of Utah Press, 2018), 28. The network has always been strongest in Turkey. By the early 2000s, its followers controlled numerous Turkish universities, media outlets, banks, and other businesses. By the end of that decade, many police, prosecutors, judges, bureaucrats, and military officers were Gülen loyalists. Until 2013, Gülenists constituted a primary source of support for the AKP's efforts to control government institutions. See Yavuz.

[36] Many analysts argue that the AKP's "new authoritarianism" has taken the place of the Kemalist "old authoritarianism." For a penetrating analysis of differences between the two versions, see Murat Somer, "Understanding Turkey's Democratic Breakdown: Old vs. New and Indigenous vs. Global Authoritarianism," *Southeast European and Black Sea Studies* 16, no. 4 (2016): 481–503.

2016 coup attempt, the parliament granted President Erdoğan sweeping powers to rule by decree. An AKP-sponsored constitutional referendum in April 2017 made some of those powers permanent and limited the role of the parliament. It also eliminated the post of prime minister and put Erdoğan in sole command of the entire executive branch. This concentration of power, coupled with the repression described in Subsection C, below, has left the Turkish political system much less democratic in 2019 than in 2002, when the AKP took office.

The AKP's populism clearly contributed to its democracy-enhancing drive to reduce the power of countermajoritarian institutions that it identified as the anti-democratic "elite." Populism may also have helped drive the AKP to push its reforms past democratic limits, until it monopolized power. While politicians of all styles aggrandize themselves, populists have an especially dark view of their political opponents, as nefariously bent on subordinating "the people" and some-times on obliterating the populist politicians themselves. The AKP leaders' experience with repression by the Kemalist military and judiciary before 2002 supported this worldview. (Erdoğan is said to have been deeply affected by his imprison-ment.) The 2007–2008 standoff over the presidency and nearly successful judicial effort to dissolve the AKP showed the party's leaders that even controlling the parliament and the executive would not fully protect them. The combination of their populist worldview and experience of repression may have convinced Erdoğan and his followers that without total power they would remain vulnerable.[37]

2 Symbolic Inclusion

The AKP also has represented previously marginalized Turks by expressing respect for them and affirming their importance and political power, through rhetoric and action. This symbolic inclusion is partly independent of the party's populist style. Whenever a politician tries to secure the votes of people who happen to have been previously marginalized, she signals that they are important. Furthermore, it is not only populists who praise the citizens whose votes they seek and validate their values and preferences. But populist political discourse may have more inclusive effects, because its central trope contrasts the virtue of the people with the corruption of the elite. Thus populist politicians are likely to extoll the positive character (and characteristics) of their constituents more often, and more passionately, than non-populists, and devote less time to other topics, such as policy priorities. In Turkey, Erdoğan and other AKP politicians regularly laud "the people," identifying them as

---

[37] This analysis does not rule out reverse or common causation: a belief in the necessity of monopolizing power may have caused the AKP's populism, or both may have been caused by the same thing, such as experience of repression. Even if one or both types of causation were present, however, it is likely that populism also helped maintain or strengthen the AKP's drive for total power, for reasons discussed in Subsection C, below.

including conservative, religious people, the working class, and the poor. Erdoğan's political and material success – he has mixed with world leaders for nearly two decades and lives in a palace larger than Versailles – may make his continued self-identification as a "Black Turk" especially significant to citizens who sensed that previous leaders regarded them merely as sources of votes.

The AKP also has demonstrated its respect for non-elite Turks across the country by engaging them directly. The party interacts far more extensively with its constituents than previous ruling parties, which made little contact with citizens except around elections. During the 1980s and 1990s, Islamist parties built grassroots networks across poor and working-class urban neighborhoods, campaigning door-to-door while their secularist competitors communicated remotely through advertising. Those networks remained active between elections, providing social services and financial aid. After taking control of the national government, the AKP continued this approach. It expanded its neighborhood-level organization across the country, down to small towns, and created parallel party branches for women and youth. It took "considerable pains to avoid assuming the lofty, detached air of previous ruling parties and act as a 'caring' government committed to effectiveness and innovation in meeting popular needs."[38] The AKP was therefore one of Turkey's first truly mass political parties, engaging directly with Turks whom the Ankara and Istanbul elite had disdained.

Symbolic representation may affect human rights in two ways. First, by proclaiming the value of previously peripheral citizens, placing them at the center of the polity, and devoting time and attention to them, populist politicians accord those people respect and recognize their dignity. Jeremy Waldron and others see those values as foundational to human rights, and part of the content of some rights.[39] Second, and more instrumentally, symbolic representation may make rights more meaningful by motivating people to use them. Citizens who feel disrespected and marginalized may be less likely to participate in politics, and thereby to exercise civil and political rights, than those who feel that at least some politicians respect and value them.[40]

3 Material Benefits and Policy Changes

The AKP has also substantively represented some of the Turks who had been marginalized geographically and politically: it has delivered economic and social benefits to the poor and working class, and changed policies to fit the preferences of

---

[38] Meltem Müftüler-Baç and E. Fuat Keyman, "Turkey under the AKP: The Era of Dominant Party Politics," *Journal of Democracy* 23, no. 1 (2012): 90.

[39] See, for example, Jeremy Waldron, *Dignity, Rank, and Rights*, ed. Meir Dan-Cohen (New York: Oxford University Press, 2012), 14–15.

[40] As I discuss in Subsection B, below, the AKP's lack of interest in its constituents' input may have reduced this mobilizing effect.

religious conservatives. Those efforts are consistent with the party's identification of those groups as "the people" in its populist rhetoric.

Since 2002, material conditions have improved for Turks in general. After repeated crises in the 1990s and early 2000s, the economy has grown rapidly and consistently, with real GDP per capita rising from $8,003 in 2004 to $14,933 in 2017, well over 4 percent per year.[41] The AKP government also has pursued policies and programs that especially benefit the traditionally marginalized groups it claims to represent. It has "focus[ed] on poverty alleviation and reaching needier parts of society as no other ruling party or coalition had done before."[42] Gaps between rich and poor in health and education have narrowed, due in part to increased government spending.[43] By 2011, the state Green Card health insurance program covered 60 percent of the poorest tenth of the population, up from 12 percent in 2003.[44] The AKP has improved government services nationwide, "assiduously practic[ing] the constituent-service politics that it learned in its early municipal-level experiences."[45] The national poverty rate fell from 30 percent in 2002 to 2 percent in 2015, after minimum wage hikes and the expansion of transfer programs for the poor.[46] Pro-development policies have fueled a massive boom in housing construction by both state and private developers. For example, the state Mass Housing Agency (MHA) built over 40,000 housing units per year from 2003 to early 2018 – compared to fewer than 2,500 per year from 1984 to 2002.[47] Previous government development projects focused on Istanbul and Ankara,

[41] "World Bank Open Data," World Bank, data.worldbank.org/ ("GDP per capita (constant 2010 US$)" variable) (accessed January 11, 2019). Dani Rodrik argues that these gains are no greater than what similarly situated countries have achieved, and he and others point to high private debt and other structural risks. See Dani Rodrik, "Turkish Economic Myths," April 16, 2015, https://rodrik.typepad.com/dani_rodriks_weblog/2015/04/turkish-economic-myths.html; Emre Deliveli, "Why Has the AKP Been So Successful?," Hürriyet Daily News, November 2, 2015, www.hurriyetdailynews.com/opinion/emre-deliveli/why-has-the-akp-been-so-successful-90598. The Turkish currency's deterioration since the 2013 Gezi Park protests, and rapid fall in 2018, reinforce their concerns. So far, however, growth has remained solid. Furthermore, even matching the performance of other developing countries represents an enormous change in Turks' economic fortunes from the 1990s and early 2000s.

[42] Müftüler-Baç and Keyman, "Turkey under the AKP," 90; see also Zehra F. Kabasakal Arat, "Human Rights," in The Routledge Handbook of Turkish Politics, ed. Alpaslan Özerdem and Matthew Whiting (New York: Routledge, 2019), 305 (noting that governments between 1980 and 2002 made "little or no effort" to fulfill social, economic, or cultural rights).

[43] World Bank, Turkey Transitions Overview (Report No. 90509-TR) (Washington, DC: World Bank, 2014), 14.

[44] Rifat Atun et al., "Universal Health Coverage in Turkey: Enhancement of Equity," The Lancet 382, no. 9886 (July 6, 2013), 77.

[45] Müftüler-Baç and Keyman, "Turkey under the AKP," 90.

[46] "World Bank Open Data," World Bank, https://data.worldbank.org/ ("Poverty headcount ratio at national poverty lines (% of population)" variable) (accessed December 20, 2018).

[47] Mert Arslanalp, "Coalitional Politics of Housing Policy in AKP's Turkey," in Social Policy in the Middle East and North Africa, ed. Marc Lynch, Melani Cammett, and Kristin Fabbe (Washington, DC: Project on Middle East Political Science, 2018), 26.

but under the AKP over 80 percent of the MHA's new affordable housing projects are located outside those metropolitan areas.[48]

The AKP has also redirected resources to more prosperous members of the conservative, religious periphery, such as businesspeople located outside the major cities. The rise of these small and medium-sized "Anatolian Tigers" has been one of the country's best-known economic development stories. It was fueled by government contracts, credits, and other benefits that previous governments had concentrated on venerable conglomerates based in Ankara, Istanbul, and İzmir.

These changes have advanced social and economic rights. Articles 12 and 13 of the International Covenant on Economic, Social, and Cultural Rights (ICESCR) provide rights to health and education, which the AKP's programs have realized at least in part. Falling poverty and new public and private housing bring people closer to the adequate standard of living guaranteed by Article 11. Expanding the geographic distribution of government aid to business helped increase employment, and therefore presumably standards of living, across Anatolia, narrowing the gap with the larger cities.[49]

The government has not framed these social and economic benefits as rights, however, and it has implemented them in ways that may undermine human rights.[50] There is evidence that the AKP has bestowed benefits disproportionately on its supporters, violating the core principle that governments must fulfill human rights without political discrimination.[51] Murat Somer argues that the AKP's simultaneous expansion of government social programs and delivery of them through channels linked to the party, such as conservative Muslim charities, has undermined democracy. Under this "new model" of welfare provision, "the benefits are believed to depend on a particular party or ideology ... rather than on impersonal state institutions and legal-institutional rights."[52] Citizens may feel dependent on the AKP's patronage and reluctant to support its opponents. The new economic and social benefits thus may have strengthened the AKP's hold on power and reduced citizens' sense of political agency.

---

[48] Arslanalp, "Coalitional Politics," 29.

[49] Some aspects of the AKP's social and economic policies have disadvantaged some poor and middle-class Turks, and some analysts suggest that the party's overall impact on them has been negative. See, for example, Arat, "Human Rights," 309–10; Cihan Tuğal, *The Fall of the Turkish Model: How the Arab Uprisings Brought Down Islamic Liberalism* (London: Verso, 2016), 149.

[50] The AKP government's catalog of its accomplishments in its first decade contained an entire chapter on "human rights" and another on "cultural rights and democratization of education" – but grouped economic development, housing, social security, and healthcare advances under the heading "Steps Taken in the Socio-Economic Field." See Republic of Turkey, *The Silent Revolution*, 4–6.

[51] See Somer, "Understanding Turkey's Democratic Breakdown," 490–491; International Covenant on Economic, Social, and Cultural Rights, December 16, 1966, 993 U.N.T.S. 3, art. 2(2).

[52] Somer, "Understanding Turkey's Democratic Breakdown," 490.

Some forms of substantive representation both express ideological preferences and deliver material benefits. The AKP has changed some government policies to suit the preferences of groups who wielded little political influence in the past, most notably religious conservatives. Reducing discrimination against religious people – particularly women who wear headscarves – represents an important improvement in human rights in Turkey that even once-skeptical secular liberals now appreciate.[53] For decades, a combination of informal norms and legal bans barred women wearing headscarves from the parliament, schools, universities, government offices, and many other settings. Millions of Turkish women thus were excluded from a wide range of jobs and public services owing to their religious beliefs. While the AKP initially played down this symbolically charged issue, it has gradually ended the informal taboos and repealed the legal bans. Other forms of religious discrimination have also declined: Islamist soldiers no longer face dismissal from the military.[54] Changes to law, policy, personnel, and norms have largely ended these forms of religious discrimination against observant Sunni Muslims. Increasing access to jobs, education, and public services for those millions advances social and economic rights. Individual women active within the AKP or conservative women's organizations say they have more opportunity to participate in politics and policymaking than they did before it came to power – although secularist feminists now feel marginalized.

The AKP articulates positions and advances policies that may be popular with conservative, religious Turks but discriminate against women and LGBTI people. It has reduced abortion services at government hospitals, and proposed allowing some child rapists to escape punishment by marrying their victims. Erdoğan and other AKP leaders express a conservative view of women that sees them as subordinate to men and emphasizes their role as wives and mothers. The President stated in 2014 that "women are not equal to men," and has repeatedly said that every Turkish woman should have at least three children.[55] This perspective conflicts with the progressive vision of women's rights embodied in the Convention on the Elimination of All Forms of Discrimination Against Women. Turkey's ratification of that

---

[53] Many secular Turks once vigorously defended headscarf bans as essential to secularism and gender equality, but most have now changed their minds and see the bans as having unnecessarily discriminated against religious women. Not all authorities agree, however: in 2004 the European Court of Human Rights held in *Leyla Şahin* v. *Turkey* that the ban on headscarves in Turkish universities did not violate the freedom of religion guaranteed by the European Convention on Human Rights.

[54] Cf. *Annual Report on International Religious Freedom*, prepared for Congress by the U.S. Department of State, December 2001, 384.

[55] Quoted in Pinar Tremblay, "Turkish Women Receive Mixed Messages on Work–Life Balance," *Al-Monitor*, January 5, 2015, www.al-monitor.com/pulse/sites/almonitor/contents/art icles/originals/2015/01/turkey-akp-mixed-messages-on-womens-place.html. For more extensive analysis of the impact of the AKP's religious conservatism on women's equality, see Yeşim Arat, "Religion, Politics and Gender Equality in Turkey: Implications of a Democratic Paradox?," *Third World Quarterly* 31, no. 6 (2010): 873–877.

treaty committed it to, among other things, work toward "the elimination of prejudices and customary and all other practices which are based . . . on stereotyped roles
for men and women."[56] AKP provincial officials restrict LGBTI Turks' freedom of
assembly and expression; they regularly deny permission for gay pride parades and
other public events and break up gatherings with force.[57]

Once-marginalized citizens, like any other group, may have preferences that
accord or clash with human rights, so aligning government policy with them may
advance or retard rights. Leaving aside the content of those preferences, however,
aligning policy with popular preferences tends to advance democracy. It fulfills the
right to political participation guaranteed by the Article 25 of the ICCPR. The UN
Human Rights Committee states that the right to "take part in the conduct of public
affairs," part of Article 25, "is a broad concept which relates to the exercise of
political power, in particular the exercise of legislative, executive, and administrative
powers [, including] the formulation and implementation of policy."[58]

B *Paternalism*

The representative dynamics generated by populism can advance and retard human
rights, but paternalism only undermines them, while exclusion, described in Subsection C, below, can do terrible damage, as it has in Turkey. The AKP's top-down
decision-making, for both the party and the government, compromises the symbolic,
and possibly the substantive, aspects of its representation of historically marginalized
constituents. Rather than soliciting and incorporating the preferences of "the
people" whom they claim to represent, AKP leaders, above all Erdoğan, make all
important decisions about personnel and policy without meaningfully consulting
ordinary citizens or the party's members. This paternalistic "caretaker attitude" and
preference for "an essentially passive people" is common among populists in power
and follows from the core populist idea of a homogeneous "national will."[59]

The three founders of the AKP, Erdoğan, Abdullah Gül, and Bülent Arinç,
initially rejected the internal authoritarianism that has characterized Turkish
political parties since 1923. The organization's initial bylaws provided that "democracy should be the primary method for carrying out internal party business."[60]
Policy choices were subject to internal debate and the party's parliamentary list

---

[56] Convention on the Elimination of All Forms of Discrimination Against Women, December
18, 1979, 1249 U.N.T.S. 13, art. 5(a).

[57] Human Rights Watch, "Turkey Has No Excuse to Ban Istanbul Pride March," June 28, 2018,
www.hrw.org/news/2018/06/28/turkey-has-no-excuse-ban-istanbul-pride-march.

[58] UN Human Rights Committee, CCPR General Comment No. 25: The Right to Participate in
Public Affairs, Voting Rights and the Right of Equal Access to Public Service, ¶ 5, CCPR/C/21/
Rev.1/Add.7 (August 27, 1996) (emphasis added).

[59] Müller, *What Is Populism?*, 30.

[60] Quoted in Caroline Lancaster, "The Iron Law of Erdoğan: The Decay from Intra-Party
Democracy to Personalistic Rule," *Third World Quarterly* 35, no. 9 (2014): 1678.

was chosen through primary elections. Although Erdoğan was always first among equals, Gül, Arinç, and other senior figures wielded considerable power at the beginning.

Once in office, however, the AKP's leaders jettisoned this commitment to internal pluralism, and recently the party has atrophied into Erdoğan's personal machine. A 2003 revision of the bylaws strengthened the leadership at the expense of the rank and file. After the 2004 local elections, the leadership dissolved fifty local party chapters for unclear reasons.[61] As Prime Minister from 2003, Erdoğan consolidated power within the AKP, appointing his loyalists to the party's parliamentary list, party leadership roles, and government positions from cabinet minister on down. In 2007, Gül resigned from the party upon assuming the presidency. Abdüllatif Şener, sometimes considered the party's fourth founder, left it in 2008. In 2014, Erdoğan pressured Gül not to run for reelection, leaving the presidency open for himself. Once elected president, Erdoğan defied the constitutional bar on partisan activity and continued to personally select candidates for the AKP electoral list. In 2015, he left Arinç, his party co-founder and former deputy prime minister, off the list entirely, effectively retiring him from politics. In 2016, after Erdoğan's protégé and successor as prime minister, Ahmet Davutoğlu, mildly resisted the President's efforts to increase his role in policymaking, Erdoğan had him replaced. As noted above, in 2017, voters approved AKP-backed constitutional amendments that eliminated the office of prime minister entirely and allocated all executive powers to the president.

The AKP's adoption of top-down, paternalistic governance is consistent with populism, although the shift in its governance style preceded the dramatic rise in populist themes in its public discourse. Populists tend toward paternalism because of the tension between their belief that "the people" possess a single, homogeneous will and the reality that preferences on policy and personnel vary considerably within whatever part of the citizenry the populists define as "the people." Populist politicians can ignore or repress this pluralism, but cannot acknowledge it, because that would contradict their belief in the homogeneity of the popular will. They therefore cannot devise processes for managing diverse views and choosing among them. The only practice consistent with their understanding of the single will is to decide for themselves what it requires – which is exactly what AKP leaders do.[62] To the extent that Erdoğan and his fellows actually believe in the single national will they describe in speeches, that idea reinforces their tendency, common among

---

[61] Sultan Tepe, "Turkey's AKP: A Model 'Muslim-Democratic' Party?," *Journal of Democracy* 16, no. 3 (July 2005): 74.

[62] Jan-Werner Müller's insight about the imperative to authoritarianism *within* populist parties – "if there is only one common good . . . then disagreement within the party that claims to be the sole legitimate representative of the common good obviously cannot be permissible" – applies more broadly, to the entire group that populists consider to constitute the people. Müller, *What Is Populism?*, 36.

long-serving leaders, to see their judgments as infallible. Even if the national will is solely a rhetorical device, and AKP leaders accept that their "people" have diverse views, they can use the national will idea to mask their authoritarian imposition of their own preferences, by claiming they perceive its content more clearly than others do.

The AKP's paternalism may undermine the positive human rights effects of representation described in the previous subsection. Government policies may have drifted away from constituents' interests and preferences because leaders have stopped listening to their voices, although electoral necessity should limit this divergence. Marginalized citizens whom the AKP initially inspired to exercise their right to political participation may have been alienated again because they sense AKP leaders' lack of interest in their views. This could be one cause of the stagnation in the AKP's vote share since 2007 in both national and local elections, its drop to 43 percent in the 2018 parliamentary elections despite the energetic support of nearly all major media outlets, and its sweeping losses in the 2019 local elections.

C *Exclusion*

The Turkish case suggests that exclusionary elements of a populist worldview can lead populists to seriously violate the human rights of their opponents, actual and perceived. Starting in the late 2000s, when populist themes became dominant in its public rhetoric, the AKP has systematically repressed its challengers and critics. This campaign broadened after the 2013 split between the party and its former ally, the Gülen movement, and turned ferocious after the failed coup attempt in 2016. Deepening and extending the analysis in Subsection A1, above, this subsection argues that three exclusionary elements of the AKP's populism contributed to the scale and brutality of the repression: the view of politics as a no-holds-barred struggle between the virtuous people and nefarious elite, the passionate anger toward the latter, and the anti-pluralist belief in a homogeneous popular will. These, coupled with fear, seem to have led Erdoğan and other AKP leaders to conclude that they had to respond to genuine threats to their power – from the military and judiciary, liberal protesters, and Gülenists – by crushing them and all other possible opponents, as well as by neutering democracy.

Whether because it saw fewer foes or because it had less power to defeat them, the AKP practiced moderate, even inclusive, politics during its early years in office. Its leaders' populist rhetoric emphasized the positive, praising the people rather than excoriating the elite. It chipped away at the Kemalist institutions' power gradually, through reforms with extensive domestic and international support. Erdoğan and his AKP colleagues seemed to view whatever resistance they faced as legitimate, or feel constrained to pretend so.

As the party has consolidated power and faced more resistance, however, it has denounced successive groups of opponents, suggesting a narrowing understanding of which groups constitute "the people" whose will should reign. Initially, AKP leaders criticized the positions of opposition politicians, journalists, and activists who opposed them on particular issues, but by the late 2000s they began to question their critics' motives, patriotism, and even entitlement to participate in political deliberations. As explained above, the AKP's idea of a unified popular will precludes it from accepting criticism as legitimate. Especially since the 2013 Gezi Park demonstrations, Erdoğan and other AKP leaders have articulated an exclusionary, majoritarian view of democracy. They cite the AKP's electoral success to dismiss opposition to their policies.[63] Erdoğan portrayed the Gezi protests as undemocratic attempts by a minority to impose its will on the majority, and compared them to past military coups. He claimed that protesters had "entered the Dolmabahçe Mosque with their beer bottles and their shoes on [and] insulted my headscarf-wearing daughters and sisters," implicitly contrasting his critics with the religiously observant Turks who epitomized the virtuous "people."[64] The Gülen movement's personnel, media outlets, and companies provided crucial support to the AKP for its first ten years in office, beyond managing the Ergenekon and Balyoz military prosecutions. After the allies split in late 2013 amid the corruption investigation, however, Erdoğan condemned the movement as a group of "spies" and "traitors" who had created a "parallel state" within the government.[65]

Repression of AKP enemies, violating their civil and political rights, has followed denunciation. As noted above, the Ergenekon and Balyoz prosecutions rested partly on fabricated evidence against the military defendants. After the Gezi protests, new laws restricted public gatherings and shielded police from accountability for excessive use of force. The government blocked social media sites, including Twitter and Facebook, during periods of political tension, and new laws in 2014 and 2018 expanded its power to regulate internet access and online expression. The dissolutions and takeovers of Gülen-linked financial, media, and industrial companies after 2013 involved dubious legal maneuvers by prosecutors and judges beholden to the AKP executive branch. Those deprived thousands of owners of their assets and undermined freedom of expression.

Repression expanded dramatically in 2016. On the night of July 15, 2016, over 200 people were killed and the parliament was bombed during a military coup

---

[63] Although the AKP has never received an absolute majority of the popular vote in a parliamentary election, its claim to represent a majority is bolstered by the fact that over 50 percent of voters backed Erdoğan in the country's first two direct presidential elections, in 2014 and 2018, and supported AKP-sponsored constitutional amendments in referenda in 2007, 2010, and 2017.

[64] "'Patience Has Its Limits,' Turkish PM Erdoğan tells Taksim Gezi Park Demonstrators," *Hürriyet Daily News*, June 9, 2013, www.hurriyetdailynews.com/patience-has-its-limits-turkish-pm-erdogan-tells-taksim-gezi-park-demonstrators-48516.

[65] Quoted in Ergun Özbudun, "AKP at the Crossroads: Erdoğan's Majoritarian Drift," *South European Society and Politics* 19, no. 2 (2014): 159.

attempt masterminded, the government has maintained, by Gülenist officers.[66] Erdoğan barely escaped a unit sent to detain him. Opposition parties united against the coup and the rebels backed down after civilians poured into the streets. Erdoğan and his government immediately launched a sweeping, brutal crackdown. Over 150,000 judges, police officers, soldiers, civil servants, and academics have been fired or arrested. Nearly all are accused of involvement in the coup attempt or connections to the Gülen movement, based on little or no evidence. Numerous detainees have been tortured. Many of those fired have lost their passports and pensions, and are unemployable owing to government blacklists and private employers' fear of being labeled Gülenist sympathizers. With the judiciary dominated by AKP appointees afraid to step out of line, the purged have virtually no way to challenge these sanctions; they are trapped in Turkey and condemned with their families to poverty.

Since the coup attempt, shockingly harsh penalties against government critics have chilled dissent, which already had been limited by AKP supporters' control of the media. Many of those purged appear to have been targeted solely for criticizing Erdoğan or his government, in some cases in a single Twitter post. Hundreds of NGOs have been closed. In early 2018, Ahmet Altan, one of the country's most famous journalists, was sentenced to life without parole for using "language evocative of a coup" during a television appearance the day before the putsch.[67] As of early 2019, Reporters Without Borders identified thirty-six journalists in prison for their work, the highest number in the world.

Erdoğan and other AKP leaders have portrayed the post-coup repression in classic populist terms, as a struggle against a shadowy group bent on taking over the country. They label it the "Fethullah Gülen Terrorist Organization," but the purges and prosecutions have also targeted liberals who have never been credibly linked to the Gülen movement. The violence of the coup attempt, and the seriousness of the threat it posed to the AKP government and Erdoğan personally, could explain the brutality of the AKP's crackdown on Gülenists in the military.[68] But what accounts for the breadth of the repression, encompassing liberals with no Gülen connection, as well as movement-affiliated academics and bureaucrats, and its viciousness toward all of them? The AKP's leaders may simply have seen an opportunity to secure themselves in power, but their populist ideology may also have contributed, first by magnifying the threat.

---

[66] For analysis of the coup attempt, including the Gülen movement's role in it, see Yavuz and Balcı, eds., *Turkey's July 15th Coup*. For details on the ensuing repression, see Arat, "Human Rights," 309; Human Rights Watch, *2019 World Report* (New York: Human Rights Watch, 2019), 588–593.

[67] J.M. Coetzee et al., "An Open Letter to President Erdoğan from 38 Nobel Laureates," *The Guardian*, February 28, 2018, www.theguardian.com/commentisfree/2018/feb/28/nobel-laureates-president-erdogan-turkey-free-writers.

[68] This explanation would not justify the violations of human rights during the crackdown. The government has not proven that Gülenists led the coup attempt, although significant evidence has come to light.

It is almost impossible to imagine an alliance between liberals such as the Gezi protesters, the Gülen movement, and the AKP's earlier nemesis, the Kemalist military and judiciary. These three groups of AKP opponents had almost no common members. Liberals saw the Kemalists' historical tutelage of civilian politics as antidemocratic and the Gülenists as a sinister cabal. Gülenists loathed Kemalists for marginalizing religion, and the Ergenekon and Balyoz prosecutions deepened the divide. Independent analysts see the three groups' challenges to the AKP as entirely distinct, and judge that the AKP has decisively defeated each.[69]

Erdoğan's and his fellows' worldview may cause them to see their opposition differently, however: viewed through the lens of Manichean populist ideology, the Kemalists, liberal protesters, and military and civilian Gülenists appear to constitute a unified and fearsome bloc. The AKP leaders' rhetoric suggests that they believe they are engaged in an existential, possibly never-ending, struggle against a single force that reconstitutes itself in different form, or perhaps against a coalition of unknown extent whose members reveal themselves sequentially as they take their turn to rise up against the AKP (and the people, whom it represents).[70]

The AKP's drive to monopolize power and its vicious repression of actual and suspected opponents could be explained largely by the combination of this fearsome specter, the party's belief in the righteousness and homogeneity of the national (popular) will as interpreted by the AKP itself, and the vindictive emotions that Erdoğan and other AKP leaders feel toward their "elite" enemies. Thus the AKP's populism may have contributed importantly to its far-reaching repression of actual and suspected opponents and its evisceration of Turkey's democratic institutions and norms.[71]

V CONCLUSION

The human rights record of the AKP government has varied over its seventeen years in office, and differs across areas of human rights. Any assessment of the effects of the

---

[69] Gülenist soldiers and civilians share a religious allegiance, and thus in a sense constitute a single force, but any threat that the civilians posed to the AKP in 2016 was distinct in nature from the violence that solders could muster. Thus the AKP's repression of Gülenist civilians also requires explanation.

[70] A more sinister, yet possible, explanation is that the AKP's leaders do not believe any of their populist rhetoric, but deploy it purely to manipulate their followers. If this is true, then it seems less likely that they genuinely fear they will be overthrown and repressed, and more likely that the scope and intensity of their human rights violations reflects a calculated strategy of rule by terror.

[71] Paradoxically, during this conflictual period, the AKP government has welcomed and supported millions of immigrants – the group attacked by many populists, particularly in Europe and the United States, as the greatest threat to "the people." Most are Syrians; the 3.6 million who have entered Turkey since 2012 constitute more than 4 percent of Turkey's population. In both absolute and relative terms, this far exceeds the numbers who reached European countries, which treated their arrival as a crisis, as well as the United States' minuscule admissions.

party's populism on it must begin with Erdoğan's recent monopolization of power and his government's assault on the civil and political rights of hundreds of thousands of Turkish citizens. As the previous subsection explained, exclusionary elements of the ruling party's populist worldview may have amplified and intensified the government's assaults on democracy and on individuals it sees as threats. Many Turks now suffer fear and political inhibition as intense as what they would feel under a full-blown authoritarian regime.

Populism may have undermined human rights in Turkey in other ways, too. AKP leaders' belief in a homogeneous popular will motivates, or helps them justify, paternalistic disregard for their constituents' views as they make decisions on policy and personnel for their party and the government. Ignoring their constituents makes AKP politicians less representative by definition and, more practically, may cause their policies to drift from their constituents' preferences, marginally reducing democracy. If their constituents sense their leaders' lack of interest, then their motivation to participate in political life may decline.

The impact of populism may not have been uniform, however: Turkey arguably provides a positive example of how populists' attention to previously marginalized groups can bolster human rights. The AKP's conviction that an elite was constraining democracy had some factual basis, although it vastly oversimplified the history of Turkish politics. The party's efforts to end military interventions in politics and moderate the judiciary's enforcement of secularism received wide support at home, including from many secular liberals, and from the European Union. Those reforms improved democracy by enhancing the power of ordinary citizens generally, and especially of conservative, religious Turks whose preferences had been underweighted for years owing to Kemalist red lines forbidding, for example, headscarves in universities. To be sure, the AKP continued this political rebalancing much too long, and power is now too concentrated in the presidency. Under different circumstances, however, the party might not have been able, or inclined, to subjugate the media, judiciary, and other potential checks on its power. In that case, its structural reforms might have left Turkey's political system in a more democratic balance than in 2002 or today.

The AKP also has represented once-marginalized groups in symbolic and substantive senses. It lauds the religious conservative "periphery" and poor and working-class Turks more generally – its version of "the people." That recognition and the party's engagement with them conveys respect and encourages them to exercise their political rights. Finally, the AKP government has redressed the state's neglect of those parts of the population and adopted public policies that fit their long-ignored preferences. These changes strengthened democracy by increasing government responsiveness to citizens. Furthermore, many specific initiatives that AKP constituents desired, such as building low-income housing and opening universities to women who wear headscarves, also happen to have enhanced human rights. (Others arguably infringe human rights, however; the views of AKP constituents, like those of most groups, do not align perfectly with human rights.)

Populism has not determined these advances and regressions; its contribution to them is uncertain and partial. The AKP government's human rights performance likely has been shaped by other factors as well, such as a mundane desire for power and its leaders' and supporters' conservative religiosity. Evaluating the causal impact of Erdoğan's and other AKP leaders' populist worldview on their decisions with high confidence would require more detailed information about their decision-making processes, and possibly Erdoğan's psychology, than may ever be publicly available. To trace the influence of populism on Turkish politics and the ramifications of that influence for human rights, this chapter has instead assessed party leaders' actions and rhetoric in their political and historical context.

The effects identified in this case study generate hypotheses that could be tested in other geographic and temporal contexts. Qualitative studies and large-sample quantitative analysis could reveal which dynamics arise often from populist rule, and what factors affect their incidence and intensity. For example, are populist rulers more repressive in countries with histories of military coups? Such research also could compare the magnitude of positive and negative effects of populism on human rights. Populists' ascent to power in the United States, Brazil, the Philippines, and Italy, among other countries, and their rising popularity elsewhere, makes these and other questions about the impact of populist rule on human rights more urgent than ever.

BIBLIOGRAPHY

Akyol, Mustafa. "Erdoganism [Noun]: From 'National Will' to 'Man of the Nation,' an Abridged Dictionary for the Post-Secular Turkish State." *Foreign Policy*, June 21, 2016. https://foreignpolicy.com/2016/06/21/erdoganism-noun-erdogan-turkey-islam-akp/.

Annual Report on International Religious Freedom. Prepared for Congress by the U.S. Department of State, December 2001.

Arat, Yeşim. "Religion, Politics and Gender Equality in Turkey: Implications of a Democratic Paradox?" *Third World Quarterly* 31, no. 6 (2010): 869–884.

Arat, Zehra F. Kabasakal. "Human Rights." In *The Routledge Handbook of Turkish Politics*, edited by Alpaslan Özerdem and Matthew Whiting, 299–314. New York: Routledge, 2019.

Arslanalp, Mert. "Coalitional Politics of Housing Policy in AKP's Turkey." In *Social Policy in the Middle East and North Africa*, edited by Marc Lynch, Melani Cammett, and Kristin Fabbe, 25–33. Washington, DC: Project on Middle East Political Science, 2018.

Atun, Rifat, Sabahattin Aydın, Sarbani Chakraborty, Safir Sümer, Meltem Aran, Ipek Gürol, Serpil Nazlıoğlu et al. "Universal Health Coverage in Turkey: Enhancement of Equity." *The Lancet* 382, no. 9886 (July 6, 2013): 65–99.

Aytaç, S. Erdem, and Ezgi Elçi. "Populism in Turkey." In *Populism Around the World*, edited by Daniel Stockemer, 89–108. Cham, Switzerland: Springer, 2019.

Bakinur, Onur. "A Key to Turkish Politics? The Center–Periphery Framework Revisited." *Turkish Studies* 19, no. 4 (2018): 503–522.

Coetzee, J.M. et al. "An Open Letter to President Erdoğan from 38 Nobel Laureates," *The Guardian*, February 28, 2018. www.theguardian.com/commentisfree/2018/feb/28/nobel-laureates-president-erdogan-turkey-free-writers.

Deliveli, Emre. "Why Has the AKP Been So Successful?" *Hürriyet Daily News*, November 2, 2015. www.hurriyetdailynews.com/opinion/emre-deliveli/why-has-the-akp-been-so-success ful-90598.

Denli, Özlem. "Freedom of Religion: Secularist Policies and Islamic Challenges." In *Human Rights in Turkey*, edited by Zehra F. Kabasakal Arat, 87–101. Philadelphia, PA: University of Pennsylvania Press, 2007.

Dinçşahin, Şakir. "A Symptomatic Analysis of the Justice and Development Party's Populism in Turkey, 2007–2010." *Government and Opposition* 47, no. 4 (2012): 618–640.

Eichler, William. "The Making of a Demagogue: How Erdoğan Became Turkey's Strong-man." *Open Democracy*, April 18, 2017. www.opendemocracy.net/william-eichler/making-of-demagogue-how-erdo.

Ergil, Doğu. "The Kurdish Question in Turkey." *Journal of Democracy* 11, no. 3 (July 2000): 122–135.

Hawkins, Kirk A., Rosario Aguilar, Erin Jenne, Bojana Kocijan, Cristóbal Rovira Kaltwasser, and Bruno Castanho Silva. Global Populism Database: Populism Dataset for Leaders 1.0, 2019. https://populism.byu.edu/Pages/Data.

Human Rights Watch. "Turkey Has No Excuse to Ban Istanbul Pride March." June 28, 2018. www.hrw.org/news/2018/06/28/turkey-has-no-excuse-ban-istanbul-pride-march.

2019 World Report. New York: Human Rights Watch, 2019.

Kalaycıoğlu, Ersin. *Turkish Dynamics: Bridge Across Troubled Lands*. New York: Palgrave Macmillan, 2005.

Kemerli, Pınar. "Religious Militarism and Islamist Conscientious Objection in Turkey." *International Journal of Middle East Studies* 47 (2015): 281–301.

Lancaster, Caroline. "The Iron Law of Erdoğan: The Decay from Intra-Party Democracy to Personalistic Rule." *Third World Quarterly* 35, no. 9 (2014): 1672–1690.

Lewis, Paul, Caelainn Barr, Seán Clarke, Antonio Voce, Cath Levett, and Pablo Gutiérrez. "Revealed: The Rise and Rise of Populist Rhetoric." *The Guardian*, March 6, 2019. www .theguardian.com/world/ng-interactive/2019/mar/06/revealed-the-rise-and-rise-of-populist-rhetoric.

Mandiraci, Berkay. "Turkey's PKK Conflict Kills Almost 3,000 in Two Years." July 20, 2017. www.crisisgroup.org/europe-central-asia/western-europemediterranean/turkey/turkeys-pkk-conflict-kills-almost-3000-two-years.

Mardin, Şerif. "Center–Periphery Relations: A Key to Turkish Politics." *Daedalus* 102, no. 1 (Winter 1973): 169–190.

McKernan, Bethan. "From Reformer to 'New Sultan': Erdoğan's Populist Evolution." *The Guardian*, March 11, 2019. www.theguardian.com/world/2019/mar/11/from-reformer-to-new-sultan-erdogans-populist-evolution.

Mudde, Cas. "Populism: An Ideational Approach." In *The Oxford Handbook of Populism*, edited by Cristóbal Rovira Kaltwasser, Paul Taggart, Paulina Ochoa Espejo, and Pierre Ostiguy, 27–47. New York: Oxford University Press, 2017.

Mudde, Cas, and Cristóbal Rovira Kaltwasser. "Populism." In *The Oxford Handbook of Political Ideologies*, edited by Michael Freeden and Marc Stears, 493–512. New York: Oxford University Press, 2013.

Müftüler-Baç, Meltem, and E. Fuat Keyman. "Turkey under the AKP: The Era of Dominant Party Politics." *Journal of Democracy* 23, no. 1 (2012): 85–99.

Müller, Jan-Werner. *What Is Populism?* Philadelphia, PA: University of Pennsylvania Press, 2016.

O'Connell, Jamie. "Common Interests, Closer Allies: How Democracy in Arab States Can Benefit the West." *Stanford Journal of International Law* 48, no. 2 (2012): 341–404.

Özbudun, Ergun. "AKP at the Crossroads: Erdoğan's Majoritarian Drift." *South European Society and Politics* 19, no. 2 (2014): 155–167.

"Democracy, Tutelarism, and the Search for a New Constitution." In *Turkey's Democratization Process*, edited by Carmen Rodríguez, Antonio Ávalos, Hakan Yılmaz, and Ana I. Planet, 293–311. New York: Routledge, 2014.

Özerdem, Alpaslan, and Matthew Whiting, eds. *The Routledge Handbook of Turkish Politics.* New York: Routledge, 2019.

"'Patience Has Its Limits,' Turkish PM Erdoğan Tells Taksim Gezi Park Demonstrators." *Hürriyet Daily News*, June 9, 2013. www.hurriyetdailynews.com/patience-has-its-limits-turkish-pm-erdogan-tells-taksim-gezi-park-demonstrators-48516.

Pope, Nicole, and Hugh Pope. *Turkey Unveiled: A History of Modern Turkey.* New York: Overlook Duckworth, 2011.

Republic of Turkey, Prime Ministry, Undersecretariat of Public Order and Security. *The Silent Revolution: Turkey's Democratic Change and Transformation Inventory, 2002–2012.* Ankara: Republic of Turkey Prime Ministry, 2013.

Rodrik, Dani. "Turkish Economic Myths." April 16, 2015. https://rodrik.typepad.com/dani_rodriks_weblog/2015/04/turkish-economic-myths.html.

Roth, Brad R. "Evaluating Democratic Progress." In *Democratic Governance and International Law*, edited by Gregory H. Fox and Brad R. Roth, 493–516. Cambridge: Cambridge University Press, 2000.

Rovira Kaltwasser, Cristóbal. "The Ambivalence of Populism: Threat and Corrective for Democracy." *Democratization* 19, no. 2 (April 2012): 184–208.

Selçuk, Orçun. "Strong Presidents and Weak Institutions: Populism in Turkey, Venezuela, and Ecuador." *Southeast European and Black Sea Studies* 16, no. 4 (2016): 571–589.

Somer, Murat. "Turkey: The Slippery Slope from Reformist to Revolutionary Polarization and Democratic Breakdown." *Annals of the American Academy of Political and Social Science* no. 681 (January 2019): 42–61.

"Understanding Turkey's Democratic Breakdown: Old vs. New and Indigenous vs. Global Authoritarianism." *Southeast European and Black Sea Studies* 16, no. 4 (2016): 481–503.

Tepe, Sultan. "Turkey's AKP: A Model 'Muslim-Democratic' Party?" *Journal of Democracy* 16, no. 3 (July 2005): 69–82.

Thomas, Heather. "Journalists Get Life in Prison for 'Subliminal Messages' Before Turkish Coup." *The Times* (London), February 19, 2018.

Tremblay, Pinar. "Turkish Women Receive Mixed Messages on Work–Life Balance." *Al-Monitor*, January 5, 2015. www.al-monitor.com/pulse/sites/almonitor/contents/articles/originals/2015/01/turkey-akp-mixed-messages-on-womens-place.html.

Tuğal, Cihan. *The Fall of the Turkish Model: How the Arab Uprisings Brought Down Islamic Liberalism.* London: Verso, 2016.

UN Human Rights Committee. CCPR General Comment No. 25: The Right to Participate in Public Affairs, Voting Rights and the Right of Equal Access to Public Service. CCPR/C/21/Rev.1/Add.7 (August 27, 1996).

Waldron, Jeremy. *Dignity, Rank, and Rights*, edited by Meir Dan-Cohen. New York: Oxford University Press, 2012.

World Bank. "World Bank Open Data." https://data.worldbank.org/.

Turkey Transitions Overview (Report No. 90509-TR). Washington, DC: World Bank, 2014.

Yabanci, Bilge. "Populism as the Problem Child of Democracy: The AKP's Enduring Appeal and the Use of Meso-Level Actors." *Southeast European and Black Sea Studies* 16, no. 4 (2016): 591–617.

Yavuz, M. Hakan. "The Three Stages of the Gülen Movement: From Pietistic Weeping Movement to Power-Obsessed Structure." In *Turkey's July 15th Coup: What Happened and Why*, edited by M. Hakan Yavuz and Bayram Balcı, 20–45. Salt Lake City, UT: University of Utah Press, 2018.

Yavuz, M. Hakan, and Bayram Balcı, eds. *Turkey's July 15th Coup: What Happened and Why*. Salt Lake City, UT: University of Utah Press, 2018.

7

Penal Populism in Emerging Markets

Human Rights and Democracy in the Age of Strongmen

Richard Javad Heydarian

I THE ASCENT OF STRONGMEN

Far from witnessing a Hegelian march towards an ideological terminus[1] where the cocktail of liberal democracy and market economy reign supreme in Kantian perpetuity,[2] the world today confronts the revenge of history: not in the form of cataclysmic wars among nations, which ravaged civilizations in the first half of the twentieth century, but instead more of a winter of discontent unraveling the foundations of modern democracies across the globe.

As collective confidence in democratic institutions wavers, a growing proportion of people have come to entrust their fate to those who Max Weber described as "charismatic" leaders: namely the political figures that are, in the eyes of their devoted supporters, "endowed with supernatural, superhuman, or at least specifically exceptional powers or qualities."[3] The type of leaders who have come to preside over the world's most powerful nations best reflects our *Zeitgeist*.

In the United States, long the bastion of democracy, Donald Trump captured the country's highest office on a right-wing populist agenda, which emphasized law and order, restricted immigration, transactional economics, and foreign policy unilateralism. Though bereft of technocratic expertise, the celebrity billionaire electrified his electoral base and mobilized a nationwide coalition by extolling his supposedly supernatural managerial skills, promising political miracles once in office. Through sheer political "genius," and his "art of the deal," Trump offered to resolve

---

[1] Francis Fukuyama, "The End of History?," *The National Interest* (1989), https://ps321.commu nity.uaf.edu/files/2012/10/Fukuyama-End-of-history-article.pdf.

[2] Fukyama's "The End of History" treatise, envisioning boredom and prosperity in a world dominated by globalization and ascendancy of democratic Western powers, echoes Immanuel Kant's confidence in a state of "perpetual peace" in a world of cosmopolitan, commercially integrated republican nations.

[3] Robert Tucker, "The Theory of Charismatic Leadership," *Daedalus* 97, no. 3 (1968): 731–756, www.jstor.org/stable/20023840.

longstanding policy conundrum, whether in the realm of trade disputes (with China and Japan), geopolitical tensions (with Iran and North Korea) or border security (with Mexico).[4]

In China, President Xi Jinping has effectively ended the two-decades-long "consociational regime" established by the former paramount leader Deng Xiaoping, who dreaded the tyranny of one-man-rule under Mao Zedong. Shortly after taking power, the Chinese leader unleashed an ambitious anti-corruption campaign, which quickly morphed into a comprehensive purge of his rivals, including Bo Xilai and Sun Zhengcai, and the establishment of a new cult of personality ("Uncle Xi"). Under Xi's watch, several former and sitting members of the Politburo and up to seventeen full and alternative members of the Central Committee and more than a hundred generals and admirals were imprisoned or faced execution.[5] He also embarked on an unprecedented effort to centralize power by placing himself at the helm of the State Security Committee, Leading Small Groups on foreign and security affairs as well as the Taiwan Affair, the Central Leading Group for Comprehensively Deepening Reforms, and numerous other newly created executive agencies, which have made the Chinese leader the "chairman of everything."[6]

Xi also tightened his subjective control over the People's Liberation Army, personally overseeing leadership reshuffles, command structure reforms, and large-scale drills from the South China Sea to Mongolia, while placing trusted allies in charge of internal security and economic policy. Xi's reforms effectively ended the more professionalized "objective control" over the armed forces. Five years into power, the Chinese leader left little doubt vis-à-vis his ambition of long-term, absolute rule over the world's most populous nation, eliminating term limits on the office of presidency while firmly maintaining his grip over the Central Military Commission and the Chinese Communist Party.[7]

In Russia, the heir of the former Soviet Empire, Vladimir Putin, has established self-styled twenty-first-century czardom, where elections have been largely reduced to a predetermined ritual of political legitimation of the status quo rather than a genuine opportunity for political change. Together with his Soviet-era colleagues from the security services, the Russian leader has established a formidable "sultanistic" regime, where a single individual in Kremlin has the final say on all key matters of decision-making.[8]

---

[4]   Bob Woodward, *Fear: Trump in the White House* (New York: Simon & Schuster, 2019).

[5]   Susan Shirk, "The Return to Personalistic Rule," *Journal of Democracy* 29, no. 2 (2018), www .journalofdemocracy.org/sites/default/files/media/29.2–Shirk–AdvanceVersion.pdf

[6]   Brad Glosserman and Denny Roy, "Asia's Next China Worry: Xi Jinping's Growing Power," *The National Interest*, July 23, 2014, nationalinterest.org/blog/the-buzz/asias-next-china-worry-xi-jinpings-growing-power-10939

[7]   Shirk, "Return to Personalistic Rule."

[8]   Masha Gessen, *The Man Without a Face: The Unlikely Rise of Vladimir Putin* (New York: Riverhead, 2012).

Crucially, over the years Putin has become an inspiration for right-wing populists and would-be strongmen across the world, ranging from Viktor Mihály Orbán in Hungary and Recep Tayyip Erdoğan in Turkey to Rodrigo Duterte in the Philippines and Donald Trump in the United States of America.[9] What all these leaders share in common is their promise of national redemption and glory, whether it be Trump's "making American great again," Xi's "Chinese Dream" and "national rejuvenation," or the clarion call by Putin – the ultimate personification of *a homo sovieticus* – for restoration of Russian imperial glory, drawing on elements of Orthodox Christianity and Soviet-era military dominance.[10]

A *Exporting Authoritarianism*

The twenty-first-century populist-authoritarian blend of leadership among global super-powers has a direct bearing on the global march of democracy. After all, historically it was precisely the great powers of the West, which actively promoted democracy across the East. As political scientists such as Samuel Huntington[11] and Larry Diamond[12] have noted, Western powers played a key role in promoting and stabilizing democracies throughout the latter half of the twentieth century. Huntington, for instance, emphasized the "key role" of the European Community (EC) "in consolidating democracy in southern Europe," particularly the democratic transitions in Portugal, Spain, and Greece, and the role of Washington as "a major promoter of democratization" in the 1970s and 1980s, thanks to the "unparalleled power of a seemingly successful US democratic model ... a 'shining city on a hill' – to inspire admiration and emulation around the world."[13] As Diamond similarly argues, it was Europe and the United States that "provided both an end state toward which emerging democracies could move, and [the necessary] support to help them get there."[14]

In stark contrast to the previous century, the US of today has instead increasingly become a symbol of political dysfunction and debilitating polarization where legislative deadlock, federal government shutdown, and divisive rhetoric have become

---

9   Ian Bremmer, "The 'Strongmen Era' Is Here. Here's What It Means for You," *Time Magazine*, May 3, 2018, time.com/5264170/the-strongmen-era-is-here-heres-what-it-means-for-you/.

10 See: Eva Hartog and Lev Gudkov, "The Evolution of Homo Sovieticus to Putin's Man," *The Moscow Times*, October 13, 2017, https://themoscowtimes.com/articles/the-evolution-of-homo-sovieticus-to-putins-man-59189; Michael Kimmage, "The People's Authoritarian," *Foreign Affairs*, July/August 2018, www.foreignaffairs.com/reviews/review-essay/2018-06-14/peoples-authoritarian; Timothy Snyder, *The Road to Unfreedom: Russia, Europe, America* (New York: Tim Duggan Books, 2018).

11 Samuel Huntington, "Democracy's Third Wave," *Journal of Democracy* 2, no. 2 (1991): 12–34, DOI: 10.1353/jod.1991.0016.

12 Larry Diamond, "Democracy after Trump: Can a Populist Stop Democratic Decline?," *Foreign Affairs*, November 2016, www.foreignaffairs.com/articles/world/2016-11-14/democracy-after-trump.

13 Huntington, "Democracy's Third Wave," 14–15.

14 Diamond, "Democracy after Trump."

ubiquitous.[15] More worryingly, the Trump administration has consciously dialed down promotion of human rights and democracy overseas, upgraded relations with authoritarian regimes such as Saudi Arabia, and downgraded diplomatic relations with traditional democratic allies, particularly in Western Europe.[16] In turn, Putin's Russia has stepped up its military assistance to authoritarian allies, particularly in Syria, and accelerated its campaign of political disruption and electoral sabotage across democracies.

Through its massive infrastructure investments, which often lack transparency and regulatory oversight, China has undermined good governance standards across the world, particularly in impoverished fledgling democracies where institutional checks and balances are underdeveloped. From Sri Lanka to Malaysia and the Maldives, a whole host of fledgling democracies have been trapped by large-scale debt to Chinese companies, which have, in turn, demanded greater control over critical infrastructure with frightening consequences for the integrity of the political institutions and the national sovereignty of host countries. This is not to mention China's export of cutting-edge surveillance technology to authoritarian regimes and would-be autocrats, who are intent on regulating and monitoring the behavior of voters.[17]

Both Russia and China have employed so-called sharp power of systematic disinformation, manipulative public diplomacy, industrial-corporate espionage, disruptive technology, and even outright bribery of political actors to degrade and destabilize democracies across the world. Xi has also actively promoted the "Chinese model" of governance, which combines authoritarian single-party rule with state-driven capitalism, chipping away at the appeal of liberal democratic values across the developing world. Crucially, the authoritarian turn among the global superpowers has coincided with a "democratic recession": In the past two decades, according to Diamond, 27 democracies have suffered either a temporary or full breakdown.[18] Thus, the rise of right-wing populists in the developing world should be understood within this milieu of global democratic retreat.

---

[15] Francis Fukuyama, *Political Order and Political Decay: From the Industrial Revolution to the Globalization of Democracy* (New York: Farrar, Straus and Giroux, 2014).

[16] "Donald Trump Is Undermining the Rules-based International Order," *The Economist*, June 7, 2018, www.economist.com/briefing/2018/06/07/donald-trump-is-undermining-the-rules-based-international-order.

[17] See: Bhrama Chellaney, "China's Creditor Imperialism," *Project Syndicate*, December 2017, www.project-syndicate.org/commentary/china-sri-lanka-hambantota-port-debt-by-brahma-chellaney-2017-12; Christopher Walker, Shanthi Kalathil, and Jessica Ludwig, "How Democracies Can Fight Authoritarian Sharp Power," *Foreign Affairs*, August 2018, www.foreignaffairs.com/articles/china/2018-08-16/how-democracies-can-fight-authoritarian-sharp-power; Ivo Daalder and James Lindsay, "The Committee to Save the World Order," *Foreign Affairs*, November/December 2018, www.foreignaffairs.com/articles/2018-09-30/committee-save-world-order; Zheping Huang, "Xi Jinping Says China's Authoritarian System Can Be a Model for the World," *Quartz*, March 2018, https://qz.com/1225347/xi-jinping-says-chinas-one-party-authoritarian-system-can-be-a-model-for-the-world/.

[18] Diamond, "Democracy after Trump."

II DEMOCRACY FATIGUE

Observing with horror the rapid collapse of democratic institutions in his home country, the early twentieth-century Italian thinker Antonio Gramsci highlighted how "incurable structural contradictions have revealed themselves," yet the ruling elite struggled to no avail "to conserve and defend the existing structure" and make "every effort to cure them."[19] The upshot was the birth of fascism, with the centrist elite rapidly fading from a political landscape drenched in violence and millenarian ideology as radical right-wing and left-wing groups tore asunder the fabric of Italian democracy.

Gramsci, a radical Marxist who eventually perished in jail under Mussolini's rule, lamented how "the old [order] is dying and the new cannot be born," correctly foreseeing "in this interregnum, a great variety of morbid symptoms [beginning to] appear." His observations on the transmogrification of the Italian society, and the spread of fascism across Europe, underscore the inherent fragility of liberal democracy, and the peaceful circulation of power anchored by an ideology of pluralism and moderation, especially in periods of immense economic and sociopolitical distress, which characterized the immediate aftermath of World War I.[20]

Almost a century after the birth of fascism in Italy, liberal democracy is once again in retreat. Across both fledgling and mature democracies, right-wing populists have outmaneuvered and, in some cases, even dislodged the mainstream elite through one electoral shock after the other, whether it is the Brexit vote in the United Kingdom, Donald Trump's unexpected victory in American presidential elections, Narendra Modi's (India) in the world's largest democracy, or Jair Bolsonaro's (Brazil) in Latin America's biggest nation.

We are confronting not so much twentieth-century fascism, but instead the specter of what American journalist Fareed Zakaria famously characterized as "illiberal democracy," where fairly competitive elections are regular yet tainted by widespread disfranchisement of minorities, fears of communal violence, and dysfunctional partisanship; where constitutionalism gives way to rule *by* law, with law becoming an instrument of executive power rather than justice; where the state becomes the expression of the will of the majority at the expense of minorities and socially constructed "others"; where communal security is pursued at the expense of civil liberties and human rights; and where institutional checks and balances are

---

[19] Antonio Gramsci, *Selections from the Prison Notebooks*, ed. Quintin Hoare and Geoffrey Nowell Smith (London: Lawrence & Wishart, 1971), 178.

[20] See Michael Mann, *Fascists* (Cambridge: Cambridge University Press, 2004); Perry Anderson, "The Heirs of Gramsci," *New Left Review* 100 (July–August 2016), https://newleftreview.org/II/100/perry-anderson-the-heirs-of-gramsci; Perry Anderson, "The Italian Disaster," *London Review of Books* 36, no. 10 (2014): 3–16, www.lrb.co.uk/v36/n10/perry-anderson/the-italian-disaster.

neutered in favor of executive supremacy.[21] This illiberal turn has been most prevalent among nations that belong to the so-called third democratic wave.[22]

Shortly after the end of the Cold War, Zakaria warned that "just as nations across the world have become comfortable with many variations of capitalism," ranging from free market capitalism in the U.S. and social democratic capitalism in Scandinavia to state capitalism in China, "they could well adopt and sustain varied forms of democracy," which depart from the standard liberal democratic template in the West, where rule of law, free and fair elections, and civil liberties and human rights are deeply embedded in the fabric of the body-politic.[23]

Questioning Fukuyama's "end of history" thesis, Zakaria doubted whether liberal democracy will be "the final destination on the democratic road," but instead "just one of many possible exits." He correctly foresaw the proliferation of hybrid regimes, which combine elements of authoritarianism with electoral politics. The rapid spread of democracy across the post-Soviet space and, later, the Arab uprisings, which deposed several aging autocrats, provided a temporary distraction from the mutation of many once-promising democracies into illiberal regimes at the dawn of the twenty-first century.

A *The Populist Puzzle*

Though unique in its genesis and subsequent manifestations, the contemporary globe-spanning revolt against liberal democracy echoes the populist explosion in the late nineteenth-century United States against the inequities of the "Gilded Age" and, more worryingly, the ascent of fascism in Europe in the early twentieth century amid the collapse of centrist-moderate political parties.[24]

But to begin with, what is populism? It is a form or style of political mobilization, which "features an appeal to 'the people' versus 'the elite', 'bad manners' and the performance of crisis, breakdown or threat."[25] A populist, therefore, tends to deploy a unique rhetoric that (i) defies conventions, namely the standard accepted "language" for the political elite; (ii) represents himself/herself as a political outsider,

---

[21] See Andrea Kendall-Taylor and Erica Frantz, "How Democracies Fall Apart: Why Populism Is a Pathway to Autocracy," *Foreign Affairs*, December 2016, www.foreignaffairs.com/articles/2016-12-05/how-democracies-fall-apart; Fareed Zakaria, "America's Democracy Has Become Illiberal," *The Washington Post*, last modified December 29, 2016, www.washingtonpost.com/opinions/america-is-becoming-a-land-of-less-liberty; Fareed Zakaria, "The Rise of Illiberal Democracy," *Foreign Affairs*, November 1997, www.foreignaffairs.com/articles/1997-11-01/rise-illiberal-democracy.

[22] Huntington, "Democracy's Third Wave."

[23] Zakaria, "Rise of Illiberal Democracy."

[24] See: David Runciman, *How Democracy Ends* (New York: Basic Books, 2018); Sarah Churchwell, *Behold America: The Entangled History of "America First" and "the American Dream"* (New York: Basic Books, 2018); Snyder, *The Road to Unfreedom*.

[25] Benjamin Moffitt, *The Global Rise of Populism: Performance, Style and Representation* (Stanford, CA: Stanford University Press, 2016), 45.

who is the true representative of the majority against a discredited ruling class; and (iii) often adopts the rhetoric of apocalypse and salvation to justify the urgency of political transformation through, and only through, his/her assumption of power.

Substantively, populism tends to rely on what Ernesto Laclau described as "empty signifiers,"[26] an appeal to universally shared sentiments and grievances through affectively resonant pronouncements, which often lack specific programmatic and evidence-based policy contents. In extreme cases, populists resort to vacuous, infeasible, and fantastical promises that mobilize disaffected sections of society, even if they defy the fundamental nature of politics as the art of the possible (rather than the impossible).

Ideologically, populism tends to come in both right-wing and left-wing varieties. The former emphasizes "law and order" over human rights and civil liberties, identitarian-nativist purity over pluralism and cosmopolitanism, and deference to an authoritarian populist figure over institutionally mediated procedural democracy. The latter, meanwhile, emphasizes redistributive policies, social justice, and class-based mobilization against systemic inequality and neoliberal governance.[27]

Other scholars, however, contend that populism is fundamentally illiberal, whether in its right-wing or left-wing variety. As Cas Mudde explains, populism is "an illiberal democratic response to undemocratic liberalism," which "criticizes the exclusion of important issues from the political agenda by the elites and calls for their re-politicization"; but this potentially corrective catharsis tends to be anchored by an "uncompromising stand [that] leads to a polarizes society ... and its majoritarian extremism denies legitimacy to opponents' views and weakens the rights of minorities [however they may be defined]."[28] Jan-Werner Müller similarly warns that populism, in all its varieties, is "an exclusionary form of identity politics," which "tends to pose a danger to democracy," since any functioning "democracy requires pluralism and the recognition that we need to find fair terms of living together as free, equal, but also irreducibly diverse citizens."[29]

The root of the problem is populism's claim to a monopoly of representation of "the people," thus the built-in exclusion of any contrarian view, no matter how legitimate and widely shared by other sections of the political class and broader society. As Müller explains, "Populists claim that they and they alone speak in the name of what they tend to call the 'real people' or the 'silent majority,'" and "accuse all other political contenders of being illegitimate."[30] Once in power, populist regimes will attempt to "hijack the state apparatus, [oversee] corruption and 'mass

[26] Ernesto Laclau, *On Populist Reason* (London: Verso, 2005).
[27] Chantal Mouffe, *For a Left Populism* (London: Verso, 2018).
[28] Cas Mudde, "The Problem with Populism," *The Guardian*, February 17, 2015, www.theguar dian.com/commentisfree/2015/feb/17/problem-populism-syriza-podemos-dark-side-europe.
[29] Jan-Werner Müller, *What Is Populism?* (Philadelphia, PA: University of Pennsylvania Press, 2016).
[30] Müller, *What Is Populism?*

clientelism' (trading material benefits or bureaucratic favors for political support by citizens who become the populists' 'clients'), and [launch] efforts systematically to suppress civil society."[31] From this perspective, any form of populism, across time and space, is on an ineluctable road towards authoritarianism and exclusionary politics, regardless of its original intent, the character of its leadership, and its ideological genesis.

How to reconcile these divergent views on populism's ontology and epistemology? Interrogating the literature on populism, Gidron and Bonikowski contend that the "challenge of defining populism is at least partially due to the fact that the term has been used to describe political movements, parties, ideologies, and leaders across geographical, historical, and ideological contexts," when it is "hard to find a common ideological denominator that connects the various ostensibly populist movements, particularly when the classification of political actors relies on the expansive lay understanding of the concept."[32]

Instead, the two Harvard scholars have classified populism broadly along three axes. The first is based on *ideology*, or "a set of ideas characterized by an antagonism between the people and the elite, as well as the primacy of popular sovereignty, whereby the virtuous general will is placed in opposition to the moral corruption of elite actors."[33] The second is based on *style* of conducting politics, whether in terms of "heated exaggeration, suspiciousness, and apocalyptic conspiratorial worldview."[34] The last is based on *strategy* of political mobilization, which concerns the relationship between the political leader and his/her constituents, specifically how "a personalistic leader seeks or exercises government power based on direct, unmediated, uninstitutionalized support from large numbers of mostly unorganized followers."[35]

Thus, it is possible for a political leader to adopt populism as an electoral strategy, but not necessarily embrace it in content and style, while others could become what I call "consummate populists" by embracing all three elements of ideology, strategy, and style. This provides a space for the many permutations of populism, which have taken root across the world, especially in fledgling democracies.

B *Emerging Market Populism*

Empirically, however, there remains a significant difference between the phenomenon of populism in Western democracies, on one hand, and in emerging market

---

[31] Müller, *What Is Populism?*
[32] Noam Gidron and Bart Bonikowski, "Varieties of Populism: Literature Review and Research Agenda," *Weatherhead Center for International Affairs* no. 13–0004 (2013), https://scholar.harvard.edu/files/gidron_bonikowski_populismlitreview_2013.pdf
[33] Gidron and Bonikowski, "Varieties of Populism," 6.
[34] Gidron and Bonikowski, "Varieties of Populism," 9.
[35] Gidron and Bonikowski, "Varieties of Populism," 1.

democracies, on the other. In the former, populism has been driven by two distinct phenomena, namely economic stagnation, especially in mostly rural and post-industrial regions hit by outsourcing and the advent of information technology, and a surge in anti-immigrant sentiment, especially among the nativist sections of the population, which tends to transcend socioeconomic divides.

Declining confidence in political institutions combined with rising income inequality has only exacerbated grievances over a seemingly unrestrained inflow of immigrants in periods of economic insecurity amid globalization as well as structural distress, thanks to the 2007–2008 Great Recession.[36] The driving forces behind populism in the West (economic stagnation and anti-immigrant sentiment), however, remain largely absent among emerging market democracies, namely nations with rapidly growing economies and a decades-long experience of electoral politics. And yet, we have witnessed the emergence of populism, mostly in their right-wing varieties, in these nations.

The first decades of the twenty-first century have seen rapid economic expansion, rather than stagnation, across emerging market democracies, from Brazil, Thailand, and Turkey to Indonesia, India, Mexico, and the Philippines. Between 2000 and 2005 alone, the gross capital inflow into these economies rose by 92 percent, a figure that surged to 478 percent over the next five years. Thanks to the unprecedented growth in capital inflows, emerging markets doubled their share of global gross domestic product, just as their growth rates also doubled (3.6 to 7.2 percent) compared to the preceding two decades.[37] While populism thrives on the grievances of "losers of globalization" in the West, emerging market democracies tend to be, at least on the macro-national level, the new "winners of globalization."

Meanwhile, emerging market democracies such as India, Indonesia, and the Philippines continue to be among the leading exporters of human capital, as millions of impoverished and middle-class citizens search for greener pastures overseas. Meanwhile, the likes of Turkey and Mexico have absorbed large-scale migration from troubled neighboring countries without significant upsurge in anti-immigrant sentiment among the local population. Thus, the advent of right-wing populism and success of political outsiders across these nations is both surprising and seemingly counterintuitive.

---

[36] See: Edward Luttwak, *Endangered American Dream* (New York: Simon & Schuster, 1994); Niall Ferguson, "Populism as a Backlash against Globalization – Historical Perspectives," *Horizons* 8 (2016), www.cirsd.org/en/horizons/horizons-autumn-2016–issue-no-8/populism-as-a-backlash-against-globalization; Robert Reich, "How Capitalism Is Killing Democracy," *Foreign Policy* (2009), http://foreignpolicy.com/2009/10/12/how-capitalism-is-killing-democracy/; Thomas Pikkety, *Capital in the Twenty First Century* (Cambridge, MA: Harvard University Press, 2014); Walter Russell Mead, "The Jacksonian Revolt: American Populism and the Liberal Order," *Foreign Affairs* (2017), www.foreignaffairs.com/articles/united-states/2017-01-20/jacksonian-Revolt.

[37] Ruchir Sharma, *Breakout Nations: In Pursuit of the Next Economic Miracles* (New York: W.W. Norton, 2013), 2–14.

If anything, the mainstream elite should have reaped the political dividends of overseeing a period of sustained economic expansion. Instead, what we are witnessing is erosion of public confidence in democratic institutions and greater preference for the authoritarian leader "who does not have to bother with elections," as an increasing share of citizens exhibits signs of "democratic fatigue."[38] According to recent Pew Surveys, a majority of citizens in Indonesia (52 percent) and India (55 percent) prefer a "strong leader," who can rule without institutional checks and balances from the legislature and judiciary, while only a small plurality of citizens in the Philippines (15 percent), Indonesia (12 percent), and India (8 percent) express categorical commitment to representative politics.[39]

The question, therefore, is why? How could a seemingly similar strand of authoritarian populism emerge outside the West across developing nations with very divergent, if not diametrically opposite, socioeconomic conditions? There are three basic factors that explain democracy fatigue, and the subsequent rise of authoritarian populism, across emerging market democracies, namely (i) democratic deficit, (ii) fragility of state institutions, and (iii) persistent politicoeconomic inequality in spite of rapid economic growth.

First of all, emerging market democracies tend to suffer from chronic institutional weaknesses, which have shredded public confidence in the overall political system. This should not have come as a surprise. As Thomas Carothers observed more than a decade after the euphoria following the collapse of the Berlin Wall, which unleashed "end of history" illusions, many third wave democracies "have some attributes of democratic political life, including at least limited political space for opposition parties and independent civil society, as well as regular elections and democratic constitutions." Yet, scratch the surface and one discovers how they "suffer from serious democratic deficits," reflected in "poor representation of citizens' interests, low levels of political participation beyond voting, frequent abuse of the law by government officials, elections of uncertain legitimacy, very low levels of public confidence in state institutions, and persistently poor institutional performance by the state."[40] Far from institutional convergence with established democracies, where checks and balances are deeply embedded in political practice, "the majority of third wave countries has not achieved relatively well-functioning

---

[38] Roberto Foa and Yascha Mounk, "The Signs of Deconsolidation," *Journal of Democracy* 28, no. 1 (2017): 5–16, DOI: 10.1353/jod.2017.0000.

[39] Zuraidah Ibrahim and John Power, "Middle Class and Frustrated in Asia? Populist Politicians are Seeking You Out in 2019," *South China Morning Post*, January 5, 2019, www.scmp.com/week-asia/politics/article/2180786/poll-dance-how-asias-politicians-are-mobilising-voting-masses; Pew Research Center, "Globally, Broad Support for Representative and Direct Democracy" (October 2017), 26, www.pewresearch.org/global/2017/10/16/globally-broad-support-for-representative-and-direct-democracy/.

[40] Thomas Carothers, "The End of the Transition Paradigm," *Journal of Democracy* 13, no. 1 (2002): 5–21, http://journalofdemocracy.org/article/endtransition-paradigm.

democracy or do not seem to be deepening or advancing whatever democratic progress they have made"[41]

In short, democratic transitions have brought about regular elections and, in many cases, liberal constitutions, but, crucially, without the corresponding presence or development of other important requisites of a robust democracy,[42] ranging from independent courts and mass-based political parties to civic culture, high social capital, and a modicum of socioeconomic justice that allows the majority of the electorate to meaningfully participate in collective decision-making.[43]

This democratic deficit has gone hand in hand with the decay of state institutions, which have failed to enforce democratic rules, protect the bureaucracy from undue influence of special interest, and discipline the rapacious local oligarchy, which tends to dominate key sectors, including telecommunications and infrastructure, among emerging market democracies, often to the consternation of the newly mobilized and increasingly self-entitled middle classes.[44]

C The "New Middle Class" Revolts

Samuel Huntington observed, fifty years ago, how throughout the mid-twentieth century, "[i]nstead of a trend toward competitiveness and democracy, there has been an 'erosion of democracy' and a tendency to [lapse into] autocratic ... regimes."[45] He correctly noted the relationship between the fragility of democratic institutions and the "decay of the administrative organization inherited from the colonial era and a weakening and disruption of the political organizations developed during the struggle for independence."

More crucially, Huntington underscored what can be termed as an "institutional-ization-aspiration gap," whereby periods of rapid economic growth tend, quite counterintuitively, to generate political instability, since the pace of political mobilization (by newly empowered middle classes and formerly marginalized sectors) for

---

[41] Carothers, "End of the Transition Paradigm," 9–10.

[42] Seymour Martin Lipset, "Some Social Requisites of Democracy: Economic Development and Political Legitimacy," *The American Political Science Review* 53 no. 1 (1959): 69–105, www.jstor .org/stable/1951731.

[43] For further analyses on the requisites of a functioning democracy, see: Robert Putnam, Robert Leonardi, and Rafaella Nanneti, *Making Democracy Work: Civic Traditions in Modern Italy* (Princeton, NJ: Princeton University Press, 1993); Robert Dahl's classic work, *Polyarchy: Participation and Opposition* (New Haven, CT: Yale University Press, 1972); and Larry Diamond, *Developing Democracy: Toward Consolidation* (Baltimore, MD: Johns Hopkins University Press, 1999).

[44] See: Francis Fukuyama, *Political Order and Political Decay: From the Industrial Revolution to the Globalization of Democracy* (New York: Farrar, Straus and Giroux, 2014); "Comparing Crony Capitalism around the World," *The Economist*, May 5, 2016, www.economist.com/ graphic-detail/2016/05/05/comparing-crony-capitalism-around-the-world.

[45] Samuel Huntington, *Political Order in Changing Societies* (London: Yale University Press, 1968).

greater representation and social expectations of improved overall living conditions (amid an economic boom) tend to overtake the ability of fragile and fraying state institutions to accommodate new social demands for political inclusion, quality public services, and law and order.

The upshot is a political Malthusian trap, whereby the exponential increase in social expectations as well as aspirations of newly empowered classes outpaces the snail-paced delivery of goods and services by state institutions. The most literally pedestrian illustration of this disruptive dynamic is the suffocating traffic in major emerging market capitals such as Manila, where economic expansion has led to a rapid expansion of car purchases, yet the government has failed to make corresponding improvements in overall public infrastructure. The upshot is the world's worst traffic congestion – though closely followed by Jakarta and New Delhi, according to the 2015 Global Driver Satisfaction Index. This has exacerbated public dissatisfaction with existing state institutions, a lingering grievance that has transformed into overall fatigue with democratic politics, which tends to emphasize compromise, transparency, and accountability, often at the expense of constant delays and deferment of major public projects, especially among developing countries.[46]

The third factor, which is closely related to the first two, is the perennial lack of inclusive development across emerging market democracies, where the gains of globalization are largely concentrated among the networked elite. Though featuring among the fastest-growing economies in the world, the Philippines saw just forty families taking home three-quarters (76 percent) of newly created growth in 2013. In places such as Indonesia, a similarly narrow yet politically connected elite continues to dominate key sectors of the economy, while India has created one of the largest collection of billionaires without a major reduction in number of those who live close to the poverty line.[47]

The primary problem is structural economic imbalances that have created low-quality growth among these nations. As Dani Rodrik explains, many rapidly developing nations such as India, Indonesia, and the Philippines tend to ignore the "manufacturing imperative," namely their overreliance on low-to-medium-end services and extractive industries as engines of growth, which lack economies of scale and fail to provide sufficient number of well-paying jobs for a booming labor market.[48] The result is high levels of underemployment and the relatively large size of the gray economy in these nations.

Historically, industrialized and newly industrialized nations managed to move up the ladder of development and bring about inclusive development through the combination of export-oriented manufacturing and modernized agricultural

---

[46] *The Economist,* "Comparing Crony Capitalism."
[47] Sharma, *Breakout Nations.*
[48] Dani Rodrik, "The Manufacturing Imperative," *Project Syndicate,* August 20, 2011, www .project-syndicate.org/commentary/the-manufacturing-imperative.

production.[49] Unlike today's emerging market democracies, the developed nations did not have to contend with structural adjustment programs, imposed by international financial institutions such as World Bank and the International Monetary Fund, which heavily curtailed their development policy space, namely flexibility in trade and industrial policies, and allowed them to nudge their infant industries up the value-chain.

It is true that sustained growth has lifted tens of millions out of extreme poverty across these nations, thanks to the expansion in precarious low-value-added employment opportunities and palliative policies such as conditional cash transfer programs for indigent families; but the true winners of globalization are not emerging markets per se, but largely their well-connected elite.[50]

The combination of concentrated development, democratic deficit, and decay of state institutions has provided a unique opening for charismatic political outsiders and populists to seize power from their liberal mainstream counterparts across major emerging market democracies. Though hailing from and operating in diverse backgrounds, these political figures, from Narendra Modi (India) to Recep Tayip Erdoğan (Turkey), Joko Widodo (Indonesia) and Rodrigo Duterte (the Philippines), share four basic characteristics.

First, railing against bureaucratic red tape and corruption, they promised decisive and effective leadership. In particular, they heavily drew on their executive background in local governance and their folksy, if not pedestrian, demeanor. As the chief minister of the state of Gujarat, the chest-thumping Modi oversaw massive investment in manufacturing, large-scale infrastructure buildup, and among the fastest growth rates anywhere in India. As the brash and tough-talking mayor of Istanbul, Erdoğan ably fixed chronic concerns with water and sewage facilities and rapidly modernized the city's public transportation system. Jokowi, the much-celebrated mayor of Solo, who garnered record votes during his mayoral stint, protected small and medium enterprises from the onslaught of conglomerates, proactively engaged grassroots organizations, and prioritized the development of local industries. As for Duterte, he drastically reduced red tape, expedited business permit processing, implemented strict rules against loitering and smoking in public places, and oversaw the transformation of Davao into the fastest-growing city in the Philippines.

---

[49] See: Jillian Keenan, "The Grim Reality Behind the Philippines' Economic Growth," *The Atlantic*, May 7, 2013, www.theatlantic.com/international/archive/2013/05/the-grim-reality-behind-the-philippines-economic-growth/275597/; Joe Studwell, *How Asia Works: Success and Failure in the World's Most Dynamic Region* (New York: Grove Press, 2014); Rodrik, "The Manufacturing Imperative."

[50] See: Dani Rodrik, *One Economics, Many Recipes: Globalization, Institutions, and Economic Growth* (Princeton, NJ: Princeton University Press, 2009); Ha-Joon Chang, *Kicking Away the Ladder: Development Strategy in Historical Perspective* (London: Anthem Press, 2002); Kevin Gallagher, *Putting Development First: The Importance of Policy Space in the WTO and IFIs* (London: Zed Books, 2005); Studwell, *How Asia Works.*

When they ran for their countries' highest officers, all four presented themselves as able executives, touting their local experiences as a model of national development. The genius of this strategy was that it impressed both the business elite as well as the aspirational middle classes, who were disillusioned by the decay and delay of public goods and services under mainstream politicians.

Meanwhile, all of them appealed to the masses by presenting themselves as political outsiders from humble backgrounds, and with a genuine heart for the poor and marginalized, whether it was Modi's relentless emphasis on his low-caste origins (son of an impoverished tea servant) and self-portrayal as *pradhan sewak* (a servant of the masses), Duterte's and Erdoğan's almost identical populist slogans of "he is one of us," or Jokowi's call for a government that serves the *orang kecil*, namely ordinary people. In this sense, they were all "hybrid" populists, who managed to gain significant support and build a large coalition across socioeconomic classes.

Second, they ran on an anti-establishment platform, which promised political transformation at the expense of a discredited ruling elite, whether in terms of Modi's attack on the long-dominant liberal Congress party; Erdoğan's Islamist-leaning moral exhortations against the centrist, Western-leaning "white Turk" parties; Jokowi's call for the replacement of the Jakarta-based Indonesian oligarchy; and Duterte's constant dismissal of the "imperial Manila" liberal elite as an out-of-touch and incompetent political class.

Third, they emphasized the importance of societal order, national greatness and collective security, even if this came at the expense of upholding and promoting human rights and basic civil liberties at home and abroad.

And crucially, they enjoyed huge appeal among the emerging-aspirational middle classes and the youth, who sought a greater voice and new opportunities amid years of rapid yet uneven economic growth. Their rallying cry is not so much freedom and democracy as effective governance and equitable delivery of public services.[51]

III THE WAR ON HUMAN RIGHTS

A salient feature of the populist politics across emerging market democracies is their illiberal lurch, often with authoritarian overtones, if not outright authoritarian policies. In India, the world's largest democracy, Modi managed to capture the highest office, with the largest electoral landslide since the times of Indira Gandhi, despite lingering concerns over his role during the 2002 pogroms in Gujarat, where

---

[51] See: Andy Marino, *Narenda Modi: A Political Biography* (New York: HarperCollins, 2014); Julio Teehankee and Mark Thompson, "The Vote in the Philippines: Electing a Strongman," *Journal of Democracy* 27 no. 4 (2016): 124–134, www.journalofdemocracy.org/article/vote-philip pines-electing-strongman; Pankaj Mishra, "Indonesia's New Economic Model," *Bloomberg*, November 5, 2012, www.bloomberg.com/opinion/articles/2012-11-04/indonesia-s-new-eco nomic-model; Soner Cagaptay, *The New Sultan: Erdogan and the Crisis of Modern Turkey* (London: I.B. Tauris, 2017).

hundreds of Muslims, including children, were massacred by Hindu extremists. He has been accused of willful neglect (if not indirectly encouraging) and outright remorselessness vis-à-vis the anti-Muslim violence, an accusation that was struck down by courts, but was credible enough to deny him visa entry to the United States throughout his stint as the chief minister of Gujarat.

The fact of Modi's roots in the hardline Hindu nationalist group Rashtriya Swayamsevak Sangh (RSS), the ideological core of the Bharatiya Janata Party (BJP) ruling party, has only reinforced widespread skepticism over his respect for religious pluralism and evenhandedness towards minorities, particularly Muslims. Modi's illiberal conviction could be best captured in his argument in favor of "modernization without westernization," namely an unshakable commitment to economic development sans liberal political values.[52]

His stint as the prime minister of India has coincided with a surge in state-backed crackdown on civil society groups and liberal intelligentsia; vigilante attacks on religious minorities groups; and the empowerment of pro-Hindutva (Hindu dominance) movements.[53] The so-called Modi wave has seen the growing prominence of authoritarian developmentalism, which is echoed on the state level by demagogic populists such as Jayalalitha Jayaram in Tamil Nadu and Mamata Banerjee in West Bengal as well as the 2017 appointment of Yogi Adityanath, a hardline Hindu monk notorious for his Islamophobic pronouncements, as the BJP's designated chief minister of Uttar Pradesh. Modi-style populism has brought about a hostile atmosphere for religious minorities and liberal figures, organizations, and movements across the country.[54]

In Turkey, after a few years of encouraging political reforms in the mid-2000s, ostensibly as part of the country's prospective membership in the European Union, Erdoğan and his Justice and Development Party (AKP) oversaw the systematic purge and marginalization of voices of dissent within the state apparatus as well as the broader political class. The authoritarian, illiberal turn took off during the so-called Ergenekan trials, a series of controversial indictments against liberal journalists and senior members of the Turkish armed forces, including numerous admirals, on largely trumped-up charges of treason and conspiracy to bring down the government.

This troubling trend accelerated following the failed 2016 coup attempt, allegedly by elements aligned to the Gülenist (*Hizmet*) movement, a former ally-turned-rival, which has been designated as a terrorist organization by the Turkish state. What followed was purge on an even larger scale, including the early retirement or

[52] Marino, *Narenda Modi*.
[53] Andrew Marszal, "Arundhati Roy Caught in the Crossfire of Indian Judicial Power Struggle," *The Telegraph*, February 6, 2016, www.telegraph.co.uk/news/worldnews/asia/india/12144154/Arundhati-Roy-caught-in-the-crossfire-of-Indian-judicial-power-struggle.html.
[54] Manjari Miller, "India's Authoritarian Streak," *Foreign Affairs*, May 30, 2018, www.foreignaffairs.com/articles/india/2018-05-30/indias-authoritarian-streak.

imprisonment of 42 percent of air force generals, 44 percent of army generals, 58 percent of admirals, as well as 586 colonels and 400 staff officers, and 20 percent of all commissioned officers. In addition, as many as 10,000 suspected Gülenist academics, officials, and government employees were also dismissed from work and faced charges of conspiracy against the state.[55]

The purge of political rivals, real and imagined, has extended to crackdown on Kurdish opposition leaders, including Selahattin Demirtas, the progressive leader of the People's Democratic Party (HDP), and shutdown or forcible takeover of various independent media outlets. The Turkish government has surpassed both China and Iran in terms of the number of journalists placed in jail. Erdoğan, having relaxed term limits and empowered the office of presidency through a newly approved constitution in 2017, has established himself as the undisputed Turkish leader for the foreseeable future, a modern neo-Ottoman "sultan," turning a once promising democracy into the latest Sultanistic regime.[56]

In Indonesia, Jokowi, though more a populist in style and strategy than in ideology, has gradually shed his progressive background, largely remaining on the sidelines during the controversial indictment of his former deputy and Jakarta Governor Basuki Tjahaja Purnama (also known as "Ahok"), a Christian of ethnic Chinese descent, on charges of religious blasphemy. To the consternation of his liberal supporters, Jokowi picked a controversial religious figure, Ma'ruf Amin, as his vice-presidential candidate for his 2019 re-election campaign.

More troublingly, he faces a renewed challenge from former rival Prabowo Subianto, a former general who has been accused of widespread human rights violations during his stint in the Indonesian military.[57] Subianto's outright embrace of right-wing populism is evident in his nostalgic call for a return to the authoritarian days of New Order under Suharto, glorification of top-down style of leadership, and desperate efforts to rally public support by resorting to apocalyptic rhetoric, where only he can supposedly save Indonesia from impending doom.[58]

---

[55] Metin Gurcan, "Turkish Military Purges Decimate Career Officer, Pilot Ranks," *Al-Monitor*, May 29, 2018, www.al-monitor.com/pulse/originals/2018/05/turkey-military-purges-career-officer-pilot.html.

[56] For an analysis of Sultanistic regimes, see Houchang Chehabi and Juan Linz (eds.), *Sultanistic Regimes* (Baltimore, MD: Johns Hopkins University Press, 1998); Cagaptay, *The New Sultan*.

[57] See: Laskmi Pamuntjak, "Jokowi, We Voted for a Humble Man. Now You've Taught a New Generation about Killing," *The Guardian*, May 5, 2015, www.theguardian.com/commentisfree/2015/may/05/jokowi-we-voted-for-a-humble-man-now-youve-taught-a-new-generation-about-killing; Lex Rieffel, "Lessons for Myanmar in Indonesian Politics," *East Asia Forum*, November 22, 2016, www.eastasiaforum.org/2016/11/22/lessons-for-myanmar-in-indonesian-politics/; Per Liljas, "Here's Why Some Indonesians Are Spooked by this Presidential Contender," *Time*, June 12, 2014, http://time.com/2836510/prabowo-subianto-human-rights-indonesia-elections.

[58] "'Ghost Fleet' Fiasco: Prabowo Defends Sci-fi Novel as 'Scenario Writing', Author, Politicians & Netizens React," *Coconut Jakarta*, March 23, 2018, https://coconuts.co/jakarta/news/ghost-fleet-fiasco-prabowo-defends-sci-fi-novel-scenario-writing-says-ok-people-dont-believe/.

The Jokowi–Prabowo rivalry will likely shift the political discourse in a rightward direction, where law and order, combined with growing concerns over religious strife and economic insecurity, becomes a central election theme. Politics of fear could increasingly overshadow a progressive vision of hope, with Jokowi sidelining political reform, defanging anti-corruption initiatives to hasten big-ticket infrastructure development, pandering to ultra-conservative Islamists, and brazenly incorporating leading illiberal figures, including Prabowo, in top cabinet positions.[59] Jokowi also raised alarm bells when he decided, early into his presidency, to restore the long-suspended implementation of the death penalty against suspected drug traffickers, a move that garnered widespread popular support.

As mentioned earlier, he has even gone so far as endorsing Duterte-style shoot-to-kill orders against suspected drug dealers, declaring in mid-2017: "The police and TNI (military) have been firm, especially when dealing with foreign drug traffickers entering the country. If they [drug dealers] resist arrest, just gun them down, show no mercy." The Indonesian president argued, "From *the practice in the field* [author's own emphasis], we see that when we shoot at drug dealers they go away. So if such a policy were implemented in Indonesia, we believe that the number of drug traffickers and users in our beloved country would drop drastically."[60]

A *Penal Populism*

By "practice in the field," the Indonesian leader was most likely referring to President Rodrigo Duterte's scorched-earth "war on drugs" in the Philippines, which has provoked global outcry and upended one of Asia's oldest and most liberal democracies. In fact, Jokowi has warmly welcomed Duterte to Jakarta on several occasions, treating him with utmost respect, with Indonesia going so far as awarding the Bintang Bhayangkara Utama (Medal of Honor), among its most prestigious government awards, to Philippine Police Chief Bato Dela Rosa, who oversaw the first two years (and most brutal phase of) the drug war in the Philippines.[61]

A year into Duterte's office, an estimated 14,000 suspected drug dealers and users were reportedly killed either during Philippine National Police (PNP) operations or at the hands of vigilante killers. Initially, authorities admitted to around 3800 cases of extrajudicial killings (EJKs), and fewer deaths during the so-called Oplan Tokhang

[59] Richard Paddock, "Indonesian General Accused of Kidnapping Is Named Defense Minister," *The New York Times,* October 23, 2019, https://www.nytimes.com/2019/10/23/world/asia/indonesia-prabowo-joko-widodo.html.

[60] "Jokowi Issues Order to Shoot Drug Traffickers," *The Star,* July 22, 2017, www.thestar.com.my/news/regional/2017/07/22/jokowi-issues-order-to-shoot-drug-traffickers/.

[61] Anne-Peralta Malonzo, "Dela Rosa Receives Highest Indonesian Government Award," *Sun-Star,* February 14, 2018, www.sunstar.com.ph/article/418944.

anti-drug operations led by the PNP,[62] but by 2018 they revealed around 23,000 Deaths Under Investigation (DUI) during Duterte's first two years of presidency.[63]

The staggeringly high number of unexplained murders across the country echoes similar policies by Thailand's former prime minister, Thaksin Shinawatra, also a controversial and highly divisive populist, who oversaw an anti-drug campaign, which claimed the lives of 1200 individuals in 2003. Former Indonesia strongman Suharto also employed a similar strategy during the early 1980s, though with a broader focus on reducing crime rates rather than illegal drug trafficking alone. And, similar to Jokowi in Indonesia, Duterte has called for the reinstitution of the death penalty in the Philippines, which was repealed in the late 2000s, especially against drug traffickers.[64]

Duterte has presented himself as the decisive and uncompromising "protector" of "law-abiding citizens" against the "bad guys," namely drug dealers and criminals. As the Filipino leader repeatedly warned during his elections campaign, nothing short of his death, not even the Philippine constitution, would prevent him from doing what was necessary to avoid the emergence of a supposed "narco-state" in the Philippines. This is a classic exercise of "penal populism," which pertains to a "process whereby politicians devise punitive penal policies, which are adjudged to be 'popular' within the general public, and are designed to mobilize votes rather than improve the crime and justice situation." No wonder, then, these forms of populism are "usually most manifest during election campaigns."[65]

Though trained as a lawyer, Duterte has shown little regard for rule of law and standard operating procedures in his anti-crime campaigns, previously in his role as the long-time mayor of Davao City and, later, as commander-in-chief of the Republic of the Philippines.[66] Human rights groups have accused Duterte of relying

---

[62] Oplan (or operation) "Tokhang" means, in Davao vernacular, knocking on the door, referring to raids by PNP officers on residences of suspected drug dealers, which, in a lot of cases, led to the death of the latter under suspicious circumstances. According to the law enforcers, the deaths were caused by "nanlaban" (armed resistance) of the suspected drug dealers, but critics doubt the veracity of such claims. See Daniel Berehulak, "They Are Slaughtering Us Like Animals," *The New York Times*, December 7, 2016, www.nytimes.com/interactive/2016/12/07/world/asia/rodrigo-duterte-philippines-drugs-killings.html.

[63] See: Francisco Tatad, "Is It the Dead End?," *The Manila Times*, September 29, 2017, www.manilatimes.net/is-it-the-dead-end/353529/; Martin Sadongdong, "PNP Insists No Policy to Kill Drug Suspects," *Manila Bulletin*, June 24, 2018, https://news.mb.com.ph/2018/06/24/pnp-insists-no-policy-to-kill-drug-suspects/.

[64] See: "'License to Kill': Philippine Police Killings in Duterte's War on Drugs," *Human Rights Watch.org*, March 3, 2017, www.hrw.org/report/2017/03/01/license-kill/philippine-police-killings-dutertes-war-drugs; Rishi Iyengar, "The Killing Time: Inside Philippine President Rodrigo Duterte's War on Drugs," *TIME.com*, last date modified August 25, 2016, http://time.com/4462352/rodrigo-duterte-drug-war-drugs-philippines-killing/.

[65] Margarita Dobrynina, "'The Roots of Penal Populism': The Role of Media and Politics," *Criminological Studies* 4 (2017): 98–124, https://doi.org/10.15388/CrimLithuan.2016.4.10729.

[66] For further analysis, see: David Johnson and Jon Fernquest, "Governing through Killing: The War on Drugs in the Philippines," *Asian Journal of Law and Society* 5 no. 2 (2018),

on a so-called Davao Death Squad (DDS) to target suspected drug dealers and petty criminals, first in his hometown and later, during his presidency, throughout the country, especially in Manila. DDS veterans such as commander Lito Patay have allegedly been assigned to the special anti-drug unit in Quezon City Police District's Station 6, which has been responsible for almost two-fifths of total deaths of suspected drug dealers at the hands of law enforcers.[67]

Whenever challenged by his critics, Duterte and other right-wing populists in emerging market democracies, most recently Brazilian President Jair Bolsonaro,[68] have repeatedly emphasized how their electoral mandate gives them the prerogative to arbitrarily impose draconian policies, even if in violation of due process. This is eerily similar to what German legal theorist Carl Schmitt, the crown jurist of the Nazi Germany regime, termed as the "state of exception," namely the suspension of normal constitutional procedures by a charismatic authoritarian leader, in favor of a more arbitrary, yet decisive response to a national emergency.

B *The Specter of Putin*

In his third State of the Nation Address in July 2018, Duterte defiantly reassured his countrymen that "the war against illegal drugs is far from over," and that it "will be as relentless and chilling, if you will, as on the day it began."[69] He reminded his critics that "[i]f you think that I can be dissuaded from continuing this fight because of demonstrations, your protests which I find misdirected, then you got it all wrong," asserting, with unshakable conviction, "Your concern is human rights, mine is human lives." For Duterte, as in Schmitt's legalist justification of absolutist rule, what makes him the commander-in-chief is his sovereign will, as the duly elected president, to transcend and defy any institutional check on his executive power in his conduct of the war on drugs.

In *The Concept of the Political*, Schmitt argues "the specific political distinction to which political actions and motives can be reduced is that between friend and enemy," where opposition is defined neither by a "previously determined general

www.cambridge.org/core/journals/asian-journal-of-law-and-society/article/governing-through-killing-the-war-on-drugs-in-the-philippines/878BFFB53E2705BEFD2373CDAC3E84F4;　Nicole Curato, "Politics of Anxiety, Politics of Hope: Penal Populism and Duterte's Rise to Power," *Journal of Current Southeast Asian Affairs* 35, no. 3 (2016), https://journals.sub.uni-hamburg.de/giga/jsaa/article/view/1011.

[67]　Clare Baldwin and Andrew Marshall, "How a Secretive Police Squad Racked Up Kills in Duterte's Drug War," *Reuters*, December 19, 2017, www.reuters.com/investigates/special-report/philippines-drugs-squad/.

[68]　Robert Tyler Valiquette and Yvonne Su, "The Rise of Duterte and Bolsonaro: Creeping Authoritarianism and Criminal Populism," *New Mandala*, December 13, 2018, www.newman-dala.org/the-rise-of-duterte-and-bolsonaro-creeping-authoritarianism-and-criminal-populism/.

[69]　A full copy of the speech can be found at: "FULL TEXT: President Duterte's 2018 State of the Nation Address," *Rappler*, July 24, 2018, www.rappler.com/nation/207989-rodrigo-duterte-sona-2018-philippines-speech.

norm nor by the judgment of a disinterested and therefore neutral third party."[70] In this sense, oppositional politics is fundamentally arbitrary and situational and, in the case of penal populism, determined by the prerogative of the charismatic leader, who almost singlehandedly defines the parameters of conflict.

The late Russian philosopher Ivan Ilyin, the chief ideologue of Putin's modern populist authoritarianism, has described this prerogative as "patriotic arbitrariness."[71] Duterte, like Trump and other populist leaders, has repeatedly praised Putin as his inspiration, role model, and "favorite hero."[72] Indeed Duterte presents almost an identical binary/Manichean conception of politics, namely that between "law-abiding citizens" and "others," namely drug dealers and criminals. His rise to power was as improbable as his ability to defy Philippines' democracy with seemingly inexhaustible impunity. A latecomer to the presidential race in 2016, entering as a replacement candidate after having failed to register ahead of the deadline, he swiftly rose up the polls, outmaneuvering better-known and well-funded mainstream rivals, including star Senator Grace Poe, then Vice-President Jejomar Binay, and former President Benigno Aquino's anointed successor and then interior secretary, Manuel Roxas III.

At the heart of Duterte's campaign was the promise of decisive leadership, vowing to end criminality within his first year in office as well as bringing about more equitable development and decentralized democracy to the Filipino people, especially those in geographic and socioeconomic peripheries. Voters were drawn most to his perceived "political will" to transform the Philippines and save the republic from apocalyptic disorder, an issue that was most resonant among aspirational middle classes who felt insecure and neglected in an impoverished nation with relatively high crime rates and poor public services.[73]

More radically, Duterte's election marked a wholesale rejection of the three-decades-long liberal democratic regime, which supplanted the Ferdinand Marcos dictatorship following the "people power" revolts in 1986. He secured a landslide electoral victory *in spite* of his repeated threats to shut down the Philippine Congress, violate the Philippine constitution, and unleash a bloody crackdown on suspected criminals. Duterte correctly anticipated the increasing tolerance of the Filipino public for authoritarian rule and draconian measures against real and perceived societal challenges.[74]

---

[70] Carl Schmitt, *The Concept of the Political: Expanded Edition*, trans. George Schwab (Chicago: University of Chicago Press, 2008), 26–27.

[71] Snyder, *The Road to Unfreedom*.

[72] Nestor Corrales, "Duterte to Meet 'Favorite Hero' Putin in Singapore," *Inquirer.net*, November 12, 2018, https://globalnation.inquirer.net/170983/duterte-to-meet-favorite-hero-putin-in-singapore

[73] For further analysis, see: Ramon Casiple, "The Duterte Presidency as a Phenomenon," *Contemporary Southeast Asia* 38, no. 2 (2016): 179–184; Teehankee and Thompson, "Electing a Strongman"; Walden Bello, "Requiem for the EDSA Republic," *Interaksyon*, June 21, 2016, www.interaksyon.com/article/129284/op-ed–requiem-for-the-edsa-republic.

[74] Bello, "Requiem for the EDSA Republic."

In office, the Duterte administration adopted a Putin-style strategy aimed at intimidating and silencing his critics, filing tax evasion charges, and employing other politically motivated legal maneuvers against prominent liberal media outlets, including *Rappler* (the country's largest online news portal), the *Philippine Daily Inquirer* (the country's newspaper of record), and the ABS-CBN Corporation (the country's largest media conglomerate). In more extreme cases, Leila De Lima, a prominent senator and chief critic of the president, was placed in indefinite pre-trial detention on dubious charges of drug trafficking, sending a clear signal to other opposition statesmen who have dared to challenge Duterte's policies.

Within his first three months in office, the Filipino president built a formidable super-majority coalition in the Philippine Congress, which has increasingly morphed into a rubberstamp chamber. Exerting growing influence over the country's judiciary, where he has had the historic opportunity to directly appoint 12 out of 15 justices,[75] the Filipino president also managed to oust (via sympathetic and quiescent justices) former Philippine Chief Justice Maria Lourdes "Meilou" Aranal Sereno through a controversial, unprecedented, and legally questionable *quo warranto* case, which has been dismissed by leading experts as unconstitutional.

Duterte's rapid concentration of power is directly related to the unwillingness of the political elite to check his power, fight for democratic principles, and their eagerness to curry favor with the new popular chief executive. Much to his satisfaction, Duterte's war on drugs has enjoyed widespread popularity, with an average of eight out of ten Filipinos expressing favorable opinion throughout the first three years of his presidency.[76]

The upshot is an imperial presidency, which has consistently enjoyed the support of seven out of ten Filipinos in authoritative polls and faces limited institutional checks and balances. The Philippines has fallen into a dangerous dialectic, where relative public apathy towards democratic rollback combined with political opportunism of the political class continually reinforce each other to create the perfect conditions for democratic breakdown at the skillful hands of charismatic and strong-willed proto-authoritarian leaders like Duterte.[77]

C *International Context*

Almost overnight, democratic nations such as the Philippines have turned into a cutting-edge laboratory for twenty-first-century authoritarianism, with Duterte serving as an inspiration for his counterparts across the region. In fact, what we see today

---

[75] Federico Pascual Jr., "Duterte to Appoint 12 of SC Members," *Philstar Global*, December 29, 2016, www.philstar.com/opinion/2016/12/29/1657695/duterte-appoint-12-sc-members.

[76] Helen Flores, "78% of Pinoys Satisfied with Drug War – SWS," *Philstar Global*, September 24, 2018, www.philstar.com/headlines/2018/09/24/1854162/78-pinoys-satisfied-drug-war-sws.

[77] Richard Javad Heydarian, *The Rise of Duterte: A Populist Revolt against Elite Democracy* (London: Palgrave Macmillan, 2018).

is a more aggressive and brutal assertion of so-called Asian values, a largely discredited ideological narrative that was forwarded by prominent regional leaders in the twilight decades of the twentieth century.

In a disturbing turn of events, prosperous Southeast Asia is rapidly turning into a den of autocracy. The Asian values doctrine rests on three premises. First, that the principles of human rights and democracy are not universal, but instead purely Western constructs, which should not be imposed on Asian societies. Second, Asian societies prioritize communitarian values and deference to authority above individualism as well as independent thought and action. Lastly, state and society are indivisible components of a holistic unit, hence opposition to the state is tantamount to an assault on the larger society. The policy implication is that liberal democracy – and its emphasis on human rights and individual civil liberties – can act as an impediment to collective stability and national development, thus the supposed necessity for authoritarian leadership.[78]

During his first stint in office in the late twentieth century, Malaysian Prime Minister Mahathir openly rejected liberal democracy as an inherently dysfunctional system, which will "result in a stalemate, in no government at all, in anarchy." He has repeatedly warned of "too much democracy," since it "will not permit development to take place for the people to enjoy the benefits of freedom and the rights that democracy promises."[79] After returning to power in 2018, however, he has sung to a different tune, presenting himself as a harbinger of democratization. And yet, he has insisted, including in an interview with the author, that he has remained "consistent" in his views and policies throughout.[80]

In a similar vein, the late Singaporean Prime Minister Lee Kuan Yew asserted: "The exuberance of democracy leads to undisciplined and disorderly conditions," often citing the Philippines' freewheeling politics and anemic economy as a cautionary tale.[81] Both leaders, however, were accused of forwarding an amorphous and self-serving ideology to justify their repressive policies amid widespread international criticism. From Nobel-laureate economist Amartya Sen[82] to South Korean activist-turned-president Kim Dae Jung,[83] a whole host of prominent figures ably

---

[78] Fareed Zakaria, "A Conversation with Lee Kuan Yew," *Foreign Affairs*, March/April 1994, www.foreignaffairs.com/articles/asia/1994-03-01/conversation-lee-kuan-yew.

[79] Terrence Toh, "Dr M: Democracy Has Its Limits," *The Star*, June 12, 2012, www.thestar.com .my/news/nation/2012/06/12/dr-m-democracy-has-its-limits/.

[80] "REPLAY: FYI with Richard Heydarian: Interview with Malaysian Prime Minister Mahathir Bin Mohamad," YouTube video, 32:31, posted by "GMANews," March 8, 2019, www.youtube .com/watch?v=PSvBTKbpPRM.

[81] Francisco Tatad, "Remembering Lee Kuan Yew," *The Manila Times*, March 25, 2015, www .manilatimes.net/remembering-lee-kuan-yew/171731/.

[82] Amartya Sen, "Human Rights and Asian Values," *The New Republic* (1997), www.nyu.edu/ classes/gmoran/SEN.pdf.

[83] Kim Dae Jung, "Is Culture Destiny? The Myth of Asia's Anti-Democratic Values," *Foreign Affairs*, November/December 199, www.foreignaffairs.com/articles/southeast-asia/1994-11-01/cul ture-destiny-myth-asias-anti-democratic-values.

dismantled any claims to a supposedly monolithic "Asia" with a singular politico-ideological heritage.

The 1997 Asian Financial Crisis heavily undermined autocratic regimes in Southeast Asia, largely sapping the traction of outspoken authoritarian leaders such as Mahathir Mohammad and Lee Kuan Yew, who were the chief ideologues of the Asian values argument. Over the years, the economic success of democratic Indonesia, Thailand, and the Philippines, not to mention, South Korea and Taiwan, further undercut their arguments. But the rise of right-wing populists is once again resuscitating the long-forgotten debate.

In the recent past, Philippine President Duterte, arguably the most prominent leader in the region, has openly rejected human rights and democracy as alien/Western principles imposed through modern imperialism. Rather than engaging in sophisticated semantics, however, Duterte has cussed at his critics with uncompromising conviction and invective-laced language, including the leaders of Western powers such as the United States and the European Union, who have opposed his scorched-earth war on drugs.

As the chairman of the Association of Southeast Asian Nations (ASEAN) in 2017, Duterte expressly forwarded a regional policy agenda that emphasizes draconian anti-crime measures, marginalizes discussions of human rights and democracy, sanctifies national sovereignty and the principle of non-interference in the domestic affairs of Southeast Asia states, and promotes regional integration in a "distinctively ASEAN Way that will guide us."[84]

His defiant rhetoric has emboldened regional autocrats and rekindled undemocratic practices across the region. In dramatic reflection of a "Duterte effect" across the region, even Indonesian President Jokowi has adopted Duterte-style rhetoric of "narcotics emergency" and, thus, the need for a shoot-to-kill approach to drug suspects. In non-democratic Southeast Asia, an even more disturbing picture has emerged. From Cambodia to Vietnam and Thailand, autocratic regimes are aggressively sniffing opposition out of existence. In Myanmar, meanwhile, the junta has waged a campaign of extermination against the minority Muslim Rohingya group. All the democratic gains of the past decade are now under question.

Duterte is both a reflection and the harbinger of what Thomas Pepinsky characterizes as "voting against disorder" across Southeast Asia, where regional leaders are "promoting not law and order, but rather order over law, and seeking legitimation for this program at the ballot box" with increasing political success.[85] The success of penal populism in the region, argues Pepinsky, "reflects elite and middle-class frustrations with unstable and ineffective governance, combined with a

---

[84] Yen Makabenta, "Dopey Drug War Recalls Asian Values Debate," *The Manila Times*, May 13, 2017, www.manilatimes.net/dopey-drug-war-recalls-asian-values-debate/326982/.

[85] Thomas Pepinsky, "Southeast Asia: Voting Against Disorder," *Journal of Democracy* 28, no. 2 (2017): 120–131, www.journalofdemocracy.org/article/southeast-asia-voting-against-disorder.

historically rooted belief that political stability and material progress require the elimination of disorderly elements."[86]

The populist–authoritarian lurch across the region has been reinforced by the West's declining influence, and America's retreat from the democracy-promotion agenda under the Trump administration, as well as China's rising influence, including its provision of advanced surveillance technology and consistent diplomatic support to beleaguered regional autocrats and right-wing populists.

For instance, China has repeatedly defended Duterte's war on drugs in international fora, including the United Nations Human Rights Council,[87] while major Chinese companies are offering cutting-edge surveillance technology to Philippine authorities, which can be deployed against critics of the government[88]. The Trump administration's outright opposition to the very existence of the International Criminal Court (ICC), meanwhile, has only strengthened the hands of right-wing populists such as Duterte, who decided to withdraw the Philippines' membership from the international judicial body ostensibly in hopes of preventing any potential investigation of and prosecution over his human rights record.[89]

IV JUDICIAL AND BUREAUCRATIC REFORM

The grip of penal populism is anchored by a curious combination of unfounded perceptions and legitimate grievances. By all measures, Duterte's war on drugs lacks both an empirically grounded basis (policy justification) as well as proven efficacy (policy outcome). From a modern public policy standpoint, it is not only ineffective but also counter-productive.

Three years into office, murders rates are up, while there is no discernible decline in number of drug users as well as supply of illegal drugs. Not even a single "big fish" drug dealer has been convicted, while the vast majority of the victims of EJKs hail from the poorest communities in the country. If anything, the government has even failed to provide a definitive account of the number of drug users and changes in supply of illegal drugs. The president himself has arbitrarily changed the number of drug users, without providing any basis for it, and fired a senior official who dared to

---

[86] Pepinsky, "Voting Against Disorder," 121.

[87] Eimor Santos, "China Vows to Defend Duterte's War vs. Drugs, Terrorism in UN," *CNN Philippines*, last date modified October 29, 2018, http://cnnphilippines.com/news/2018/10/29/China-Duterte-drug-war-terrorism-United-Nations.html.

[88] Paolo Romero, "DILG, Chinese Firm to Install 20-Billion CCTV Network," *Philstar Global*, last date modified December 13, 2018, www.philstar.com/headlines/2018/12/13/1876639/dilg-chinese-firm-install-p20-billion-cctv-network.

[89] Lian Buan, "What the ICC Pullout Case Means for Duterte and the Supreme Court," *Rappler*, last date modified December 17, 2018, www.rappler.com/newsbreak/iq/210663-meaning-of-international-criminal-court-withdrawal-for-duterte-supreme-court.

provide contradictory, albeit more authoritative, numbers.[90] Above all, the Philippine government has yet to address the elephant in the room, namely the large-scale import of *Shabu* (crystal methamphetamine) from Mainland China, a country that has been particularly friendly with the Filipino president.[91] As Duterte himself admitted in an interview, "Others can't do it. How can we? [Those drugs], we can't control it."[92]

Throughout his presidential campaign, and early during his term in office, the Filipino leader repeatedly warned about the prospect of the Philippines turning into a Mexico-style narco-state, where retail-level drug kingpins run large portions of the society and systematically infiltrate core elements of the state apparatus, including security services and top elected offices. In fact, one of Duterte's favorite books is *El Narco* by British journalist Ioan Grillo, who has closely examined the rise of Joaquin Archivaldo "El Chapo" Guzmán Loera and the broader drug war in Mexico, which has claimed tens of thousands of lives over the past two decades.[93]

Comparing himself to Hitler, Duterte asserted that there are as many as four million drug users in the country, who should be killed lest they "contaminate another 10 million." But according to the Dangerous Drugs Board (DBB), a specialized agency under the Office of the President, the number of "users," which is liberally defined as anyone who has tried (rather than is chronically dependent on) any illegal drugs in recent history, is closer to 1.7 million. This means that drug prevalence in the Philippines, which hovers between 1.7 and 2.3 percent, ranks well below the global average of 5.2 percent. As United Nations Office on Drugs and Crime (UNODC) data shows, illicit opioid use in the Philippines (0.05 percent) pales in comparison to that in the US (5.41 percent) and Australia (3.30 percent); amphetamine use in the Philippines (2.35 percent) is at almost same level as in the US (2.2 percent), but significantly lower than in Australia (2.9 percent); and cocaine use in the Philippines (0.03 percent) is also relatively low, and of a different order of magnitude, when compared to such developed nations as the US (2.1 percent), Australia (2.1 percent), and the UK (2.4 percent).

Duterte's rhetoric on a crime epidemic in the country is also questionable. For instance, the Philippines registered a lower number (232,685) of crimes involving physical injury than the UK (375,000). Reported cases of rape in the Philippines

---

[90] Jonathan de Santos, "Duterte Fires Drugs Board Chair for 'Contradicting Government,'" *Philippine Star*, May 24, 2017, www.philstar.com/headlines/2017/05/24/1703250/duterte-fires-drugs-board-chair-contradicting-government

[91] John Chalmers, "Meth Gangs of China Play Star Role in Philippines Drug Crisis," *Reuters*, December 16, 2016, www.reuters.com/investigates/special-report/philippines-drugs-china/.

[92] "Duterte: We Can't Control Drug Problem," CNN *Philippines*, August 12, 2017, http://cnnphilippines.com/news/2017/08/12/Duterte-war-on-drugs-cant-control-drug-problem.html.

[93] Ioan Grillo, *El Narco: Inside Mexico's Criminal Insurgency* (New York: Bloomsbury Press, 2011) and *Gangster Warlords: Drug Dollars, Killing Fields, and the New Politics of Latin America* (New York: Bloomsbury Press, 2019).

(10,294) were also lower than in France (12,157) and the UK (30,000). The reported number of robberies (52,798) in the Philippines mirrored Latin America's most peaceful country, Costa Rica, which only has a population of 4.7 million people, less than half of the population of Metro Manila. One area of concern, however, is homicide rates, where the Philippines (9 per 100,000) is on par with Russia and higher than in the US. Yet, widespread EJKs under Duterte have only exacerbated this problem, showing the counterproductive nature of his anti-crime policy. Above all, there is also no conclusive evidence to suggest that transnationally active drug kingpins have infiltrated the Philippine state apparatus as has been the case of Mexico and Columbia in past decades.[94]

Obviously, there are concerns over the possibility of under-reporting of crimes in conservative societies like the Philippines, where cultural subtlety is highly prized (especially in cases involving rape and the stigma that comes with reporting it to authorities), vigilante justice is common, trust in law enforcers is low, and the culture of litigation is nascent. Yet there is no evidence to suggest that the Philippines is facing a crime epidemic on the scale that Duterte and his supporters claim.

The gap between perception and reality is also reflected in longitudinal surveys by the Social Weather Stations (SWS), a leading polling agency in the Philippines. Between 1986 and 2016, beginning with the reformist-liberal administration of Cory Aquino and ending with her son's (Benigno) term, reported rates of victimization by Filipino families saw a dramatic downward swing from a high of 38 percent to a low of 6 percent, settling at 11 percent just before Duterte took office. Yet, between 2006 and 2016, the rate of *fear* of victimization surged from 37 percent to more than 60 percent. The period also saw a greater number of respondents expressing concern over the "presence" of drug users and proliferation of illegal drugs in their communities. In mid-2016, more than half of the respondents (52 percent) in a Pulse Asia survey identified clamping down on crime and drugs as one of their most urgent policy concerns.[95]

One potential culprit for this dramatic increase in collective sense of insecurity is the sensationalist Philippine media, which has increasingly bombarded its audience with gruesome news of murder, rape, and drug use in its prime-time reportage and headlines. Paradoxically, Duterte's penal populism was enabled and strengthened by the very institution (media) that he has vilified as the enemy of the people. A sustained period of economic growth has also created an increasingly wealthy

---

[94] For further analysis, see Camille Diola, "Duterte Hikes Drug Use Figure Anew Despite Little Evidence," *Inquirer.net*, last date modified September 23, 2016, www.philstar.com/headlines/2016/09/23/1626648/duterte-hikes-philippines-drug-use-figure-anew-despite-little-evidence; Iyengar, "The Killing Time."

[95] Patricia Lourdes Viray, "Pulse: Fewer Filipinos See Crime as Major National Concern," *Philippine Star*, October 17, 2017, www.philstar.com/headlines/2016/10/17/1634321/pulse-fewer-filipinos-see-crime-major-national-concern.

middle class that has become ever more worried about the safety of its property and life.

It is no wonder, then, that it is the middle classes who have consistently identified fighting crime as one of their top priorities, while poorer classes have been primarily concerned with inflation and unemployment.[96] It is precisely this milieu of impending social panic that offered Duterte the opportunity to rally public support through a law and order campaign, where illegal drugs are supposedly the source of all social maladies.[97]

A *The Real Law and Order Crisis*

Public concern over law and order, however, has not been completely baseless. If anything, Duterte correctly identified pervasive social anxieties over lack of functioning judicial institutions in the country. His chief failure, however, was mistaking the symptom for the cause. The prevalence of illegal drugs and high rights of murder are only reflections of a more fundamental problem in the Philippine political system.

The country's real law and order problem lies in the lack of investment in the capacity of the country's penal system and judiciary to safeguard basic civil liberties and protect human rights. The upshot is declining public confidence in the justice system, and the consequent rise of Duterte-style penal populism, where vigilante killings and violation of due process have become ubiquitous amid widespread public apathy.

Duterte's war on drugs is popular, mainly because there is little public confidence in standard, constitutionally prescribed procedures. In fairness, the Duterte administration decided to increase both the budget of law enforcement agencies (24.6 percent) and the judiciary (21.5 percent) in his first year in office. Yet, the judiciary's share of total national budget in 2017 stood at less than 1 percent. In the Philippines, there is only one court per 50,000 individuals, with lower courts overwhelmed by an average of 4000 cases daily. A single judge in the Philippines is responsible for an average of 644 cases annually. This largely explains the dysfunctional judicial system in the Philippines, which has been

---

[96] See Pulse Asia's "most urgent concerns" surveys, www.pulseasia.ph/march-2018-nationwide-survey-on-urgent-national-concerns-and-national-administration-performance-ratings-on-selected-issues/.

[97] For further analysis, see: Mahar Mangahas, "Survey of Public Safety," *Inquirer.net*, last date modified August 20, 2016, http://opinion.inquirer.net/96633/surveys-of-public-safety; Peter Shadbolt, "Philippines Raid Reveals Mexican Drug Cartel Presence in Asia," *CNN.com*, last date modified February 25, 2014, http://edition.cnn.com/2014/02/24/world/asia/philippines-mexico-sinaloa-cartel/; Pia Ranada, "A Look at the State of Crime, Drugs in the Philippines," *Rappler.com*, last date modified January 5, 2016, www.rappler.com/nation/118004-crime-drugs-philippines; Pia Ranada, "Is Duterte's '4 Million Drug Addicts' a 'Real Number'?," *Rappler.com*, last date modified May 8, 2017, www.rappler.com/rappler-blogs/169009-duterte-drug-addicts-real-number.

hobbled by delay, corruption, and widespread public distrust. The Philippines' penitentiary system is even more overburdened. On average, prisons struggle with an overcapacity rate of 380 percent, with some major facilities reaching an overcapacity rate of up to 2000 percent. With pre-trial detainees constituting at least 64 percent of the prison population, the Philippines has the second worst rate of pre-trial incarceration in the whole of Asia.[98]

In fact, the Philippines has the world's most crowded incarceration system, according to the World Prison Brief's list.[99] In the Manila City Jail, one of the largest in the country, there was only a single correctional officer for every 528 inmates, far lower that the government's recommended ratio of one officer for every seven inmates. The result is the emergence of intra-jail gangs, who effectively take over basic operations, including security and provision of food, within the jail system. In one recent raid, jail administrators found a single gang in possession of as much as \$13,700, which is often used for purchase of food and other basic necessities of inmates. Another major concern is the number of minors, with many pre-trial detainees who should been placed in specialized facilities for juvenile delinquents finding themselves in overcrowded jails, where they are often subject to torture, rape, and other forms of violence.[100]

The policy implication is clear: The Philippines will need to invest in the capacity of its overburdened and malfunctioning judicial institutions if it seeks to restore public confidence in its democratic constitution and, accordingly, push back against Duterte's penal populism.

The problem, however, is that Duterte's authoritarian lurch and frontal assault on democratic institutions will likely further erode the independence, self-confidence, and credibility of the country's judicial institutions, which have grappled with limited budgets, lack of political support from civil society and the ruling class, and executive encroachments.

As surveys show, a large majority of Filipinos have expressed their preference for drug suspects to be kept alive, while fearing the prospect of ending up as victims of EJK themselves (GMA 2016).[101] What they seek is not the negation of human rights, but instead renewed confidence in the country's besieged judicial institutions.

---

[98] Agree Abadines, "Philippine Judiciary and Criminal Justice System under Pressure: An Inside Look," *ASEANtoday.com*, last date modified February 6, 2017, www.aseantoday.com/2017/02/.

[99] "Highest to Lowest: Occupancy Level (Based on Official Capacity)," *World Prison Brief*, www .prisonstudies.org/highest-to-lowest/occupancy-level?field_region_taxonomy_tid=All.

[100] Aurora Almendral, "Where 518 Inmates Sleep in Space for 170, and Gangs Hold It Together," *The New York Times*, January 7, 2019, www.nytimes.com/2019/01/07/world/asia/philippines-manila-jail-overcrowding.html.

[101] "Eight out of 10 Pinoys Worry about Extrajudicial Killings – SWS Survey," *GMA News*, last date modified December 19, 2016, www.gmanetwork.com/news/news/nation/592936/eight-out-of-10-pinoys-worry-about-extrajudicial-killings-sws-survey/story/.

BIBLIOGRAPHY

"Comparing Crony Capitalism Around the World." *The Economist*, May 5, 2016. www .economist.com/graphic-detail/2016/05/05/comparing-crony-capitalism-around-the-world.

"Donald Trump Is Undermining the Rules-based International Order." *The Economist*, June 7, 2018. www.economist.com/briefing/2018/06/07/donald-trump-is-undermining-the-rules-based-international-order.

"Duterte: We Can't Control Drug Problem." *CNN Philippines*, August 12, 2017. http://cnn philippines.com/news/2017/08/12/Duterte-war-on-drugs-cant-control-drug-problem.html.

"Eight out of 10 Pinoys Worry about Extrajudicial Killings – SWS Survey." *GMA News*. Last date modified December 19, 2016. www.gmanetwork.com/news/news/nation/592936/ eight-out-of-10-pinoys-worry-about-extrajudicial-killings-sws-survey/story/.

"FULL TEXT: President Duterte's 2018 State of the Nation Address." *Rappler*, July 24, 2018. www.rappler.com/nation/207989-rodrigo-duterte-sona-2018-philippines-speech.

"'Ghost Fleet' Fiasco: Prabowo Defends Sci-fi Novel as 'Scenario Writing', Author, Politicians & Netizens React." *Coconut Jakarta*, March 23, 2018. https://coconuts.co/jakarta/news/ghost-fleet-fiasco-prabowo-defends-sci-fi-novel-scenario-writing-says-ok-people-dont-believe/.

"Highest to Lowest: Occupancy Level (Based on Official Capacity)." *World Prison Brief*. www .prisonstudies.org/highest-to-lowest/occupancy-evel?field_region_taxonomy_tid=All.

"Jokowi Issues Order to Shoot Drug Traffickers." *The Star*, July 22, 2017. www.thestar.com .my/news/regional/2017/07/22/jokowi-issues-order-to-shoot-drug-traffickers/.

"'License to Kill' Philippine Police Killings in Duterte's War on Drugs." *Human Rights Watch.org*, March 3, 2017. www.hrw.org/report/2017/03/01/license-kill/philippine-police-killings-dutertes-war-drugs.

Abadines, Argee. "Philippine Judiciary and Criminal Justice System Under Pressure: An Inside Look." ASEANtoday.com. Last date modified February 6, 2017. www.aseantoday .com/2017/02/.

Almendral, Aurora. "Where 518 Inmates Sleep in Space for 170, and Gangs Hold It Together." *The New York Times*, January 7, 2019. www.nytimes.com/2019/01/07/world/ asia/philippines-manila-jail-overcrowding.html.

Anderson, Perry. "The Heirs of Gramsci." *New Left Review* 100 (July–August 2016). newleftre view.org/II/100/perry-anderson-the-heirs-of-gramsci.

——. "The Italian Disaster." *London Review of Books* 36, no. 10 (2014): 3–16. www.lrb.co.uk/v36/ n10/perry-anderson/the-italian-disaster.

Baldwin, Clare, and Andrew Marshall. "How a Secretive Police Squad Racked Up Kills in Duterte's Drug War." *Reuters*, December 19, 2017. www.reuters.com/investigates/special-report/philippines-drugs-squad/.

Bello, Walden. "Requiem for the EDSA Republic." *Interaksyon*, June 21, 2016. www.inter aksyon.com/article/129284/op-ed-requiem-for-the-edsa-republic.

Berehulak, Daniel. "They Are Slaughtering Us Like Animals." *The New York Times*, December 7, 2016. www.nytimes.com/interactive/2016/12/07/world/asia/rodrigo-duterte-philippines-drugs-killings.html.

Bremmer, Ian. "The 'Strongmen Era' Is Here. Here's What It Means for You." *Time Magazine*, May 3, 2018. https://time.com/5264170/the-strongmen-era-is-here-heres-what-it-means-for-you/.

Buan, Lian. "What the ICC Pullout Case Means for Duterte and the Supreme Court." *Rappler*. last date modified December 17, 2018. www.rappler.com/newsbreak/iq/210663-meaning-of-international-criminal-court-withdrawal-for-duterte-supreme-court.

Cagaptay, Soner. *The New Sultan: Erdogan and the Crisis of Modern Turkey.* London: I.B. Tauris., 2017.

Carothers, Thomas. "The End of the Transition Paradigm." *Journal of Democracy* 13, no. 1 (2002): 5–21. http://journalofdemocracy.org/article/endtransition-paradigm.

Casiple, Ramon. "The Duterte Presidency as a Phenomenon." *Contemporary Southeast Asia* 38, no. 2 (2016): 179–184.

Chalmers, John. "Meth Gangs of China Play Star Role in Philippines Drug Crisis," *Reuters,* December 16, 2016. www.reuters.com/investigates/special-report/philippines-drugs-china/.

Chang, Ha-Joon. *Kicking Away the Ladder: Development Strategy in Historical Perspective.* London: Anthem Press, 2002.

Chehabi, Houchang, and Juan Linz (eds.). *Sultanistic Regimes.* Baltimore, MD: Johns Hopkins University Press, 1998.

Chellaney, Bhrama. "China's Creditor Imperialism." *Project Syndicat,* December 2017. www.project-syndicate.org/commentary/china-sri-lanka-hambantota-port-debt-by-brahma-chellaney-2017-12.

Churchwell, Sarah. *Behold America: The Entangled History of "America First" and "the American Dream."* New York: Basic Books, 2018.

Corrales, Nestor. "Duterte to Meet 'Favorite Hero' Putin in Singapore." *Inquirer.net,* November 12, 2018. https://globalnation.inquirer.net/170983/duterte-to-meet-favorite-hero-putin-in-singapore.

Curato, Nicole. "Politics of Anxiety, Politics of Hope: Penal Populism and Duterte's Rise to Power." *Journal of Current Southeast Asian Affairs* 35, no. 3 (2016). https://journals.sub.uni-hamburg.de/giga/jsaa/article/view/1011.

Daalder, Ivo, and James Lindsay. "The Committee to Save the World Order." *Foreign Affairs,* November/December 2018. www.foreignaffairs.com/articles/2018-09-30/committee-save-world-order.

Dahl, Robert. *Polyarchy: Participation and Opposition.* New Haven, CT: Yale University Press, 1972.

De Santos, Jonathan. "Duterte Fires Drugs Board Chair for 'Contradicting Government.'" *Philippine Star,* May 24, 2017. www.philstar.com/headlines/2017/05/24/1703250/duterte-fires-drugs-board-chair-contradicting-government.

Diamond, Larry. "Democracy after Trump: Can a Populist Stop Democratic Decline?" *Foreign Affairs* (2016). www.foreignaffairs.com/articles/world/2016-11-14/democracy-after-trump.

Developing Democracy: Toward Consolidation. Baltimore, MD: Johns Hopkins University Press, 1999.

Diola, Camille. "Duterte Hikes Drug Use Figure Anew Despite Little Evidence." *Inquirer.net.* Last date modified September 23, 2016. www.philstar.com/headlines/2016/09/23/1626648/duterte-hikes-philippines-drug-use-figure-anew-despite-little-evidence.

Dobrynina, Margarita. "'The Roots of Penal Populism': The Role of Media and Politics." *Criminological Studies* 4 (2017): 98–124. DOI: 10.15388/CrimLithuan.2016.4.10729.

Ferguson, Niall. "Populism as a Backlash against Globalization – Historical Perspectives." *Horizons* 8 (2016). www.cirsd.org/en/horizons/horizons-autumn-2016–issue-no-8/populism-as-a-backlash-against-globalization.

Flores, Helen. "78% of Pinoys Satisfied with Drug War – SWS." *Philstar Global,* September 24, 2018. www.philstar.com/headlines/2018/09/24/1854162/78-pinoys-satisfied-drug-war-sws.

Foa, Roberto Stefan, and Yascha Mounk. "The Signs of Deconsolidation." *Journal of Democracy* 28, no. 1 (2017): 5–16. DOI: 10.1353/jod.2017.0000.

Fukuyama, Francis. "The End of History?" *The National Interest* 16 (1989): 3–18. www.jstor
.org/stable/24027184.
*Political Order and Political Decay: From the Industrial Revolution to the Globalization of
Democracy.* New York: Farrar, Straus & Giroux, 2014.
Gallagher, Kevin. *Putting Development First: The Importance of Policy Space in the WTO and
IFIs.* London: Zed Books, 2005.
Gessen, Masha. *The Man Without a Face: The Unlikely Rise of Vladimir Putin.* New York:
Riverhead, 2012.
Gidron, Noah, and Bart Bonikowski. "Varieties of Populism: Literature Review and Research
Agenda." *Weatherhead Center for International Affairs* no. 13-0004 (2013). https://scholar
.harvard.edu/files/gidron_bonikowski_populismlitreview_2013.pdf.
Glosserman, Brad, and Denny Roy. "Asia's Next China Worry: Xi Jinping's Growing Power."
The National Interest, July 23, 2014. https://nationalinterest.org/blog/the-buzz/asias-next-
china-worry-xi-jinpings-growing-power-10939.
Gramsci, Antonio. *Selections from the Prison Notebooks.* Edited by Quintin Hoare and
Geoffrey Nowell Smith. London: Lawrence & Wishart, 1971.
Grillo, Ioan. *El Narco: Inside Mexico's Criminal Insurgency* (New York: Bloomsbury Press,
2011)
Gangster Warlords: Drug Dollars, Killing Fields, and the New Politics of Latin America.
New York: Bloomsbury Press, 2019.
Gurcan, Metin. "Turkish Military Purges Decimate Career Officer, Pilot Ranks." *Al-Monitor,*
May 29, 2018. www.almonitor.com/pulse/originals/2018/05/turkey-military-purges-career-
officer-pilot.html.
Hartog, Eva, and Lev Gudkov. "The Evolution of Homo Sovieticus to Putin's Man." *The
Moscow Times,* October 13, 2017. themoscowtimes.com/articles/the-evolution-of-homo-
sovieticus-to-putins-man-59189.
Heydarian, Richard Javad. *The Rise of Duterte: A Populist Revolt against Elite Democracy.*
London: Palgrave Macmillan, 2018.
Huang, Zheping. "Xi Jinping Says China's Authoritarian System Can Be a Model for the
World." *Quartz,* March 2018. https://qz.com/1225347/xi-jinping-says-chinas-one-party-
authoritarian-system-can-be-a-model-for-the-world/.
Huntington, Samuel. *Political Order in Changing Societies.* London: Yale University Press,
1968.
"Democracy's Third Wave." *Journal of Democracy* 2, no. 2 (1991): 12–34. DOI: 10.1353/
jod.1991.0016.
Ibrahim, Zuraidah, and John Power. "Middle Class and Frustrated in Asia? Populist Politicians are Seeking You Out in 2019." *South China Morning Post,* January 5, 2019. www
.scmp.com/week-asia/politics/article/2180786/poll-dance-how-asias-politicians-are-mobilis
ing-voting-masses.
Iyengar, Rishi. "The Killing Time: Inside Philippine President Rodrigo Duterte's War on
Drugs." *TIME.com.* Last date modified August 25, 2016. http://time.com/4462352/rodrigo-
duterte-drug-war-drugs-philippines-killing/.
Johnson, David, and Jon Fernquest. "Governing through Killing: The War on Drugs in the
Philippines." *Asian Journal of Law and Society* 5, no. 2 (2018). www.cambridge.org/core/
journals/asian-journal-of-law-and-society/article/governing-through-killing-the-war-on-
drugs-in-the-philippines.
Keenan, Jillian. "The Grim Reality Behind the Philippines' Economic Growth." *The Atlantic,* May 7, 2013. www.theatlantic.com/international/archive/2013/05/the-grim-reality-
behind-the-philippines-economic-growth/275597/.

Kim, Dae Jung. "Is Culture Destiny? The Myth of Asia's Anti-Democratic Values." *Foreign Affairs*, November/December 1994. www.foreignaffairs.com/articles/southeast-asia/1994-11-01/culture-destiny-myth-asias-anti-democratic-values.

Kimmage, Michael. "The People's Authoritarian." *Foreign Affairs*, July/August 2018. www.foreignaffairs.com/reviews/review-essay/2018-06-14/peoples-authoritarian.

Laclau, Ernesto. *On Populist Reason*. London: Verso, 2005.

Liljas, Per. "Here's Why Some Indonesians Are Spooked by this Presidential Contender." *Time*, June 12, 2014. http://time.com/2836510/prabowo-subianto-human-rights-indonesia-elections.

Lipset, Seymour Martin. "Some Social Requisites of Democracy: Economic Development and Political Legitimacy." *The American Political Science Review* 53, no. 1 (1959): 69–105. www.jstor.org/stable/1951731.

Luttwak, Edward. *Endangered American Dream*. New York: Simon & Schuster, 1994.

Makabenta, Yen. "Dopey Drug War Recalls Asian Values Debate." *The Manila Times*, May 13, 2017. www.manilatimes.net/dopey-drug-war-recalls-asian-values-debate/326982/.

Malonzo, Anne-Peralta. "Dela Rosa Receives Highest Indonesian Government Award." *SunStar*, February 14, 2018. www.sunstar.com.ph/article/418944.

Mangahas, Mahar. "Survey of Public Safety." *Inquirer.net*. Last date modified August 20, 2016. http://opinion.inquirer.net/96633/surveys-of-public-safety.

Mann, Michael. *Fascists*. Cambridge: Cambridge University Press, 2004.

Marino, Andi. *Narenda Modi: A Political Biography*. New York: HarperCollins, 2014.

Marszal, Andrew. "Arundhati Roy Caught in the Crossfire of Indian Judicial Power Struggle." *The Telegraph*, February 6, 2016. www.telegraph.co.uk/news/worldnews/asia/india/12144154/Arundhati-Roy-caught-in-the-crossfire-of-Indian-judicial-power-struggle.html.

Mead, Walter Russell. "The Jacksonian Revolt: American Populism and the Liberal Order." *Foreign Affairs* (2017). www.foreignaffairs.com/articles/united-states/2017-01-20/jacksonian-Revolt.

Miller, Manjari. "India's Authoritarian Streak." *Foreign Affairs*, May 30, 2018. www.foreignaffairs.com/articles/india/2018-05-30/indias-authoritarian-streak.

Mishra, Pankaj. "Indonesia's New Economic Model." *Bloomberg*, November 5, 2012. www.bloomberg.com/opinion/articles/2012-11-04/indonesia-s-new-economic-model.

Moffitt, Benjamin. *The Global Rise of Populism: Performance, Style and Representation*. Stanford, CA: Stanford University Press, 2016.

Mouffe, Chantal. *For a Left Populism*. London: Verso, 2018.

Mudde, Cas. "The Problem with Populism." *The Guardian*, February 2015. www.theguardian.com/commentisfree/2015/feb/17/problem-populism-syriza-podemos-dark-side-europe.

Müller, Jan-Werner. *What Is Populism?* Philadelphia, PA: University of Pennsylvania Press, 2016.

Paddock, Richard. "Indonesian General Accused of Kidnapping Is Named Defense Minister." *The New York Times*, October 23, 2019. https://www.nytimes.com/2019/10/23/world/asia/indonesia-prabowo-joko-widodo.html.

Pamuntjak, Laskmi. "Jokowi, We Voted for a Humble Man. Now You've Taught a New Generation about Killing." *The Guardian*, May 5, 2015. www.theguardian.com/commentisfree/2015/may/05/jokowi-we-voted-for-a-humble-man-now-youve-taught-a-new-generation-about-killing.

Pascual Jr., Federico, "Duterte to Appoint 12 of SC Members." *Philstar Global*, December 29, 2016. www.philstar.com/opinion/2016/12/29/1657695/duterte-appoint-12-sc-members.

Pepinsky, Thomas. "Southeast Asia: Voting Against Disorder." *Journal of Democracy* 28, no. 2 (2017): 120–131. www.journalofdemocracy.org/article/southeast-asia-voting-against-disorder.

Pew Research Center, "Globally, Broad Support for Representative and Direct Democracy" (October 2017). www.pewresearch.org/global/2017/10/16/globally-broad-support-for-repre sentative-and-direct-democracy/.

Pikkety, Thomas. *Capital in the Twenty First Century*. Cambridge, MA: Harvard University Press, 2014.

Putnam, Robert, Robert Leonardi, and Rafaella Nanneti. *Making Democracy Work: Civic Traditions in Modern Italy*. Princeton, NJ: Princeton University Press, 1993.

Ranada, Pia. "A Look at the State of Crime, Drugs in the Philippines." *Rappler.com*. Last modified January 5, 2016. www.rappler.com/nation/118004-crime-drugs-philippines.

"Is Duterte's '4 Million Drug Addicts' a 'Real Number'?" *Rappler.com*. Last date modified May 8, 2017. www.rappler.com/rappler-blogs/169009-duterte-drug-addicts-real-number.

Reich, Robert. "How Capitalism Is Killing Democracy." *Foreign Policy* (2009). http://foreign policy.com/2009/10/12/how-capitalism-is-killing-democracy/.

Rieffel, Lex. "Lessons for Myanmar in Indonesian Politics." *East Asia Forum*, November 22, 2016. www.eastasiaforum.org/2016/11/22/lessons-for-myanmar-in-indonesian-politics/.

Rodrik, Dani. *One Economics, Many Recipes: Globalization, Institutions, and Economic Growth*. Princeton, NJ: Princeton University Press, 2009.

"The Manufacturing Imperative." *Project Syndicate*, August 20, 2011. www.project-syndi cate.org/commentary/the-manufacturing-imperative/.

Romero, Paolo. "DILG, Chinese Firm to Install 20-Billion CCTV Network." *Philstar Global*. Last date modified December 13, 2018. www.philstar.com/headlines/2018/12/13/1876639/dilg-chinese-firm-install-p20-billion-cctv-network.

Runciman, David. *How Democracy Ends*. New York: Basic Books, 2018.

Sadongdong, Martin. "PNP Insists No Policy to Kill Drug Suspects." *Manila Bulletin*, June 24, 2018. news.mb.com.ph/2018/06/24/pnp-insists-no-policy-to-kill-drug-suspects/.

Santos, Eimor. "China Vows to Defend Duterte's War vs. Drugs, Terrorism in UN." *CNN Philippines*. Last date modified October 29, 2018. http://cnnphilippines.com/news/2018/10/29/China-Duterte-drug-war-terrorism-United-Nations.html.

Schmitt, Carl. *The Concept of the Political: Expanded Edition*. Translated by George Schwab. Chicago: University of Chicago Press, 2008.

Sen, Amartya. "Human Rights and Asian Values." *The New Republic* (1997). www.nyu.edu/classes/gmoran/SEN.pdf.

Shadbolt, Peter. "Philippines Raid Reveals Mexican Drug Cartel Presence in Asia." *CNN.com*. Last date modified February 25, 2014. http://edition.cnn.com/2014/02/24/world/asia/philippines-mexico-sinaloa-cartel/.

Sharma, Ruchir. *Breakout Nations: In Pursuit of the Next Economic Miracles*. New York: W.W. Norton, 2013.

Shirk, Susan. "The Return to Personalistic Rule." *Journal of Democracy* 29, no. 2 (2018). www.journalofdemocracy.org/sites/default/files/media/29.2–Shirk–AdvanceVersion.pdf.

Snyder, Timothy. *The Road to Unfreedom: Russia, Europe, America*. New York: Tim Duggan Books, 2018.

Studwell, Joe. *How Asia Works: Success and Failure in the World's Most Dynamic Region*. New York: Grove Press, 2014.

Tatad, Francisco. "Remembering Lee Kuan Yew." *The Manila Times*, March 25, 2015. www.manilatimes.net/remembering-lee-kuan-yew/171731/.

"Is It the Dead End?" *The Manila Times*, September 29, 2017. www.manilatimes.net/is-it-the-dead-end/353529/.

Taylor, Andrea, and Erica Frantz. "How Democracies Fall Apart: Why Populism Is a Pathway to Autocracy." *Foreign Affairs* (2016). www.foreignaffairs.com/articles/2016-12-05/how-democracies-fall-apart.

Teehankee, Julio, and Mark Thompson. "The Vote in the Philippines: Electing A Strongman." *Journal of Democracy* 27, no. 4 (2016): 124–134. www.journalofdemoc racy.org/article/vote-philippines-electing-strongman.

Toh, Terrence. "Dr M: Democracy Has Its Limits." *The Star*, June 12, 2012. www.thestar.com .my/news/nation/2012/06/12/dr-m-democracy-has-its-limits/.

Tucker, Robert. "The Theory of Charismatic Leadership." *Daedalus* 97, no. 3 (1968): 731–756. www.jstor.org/stable/20023840.

Valiquette, Robert Tyler, and Yvonne Su. "The Rise of Duterte and Bolsonaro: Creeping Authoritarianism and Criminal Populism." *New Mandala*, December 13, 2018. www .newmandala.org/the-rise-of-duterte-and-bolsonaro-creeping-authoritarianism-and-criminal-populism/.

Viray, Patricia Lourdes. "Pulse: Fewer Filipinos See Crime as Major National Concern," *Philippine Star*, October 17, 2017. www.philstar.com/headlines/2016/10/17/1634321/pulse-fewer-filipinos-see-crime-major-national-concern.

Walker, Christopher, Shanthi Kalathil, and Jessica Ludwig. "How Democracies Can Fight Authoritarian Sharp Power." *Foreign Affairs*, August 2018. www.foreignaffairs.com/art icles/china/2018-08-16/how-democracies-can-fight-authoritarian-sharp-power.

Woodward, Bob. *Fear: Trump in the White House*. New York: Simon & Schuster, 2019.

Zakaria, Fareed. "A Conversation with Lee Kwan Yew." *Foreign Affairs*, 1994. www.foreign affairs.com/articles/asia/1994-03-01/conversation-lee-kuan-yew.

"The Rise of Illiberal Democracy." *Foreign Affairs*, 1997. www.foreignaffairs.com/articles/ 1997-11-01/rise-illiberal-democracy.

"America's Democracy Has Become Illiberal." *The Washington Post*. Last modified December 29, 2016. www.washingtonpost.com/opinions/america-is-becoming-a-land-of-less-liberty

8

The Populist Threat to Democracy in Myanmar

Yee Mon Htun

I INTRODUCTION

Discussions about populism in Southeast Asia often include the Philippines and Duterte's brutal war on drugs or Thailand's former Prime Minister Thaksin Shinawatra and his supporters in the *Pheu Thai* party's bid to return to power in the 2019 general elections. And despite global attention and condemnation surrounding the catastrophic Rohingya crisis, the populist social movement in my country of birth, Myanmar, and its role in bringing about the aforementioned crisis is under-examined. In fact, monks affiliated with the 969 movement ("969") like U Wirathu and *MaBaTha* (the Association for the Protection of Race and Religion) in Myanmar are rarely mentioned in the same vein as other Southeast Asian populist actors. International reporting has often mischaracterized them as a Buddhist nationalist movement, and that the country, opening up from more than five decades of oppressive, isolated military rule, has somehow unleashed simmering resentment between Myanmar's Buddhist majority and ethnic Muslim minorities. While 969 and *MaBaTha* have used Buddhism as a ploy, I argue, using Cas Mudde's ideational approach, that they are in fact populists working in conjunction with the Myanmar military, known as the *Tamadaw*, to stoke fear and incite violence for political gain.[1]

As of September 2018, more than 725,000 Rohingya refugees have been forced to flee to Bangladesh after the *Tamadaw* launched a "clearance operation" in 2017, destroying hundreds of Rohingya villages in northern Rakhine state. The military claims it is pursuing the Arakan Rohingya Salvation Army ("ARSA") and terrorist elements, after a coordinated attack on thirty border police outposts left twelve

---

[1] Cas Mudde, "Populism: An Ideational Approach," in *The Oxford Handbook on Populism*, ed. Cristóbal Rovira Kaltwasser, Paul Taggart, Paulina Ochoa Espejo, and Pierre Ostiguy (Oxford: Oxford University Press, 2017), 27–47.

dead.[2] Harrowing accounts from Rohingya survivors tell another story. They reveal a brutal military operation identical to the other *Tamadaw* campaigns waged over the decades against civilians in other ethnic regions, with indiscriminate targeting and killing of civilians, widespread use of sexual violence, dehumanizing, racist rhetoric, and complete impunity for its actions.

The UN Independent International Fact-Finding Mission on Myanmar ("FFM") was established in response to the Rohingya crisis and ongoing armed conflict in Kachin and Shan states.[3] The FFM presented its findings in August 2018, recommending that senior generals in the *Tamadaw* be investigated and prosecuted for genocide, crimes against humanity, and war crimes.[4] At the time of writing, the Office of the Prosecutor at the International Criminal Court ("ICC") has opened a preliminary examination into the alleged deportation of the Rohingyas from Myanmar to Bangladesh.[5] These developments towards accountability for the *Tamadaw*'s atrocities should have been welcome news in a country that has languished under a repressive military rule and long struggled for democracy and human rights.

Instead, the reaction from inside Myanmar is one of denial and rejection. The civilian government, including its de facto leader, State Counsellor Aung San Suu Kyi, refuse to condemn the *Tamadaw*. The UN and international human rights system that had once been held in positive regard by the general public has been deemed "biased," and seeking to interfere and encroach upon Myanmar's sovereignty.[6] Most shocking of all is that the populist social movement has successfully used the Rohingya crisis to galvanize support domestically for the *Tamadaw*, despite it being one of the most reviled institutions in Myanmar.

This chapter examines the Rohingya crisis and how Myanmar's promising transition to democracy has so far been disrupted by 969, *MaBaTha*, and the *Tamadaw*. It begins with some background on Myanmar – a historical discussion around Myanmar identity and "belonging" – to provide context as to why the populist social movement's narrative is at present resonating with the Buddhist Burman majority in

[2] Wa Lone and Shoon Naing, "At Least 71 Killed in Myanmar as Rohingya Insurgents Stage Major Attack," *Reuters*, August 24, 2017, www.reuters.com/article/us-myanmar-rohingya/at-least-71-killed-in-myanmar-as-rohingya-insurgents-stage-major-attack-idUSKCN1B507K.

[3] Human Rights Council resolution 34/22, "Situation of Human Rights in Myanmar," A/HRC/RES/34/22, available from undocs.org A/HRC/RES/34/22.

[4] "Myanmar: Tatmadaw Leaders Must be Investigated for Genocide, Crimes against Humanity and War Crimes," Office of the United Nations High Commissioner for Human Rights, www.ohchr.org/EN/HRBodies/HRC/Pages/NewsDetail.aspx?NewsID=23475&LangID=E (accessed August 28, 2018).

[5] "Statement of ICC Prosecutor, Mrs Fatou Bensouda, on opening a Preliminary Examination concerning the alleged deportation of the Rohingya people from Myanmar to Bangladesh," International Criminal Court, www.icc-cpi.int/Pages/item.aspx?name=180918-otp-stat-Rohingya (accessed September 18, 2018).

[6] "Myanmar Army Chief Says 'No Right to Interfere' as UN Weighs Rohingya Crisis," *The Irrawaddy*, September 25, 2018, www.irrawaddy.com/news/burma/myanmar-army-chief-says-no-right-interfere-un-weighs-rohingya-crisis.html.

Myanmar. This is followed by an examination of Myanmar's populist social movement, its exclusionary rhetoric, and the sociopolitical factors that gave rise to it. I will also present the strategic value of the Rohingya crisis for strengthening authoritarianism, and its effects on undermining human rights and shrinking civil society space in Myanmar. The chapter will end with a series of recommendations on how to respond to the populist movement, which, if left unchecked, threatens the future of peace and democracy in Myanmar.

II FORGING THE MYANMAR IDENTITY: FEAR AND LOATHING IN THE "GOLDEN LAND"

People in Myanmar refer to their country as the "Golden Land" because of the countless golden pagodas scattered across the country. Sharing a border with Bangladesh and India in the west, China in the north, and Laos and Thailand in the east, Myanmar is inhabited by a large number of groups with various ethnic, cultural, linguistic, and religious backgrounds. With 135 "official" ethnic groups, it is one of the most ethnically diverse countries in Southeast Asia.[7] The *Bamar*/Burman make up nearly 70 percent of the total population. There are seven other ethnic groups: Chin, Kachin, Karen, Karenni, Mon, Rakhine, and Shan, residing in various states bordering the aforementioned countries. Some 89 percent of Myanmar's 51.4 million people are Theravada Buddhists.[8] Christians and Muslims make up approximately 4 percent each, while the remaining 3 percent are practitioners of indigenous Animist *Nats* or other religions, including Hinduism and Bahai.[9] Given how sensitive ethnic and religious demography is in Myanmar, these estimates from the Ministry of Immigration and Population are likely to be an underestimation.[10]

Just as populism employs an exclusionary notion of the "pure people," in direct opposition to "the corrupt elite,"[11] concepts of identity and belonging have been at the heart of interethnic conflicts between the *Tamadaw* and ethnic armed organizations ("EAOs") in Myanmar. Home to the world's longest-running civil war, Myanmar has known little peace and violence has long plagued it. The contestation around national identity between Myanmar's majority and minority communities must be resolved inclusively if the country is to have peace. The danger posed by the 969 and *MaBaTha*'s exclusionary populist social movement is that it seeks to

---

[7] Bruce Matthews, "Religious Minorities in Myanmar – Hints of the Shadow," *Contemporary South Asia* 4 (1995): 287–308.

[8] Ministry of Labour, Immigration and Population, "Population and Housing Census of Myanmar: Union Report," www.dop.gov.mm/en/publication-category/census (accessed October 3, 2018).

[9] Ministry, "Population and Housing Census."

[10] International Crisis Group, "Counting the Costs: Myanmar's Problematic Census," www.crisis group.org/asia/south-east-asia/myanmar/counting-costs-myanmar-s-problematic-census (accessed October 3, 2018).

[11] Mudde, "Ideational Approach."

continue the *Tamadaw's* policies: institutionalization of Buddhist *Bamar* hegemony at the expense of ethnic and religious minorities' rights. So how did Buddhist Burman nationalism come about in a multi-ethnic, multi-faith nation? It, along with the discriminatory attitudes towards the Rohingyas, in some ways developed in opposition to British colonial rule.

A A Nation Divided: Legacies of Colonial Rule

The British colonized Myanmar in 1886 following three Anglo-Burmese wars.[12] They employed a divide-and-rule strategy, exiling the Burmese King Thibaw to India, and administered the ethnic majority *Bamar* under "Ministerial Burma." The ethnic minorities of the "Frontier Areas," on the other hand, were administered through indirect rule and permitted a degree of self-governance.[13] *Bamar* political and cultural systems were dismantled by the British whereas ethnic minorities were able to maintain their traditional practices.[14] The British also brought in Indian civil servants from the British Raj and foreign workers from the South Asian continent to administer and run commercial operations in Myanmar.[15] The "foreigners'" favored status and monopoly over the economy made them targets of *Bamar* anger. *Bamar* resentment towards them grew during the colonial era as they felt excluded and their way of life threatened, evident from the public proclamation in *Hluttaw* (Parliament): "Those heretics the English *kalars* having most harshly made demands calculated to bring about the impairment and destruction of our religion, the violation of our national traditions and customs, and the degradation of our race."[16]

The Rohingya are Muslim minorities from northern Rakhine state bordering Bangladesh. They constitute around half of the total Muslim population in Myanmar.[17] Globally, they are known as "the most persecuted people on earth," but in Myanmar they are deemed foreign interlopers.[18] There are varying accounts and political debates around the origin of the Rohingya. Even though there is historical evidence to suggest their presence in Rakhine state since the late eighteenth century,[19] populists seeking to exclude them as ethnic minorities often suggest they

[12] Ni Ni Myint, *Burma's Struggle against British Imperialism 1885–1895* (Yangon: The Universities Press, 1983).

[13] Myint, *Burma's Struggle*.

[14] Myint, *Burma's Struggle*.

[15] Nalini R. Chakravarti, *The Indian Minority in Burma: The Rise and Decline of an Immigrant Community* (London: Institute of Race Relations, 1971).

[16] Kei Nemoto, "The Concepts of Dobama (Our Burma) and Thudo-Bama (Their Burma) in Burmese Nationalism, 1930–1948," *Journal of Burma Studies* 5 (2000): 5.

[17] Matthews, "Religious Minorities."

[18] Matthews, "Religious Minorities."

[19] Francis Buchanan, "A Comparative Vocabulary of Some of the Languages Spoken in the Burma Empire," *Asiatic Researches* (1799): 223–237.

are not *taiyingtha*. *Taiyingtha* (sons of the soil) refers to ethnic groups deemed "indigenous" to Myanmar.[20] To be included as a *taiyingtha*, an ethnic group must prove that it existed in Myanmar prior to 1823 (the date of the first occupation by the British).[21] In the populist social movement's eyes, the Rohingya were brought in by the British from what is now Bangladesh and therefore are not part of "the people."[22] Even the community's chosen name of Rohingya is rejected; derogatory names like "*Bengali*" and/or "*kalar*" are used instead, to suggest they are foreign interlopers who do not "belong."

Religion was another important aspect of identity, and the *Bamar* felt that, like ethnicity, it was threatened by colonial policies. Without patronage from the monarchy, Buddhism and its monastic tradition of educating the masses declined. The British refused to support the Buddhist monastic schools and instead encouraged Christian missionary schools to proliferate.[23] The *sanga* (monastic community), outraged at the prospect of losing their religion and cultural traditions, were among the first to mobilize and rebel against the British. Monks like U Ottama, U Wisara, and former monk Saya San led a nationalist movement.[24] From that point on, Buddhism and Burman nationalism became synonymous with one another, and cemented the historical precedent of the *sanga*'s role in protecting race and religion from foreign threats.[25] This is particularly relevant in our later discussions around 969 and *MaBaTha*.

The anti-British rebellions were crushed by ethnic minority soldiers of the British Burma Army, which furthered interethnic tensions.[26] Nationalist movements like the *Dobama Asiayone* (Our Burma Association) began propagating quantifiers of "belonging." To be a "*dobama*" is to be both Buddhist and *Bamar*, which excluded ethnic minorities on both ethnic and religious grounds. Ethnic minorities and immigrants became associated with "*thudo bama*" (the Colonials' Burma). An excerpt from their pamphlet reads like a populist manifesto: "If there exist *dobamas*, there also exist *thudo bama*. Be aware of them. *Thudo bama* do not cherish our Buddhism, do not respect it."[27]

The interethnic divisions only grew with the outbreak of World World II. The ethnic *Bamar*, including Aung San (Aung San Suu Kyi's father), formed the anti-British Burmese Independence Army, deployed with the Japanese to drive the

---

[20] Nick Cheesman, "How in Myanmar 'National Races' Came to Surpass Citizenship and Exclude Rohingya," *Journal of Contemporary Asia* 7, no. 3 (2017): 461–483.

[21] Cheesman, "National Races."

[22] Cheesman, "National Races."

[23] Donald E. Smith, *Religion and Politics in Burma* (Princeton, NJ: Princeton University Press, 1965).

[24] Myint, *Burma's Struggle*.

[25] Myint, *Burma's Struggle*.

[26] John S. Furnivall, *Colonial Policy and Practice: A Comparative Study of Burma and Netherlands India* (Cambridge: Cambridge University Press, 1948).

[27] Furnivall, "Colonial Policy."

British out of Myanmar.[28] The Karen, Karenni, Kachins, and Chins remained loyal to the British, waging guerrilla warfare against the Japanese and *Bamar*. The Rohingya also sided with the British and supported the underground forces during the "Burma Campaign."[29] The Buddhist Rakhine, on the other hand, joined the *Bamar*. The Rohingya and Rakhine clashed during and after the war, resulting in historic animosity that persists to today.

Aung San's Anti-Fascist People's Freedom League ("AFPFL") forces eventually rejoined the British to drive the Japanese out of Myanmar and negotiated independence.[30] As the father of independence, Aung San sought national unity between the *Bamar* and ethnic minorities. He strove to build a secular state, and perceptively warned the *Bamar* not to interpret Buddhist Burman nationalism of the colonial era too narrowly as this could have dire consequence for the future of the country.[31] Aung San's 11-member executive interim government included not only *Bamar* but also ethnic and religious minorities.[32] In his 1945 statement "Defense of Burma," Aung San called for "unity of the entire people, irrespective of race, religion, sex and sectarian and party interests, in action and not in words for national tasks and objectives."[33] Aung San convinced ethnic leaders of the "Frontier Areas" to join the union, promising them full autonomy, protection of minority rights, and the right to secession. They signed the *Panglong* Agreement in 1947, laying the foundation for a federal, democratic Myanmar.[34] However, before it could be fully realized, Aung San and members of his interim government were assassinated.[35]

Myanmar gained independence the following year. Prime Minister U Nu pursued Buddhist nationalist policies to re-establish Myanmar as it was before colonization.[36] Buddhism was installed as the state religion in 1961, alienating non-Buddhist ethnic groups.[37] Unlike Aung San, U Nu opposed "minority rights," seeing them as remnants of British imperialism and as undermining "national unity."[38] National unity for U Nu's central government meant assimilating everyone under the Buddhist *Bamar* mono-ethnic, national identity.[39] Protection of minority rights and

---

[28] Martin Smith, *Burma: Insurgency and the Politics of Ethnicity* (London: Zed Books, 1991), 64.

[29] Smith, *Insurgency*.

[30] Josef Silverstein, *The Political Legacy of Aung San* (New York: Cornell University Press, 1972), 13.

[31] Silverstein, *Political Legacy*, 13.

[32] Thant Myint-U, *The River of Lost Footsteps: A Personal History of Burma* (New York: FSG, 2006), 111–112.

[33] Myint-U, *River of Lost Footsteps*.

[34] Thant Myint-U, *The Making of Modern Burma* (Cambridge: Cambridge University Press, 2001), 14.

[35] Silverstein, *Political Legacy*, 13.

[36] Mikael Gravers, *Nationalism as Political Paranoia in Burma* (Richmond, Surrey: Curzon Press, 1999), 42.

[37] Gravers, *Nationalism*, 57.

[38] Gravers, *Nationalism*, 55.

[39] Gravers, *Nationalism*, 55.

autonomy were key guarantees of the *Panglong* Agreement, and when the central government failed to honor them, ethnic armed organizations (EAOs) rebelled, seeking secession.[40] By 1958, General Ne Win and the *Tamadaw* were brought in by U Nu to temporarily maintain internal peace and restore order. They staged a coup in 1962 and permanently deposed the civilian government.[41]

B *Maintaining Power through Fear and Paranoia:* Tamadaw *in Action*

Ne Win and the *Tamadaw* held themselves out as "saviors" who were keeping Myanmar from disintegration against the internal (EAOs) and external (foreign) forces seeking to destroy it.[42] In reality, the military campaigns against the EAOs were less about preserving the union and more about asserting Buddhist *Bamar* centralized governance over the "Frontier Areas."[43] The junta closed off Myanmar, "safeguarding" it against foreign threats and pursued policies to quell the "enemy within."[44] They dismantled parliament and the judiciary, established a one-party rule, and nationalized the economy. The junta restricted political activities, suppressing those that challenged its hold on power. From EAOs seeking autonomy to political opponents and civilian protestors, all forms of dissent were deemed threats to be crushed. The country's human rights record became marred with systemic abuse and violations spanning the spectrum of civil, political, economic, social, and cultural rights.

State-controlled media outlets like the "New Light of Myanmar" celebrated the *Tamadaw*'s military glories against the enemies besieging the country. It failed to mention the *Tamadaw*'s excessive use of force, extrajudicial killings, enforced disappearances, sexual violence, torture, arbitrary detention, forced labor, land confiscation, internal displacement, and mass expulsion of ethnic and religious minorities. Citizens were instead warned to be vigilant against threats that sought to destroy Myanmar. If I were to catalogue all the threats that we were taught to fear in Myanmar, the list would include: communists, EAOs, the pro-democracy movement, the National League for Democracy ("NLD"), and the international community with its neo-colonial agenda.

With full control of the country, Ne Win and the *Tamadaw* institutionalized Buddhist *Bamar* hegemony in Myanmar.[45] Buddhist *Bamar* cultural identity became the Myanmar national identity, permeating all facets of civil, political,

---

[40] Bertil Lintner, *Land of Jade: A Journey through Insurgent Burma* (Edinburgh: Kiscadale Publications, 1990), 167.

[41] Gravers, *Nationalism*, 55.

[42] Gravers, *Nationalism*, 65.

[43] Robert H. Taylor, "Perceptions of Ethnicity in the Politics of Burma," *Southeast Asian Journal of Social Science* 10, no. 1 (1982): 8–9.

[44] Gravers, *Nationalism*, 22.

[45] Lintner, *Land of Jade*.

and cultural life. From the education system to citizenship laws, each were designed to maintain Buddhist *Bamar* privilege, and perpetuate systemic discrimination and distrust of "others." Schools and university, even in ethnic regions, taught only in Burmese. The curriculum reflected *Bamar* history and military nationalist propaganda. Ethnic minorities were demonized for their past collaboration with British colonialists and attempts by EAOs to destroy national unity.[46]

The *Tamadaw* utilized citizenship as another a way of determining who belonged and who didn't. People were categorized along their ethnic, blood lines and religious affiliation. The "pure blood" Buddhist *Bamar* faced little difficulty acquiring identity cards, unlike the *thwe-hnaw* (mixed blood, with a racist connotation of impureness), who had to prove their loyalty and ethnic ties to Myanmar. An excerpt from Ne Win's speech is worth quoting as it captures the rhetoric the *Tamadaw* utilized to sow fear and paranoia in order to maintain control of Myanmar:

> Today you can see that even people of pure blood are being disloyal to the race and country but are being loyal to others. If people of pure blood act this way, we must carefully watch people of mixed blood. Some people are of pure blood, pure Burmese heritage and descendants of genuine citizens. Karen, Kachin and so forth, are of genuine pure blood. But we must consider whether these people are completely for our race, our Burmese people: and our country, our Burma.[47]

C *The Rohingya*

Out of all the ethnic minority communities vilified by the *Tamadaw*, none bear the brunt more so than the Rohingya. I speculate that 969 and the *MaBaTha* populist movement targeted them because they had committed a triple sin: being "the others," "and the enemy within," while also lacking legal status, unlike the EAOs. Decades of military propaganda about their failed Mujahid rebellion have no doubt furthered fear and resentment towards them. The Mujahid rebellion of the Rohingya formed in 1947 with the main purpose of absorbing Northern Rakhine state into the newly created East Pakistan. A number of Rohingya leaders even met with Muhammad Ali Jinnah to discuss the matter. However, Jinnah, not wishing to create hostility with Myanmar, informed Aung San of his support for Rohingya integration in Myanmar.[48]

The five demands by the Mujahid were: declaring their territory as an autonomous "Free Muslim State" under the sovereignty of Myanmar; recognizing Urdu as the language of the state; establishing independent schools taught in Urdu; releasing

---

[46] Robert Taylor, "Do States Make Nations? The Politics of Identity in Myanmar Revisited," *South East Asia Research* 13, no. 3 (2017): 261–286.

[47] Smith, *Insurgency*, 37.

[48] Moshe Yegar, *The Muslims of Burma: A Study of a Minority Group* (Wiesbaden: Otto Harrassowitz, 1972), 34.

prisoners; and granting legal status to the Mujahid movement.[49] The *Tamadaw* ignored these demands and conducted a series of military operations against the rebellion. The rebellion's numbers dwindled and, by 1961, only 300 or so individuals were left to surrender.[50]

Once full members of Myanmar society, the Rohingya have gradually lost their citizenship following the passage of laws and military operations in the late 1970s and early 1980s. The 1975 State Protection Law authorized, ". . . as may be necessary, restricting any fundamental right of any person suspected of having committed or believed to be about to commit, any act which endangers the sovereignty and security of the state or public peace and tranquility."[51] Using this law, the *Tamadaw* began Operation *Naga Min* (King Dragon) to purge Myanmar of foreign elements and remnants of colonial rule.[52] Their justification was that they were protecting Buddhist *Bamar* from internal and external threats. The national military operation went state by state scrutinizing individuals and identifying them as either citizen or "illegal immigrant."[53] By 1978, Operation *Naga Min* reached Rakhine state. It led to widespread violence and human rights abuses against the Rohingya, causing many to flee to Bangladesh. A bilateral agreement with Bangladesh a year later led to the repatriation of 180,000 Rohingya.[54] In 1991 250,000 Rohingya would return to Bangladesh as a result of Operation *Pyi Thaya* (beautiful country), which displaced Rohingya villages and settled Buddhists in their place.[55]

The persecution and injustices visited upon the Rohingya in Myanmar have been enabled by their lack of legal status under the 1982 Citizenship Law. The law recognized 135 *taiyingtha* (ethnic groups), but not the Rohingya. They are instead deemed "illegal Bengali immigrants" who arrived with the British after 1823. Even though many generations have lived in Myanmar, in the eyes of the *Tamadaw*, they are perpetual "crows living among peacocks, who cannot become peacocks."[56] Peacocks are a national symbol representing Myanmar identity. Without citizenship rights, stateless Rohingya are not afforded protection or rights and are vulnerable to systemic discrimination, suffering restrictions affecting their movement, marriage, and access to health and education. Dire conditions would drive many Rohingya "boat people" to journey perilously to neighboring countries like Malaysia and

---

[49] Yegar, *Muslims of Burma*, 34.

[50] Jean A. Berlie, *The Burmanization of Myanmar's Muslims* (Bangkok: White Lotus Press, 2008), 56.

[51] Peter Gutter and B.K. Sen, *Burma's State Protection Law: An Analysis of the Broadest Law in the World* (Bangkok: Burma Lawyer's Council, 2001), 22.

[52] Azeem Ibrahim, *The Rohingyas: Inside Myanmar's Hidden Genocide* (London: Hurst, 2016), 51.

[53] Gutter and Sen, *Burma's State Protection Law*, 22.

[54] Mark Cutts, *The State of the World's Refugees, 2000: Fifty Years of Humanitarian Action* (Oxford: Oxford University Press, 2000), 75.

[55] Eileen Pittaway, "The Rohingya Refugees in Bangladesh: The Failure of the International Protection System," in H. Adelman (ed.), *Protracted Displacement in Asia: No Place to Call Home* (Aldershot: Ashgate, 2008), 87.

[56] Cheesman, "National Races."

Thailand over the years but for those who could not leave, they remain confined to Rakhine state with Buddhist Rakhine. These two oppressed ethnic communities eked out an existence. By 2012, 969 and *MaBaTha* revived *Tamadaw*'s Buddhist *Bamar* nationalist propaganda and plunged Rakhine state into chaos. The next section will examine the Myanmar populist movement, its exclusionary rhetoric, and the sociopolitical factors that gave rise to it.

III PREACHING HATE: MYANMAR POPULIST MOVEMENT IN ACTION

Monks are perhaps not what one thinks of when envisioning an exclusionary populist movement. I hope to shift this conversation by presenting 969 and *MaBaTha*'s populist social movement and highlighting their impact on human rights and democratic transition in Myanmar. Before delving into the Myanmar populist movement, I want to first start by defining the ideational approach to populism.

A *Defining Populism*

Mudde defines populism as a "thin-centered ideology that considers society to be ultimately separated into two homogeneous and antagonistic groups: 'the pure people' versus 'the corrupt elite,' and which argues that politics should be an expression of the general will of the people."[57] As a thin-centered ideology, populism attaches to other ideological concepts including nationalism and socialism. The distinction between inclusionary populism and exclusionary populism hinges on how populism combines with its "host ideologies."[58] Left-wing, inclusionary populists combine with socialism while right-wing exclusionary populists combine with nationalism.[59] Mudde and Rovira Kaltwasser's study states that Latin America has a history of left-wing inclusionary populism dating back to 1940s while right-wing, exclusionary populists are found in contemporary Europe.[60] According to the aforementioned study, the two types of populism differ on how they "include" or "exclude" based on material, political, and symbolic dimensions.[61]

On the material dimension, left-wing, inclusionary populists seek to include by distributing monetary and non-monetary resources, while right-wing exclusionary populists are concerned with "protecting" these resources and excluding them from "threats," i.e., immigrants who are not considered part of "the people." Politically,

---

[57] Cas Mudde and Cristóbal Rovira Kaltwasser, *Populism: A Very Short Introduction* (Oxford: Oxford University Press, 2017),18.

[58] Cas Mudde and Cristóbal Rovira Kaltwasser, "Exclusionary vs. Inclusionary Populism: Comparing Contemporary Europe and Latin America," *Government and Opposition* 48, no. 2 (2013): 147–174.

[59] Mudde and Rovira Kaltwasser, "Exclusionary vs. Inclusionary Populism," 150.

[60] Mudde and Rovira Kaltwasser, "Exclusionary vs. Inclusionary Populism," 156.

[61] Mudde and Rovira Kaltwasser, "Exclusionary vs. Inclusionary Populism," 158.

right-wing populists oppose extending political rights to non-citizens and seek to "exclude"/limit their political and religious participation in society while left-wing populists target certain groups ignored by the political establishment. The least tangible dimension of the three is the symbolic, namely the determination of "the people." In some ways, this is one of the most crucial aspects as the boundaries of "who belongs" and "who doesn't" determine whether one is included or excluded within the populists' definition of society.[62]

For right-wing exclusionary populists like Le Pen in France and Trump in the United States, the long list of groups excluded from "the people" range from refugees and asylum seekers, foreign workers, visible minorities and people of foreign descent, to political elites. Generating fear of "the others," and safeguarding the nation against external and internal threats, have resulted in policies that infringe ethnic and religious minorities' rights. From the Muslim travel bans and exclusionary immigration policies, to debates in Europe around burqa, niqab, and hijab, right-wing exclusionary populists also feature an anti-Muslim and immigration dimension. These aforementioned markers are all found in 969 and *MaBaTha*'s movement. Their quest to exclude the Rohingya and other Muslims from Myanmar's material, political, and symbolic dimensions leads me to believe they are right-wing exclusionary populists hiding behind the saffron robes of Buddhism.

B 969 *and* MaBaTha

As discussed in the preceding sections, monks have played an important role in the political life of Myanmar. They were among the first to lead a rebellion against the British colonial forces, and were also part of the 1988 democratic uprising. In 2007, tens of thousands of monks across Myanmar took to the streets to protest economic hardship resulting from the military government's removal of fuel subsidies. They challenged the military and refused alms. The monk-led "Saffron Revolution," like many pro-democratic uprisings before it, ended when the military cracked down, killing and injuring monks, raiding monasteries and jailing those who had been part of the movement.[63] Outside of the political arena, the monastic community, as the reservoir of Buddha's teachings, is afforded reverence and unquestioned authority. Monks serve as community leaders, and monasteries play a vital role providing much-needed social services. They operate orphanages and monastic schools, run free clinics and even step in, when government agencies fail, to assist with disaster relief.

However, since 2012, monks from 969 and *MaBaTha* have been the main drivers of an exclusionary populist movement sweeping Myanmar. I have witnessed first-hand the impact that 969 and *MaBaTha* have had on Myanmar. In the span of

[62] Mudde and Rovira Kaltwasser, "Exclusionary vs. Inclusionary Populism," 164.

[63] "Myanmar's Saffron Revolution: 10 Years Later," *Radio Free Asia*, www.rfa.org/english/news/special/saffron/ (accessed November 2, 2018).

a few years, they have managed to create an atmosphere of intolerance, pass a series of discriminatory laws, and set off anti-Muslim riots across Myanmar, culminating in the Rohingya crisis of 2017. Central to their xenophobic campaigns is a Myanmar reserved for Buddhist *Bamar*. 969 and *MaBaTha*, like other populist movements, seek to create what Mudde and Rovira Kaltwasser call "ethnocracy": a state belonging to a single ethnic group, forsaking the rights of ethnic and religious minorities.[64] In a way, 969 and *MaBaTha* have incorporated decades of *Tamadaw*'s nationalist propaganda and repackaged it so that the rhetoric of "who belongs" and "the enemy within" is espoused by monks instead of the generals. They have also replicated the military's playbook, utilizing fear and division between communities as a means of maintaining control.

If I were to distill the essence of the Myanmar populist movement into definitional terms, the "pure people" for 969 and *MaBaTha* are Buddhists. The Rohingya and other Muslims represent "the enemy within." The general will of the people of Myanmar is to protect race and religion from threats. As for the antagonistic "elites," this covers everyone who has stood in their way, including the civilian government, the international community and international human rights system, journalists, and civil society. 969 and *MaBaTha* often label local opposition to their cause as "race traitors" and/or *Dollar zah* (professionals paid in "Dollars" as opposed to Myanmar *Kyat*), indicating that their loyalty is not to Myanmar but rather "foreign elements" who have purchased it.

969 and *MaBaTha* began mobilizing in 2011, taking advantage of the increased political space as Myanmar began its transition from military rule and emerged from its pariah status. A series of developments in 2010 led to international re-engagement. National elections were held that year, and the junta's proxy party, the Union Solidarity and Development Party ("USDP"), led by retired military General Thein Sein, won, fulfilling a key step in the junta's "roadmap to democracy."[65] President Thein Sein's quasi-civilian government released political prisoners, including Nobel Laureate Aung San Suu Kyi and members of her opposition party, the National League for Democracy ("NLD").

It was a time of drastic sociopolitical changes in Myanmar. Many in the country were anxious about Myanmar's future as it emerged from five decades of isolated military rule. I posit that people, especially the rural poor (969 and *MaBaTha*'s main base of supporters) turned to monks as familiar symbols of religion and culture in the face of uncertainty. The numbers in 969 are a shorthand way of referring to "the triple gems" in religious scripture: the nine qualities of Buddha, the six qualities of the teaching or *dhamma*, and the nine qualities of the *sanga*.[66]

---

[64] Mudde and Rovira Kaltwasser, *Very Short Introduction*, 85.

[65] "Pro-Military Party 'Wins' Burmese Election," *BBC News*, November 9, 2010, www.bbc.com/news/world-asia-pacific-11715956.

[66] Benjamin Schonthal and Matthew J. Walton, "The (New) Buddhist Nationalisms? Symmetries and Specificities in Sri Lanka and Myanmar," *Contemporary Buddhism* 17, no. 1 (2016): 85.

While 969 is a decentralized social movement made up of monks and lay Buddhists, *MaBaTha* (an acronym for *Amyo Batha Thathana Saun Shauq Ye Ah Phwe*, the Association for the Protection of Race and Religion) is a centralized organization. Formed in 2014, it "officially" undertakes activities to protect, strengthen, and promote Buddhism. *MaBaTha* operates monastic schools, offers scholarships, and provides charity ranging from blood donation drives to free funeral services. The organization is well resourced, with a vast network extending throughout Myanmar. When mobilizing, it strategically engages with both policy-makers and grassroots communities, especially the rural poor. Civil society actors have repeatedly alluded to ties between *MaBaTha* and hardliners within the *Tamadaw*, cronies, and deep-state actors, but it is hard to find conclusive evidence of it.

C *Escalation of Violence and Discrimination against Muslims*

969 emerged on the national stage by encouraging people to support Buddhist-owned businesses instead of Muslim-owned ones. Muslims have been well represented in the mercantile community since the colonial era. The 969 campaign took advantage of the economic disparity and historic resentment between the Buddhists and financially successful Muslims. 969 handed out stickers with their logo bearing Buddhist iconography to Buddhist-owned business aimed at countering 786 stickers displayed by Muslim-owned restaurants. Walton states that 786 is numerical reference to *Bismillah ar-Rahman ar-Rahim* (in the name of Allah), and restaurants display it to signal that they serve halal food.[67] The message of 969 was that Buddhists had to support each other or else the foreign "others" would become powerful and dominate the Myanmar economy.

The power of 969's messages lies in the fact that they tap into historic interethnic tension and fears – mixing the past with lies. This is further compounded by having monks deliver the message. And no one in the 969 and *MaBaTha* has preached hate quite like Mandalay-based monk U Wirathu. He was jailed for nine years for inciting anti-Muslim violence. Styling himself as the "Burmese Bin Laden,"[68] he has vowed to patriotically defend Myanmar and Buddhism against Islam and the "enemy within." U Wirathu began mobilizing soon after his release from prison, giving sermons throughout Myanmar.

By June 2012, the rape and murder of Thida Htwe, a Buddhist woman, at the hands of three Muslim men in Rakhine state would become the vehicle 969 and U Wirathu sought to incite and unleash violence against Muslim minorities. The rape of Thida Htwe was deemed an honor crime by 969, and graphic photos of

---

[67] Schonthal and Walton, "(New) Buddhist Nationalisms," 85.

[68] Hannah Beech, "The Face of Buddhist Terror," *Time*, July 1, 2013, http://content.time.com/time/subscriber/article/0,33009,2146000-3,00.html.

her dead body along with incendiary remarks about her killers' identity and religious affiliations were disseminated on social media. Rakhine Buddhist mobs attacked and killed 10 Muslim pilgrims in retaliation for Thida Htwe, setting off a series of riots between Buddhists and Muslims that spread across Rakhine state. The first wave of violence lasted until August 2012, to be followed by a second series of attacks in October 2012. The last incident of violence occurred in 2013. The riots affected 12 townships and three communities: the Rohingya, Rakhine, and Kaman (another Muslim community in Rakhine, but who, unlike the Rohingya, are citizens under the 1982 Citizenship Law). The UN estimates that over 140,000 were displaced by the riots, and that 95 percent of the displaced were Rohingya, who were then confined to internally displaced person ("IDP") camps in Rakhine.[69]

The 2012–2013 riots in Rakhine state, though significant, could be attributed to longstanding tensions between the Rakhine Buddhists and Rohingya Muslims dating back to the colonial era. But soon violence against Muslims began erupting in Myanmar towns that had no historic tensions, resulting in deaths, injuries, destruction of property, and strained communal relations. A jewelry store dispute between a Buddhist and a Muslim, and the murder of a Buddhist monk by a group of Muslims in March 2013, led to riots in Meikhtila. This was followed by a riot in Okkan in April, when a Muslim woman bumped a Buddhist monk with her bicycle and knocked over his alms bowl. The May riot in Lashio occurred after a Muslim man poured gasoline on a Buddhist woman and threatened to set her on fire. Buddhist mobs attacked in retaliation. A riot broke out in Htan Gon in August after rumors of an attempted sexual assault of a Buddhist woman by a Muslim man. The following year, a similar allegation of rape of a Buddhist women by her Muslim employers led to riots in Mandalay, and the killing of a Muslim and a Buddhist man. The allegation later turned out to be false.

I interviewed numerous eyewitnesses (including the two widows) and interfaith peace activists in Mandalay, and other civil society actors in Myanmar, uncovering a pattern associated with the various riots.[70] According to them, each riot has been preceded by an allegation of a rape or incident of offence to Buddhism. The alleged perpetrator is usually a Muslim while the victim is a Buddhist. 969 monks including U Wirathu then spread the news via social media regardless of whether the allegation was true. The online posts are also accompanied by a call to Buddhists to take action and defend their race and religion. A public rally is then held by 969 supporters, which subsequently leads to rioting. It is worth noting that in Mandalay, like other towns, riot police in full gear stood by while Buddhist mobs attacked and

---

[69] "Area-Based Programming: UNDP in Rakhine," UNDP, www.mm.undp.org/content/myan mar/en/home/area-based-programming/rakhine.html (accessed November 18, 2018).
[70] Justice Trust, *Hidden Hands Behind the Communal Violence in Myanmar* (Bangkok: Justice Trust, 2015).

destroyed mosques, Muslim shops and homes. Furthermore, local activists stated that almost every major outbreak of violence since 2012 was preceded by a 969-sponsored sermon tour of the area, usually by U Wirathu himself.

Once the violence of the riots subsided, 969 and *MaBaTha* turned their attention to passing a series of discriminatory laws known as the four laws, in order to "safeguard nationality and religion." They petitioned President Thein Sein in June 2013, claiming they had more than 1.3 million signatures from Myanmar citizens. The "Buddhist Women's Special Marriage Law" placed restrictions on interfaith marriages and limited non-Buddhist men from rights, including custody. The "Population Control Healthcare Law" required 36-months' birth spacing for couples. The "Religious Conversion Law" created a new system of state oversight for those changing religion. Lastly, the "Monogamy Law" prohibited polygamy. And even though the laws do not explicitly mention Muslims or the Rohingya, they are designed with discriminatory intent and anti-Muslim stereotypes, namely that Muslims in Myanmar are polygamous and have high birth rates. They also seek to marry Buddhist women and convert them to Islam.

The women's rights movement in Myanmar voiced their opposition and mobilized against the discriminatory laws. They held public events and press conferences asserting that the four laws contravene Myanmar's obligations under the Convention on the Elimination of all Forms of Discrimination Against Women (CEDAW). 969 and *MaBaTha* labelled the protestors "race traitors," and threatened them with violence. Several prominent women rights leaders I knew closely reported having their social media, email, and phone hacked. Others received threatening messages and texts. Several tried to open first information reports with the police but were turned away. Ultimately, the four laws were passed in 2015.

It is worth noting that women's bodies and allegations of rape and dishonor at the hands of Muslims have been used by 969 and *MaBaTha* to incite violence, and yet the draft "Prevention of Violence Against Women Law" has been stalled since 2014. The four laws, on the other hand, managed to get passed in record time as 969 and *MaBaTha* were extremely effective at shaping public opinion. Their sermons, statements, publications and periodicals, social media posts and videos are designed to stoke fear, incite violence, and normalize persecution. Their hate speech has enabled and excused riots, discriminatory law, and even a potential genocide against the Rohingya.

D *Hate Speech*

The 969 and *MaBaTha* materials I have managed to obtained and sermons I have studied follow a few key rhetorical tropes.[71] The first is that Muslims are planning to take over Myanmar through a "slow invasion." According to 969 and *MaBaTha*,

---

[71] *MaBaTha* pamphlets and DVDs in author's possession.

Muslims plan to eliminate the Buddhist Myanmar way of life by marrying Buddhist women, and gaining economic power. Excerpts and copies of a banned book published in the 1980s entitled *A Myo Pyaut Mhar Soe Kyaut Sayar* (Fearing the extinction of our race) have reappeared. This book states that the greatest threat to Buddhism is Islam, and that inaction will lead to the disappearance of Buddhism and Myanmar in a hundred years. The book singles out Buddhist women and children as being particularly vulnerable and therefore should not associate with non-Buddhists.

A quote from *A Myo Pyaut Mhar Soe Kyaut Sayar* states: "When we study world history, we can see that different races of the world did not become extinct, swallowed by the earth, but only by other humans." These messages often point to countries like Afghanistan, Bangladesh, and Indonesia, which were once Buddhist but are now Muslim. A 2013 sermon by U Wirathu captures the essence of the "Muslim conspiracy" in Myanmar:

> Muslims have a lot of money and no one knows where that money mountain is. They use that money to get our young Buddhist women. They show that money to attract our young women ... That money will be used to get a Buddhist-Burmese woman, and she will very soon be coerced or even forced to convert to Islam ... And the children born of her will become Bengali Muslims and the ultimate danger to our Buddhist nation, as they will eventually destroy our race and our religion. Once they become overly populous, they will overwhelm us and take over our country and make it an evil Islamic nation.[72]

The second major theme pushed by 969 and *MaBaTha* is that Islam is inseparable from jihadism. They claim that if Myanmar does not take security precautions against jihadism, it too is at risk in the larger global war on terror. The materials produced around this message often sensationalize terrorist attacks and share graphic videos and photos from ISIS and Al-Qaeda, which are designed to conflate Islam with terrorism. According to U Wirathu, "whatever they do, they do it from their Islamic point of view ... Everywhere in the world, the Muslims themselves are the violators of basic human rights. They have brutally violated freedom of religion in every society they control."

The failed Mujahid rebellion of the Rohingya is often used to remind people that Muslims have tried in the past, and if given a chance, they will do so again. And like the *Tamadaw*, the 969 and *MaBaTha* messaging around the impending jihad conveys a sense that Myanmar is besieged by "the enemy within." Wirathu on his now defunct personal blog had a whole series of videos dedicated to jihad including: "Defend against the dangers of Jihad"; "Jihad and the future"; and "Jihad war and future Myanmar."[73]

---

[72] 969 [Untitled DVD] (2013).
[73] On file with civil society activists in Myanmar.

The final focus of their messages is around the Rohingya, emphasizing that they are not a real ethnic community but rather a term invented by illegal immigrants from Bangladesh to attain *taiyingtha* ethnic status in Myanmar. Rohingya are routinely subjected to dehumanizing language by 969 and *MaBaTha*. Outside of the derogatory term *"Bengali"* and the many derivatives of *"kalar,"* they have been called everything from fleas, dogs, weeds, and carps that spread uncontrollably, to floating garbage of unknown origin (*Yay Myaw Kan Tin*). Accompanying this theme is the idea that serious human rights violations against the Rohingya are exaggerated fabrications designed to gain sympathy from the international community and that the *real* victims of the violence in Rakhine state are Buddhist Rakhine.

The international community is also cast in a negative light. They are painted as biased "outsiders" who do not understand the threats that Rohingya and Muslims pose to Myanmar's race and religion. 969 and *MaBaTha* comments on the UN and international human rights organizations follow the line that they have been "hijacked by Arabs"[74] and are trying to force Myanmar to give citizenship rights and *taiyingtha* status to foreign illegal immigrants. UN Special Rapporteurs have been threatened, attacked, and barred from entering Myanmar. This level of rejection of the international community has not been seen since the military-era policies of non-engagement.

Anti-international attitudes and withdrawal from international human rights institutions have increased in Myanmar in recent years. In 2013, former Special Rapporteur Quintana attempted to visit Meiktila following communal riots. Protestors surrounded his convoy, punching his vehicles' doors and windows.[75] A year later, 30 UN and INGO offices were attacked in Rakhine state, resulting in the temporary evacuation of more than 300 humanitarian workers. There was extensive damage, and various program activities were suspended for four weeks.[76]

Groups like 969 and *MaBaTha* continue to fuel rumors of unfair international aid distribution, which have resulted in impeded access and attacks on humanitarian shipments bound for the Rohingya refugees and IDPs.[77] At a public rally in 2015, U Wirathu called current Special Rapporteur on Myanmar, Professor Yanghee Lee a "bitch" and a "whore," and threatened her with violence.[78] The Myanmar authorities have denied Professor Lee entry into the country since 2017. The Myanmar government similarly refused to cooperate with the FFM and blocked its investigators from entering Myanmar.

---

74 Beech, "Face of Buddhist Terror."
75 "Burma 'Failed to Protect' UN Rights Envoy," *BBC News*, August 21, 2013, www.bbc.com/news/world-asia-23787470.
76 "Mobs Attack Offices of UN, Aid Groups in Myanmar's Rakhine State," *Radio Free Asia*, March 27, 2013, www.rfa.org/english/news/myanmar/flag-03272014173432.html.
77 "Myanmar Mob Attacks Aid Shipment Bound for Rohingya Area," *Associated Press*, September 21, 2017, www.theindependentbd.com/home/printnews/115178.
78 The footage can be found at: www.youtube.com/watch?v=comAfSalvEY.

E *The Role of Social Media in Dissemination of Exclusionary Rhetoric*

The transition period in Myanmar brought forth many changes but the liberalization of telecommunications is perhaps the one that has utterly transformed Myanmar society in both a positive and negative way. On the one hand, it led to greater connectivity and information owing to cheap and readily available SIM cards and smartphones from China. A World Bank study found that the SIM card price in Myanmar dropped from $250 in 2012 to a less than $2 in 2016.[79] By 2017, Myanmar leapfrogged from being one of the least connected countries in the world, having no phones, to 33 million mobile users and 80 percent smartphone usage.[80] People joined social media platforms, particularly Facebook, which enjoys a 90 percent monopoly over other platforms.[81] For many in Myanmar, Facebook *is* the internet. It is their main source for news, information, entertainment, videos and the messaging system. Government officials, key ministries, and news agencies all utilize Facebook to communicate directly with the public.

The negative aspect of increased connectivity is that it has enabled 969, *MaBaTha* and its supporters to disseminate misinformation and their virulent rhetoric easily and quickly. Hateful rhetoric and incitement of violence towards the Rohingya and Muslims can be found in news feeds, fake news, inflammatory posts, poems, articles, comments, graphic images, and propaganda videos primed for "liking" and "sharing" widely with others. Civil society groups in Myanmar report that there is a constant barrage of negative information on the Muslim conspiracy to take over Myanmar, the jihadist threats posed by Islam, Rohingyas that lie, and a biased international community that believes those lies.

Part of the problem is that social media is a new tool and people lack the necessary digital literacy. Furthermore, a poor education system, based on rote memorization, has not strengthened critical thinking skills, which could potentially offset people's susceptibility to manipulation. While there are positive messages and local campaigns like Myanmar ICT for Development Organization's "Flower Speech," reminding people to spread positivity instead of hate, and the "My Friend Campaign," highlighting interfaith friendships, the volume of content generated cannot match the volume of messages fueling hate and intolerance.

In October 2018, the *New York Times* uncovered a systematic online campaign by *Tamadaw* personnel to create negative content aimed at the Rohingya and Muslims

---

[79] "Myanmar: Investment Analysis and Implementation Options for Proposed Digital Government Project," World Bank, http://documents.worldbank.org/curated/en/528481530162210035/Myanmar-Investment-Analysis-and-Implementation-Options-for-Digital-Government-Project (accessed November 12, 2018).

[80] "Digital Landscapes, Mobile Research," Digital in Asia, https://digitalinasia.com/2017/01/09/myanmar-33-million-mobile-users-smartphone-usage-80/(accessed November 12, 2018).

[81] "Social Media Statistics Myanmar," GlobalStats, http://gs.statcounter.com/social-media-stats/all/myanmar (accessed November 12, 2018).

in Myanmar. According to the article, "hundreds of military personnel created troll accounts and news and celebrity pages on Facebook and then flooded them with incendiary comments and posts timed for peak viewership … officers were also tasked with collecting intelligence on popular accounts and criticizing posts unfavorable to the military."[82] Facebook's head of cybersecurity confirmed that there had been "clear and deliberate attempts to covertly spread propaganda that were directly linked to the Myanmar military."[83] The Russian military is attributed as assisting the *Tamadaw*'s online influencing campaigns. This is unsurprising given that the two countries have maintained close military relations dating back to the military dictatorship era, and most of the *Tamadaw*'s weapons acquired are from Russia and China.

The FFM findings on the Rohingya crisis pointed out Facebook's role in spreading hate speech and inciting violence. The company responded by taking down the social media accounts of U Wirathu and senior military leaders, including the Commander-in-Chief Min Aung Hlaing. However, the messages of hate against the Rohingyas, Muslims, the international community and "race traitors" in Myanmar have not subsided. Facebook could and needs to be doing a lot more for Myanmar. It needs to work with local experts, civil society organizations, and human rights activists to develop strategies that are responsive to Myanmar context. Local groups I interviewed, including *Phandeeyar*, *Athan*, and Muslim grassroots organizations wishing to remain anonymous stated that Facebook's current model of relying on users to flag negative content is slow and ineffective. Many expressed frustrations that even when they flag content that clearly violates Facebook's community standard, the content-monitoring team disagrees and does not remove it.

The Myanmar authorities have also stated that they are preparing a bill for protecting against hate speech, but no official detail has been given about the proposed law. They have also approved a 6.4 billion Kyat budget for the creation of a "Social Media Monitoring Team." Civil society actors are concerned that the aforementioned draft law, like section 66(d) of the Telecommunications Act, will be disproportionately used against activists voicing dissent. They believe the "Social Media Monitoring Team" is simply a ruse to surveil activists and curtail freedom of expression in Myanmar.

Responding to the populist social movement in Myanmar requires both online and offline strategies to counter the content generated by 969, *MaBaTha*, and military troll farms. For now, 969 and *MaBaTha*'s exclusionary populist movement have successfully inflicted atrocities upon the Rohingya and managed to deport over

---

[82] Paul Mozur, "A Genocide Incited on Facebook, with Posts from Myanmar's Military," *New York Times*, www.nytimes.com/2018/10/15/technology/myanmar-facebook-genocide.html (accessed November 2, 2018).

[83] Mozur, "Genocide Incited on Facebook."

725,000 people to Bangladesh. And the general population fed on a diet of fear and hate have stood by. If the online culture of hate continues to feed into an offline culture of anti-pluralist intolerance, then the prospect of the Rohingya repatriating home to Myanmar in a voluntary, safe, and dignified manner remains dubious.

IV THE AFTERMATH OF THE ROHINGYA CRISIS:
A RETURN TO AUTHORITARIANISM?

The final section of this chapter examines the Rohingya crisis to explore who has benefitted and lost as a result of it. Leading up to the 2015 elections, 969 and *MaBaTha* campaigned alongside the incumbent quasi-civilian government's Union Solidarity and Development Party ("USDP") and NLD party. Even though they were not explicit which party they were supporting, monks including U Wirathu urged people to vote for a party that would better protect race and religion. They conducted "voter education" sessions telling followers to ask the candidates six questions: are they Buddhist?; do they support the four laws and pledge not to repeal them?; will they try and change the 1982 Citizenship Law?; would they change section 59(f) of the 2008 Constitution that bars Suu Kyi from the presidency?; and would they protect race and religion? The underlying message from 969 and *MaBaTha* was that a vote for NLD could potentially undo the four laws, grant citizenship rights to the Rohingya, and make Myanmar vulnerable to the Muslim threat.

The NLD could have and should have faced the populist social movement directly and spoken out about the dangers of intolerance and the threats such a culture would have on peace and democracy in Myanmar. They should have built their campaign around fundamental human rights for all regardless of ethnic and religious affiliations. The NLD, afraid of losing support, instead chose not to engage and let the populist social movement dictate the terms and narratives of the election. I feel it was a major missed opportunity and travesty that, for the first time in the history of Myanmar, not a single Muslim candidate (including those who were in the NLD) was permitted to run for office, and the Parliament seated in 2016 is the first to have no Muslim members. Those who disagree with me say that Aung San Suu Kyi and the NLD were strategic and won a decisive victory, forming Myanmar's first civilian government in over fifty years.[84] While that may be true, I fear that 969 and *MaBaTha*'s campaign of hate remained intact and the 2015 elections, if anything, normalized and affirmed its power to shape national discourse.

Even though support for the *Tamadaw* and its role in Myanmar society was uncertain following the election, the exclusionary populist social movement and the Rohingya crisis has helped increase support domestically for the *Tamadaw*. The

---

[84] "Myanmar's 2015 Landmark Elections Explained," *BBC News*, December 3, 2015, www.bbc .com/news/world-asia-33547036.

Tamadaw has used the ARSA attacks and clearance operations against "terrorism" in Rakhine state to re-establish its image as the "savior" and protector of the nation from "external" and "internal" threats. The threat of terrorism is also strategic because it offers the military the potential to assume power should a State of Emergency be declared under section 412 of the military-drafted 2008 Constitution. That said, a State of Emergency might not even be warranted as the *Tamadaw*'s USDP party is capitalizing on its newfound popularity and vying for a comeback in the 2020 elections. In fact, USDP managed to steal a few seats from the NLD during the by-elections in November 2018.

The Rohingya crisis has been fraught for Aung San Suu Kyi and her party. Her inaction and silence has irreparably transformed her from a global human rights icon to a pariah. Countless articles have been written about the Nobel Laureate who did nothing to stop the *Tamadaw*'s atrocities. She has been stripped of major human rights awards including Amnesty International's Ambassador of Conscience Award, the US Holocaust Memorial Museum's Elie Wiesel Award, and Honorary Canadian Citizenship, and there have even been calls to revoke her Nobel Peace Prize. Her popularity in Myanmar coupled with the international community's support made her a formidable adversary against the military. The Rohingya crisis has diminished the latter, isolating her with fewer international allies.

Even though I too am disappointed by Aung San Suu Kyi and NLD's response to the Rohingya crisis, I recognize that there are constitutional barriers preventing the civilian government from acting. For instance, the key ministries that could resolve the Rohingya crisis – Defence, Border Affairs, and Home Affairs – are not under the civilian government purview. These ministries do not report to the civilian government and are instead overseen by the Commander-in-Chief, Min Aung Hlaing. While the NLD has the majority number of seats, 25 percent of the seats in each house of parliament are reserved for military members of parliament ("MP"). The 2008 Constitution requires a 75 percent vote before any constitutional amendments can be adopted, so the civilian government is kept in check by the military MPs' effective veto power. And because these unelected MPs are appointed by the *Tamadaw*, it is foreseeable that anyone who votes contrary to the *Tamadaw*'s interests could be replaced.

China is another party that has benefitted from the Rohingya crisis. It was one of Myanmar's main trade partners during the military dictatorship era. However, as the country opened up, and Myanmar strengthened ties with other Western countries, China's foreign relations influence waned. The Rohingya crisis has given China (along with Russia) an opportunity to restore close relations with Myanmar. China has so far expressed support for Myanmar's handling of the Rohingya crisis internationally. It could even leverage its permanent seat on the UN Security Council to buffer Myanmar from punitive measures. Winning the Myanmar government's support is important for China given its economic interests in Myanmar. Myanmar and specifically Rakhine state is crucial for its "One Belt, One Road" initiative.

China plans to install a major deep port at Kyaukphyu, connecting to a road, rail, and pipeline network that would move energy and other materials from the Bay of Bengal through Myanmar to Yunnan Province. China's other mega projects in Myanmar include a series of dams on the Irrawaddy river and a copper mine in Letpadaung.

Given that I have already discussed at length the negative impact that the exclusionary populist social movement and *Tamadaw*'s increased popularity have had on the rights of Rohingya and religious minorities, I will dedicate this last portion to civil society actors, activists, journalists, lawyers, and human rights defenders. These individuals who seek to tell the truth and/or are critical of the *Tamadaw* do so at significant risk to their personal safety and liberty. While rampant hate speech by populist actors like U Wirathu and riots have been permitted by authorities, a series of laws exists to silence, intimidate, and stifle dissent. These include the Official Secrets Act; criminal defamation provisions within the Penal Code: section 505(b) and the Telecommunications Act: section 66(d); and section 143–147 of the Penal Code and Peaceful Assembly and Peaceful Procession Act limiting the right to peaceful assembly. Below are a few examples of the shrinking civil society space in Myanmar in the 2017 to 2019 period alone:

- U Ko Ni, a prominent Muslim lawyer and legal advisor to NLD was assassinated at the Yangon International Airport in January 2017. He had been calling for constitutional reforms to reduce the military's role. As one of Myanmar leading lawyers, he found the legal solution circumventing the constitutional bar prohibiting Aung San Suu Kyi from becoming President and instead enabled her to become the State Counsellor. The trial took more than two years before the gunman, Kyi Lin, and his conspirators, Aung Win Zaw, Aung Win Tun, and Zeya Phyo, who are all ex-military officers, were found guilty. Kyi Lin and Aung Win Zaw were sentenced to death while Aung Win Tun and Zeya Phyo received a three-year sentence for harboring a fugitive. At the time of writing, the alleged mastermind, Lieutenant Colonel Aung Win Khaing, still remains at large.
- Reuters journalists Wa Lone and Kyaw Soe Oo were set up and arrested by police for their investigative work implicating security forces in the killing of 10 Rohingya men and boys in Rakhine state. They were charged under the Official Secrets Act. The court convicted and handed them a seven-year sentence. The two reporters' appeal to the Yangon High Court was rejected (in December 2018), and the Supreme Court similarly upheld the lower courts' decisions in April 2019. The two journalists had served 511 days in jail before they were released by a presidential amnesty in May 2019. The two journalists received a 2019 Pulitzer Prize for their work.

- Pulitzer-winning Associated Press journalist Esther Htusan received death threats over her critical reporting of the military operations in Rakhine state and the civilian government's handling of the Rohingya crisis. The death threats and accompanying call to action were widely shared on Facebook. This, coupled with incidents of in-person intimidation, caused her to flee Myanmar in 2017.
- The *Voice Daily*'s editor-in-chief Kyaw Min Swe and satirical columnist Ko Kyaw Zwa Naing were arrested and charged with defamation in May 2017. The latter had written a piece entitled "Oath of the Nation of Bullets," which had mocked a military propaganda film entitled "Union Oath." The *Voice Daily* published a formal apology and issued a correction. The charges were dropped four months later.
- Three journalists, Aye Niang, Pyae Phone Naing, and Thein Zaw, from the Democratic Voice of Burma and *The Irrawaddy*, were arrested for covering an EAO drug-burning ceremony held as part of the U.N.'s International Day Against Drug Abuse in June 2017. They were charged under the 1908 Unlawful Associations Act and if convicted, could face up to three years in prison.
- In April 2018, eight students were convicted of criminal defamation for performing a satirical anti-war play, and the man who live-streamed the play on Facebook was sentenced to three months in jail for violating section 66(d) of the Telecommunications Act.
- In July 2018, 47 youth anti-war activists were arrested in Meiktila and Yangon for participating in a peace protest highlighting the plight of IDPs in Northern Myanmar. The three main youth organizers were found guilty of criminal defamation under the penal code. The court handed down a six-month sentence and fined them.
- Min Htin Ko Ko Gyi, a filmmaker and co-founder of the Human Rights, Human Dignity International Film Festival in Yangon, was arrested and charged for allegedly defaming the *Tamadaw* in April 2019. He had written a series of Facebook posts criticizing the 2008 Constitution and the military's dominant role in politics. He remains in custody to this day as his lawyer's request for bail on medical grounds has been denied twice, despite Min Htin Ko Ko Gyi's failing health due to liver cancer.
- Kay Khine Tun, Zeyar Lwin, Paing Ye Thu, Phoe Thar, and Paing Phyo Min of the *Daungdoh Myoset* (Peacock Generation) performance troupe were also arrested and charged with defamation in April 2019 for performing and Facebook livestreaming a satirical *thangyat*. *Thangyats* are typically satirical songs, chants, and dance performed during Myanmar new year festivities that critique various social issues and behaviors. The *Daungdoh Myoset* troupe were found guilty of undermining the military and its members received a one-year sentence.

A *The Road Ahead*

Mudde and Rovira Kaltwasser have stated that populism's effect on democracy is that democracy can be diluted or even abolished.[85] The exclusionary populist social movement in Myanmar and the aftermath of the Rohingya crisis certainly feel like a return to authoritarianism. For instance, the persecution of ethnic and religious minorities, which have been occurring for decades, persists. The *Tamadaw*'s culture of impunity for gross violations of human rights is intact even after they have committed potential acts of genocide against the Rohingya. Myanmar refuses to cooperate with the international community and is rejecting international human rights systems when they should be embracing them to build a stronger democracy and rights-respecting culture. Furthermore, authoritarian allies like Russia and China continue to shield them at the international level just as they have done in the past.

The rhetoric of "belonging" defined around Buddhist *Bamar* national identity is stronger than ever thanks to new technology and platforms like Facebook, and 969 and *MaBaTha*'s mobilization. This does not bode well for EAOs engaging in peace talks or for the Rohingya refugees' repatriation. A national identity that is anti-pluralist runs counter to the ethnic minority groups' hope of a federal, democratic state as originally promised by the *Panglong* Agreement. If the peace negotiations and terms between the *Tamadaw* and the EAOs break down, then the nationwide ceasefire agreements would no longer hold and Myanmar could easily be plunged back into a state of conflict.

It is imperative that Myanmar takes the correct course if democracy and peace are to have a chance. Below are some recommendations that could be utilized to respond to the populist movement in Myanmar before it is too late. Given that the 2020 general elections could potentially be a flashpoint for violence, incitement, hate speech, misinformation, and harassment designed to undermine the political process, I have separated these time-sensitive recommendations from longer-term institutional reforms and local–international cooperation, as measures that should be undertaken before the elections.

V RECOMMENDATIONS

A *Before the 2020 General Elections*

A vibrant civil society, local interfaith peace movements, and moderate voices within the religious community exist in Myanmar. They have the potential of opposing the populist social movement's rhetoric of hate, but they lack the resources to spread their counter-narratives. Supporting these groups' efforts and designing

---

[85] Mudde and Rovira Kaltwasser, *Very Short Introduction*, 91.

culturally relevant campaigns could educate and transform Myanmar society. These national campaigns could emphasize the power of peaceful coexistence and urge the importance of communities coming together to build a rights-respecting culture or risk returning to oppressive military rule. Social media platforms like Facebook, which have been utilized by populists to spread hate, could assist civil society organizations and the interfaith peace movement to disseminate its messages of peace and tolerance, and de-escalate tensions.

969, *MaBaTha*, and *Tamadaw* prey on people's fears, prejudices, and ignorance. Building up people's capacity and making them informed citizens would deprive these groups of potential supporters. Such efforts could include peace education; educating the Buddhist *Bamar* majority about privilege; transitional justice mechanisms, including truth-telling the *Tamadaw*'s past and ongoing persecution of ethnic and religious minority communities; fostering understanding and respect of different religions; and building up people's digital literacy skills and critical thinking skills, which would also make them less susceptible to the populist campaigns.

The civilian government needs to take steps to protect civil society actors, journalists, lawyers, and human rights defenders. It can start by releasing all political prisoners. And to ensure new charges will not be brought, the civilian government should repeal and reform laws like the Official Secrets Act, Peaceful Assembly and Peaceful Procession Act, and provisions within the Penal Code and the Telecommunications Act.

B *Longer-Term Institutional Reforms and Local–International Cooperation*

The civilian government and the international community need to re-engage and cooperate with one another or risk returning Myanmar to its previous pariah state. Rule of law is an area that both the civilian government and the international community have repeatedly mentioned and could be a potential collaborative space. The NLD have announced its plans for constitutional reform. Local and international constitutional law experts could assist them ensuring that the legislative reforms build a federal democratic Myanmar and are protective of ethnic and religious minorities' rights.

I believe the civilian government and the international community could work together to strengthen the legal profession, judiciary, and criminal justice system in Myanmar. Equitable administration of justice requires better-trained judges and police officers empowered to protect the people of Myanmar and serve them rather than the *Tamadaw* and the powerful. An impartial legal system is also the best strategy to ending impunity in Myanmar, and is an investment if there is ever to be domestic accountability for gross crimes and atrocities.

That said, the international community needs to ensure powerful states like China and Russia and their economic interest do not sway them from pursuing all punitive measures against the *Tamadaw*, not just for its role in the Rohingya crisis, but its war crimes and crimes against humanity in Myanmar against all ethnic and religious minority communities. Targeted sanctions against the military leaders need to be reinstalled. A global arms embargo should also be placed upon Myanmar. The international community needs to contribute to humanitarian aid for the Rohingya refugees. And it needs to ensure that any discussion of repatriation is not premature or driven purely by political interests, but only a safe, dignified, and voluntary return to Myanmar in the best interests of the Rohingyas. If such an option is not possible, the international community needs to work with Bangladesh on either local integration or offering refugee resettlement for the Rohingya.

These recommendations and their holistic approach offer a chance of stopping the populist social movement and undoing the decades of harms from the *Tamadaw*'s divisive identity politics. However, its chance of success requires coordination and an alliance between local and international actors, with the former taking the lead and the latter playing a supportive role.

BIBLIOGRAPHY

"Area-Based Programming: UNDP in Rakhine." UNDP. www.mm.undp.org/content/myan mar/en/home/area-based-programming/rakhine.html (accessed November 18, 2018).
"Burma 'Failed to Protect' UN Rights Envoy." *BBC News*, August 21, 2013. www.bbc.com/ news/world-asia-23787470.
"Digital Landscapes, Mobile Research." Digital in Asia. https://digitalinasia.com/2017/01/09/ myanmar-33-million-mobile-users-smartphone-usage-80/ (accessed November 12, 2018).
"Mobs Attack Offices of UN, Aid Groups in Myanmar's Rakhine State." *Radio Free Asia*, March 27, 2013. www.rfa.org/english/news/myanmar/flag-03272014173432.html.
"Myanmar Army Chief Says 'No Right to Interfere' as UN Weighs Rohingya Crisis." *The Irrawaddy*, September 25, 2018. www.irrawaddy.com/news/burma/myanmar-army-chief-says-no-right-interfere-un-weighs-rohingya-crisis.html.
"Myanmar: Investment Analysis and Implementation Options for Proposed Digital Government Project." *World Bank*. http://documents.worldbank.org/curated/en/52848153016221 0035/Myanmar-Investment-Analysis-and-Implementation-Options-for-Digital-Government-Project (accessed November 12, 2018).
"Myanmar Mob Attacks Aid Shipment Bound for Rohingya Area." *Associated Press*, September 21, 2017. www.theindependentbd.com/home/printnews/115178.
"Myanmar's 2015 Landmark Elections Explained." *BBC News*, December 3, 2015. www.bbc .com/news/world-asia-33547036.
"Myanmar's Saffron Revolution: 10 Years Later." *Radio Free Asia*. www.rfa.org/english/news/ special/saffron/ (accessed November 2, 2018).
"Myanmar: Tatmadaw Leaders Must be Investigated for Genocide, Crimes against Humanity, War Crimes – UN Report." *Office of the United Nations High Commissioner for Human Rights*, August 27, 2018. www.ohchr.org/en/NewsEvents/Pages/DisplayNews.aspx? NewsID=23475&LangID=E.
"Pro-Military Party 'Wins' Burmese Election." *BBC News*, November 9, 2010. www.bbc.com/ news/world-asia-pacific-11715956.
"Social Media Statistics Myanmar." GlobalStats. http://gs.statcounter.com/social-media-stats/ all/myanmar (accessed November 12, 2018).

Beech, Hannah. "The Face of Buddhist Terror." *Time*, July 1, 2013. http://content.time.com/time/subscriber/article/0,33009,2146000-3,00.html.

[Bensouda, Fatou], "Statement of ICC Prosecutor, Mrs Fatou Bensouda, on opening a Preliminary Examination concerning the alleged deportation of the Rohingya people from Myanmar to Bangladesh." International Criminal Court. www.icc-cpi.int/Pages/item.aspx?name=180918-otp-stat-Rohingya (accessed September 18, 2018).

Berlie, Jean A. *The Burmanization of Myanmar's Muslims*. Bangkok: White Lotus Press, 2008.

Buchanan, Francis. "A Comparative Vocabulary of Some of the Languages Spoken in the Burma Empire." *Asiatic Researches* 5 (1799): 223–237.

Chakravarti, Nalini R. *The Indian Minority in Burma: The Rise and Decline of an Immigrant Community*. London: Institute of Race Relations, 1971.

Cheesman, Nick. "How in Myanmar 'National Races' Came to Surpass Citizenship and Exclude Rohingya." *Journal of Contemporary Asia* 7, no. 3 (2017): 461–483.

Cutts, Mark. *The State of the World's Refugees, 2000: Fifty Years of Humanitarian Action*. Oxford: Oxford University Press, 2000.

Furnivall, John S. *Colonial Policy and Practice: A Comparative Study of Burma and Netherlands India*. Cambridge: Cambridge University Press, 1948.

Gravers, Mikael. *Nationalism as Political Paranoia in Burma*. Richmond, Surrey: Curzon Press, 1999.

Gutter, Peter, and B.K. Sen. *Burma's State Protection Law: An Analysis of the Broadest Law in the World*. Bangkok: Burma Lawyer's Council, 2001.

Ibrahim, Azeem. *The Rohingyas: Inside Myanmar's Hidden Genocide*. London: Hurst, 2016.

International Crisis Group, *Counting the Costs: Myanmar's Problematic Census*. Asia Briefing 144 (2014). www.crisisgroup.org/asia/south-east-asia/myanmar/counting-costs-myanmar-s-problematic-census (accessed October 3, 2018).

Justice Trust. *Hidden Hands Behind the Communal Violence in Myanmar*. Bangkok: Justice Trust, 2015.

Lintner, Bertil. *Land of Jade: A Journey Through Insurgent Burma*. Edinburgh: Kiscadale Publications, 1990.

Lone, Wa, and Shoon Naing. "At Least 71 Killed in Myanmar as Rohingya Insurgents Stage Major Attack." *Reuters*, August 24, 2017. www.reuters.com/article/us-myanmar-rohingya/at-least-71-killed-in-myanmar-as-rohingya-insurgents-stage-major-attack-idUSKCN1B507K.

Matthews, Bruce. "Religious Minorities in Myanmar – Hints of the Shadow." *Contemporary South Asia* 4, no. 3 (1995): 287–308.

Ministry of Labour, Immigration and Population. "Population and Housing Census of Myanmar: Union Report." www.dop.gov.mm/en/publication-category/census (accessed October 3, 2018).

Mozur, Paul. "A Genocide Incited on Facebook, with Posts from Myanmar's Military," *New York Times*, October 15, 2018. www.nytimes.com/2018/10/15/technology/myanmar-facebook-genocide.html (accessed November 2, 2018).

Mudde, Cas. "Populism: An Ideational Approach." In *The Oxford Handbook on Populism*, edited by Cristóbal Rovira Kaltwasser, Paul Taggart, Paulina Ochoa Espejo, and Pierre Ostiguy, 27–47. Oxford: Oxford University Press, 2017.

Mudde, Cas, and Cristóbal Rovira Kaltwasser. *Populism: A Very Short Introduction*. Oxford: Oxford University Press, 2017.

"Exclusionary vs. Inclusionary Populism: Comparing Contemporary Europe and Latin America." *Government and Opposition*, 48, no. 2 (2013): 147–174.

Myint, Ni Ni. *Burma's Struggle against British Imperialism 1885–1895*. Yangon: The Universities Press, 1983.

Myint-U, Thant. *The Making of Modern Burma*. Cambridge: Cambridge University Press, 2001.

The River of Lost Footsteps: A Personal History of Burma. New York: FSG, 2006.

Nemoto, Kei. "The Concepts of Dobama (Our Burma) and Thudo-Bama (Their Burma) in Burmese Nationalism, 1930–1948." *Journal of Burma Studies* 5 (2000): 1–16.

Pittaway, Eileen. "The Rohingya Refugees in Bangladesh: The Failure of the International Protection System." In *Protracted Displacement in Asia: No Place to Call Home*, edited by H. Adelman, 83–106. Aldershot: Ashgate, 2008.

Schonthal, Benjamin, and Matthew J. Walton. "The (New) Buddhist Nationalisms? Symmetries and Specificities in Sri Lanka and Myanmar." *Contemporary Buddhism* 17, no. 1 (2016): 81–115.

Silverstein, Josef. *The Political Legacy of Aung San*. New York: Cornell University Press, 1972.

Smith, Donald E. *Religion and Politics in Burma*. Princeton, NJ: Princeton University Press, 1965.

Smith, Martin. *Burma: Insurgency and the Politics of Ethnicity*. London: Zed Books, 1991.

Taylor, Robert. "Do States Make Nations? The Politics of Identity in Myanmar Revisited." *South East Asia Research* 13, no. 3 (2017): 261–286.

Taylor, Robert H. "Perceptions of Ethnicity in the Politics of Burma." *Southeast Asian Journal of Social Science* 10, no. 1 (1982): 7–22.

Yegar, Moshe. *The Muslims of Burma: A Study of a Minority Group*. Wiesbaden: Otto Harrassowitz, 1972.

9

In Defense of Democratic Populism

Douglas A. Johnson[1]

(K)eep close to the people. They are always right and will mislead no one.[2]

Abraham Lincoln

I INTRODUCTION

Much of current academic literature largely construes populism as a threat to liberal institutions and the rule of law, and thus damaging to international human rights norms and practice. This understanding of "populism" appears to equate it with authoritarian manipulations to entrench anti-democratic forces in power. However, before acceding to this view, I want to consider alternative understandings of populism as quintessentially democratic politics, and to ask, given the current and alarming rise of authoritarian discourse as a powerful political force, what the human rights movement might learn from both democratic and authoritarian populisms.

When the question was first posed to me about whether populism was a threat to human rights, I immediately thought of Tom Harkin. Harkin called himself a "prairie populist." A Member of the U.S. Congress in the 1970s, Harkin wrote some of the first human rights legislation, requiring the US government to respect and

[1] I would like to thank several people helpful to me in writing this chapter. Gerald Neuman, our editor and colleague, encouraged me to be part of his project, and his thoughtful comments, patience, and missed deadlines kept me going. Jane Mansbridge provided ideas and editing at an important juncture. Pippa Norris shared her syllabus for her course on "Authoritarian Populism" and continues to forward research and articles. I thank William Schulz for a series of helpful clarifications and conceptual suggestions. I especially thank Kathryn Sikkink for her support, editing, and conceptual challenges. Even with this help, the errors of judgment and fact are strictly my own.
[2] Carl Sandburg, *Abraham Lincoln: The Prairie Years and The War Years* (New York: Harcourt, Brace and World, 1954), 593.

promote human rights. He helped lay the groundwork that made it possible for Jimmy Carter to make human rights central to his foreign policy message. Later as a US Senator, Harkin continued working to protect human rights by voice, vote, and advancing new legislation. He is regarded as the heart and architect of the Americans with Disabilities Act, which later became a model used to draft the UN Convention on the Rights of Persons with Disabilities. Harkin's career embodied the moral values and expanded the institutional frameworks to protect human rights. Harkin started the Populist Caucus in the U.S. House of Representatives in 1983. He was a proponent of what I will call "democratic populism," though as a boy from Kansas, I still resonate with the term "prairie populists."

George McGovern was "widely described as a 'prairie populist' for his strong commitment to social justice and resolute critique of the corrupting effects of power."[3] Like Tom Harkin, other political leaders from the Midwest consciously identified themselves in this tradition. I learned as a child that the prairie populist movement was a progressive force at a time when unregulated monopolies squeezed rents out of farmers and laborers in the Midwest. The official Populist Party folded into the Democrats in the early 1900s, moving that party from its stance against post-Civil War Reconstruction into the liberal party of Franklin Roosevelt. Although the Progressive Republicans, including Teddy Roosevelt, abhorred the populists, their issues raised a constituency that then flowed to the Republicans when the Progressives became briefly dominant in that Party. Thus, populism as a political force was a key contributor to the great surge of democracy during the Progressive Era.[4]

Viktor Orbán of Hungary is now viewed as the poster-child of populism. For years, the press has identified Elizabeth Warren as a populist. What is the meaning of a word that covers such broad personal and ideological territory? Each of these cases and many discussed in this book are often labels used by others to describe someone they do not like. I will consider these cases, but also look to those who label themselves as populists, as Harkin does, to understand what they mean when they do so.

Richard Haass called President Trump the "world's most prominent populist."[5] Trump's political discourse surely fits into the frame used throughout this book as someone with authoritarian tendencies. But is he a populist?

In response to a reporter's question, Barak Obama challenged that view without specifically naming candidate Trump: "I'm not prepared to concede the notion that some of the rhetoric that is popping up is populist." After describing his own policies, he declared, "I suppose that that makes me a populist." President Obama

---

[3] Bart Bonikowski and Noam Gidron, "The Populist Style in American Politics: Presidential Campaign Discourse, 1952–1996," *Social Forces* 94, no. 4 (2016): 1606.

[4] Lawrence Goodwyn, *Democratic Promise: The Populist Moment in America* (New York: Oxford University Press, 1976).

[5] Richard Haass, "What the Global Elite Can Learn from the Donald," *Time*, February 5, 2018, 31.

did not denounce candidate Trump as a populist; he refused to give him the honor of the label. Obama continued:

> So, I would advise everybody to be careful about suddenly attributing to whoever pops up at a time of economic anxiety the label that they're "populist." Where have they been? Have they been on the front lines working on behalf of working people? Have they been carrying the labor to open opportunity for more people? There are people like Bernie Sanders, I think, who genuinely deserve the title, because he has been in the vineyards fighting on behalf of these issues.[6]

As I began to review the literature about populism, I was struck by the many definitions of populism, each becoming more negative and alarming. However, these seemed to me shaped without asking those who call themselves "populists" what they mean by it.

II DEFINITIONS: SO, WHAT IS POPULISM?

President Obama saw populism as an orientation to the needs of ordinary citizens, as a struggle on behalf of working people. Academics have more complex views but largely use the term pejoratively. Cas Mudde writes: "the very notion of populism tends to receive a negative connotation in both the scholarly and public debate, since it is commonly analysed as a pathological phenomenon."[7] Some point out that populist movements, such as the Tea Party or what Pippa Norris calls "authoritarian populists" now building in Europe, contrast the deserving "people" with the undeserving outsider.[8] Mudde says right-wing populism involves nationalism or xenophobia and a strong state that delivers social welfare, but which excludes minorities and other "outsiders," a phenomenon he calls "welfare chauvinism."[9] He defines populism as "a thin-centred ideology that considers society to be ultimately separated into two homogeneous and antagonistic groups, 'the pure people' versus 'the corrupt elite,' and which argues that politics should be an expression of the volonté générale (general will) of the people."[10] Similarly, Gerald Neuman, earlier in this volume, "favors the "ideational approach," which understands populism as employing an exclusionary notion of the people – the 'real people,' as

---

[6] Joint news conference with the Mexican President Peña Nieto and Canadian Prime Minister Justin Trudeau at the "Three Amigos" summit on June 29, 2016, in Ottawa, Canada. Transcript by Douglas A. Johnson from the YouTube video: www.youtube.com/watch?v=QSOWEC1qZRE.

[7] Cas Mudde and Cristóbal Rovira Kaltwasser, "Exclusionary vs. Inclusionary Populism: Comparing Contemporary Europe and Latin America," *Government and Opposition* 48, no. 2 (2013): 149.

[8] Michael Minkenberg, "The Tea Party and American Populism Today: Between Protest, Patriotism and Paranoia," *Der Moderne Staat – DMS: Zeitschrift für Public Policy, Recht und Management* 4, no. 2 (2011): 284; Pippa Norris and Ronald Inglehart, *Cultural Backlash: Trump, Brexit and Authoritarian Populism* (Cambridge: Cambridge University Press, 2019).

[9] Cas Mudde, *Populist Radical Right Parties in Europe* (Cambridge: Cambridge University Press, 2007), 18–23.

[10] Mudde and Rovira Kaltwasser, "Exclusionary vs. Inclusionary Populism," 150.

opposed to disfavored groups that are unworthy – and that purports to rule on behalf of the 'real people,' whose will should not be constrained.'"[11] Jan-Werner Müller says that all populists are "anti-elitist, populists are always anti-pluralist. Populists claim that they, and they alone, represent the people."[12] Each of these attempts and others cast populism as a dangerous force. While these approaches capture something important about populism, they do not help us understand why someone with Obama's gifts of political communication would say, "I guess I am a populist."

Indeed, populist messaging has been important to mainstream political leaders in the US. In their study of presidential speeches from 1950 to 1996, Bonikowski and Gidron found that both Republican and Democratic candidates used discourse "predicated on a moral vilification of elites and a concomitant veneration of the common people."[13] They argue that efforts to classify political parties as populist or non-populist miss seeing populist discourse as a strategic tool of claims-making in democratic societies with competitive elections. Thus, populism is not an ideology, thick or thin, but a style of discourse which, they note from their research, was used most frequently by the opponent outside of power, such as Dwight Eisenhower in 1952, but diminishes in their rhetoric as the incumbent (Eisenhower in 1956).[14] The notion of strategic discourse raises a critique of populists that is implicit in the many definitions, namely that "the veneration of the common people" is a political and dishonest mask. As we see authoritarian populists entrenching themselves in power, this cynical view seems well supported. It does not leave room for our modern imaginations to see "the people," as Lincoln does, as a source of moral strength on which a political leader draws inspiration and hope.

Within those descriptions of populism considering elements of charismatic single leadership, of claims to embody a unified "people," of scapegoating minorities and immigrants, and – most importantly for this argument – disregarding rights and the rule of law, I argue that these characterize *some* populist movements and not others. I will thus distinguish between democratic populism and authoritarian populism. Many of the examples cited in this volume are authoritarians who disregard rights and the rule of law, but this is not the case of democratic populists. I argue that often-ascribed characteristics of populism, the single charismatic leader and the opposition to corrupt elites, lie on a spectrum in which one end is authoritarian and on the other is action legitimately appropriate to the role of social movements in a democratic society. What concerns me about the tenor of critique characterizing populism in opposition to human rights is that the leaders, institutions, and movements for human rights should not put themselves in a position of saying that the critiques of elites and the popular movements challenging the power of elites are

---

[11] Chapter 1 (in this volume).
[12] Jan-Werner Müller, *What Is Populism?* (Philadelphia, PA: University of Pennsylvania Press, 2016), 9.
[13] Bonikowski and Gidron, "Populist Style," 1594.
[14] Bonikowski and Gidron, "Populist Style," 1605.

illegitimate. Whether the power of elites is inordinate and corrupt is an empirical question, but the global trend of concentration of wealth threatens efforts to protect and promote human rights, especially economic, social, and cultural rights. At its deepest level, I believe that human rights must be a challenge to arbitrary uses of power and those many defenders on the local and international stages should embody hope to social movements that challenge power.

III DEMOCRATIC AND AUTHORITARIAN POPULISM CONTRASTED

A *Democratic Populism*

1 The Early Democratic Populists

To understand populism, we should begin with the meaning understood by those who actually call themselves "populist." Populism is a historical force in the United States, necessitated by the essentially conservative structure of the American federal system. Voting rights were highly limited, with each state determining who qualified to participate in the American experiment. Slaves and women were, by definition, disqualified. But in many states, only propertied males or the literate were granted voting rights. Thus, from the beginning there is a struggle between the ideals set out in the Declaration of Independence and the system of governance established by the Constitution.

Thomas Jefferson, as the author of the Declaration and as President and political agitator, framed the early debate in the US contrasting the rights of the common people to elites, though he was of the slaveholding elite. However, his stirring words represented an aspiration taken on by social movements to expand freedom and voting rights.[15] Andrew Jackson, both a slaveholder and responsible for the "Trail of Tears" against native peoples, styled himself as "a man of the people" and is credited as an early populist leader who rallied against the financial and political elites. Both their political rhetoric and projects were oriented to the "yeoman" they conceived as the builders of a strong agriculturally based culture and economy. While Alexander Hamilton and the Federalists favored selling land for high prices to fund Federal economic infrastructure projects, Jefferson's policy was to sell lands cheaply and get them into the hands of small farmers. As the western lands began to fill with small farmers and town-based traders, Jackson pushed for the expansion of voting rights to expand democracy, rather than inhibit it. This orientation of public policy to "the common man" rather than the moneyed interests of the East continued as a theme

---

[15] For an fascinating discussion of Jefferson's views that laws should expire each generation to prevent the dead from unduly influencing a democracy of the living, see Astra Taylor, "Traditions of the Future," *Le Monde diplomatique*, May 9, 2019, https://mondediplo.com/openpage/traditions-of-the-future.

in American politics.[16] This theme was overshadowed in the 1850s by the debate over slavery but reemerged in the post-Civil war period.

2 Background to the Rise of the US Populist Party

During the Civil War, US industrial policy favored the development of capital investment in railroads, telegraphs, and all production that aided the war effort, including arms and ammunition, of course, but also food production and processing, clothing and leather manufacture, transportation, and energy, especially coal mining. Although the demand for increasing troop strength was constant, this industrial growth also required a dramatic growth in an urban working class. Even though Lincoln bent himself to the production of resources needed to fight the war, he remained interested in the protection of the working classes.[17] As he was raised a yeoman farmer, his rhetoric remained oriented to the concept of the ordinary citizen as the basis of the moral value of the American form of government.

The war effort and the expansion of the railroads encouraged a shift from subsistence agriculture to cash crops, making farmers increasingly subject to market conditions. New levels of farm mechanization allowed the production of more crops; it also required capital investment that put farmers into debt. Dramatic increases in crop levels led to a fall in crop prices that deeply affected the livelihoods of farm families. It also brought them into direct contact with two politically powerful sets of institutions, railroads and banks, that were seen as corrupt and exploitative as monopolies can be without regulation.[18]

In this context and building on previous farmer-organizing efforts such as The Grange, the Populist Party began as a loose network of farmer and labor organizations and coalesced into an official party in 1892.[19] It appears that this is the first use of the term "populist" in the name of a political party. Officially, the People's Party, they embraced the Populist Party name. It adopted the statement of purposes and goals, "the Omaha Platform," at its national convention on July 4, 1892. The declaration begins, "We meet in the midst of a Nation brought to the verge of moral, political, and material ruin. Corruption dominates the ballot box, the

---

[16] Robert W. Merry, "Andy Jackson's Populism," *The American Conservative*, www.theamerican conservative.com/articles/andy-jacksons-populism/(accessed May 23, 2019).

[17] "And, inasmuch [as] most good things are produced by labor, it follows that [all] such things of right belong to those whose labor has produced them. But it has so happened in all ages of the world that some have labored, and others have, without labor, enjoyed a large portion of the fruits. This is wrong and should not continue. To [secure] to each laborer the whole product of his labor, or as nearly as possible, is a most worthy object of any good government." *From Lincoln in His Own Words*, ed. Milton Meltzer (London: Sandpiper, 2009), 60.

[18] Philip L. Darg, "The Farmer-Labor Party in Minnesota Politics: 1918–1948," PhD dissertation, University of North Dakota, 2015, https://search-proquest-com.ezp-prod1.hul.harvard.edu/doc view/1775525061/?pq-origsite=primo, 6.

[19] Darg, "Farmer-Labor Party," 7.

Legislature, the Congress, and touches even the ermine of the bench."[20] The Populist Party's overall purpose was "to restore the government of the Republic to the hands of 'the plain people,' with which class it originated."[21] Here is the contrast discussed throughout this volume: the orientation to the common person in opposition to corrupt elites.

As the first formal statement of the populists' purpose, the Populist Party's platform helps us understand their political aspirations. First and foremost, the platform calls for the expansion of the money supply:

> Our country finds itself confronted by conditions for which there is no precedent in the history of the world; our annual agricultural productions amount to billions of dollars in value, which must, within a few weeks or months, be exchanged for billions of dollars' worth of commodities consumed in their production; the existing currency supply is wholly inadequate to make this exchange; the results are falling prices, the formation of combines and rings, the impoverishment of the producing class.[22]

This is not the call of irresponsible spending for the benefit of political clients as often ascribed to populists, but rather recognition that the tight money supply based on the gold standard constricted trade to the benefit of the banking elites. "(A) national currency, safe, sound, and flexible, issued by the general government only," not involving the banks in its issuance, was a key part of the platform. Although this might appear to modern eyes as a technical issue without public appeal, it is because government tactics to manage the money supply have become commonplace.

Addressing the unequal power of the railroads, the Omaha Platform called for the nationalization of the railroads: "the time has come when the railroad corporations will either own the people or the people must own the railroads,"[23] In a similar vein, "given the importance of free commerce to the common citizens," the platform also said that telephone and telegraph services should be owned and operated by the government along the lines of the U.S. Postal Service. That agency is identified as a trusted institution, and to remove the power of the banks from daily life, the platform called for the establishment of postal savings banks to democratize the capacity to protect savings. Given the corrupting influence of the political patronage system, the

---

[20] "The Omaha Platform: Likely to Serve as a Basis for the St. Louis Declarations," *New York Times*, July 22, 1896, 2, www.nytimes.com/1896/07/22/archives/the-omaha-platform-likely-to-serve-as-a-basis-for-the-st-louis.html.

[21] "The Omaha Platform: Launching the Populist Party," http://historymatters.gmu.edu/d/5361/ (accessed January 13, 2019). This project of George Mason University includes the full text of the platform.

[22] "The Omaha Platform: Launching the Populist Party." All quotes in this paragraph are taken from this document.

[23] "The Omaha Platform: Launching the Populist Party." All quotes in this paragraph are taken from this document.

Populists called for a Constitutional amendment to establish a "civil-service regulation of the most rigid character." Far from attacking the institutions of liberal democracy, the Populist or People's Party wanted to increase its capacity to control wealthy and corrupt elites and, with some very practical ideas, increase the stability and influence of farmers and labor: "We believe that the power of government – in other words, of the people – should be expanded (as in the case of the postal service) as rapidly and as far as the good sense of an intelligent people and the teachings of experience shall justify, to the end that oppression, injustice, and poverty shall eventually cease in the land."

Other aspects of the once radical Populist political reform demands have made their way into accepted norms and institutions:

- Direct election of U.S. Senators;
- The secret ballot, "fairly counted";
- A graduated income tax;
- The 8-hour working day;
- The abolishment of "private armies," such as the Pinkerton guards, used by corporations to break strikes;
- The development of referendum and ballot initiatives.[24]

Two aspects of the Omaha platform, both focused on non-citizens, would give concern to our international human rights regime. The platform called for all land to be owned by citizens, rather than "aliens," a policy directed at wealthy foreigners and land speculators. The platform also called for restrictions on immigration that echo some of the most exclusionary language of current nationalists: "we condemn the fallacy of protecting American labor under the present system, which opens our ports to the pauper and criminal classes of the world and crowds out our wage-earners; and we denounce the present ineffective laws against contract labor, and demand the further restriction of undesirable emigration."[25] This is very much in the tradition of the "Know Nothing" party of the 1840s, a current running through parties of the left and the right at various times in the nation's history. The Populist opposition to immigration was driven by the political context: the labor movement was being violently repressed and wages were suppressed by the rapid growth of supply. It would be another forty years before the right to organize and to strike was recognized in Federal law.[26]

The Populists experienced success in elections of 1892 in the South, Midwest, and West, garnering over a million votes, winning four states and gaining 22 votes in the electoral college for its Presidential candidate, James B. Weaver. They won eleven seats in the U.S. House of Representatives, in addition to governors and majorities in

[24] "The Omaha Platform: Launching the Populist Party."
[25] "The Omaha Platform: Launching the Populist Party."
[26] National Labor Relations Act of 1935, 49 Stat. 449.

three state legislatures.[27] Attempts to appeal to the farmers of the Northeast and urban labor were not successful, however, even with labor leaders like Eugene Debs backing the Populists. William Jennings Bryan, famous for the "Cross of Gold" speech, won the Democratic nomination for President in the elections of 1896, and the Populist Party made an electoral alliance to achieve their platform demand of an expanded money supply, given their belief that the gold standard was the "cross" that crucified the working class. The alliance with the Democrats split the organizing energy of the People's Party, which was formally disbanded in 1908.

Many of the Populist Party's issues were taken up by the Progressive Movement, influencing reformers such as Theodore Roosevelt and Robert La Follett. This non-partisan reform movement developed a broader agenda than the Populists, including concern for abuse of corporate power beyond the banks and railroads, and the need to develop regulations to curb their abuses. The movement took up issues from the Populists like civil service reform, but also challenged the moneyed interests within their own parties to make them more democratic. The enthusiasm and mobilization of the Progressives became the more viable organizing option for the populists, although Roosevelt opposed the Populist Party for its more radical, class-based program, and the party continued to put up presidential candidates until 1908.[28] Teddy Roosevelt handily won every state where the populists were strongest.[29]

My purpose here is not to give a detailed history of the Populist Party but rather to point out that some of its distinguishing features remain central to modern definitions of populism, such as the focus on corrupt elites versus the people as a broad category. In contrast to views of populism as a tool of charismatic leaders, they did not rely on a charismatic leader who spoke "for the people" and who manipulated popular support to undermine institutions and entrench themselves in power. Quite the contrary. Populism was based on organizing among affected citizens (farmers and laborers) in networks that became more institutionalized, and they favored the expansion of American institutions to guarantee their rights. Bryan was certainly a charismatic orator, but the Populist Party endorsed him because he adopted the most important part of their political platform – the expansion of the money supply – and they did not continue with him in his multiple attempts at the Presidency. "Populism was the most significant mass movement challenging the foundations of corporate capitalism in US history. For this reason, it offered the greatest promise of a democratically organized society,"[30] notes J. Craig Jensen, creating an influence

---

[27] Darg, "Farmer-Labor Party," 8. The People's Party won the states of Colorado, Kansas, Idaho, and Nevada, and received Electoral College votes from North Dakota and Oregon.

[28] Darg, "Farmer-Labor Party," 9.

[29] "1904 United States Presidential Election," *Wikipedia*, January 8, 2019, https://en.wikipedia .org/w/index.php?title=1904_United_States_presidential_election&oldid=877442318.

[30] J. Craig Jenkins, review of *Radical Protest and Social Structure: The Southern Farmer's Alliance and Cotton Tenancy, 1880–1890*, by Michael Schwartz, and *Democratic Promise: The Populist Movement in America*, by Lawrence Goodwyn, *Theory and Society* 11, no. 5 (1982): 716.

that continues to inspire current political movements. This model of organizing for the interests of the ordinary citizens continued after the formal collapse of the party. Labor organizing, constantly under repression by corporations and government allies, nonetheless continued, as did cooperatives and institution building by the agrarian protest movement. "The goal of these disempowered classes was to maintain their concept of economic fairness and democracy through mass communication and organization."[31]

3 The Farmer-Labor Party of Minnesota

Perhaps the most successful of these post-Populist Party groups was the Farmer-Labor Party of Minnesota that sought to fuse together the political power of two citizen forces, farmers and labor. This was a difficult thing to do. Farmers were property holders who favored a reduction of property taxes in a local and state framework dependent on these taxes. Laborers had no property, but wanted expanded government programs and investments, such as job creation through public works and education that benefitted from higher taxes. Nonetheless, through grassroots organizing and mutual concern about the dominant power of corporations over both sectors, the party had electoral success in Minnesota. Initially the party ran in the Republican primaries in Minnesota and, when the candidates failed to win, ran again as a new party. Mindful of the fading nature of third parties, however, the leadership established the Farmer-Labor Federation in 1923 to organize local clubs and support the party but as a separate organization. "The official purpose of the organization was to promote political education designed to instill 'values of democracy and citizenship' and resist the influence of corporate interests."[32] Because the Federation was not a political party, trade unions were able to join, pay dues, and help build a robust organization.[33] At its height in the mid-1930s, the clubs' membership rose to over 20,000.[34]

In the elections of 1922, the Minnesota Farmer-Labor Party won a U.S. Senate and two House seats, its first successful bid, and became the main opposition party in the state.[35] Winning a special election in 1923, Magnus Johnson became the second Farmer-Labor Senator by defeating the sitting Republican governor.[36] With this electoral success, the Farmer-Labor Federation (later renamed the Association) began to consolidate the organization of a long-term grassroots political movement and party, calling for state and federal activism in support of small farmers and the

---

[31] Darg, "Farmer-Labor Party," 18.
[32] Darg, "Farmer-Labor Party," 167.
[33] Paul S. Holbo, "The Farmer-Labor Association, Minnesota's Party within a Party," *Minnesota History* 38, no. 7 (1963): 302.
[34] Holbo, "Farmer-Labor Association," 303.
[35] Darg, "Farmer-Labor Party," 155.
[36] Darg, "Farmer-Labor Party," 166.

working class. Like the Populist Party before it, "Farmer-Labor policy was based on perceptions of economic injustice which both the party's leaders and its members saw being committed by entrenched corporate interests in league with a corrupted (or corruptible) government at the expense of the common farmer and laborer."[37] The specific demands included government ownership of key aspects of economic infrastructure that would diminish the price-setting power of corporations, such as grain elevators where farmers could store their grain until prices recovered.[38] Although details changed over time, Farmer-Labor policy "was based on perceptions of economic injustice" by powerful corporate interests in combination with corrupt government, and "The solutions often proposed in answer to this situation was government intervention into the economic sphere as an agent that would put common 'producers' and 'consumers' on even ground with the corporate giants."[39]

The Farmer-Labor Party was a populist party by intent and purpose. Yet it does not meet the definition now in vogue defining a "populist leader" claiming to speak for the will of the people and relying on charisma. A party of the left, it created a robust organization of grassroots members that had both state and national agendas. Though it had many leaders, Floyd B. Olson was doubtless the most popular and effective. Beginning in 1930, Olson won the governorship with nearly 57 percent of the popular vote[40], was re-elected two more times, and was considered a viable presidential candidate. He died in office in 1936 from stomach cancer and was followed by two more Farmer-Labor governors.[41] The party produced four U.S. Senators, eight members of Congress, and a majority of the Minnesota legislature. Facing declining political prospects in the late 1930s, it merged with the Democratic Party in 1944 to become the Minnesota Democratic-Farmer Labor Party, which it remains to this day.[42]

The Populist and Farmer-Labor Parties were two manifestations of what has become known as "prairie populism," a belief that government policy should be oriented to the needs of common, ordinary citizens, and that popular organizing in social movements and political parties is necessary to overcome the privilege of economic elites. It is worth noting that neither of these early populist parties relied on a single charismatic leader; both focused on organizing within communities and uniting pre-existing networks of farmers and laborers. They opposed the traditional political party rule by bosses and sought more democratic means of conducting party business. Nor did they use their power on the state level to create authoritarian measures that would favor their hold on power. They did not attempt to disrupt the

---

37 Darg, "Farmer-Labor Party," 179.
38 Darg, "Farmer-Labor Party," 171–172.
39 Darg, "Farmer-Labor Party," 180.
40 Darg, "Farmer-Labor Party," 228.
41 Darg, "Farmer-Labor Party," 217–287.
42 Darg, "Farmer-Labor Party," 357–367.

national constitutional order but proposed new institutions designed to protect the interests of the working classes.

This tradition is not opposed to government institutions but seeks to make them more responsive to the needs of society at large. By tradition, it was largely a progressive movement.

It is this tradition to which President Obama referred. When Tom Harkin started the Populist Caucus in the U.S. House of Representatives in 1983, he said, "Populists are in favor of a strong government in the area of antitrust and regulating those natural kinds of monopolies that have control of natural resources."[43] As an example, he pointed to the need for the Federal government to regulate natural gas.[44] That caucus disappeared when Harkin moved to the Senate, but was later reestablished by another Iowa Democratic House Member, Bruce Braley, who said, "A populist is someone who fights for common sense economic policies that sustain and expand the middle class. The Populist Caucus is intended to bring members of Congress together around a few core economic issues to strengthen the middle class. Generally speaking, populists in history have championed the needs of working people and advocated a more democratic society."[45] There was a large overlap with the House Progressive Caucus, so the Populist Caucus went defunct in 2014.[46] But this did not end the view that populism was a positive force in American politics. As Mounk says, "For those who wish to usher in a new period of relative democratic stability, the challenge will be to harness the passion of the populists to the cause of reinvigorating governance, but without helping them kindle the flames of an antidemocratic revolt."[47]

This analysis has relied heavily on the history of American populists, pointing to specific human rights leadership of self-identified populists. There is a growing call among US progressives to see that populist messaging, especially policies to aid the broad majority of middle-class and poor citizens, is an essential element to halt the nativism of Trump. But democratic populist movements are developing in other parts of the world as a counter to both neoliberal economic policies and authoritarian populism. "Podemos" of Spain and Syriza in Greece are such movements. There is also theorizing on what a left-wing populism should be, for example, as in the work of Argentine Ernesto Laclau and Belgian Chantal Mouffe, which demonstrates how far it is from the exclusionary form of authoritarian parties.

---

[43] Julia Malone, "Modern-day Populist Movement Sprouts among House Democrats," *Christian Science Monitor*, February 28, 1983, www.csmonitor.com/1983/0228/022847.html (quoting Harkin).

[44] Malone, "Modern-day Populist Movement."

[45] Chris Weigant, "Exclusive Interview with Rep. Bruce Braley, Populist Caucus Founder and Chairman," *Huffington Post*, March 11, 2009. www.huffingtonpost.com/chris-weigant/exclusive-interview-with_b_174033.html.

[46] "Populist Caucus," *Wikipedia*, en.wikipedia.org/wiki/Populist_Caucus.

[47] Yascha Mounk, "Pitchfork Politics: The Populist Threat to Liberal Democracy," *Foreign Affairs* 93, no. 5 (2014): 35.

Reviewing their ideas, John B. Judis says that "the couple argued that a left must build a historical bloc out of diverse classes – the white-collar as well as blue-collar working class and the small business sector – and diverse struggles (including feminism, antiracism, anti-war, and ecology) that can't be reduced to a struggle between classes."[48]

B *Authoritarian Populists*

Concerns about demagogues and their capacity to influence and manipulate the populace are at least as old as Socrates and Athenian democracy. There is a constant struggle between ideals within democracies about creating policies that work for all in society versus the powerful few, and protection of individuals with institutions of law that prevent mob rule and disorder. Socrates' choice of a death penalty over exile made him the poster-child of free speech, obscuring both his authoritarian, non-democratic views and their influence on some of his disciples carrying out bloody, repressive coups against Athenian democracy.[49]

Steeped in the Socratic virtues, British and American political elites were keen to promote stability by limiting the impact of what they characterized as mob rule in favor of a system with strongly undemocratic features. Those protected by this stability included small and sparsely populated states at the expense of populous states and a slave-holding minority in the South. In contrast, Lincoln believed in the ultimate fairness of the people, and championed the interest of working people over capital. American history, as well as that of other democracies around the world, involves the struggle to expand the franchise to include more and more of the populace. At each phase, a social movement promoted the change, always having to overcome the resistance of those already included. Many of the great moral advances in human rights, from the end of slavery to voting rights first for racial minorities and then for women, came as a result of social movements that challenged their elites.

Socrates could have spent his time thinking of ways to channel democratic governance into careful deliberation and decision-making. He would, of course, have had to hide more effectively his contempt for ordinary people. However, he chose, and his acolyte Plato chose, to champion authoritarianism and dictatorship of "the wise." "Respect for authority" is one of the identified "five universal moral instincts,"[50] so we should not be surprised that some elevate this to justify strongman leadership.

---

[48] John Judis, "Rethinking Populism," *Dissent* 63, no. 4 (2016): 118, DOI: 10.1353/dss.2016.0082.

[49] I.F. (Isidor Feinstein) Stone, *The Trial of Socrates* (Boston: Little, Brown, 1988), 111. "For the overthrow of the democracy in 411 B.C. was initiated by his favorite, Alcibiades, and the overthrow of 404 B.C. was led by Critias and Charmides, who appear as associates of Socrates in the dialogues of Plato, a cousin of Critias and a nephew of Charmides."

[50] Steven Pinker, "The Moral Instinct," *New York Times*, Magazine, January 13, 2008.

What I find most important about the "authoritarian populists,"[51] as compared to authoritarians in the past, is that they rely in new ways on elections. By relying on electoral support, they gain greater credibility and legitimacy because of the more widespread and modern value that leaders should be chosen by citizens, by majorities. Winning elections requires finding popular messages that appeal to voters' perceptions of their needs and wants. There are competing descriptions and explanations for this new breed of authoritarians: competitive authoritarians,[52] stealth authoritarians,[53] autocratic legalism.[54] Viktor Orbán took the warning label of "illiberal democracy"[55] and transformed it into a title of a respectable political project. It is tempting to use this labeling to distinguish between "liberal populism" and "illiberal populism." What these descriptors hold in common is the understanding of the essentially authoritarian nature of these regimes.

Authoritarians have always focused on messages of threat to justify both their rule and their rules. The Argentine junta came to power with public support because it promised to end "subversion" and violence of the revolutionary left. The Pinochet regime made the same promise, though it faced not violence but what it perceived as the chaos of social mobilization. The Soviet Union and Cuba emphasized the external threat of the West, especially the United States. The legitimacy of these regimes fell over time as they proved to be not only undemocratic but also incompetent to rule fairly, and morally weakened by corruption. At the same time, the values of democracy in the world gained increasing legitimacy. This appeal to internal and external threat has been an effective tool of legitimizing authoritarians throughout human history. What is new is the perceived need to add the legitimacy of elections to the autocrat's toolkit. Of course, elections were held in the Soviet Union, with candidates preselected by the ruling elite. Atatürk famously dealt with political divisions in his society by founding multiple parties with himself as leader. The growth of international institutions committed to free and fair elections, such as the Organization for Security and Cooperation in Europe, also elaborated more specific standards of what democracy meant in operational terms. These and other parts of the human rights framework established guiderails that defined democratic regimes. The new authoritarians have developed tactics to stay close to those guidelines while subverting them.

---

[51] Ronald Inglehart and Pippa Norris, "Trump and the Populist Authoritarian Parties: *The Silent Revolution* in Reverse," *Perspectives on Politics* 15, no. 2 (2017): 443–454, DOI: 10.1017/S1537592717000111. I am grateful to Prof. Norris for sharing her wisdom and her syllabus of her course "Authoritarian Populism" at the Harvard Kennedy School, 2018.

[52] Steven Levitsky and Lucan Way, "The Rise of Competitive Authoritarianism," *Journal of Democracy* 13, no. 2 (2002): 51–65, DOI: 10.1353/jod.2002.0026.

[53] Ozan O. Varol, "Stealth Authoritarianism," *Iowa Law Review* 100, no. 4 (2015): 1673–1742.

[54] Kim Lane Scheppele, "Autocratic Legalism," *The University of Chicago Law Review* 85, no. 2 (2018): 545–584.

[55] Fareed Zakaria, "The Rise of Illiberal Democracy," *Foreign Affairs* 76, no. 6 (1997): 22–43.

These new authoritarians, like the old, take advantage of the human tendency to divide the world into insiders and outsiders, to use nationalism and xenophobia to define others as unclean, foreign, not fully human, and therefore a threat to the people. Judis notes that "in Western Europe, the term 'populist' has been primarily used in a pejorative way – to refer to demagogic appeals by right-wing parties that, according to their detractors, exploit the public's ignorance and ethnic and religious resentments."[56] Orbán denigrated first the Roma but found that Muslim refugees were an even more effective target group for mobilizing fear and hatred of others. Narendra Modi, the current authoritarian Prime Minister of India, defined Muslims as external invaders who gained too much power over a pure Hindu culture. Rodrigo Duterte, authoritarian populist President of the Philippines, dehumanized as outsiders not just criminals and drug dealers but drug users, and said they needed to be expunged from society. Trump found dehumanizing outsiders, especially immigrants, an equally effective mobilizing tool.

Yet President Obama refuses to grant Trump the honor of the title of "populist." Rather, he is a nativist, in Obama's words, a tribalist who legitimizes only a minority of the country; Trump calls himself a nationalist, but it is the tribe, not the nation that he represents. Moreover, if Obama is right to challenge the notion that Trump is a populist, perhaps this is also true for Duterte, Erdoğan, Modi, and Orbán. Fundamentally, they are nativist authoritarians.

Authoritarian populists also differ from conservatives. Mainstream conservatives believe in the primacy of the status quo, and thus the protection of the political and economic institutions that maintain it.[57] Conservatives believe that government should be restricted in its size and scope, especially in what they might call "redistributive" policies. They believe in the authority of the economic and political elites as the creators of value and stability. From his study of European conservative parties, Daniel Ziblatt thinks "that when one looks around the world historically, at key moments, conservatives have been a hinge of history. Their reaction to forces of change shape whether or not a democracy survives."[58] The key, says Ziblatt, is the capacity to form a coherent political party that can contain the far right as well as providing the opportunity to win elections. In those cases, he argues, conservative parties have helped to consolidate democracies, or, when they fail and make coalitions with right-wing authoritarian movements, they weaken it.

Again, Orbán is instructive. When a radical right-wing movement, Jobbik, gained increasing prominence to challenge his supermajority in the 2014 elections, Orbán moved his political party, Fidesz, towards the radical right. He so effectively took control of that political space that Jobbik relocated itself as a more centrist party

---

[56] Judis, "Rethinking Populism," 5.

[57] I want to thank William Schultz for helping me to clarify this distinction.

[58] Uri Friedman, "Why Conservative Parties Are Central to Democracy," *The Atlantic*, June 14, 2017, www.theatlantic.com/international/archive/2017/06/ziblatt-democracy-conservative-parties/ 530118/.

in 2018,[59] coming in second place in the elections with a moderate platform. Orbán's principle was simply to win elections and cement his control to further his authoritarian state; his coalition once again controlled a super-majority in Parliament, sufficient to change the constitution at will. He used nativist arguments to appeal to voters, reinforced by providing one million passports and voter rights to the Hungarian diaspora, primarily in Romania and other Hungarian linguistic remnants in Eastern Europe likely to vote for him. He made no other promises of social welfare nor economic benefits to this expanded constituency. In contrast, facing a declining workforce in Hungary because young people are leaving his new society, rather than desert his opposition to augmenting a workforce through immigration, Orbán's new Parliament passed legislation requiring Hungarian workers to work 400 hours of overtime without compensation. Dubbed the "slave law," this sparked a series of protest demonstrations by popular movements.[60]

While mainstream conservatives champion elites, keep the government from interfering with the economic system, and propose judicial restraint, elected authoritarians such as Orbán blatantly use government to reshape public institutions – the judiciary, the electoral system in its entirety, the media, the civil service, even governance of the universities – to further their political and economic dominance. These tactics of domination are now so widely used by today's elected authoritarians that academics have identified their shared repetitive steps, such as Larry Diamond's 12-step program for autocrats.[61] There are, of course, other forms of authoritarian regimes, including outright dictatorship and rogue regimes. However, the emerging trend in authoritarianism relies on elections to support its legitimacy and justify its activities as democratic decision-making. What unites the "exclusionary populism" common to the right-wing parties of Europe and the "inclusionary populism" of Latin America[62] are the authoritarian tactics they put into place to cement an election outcome into permanent control of the resources of the state.

IV WHY DO WE NEED DEMOCRATIC POPULISM?

"Populism is Democracy's Way of Saying 'Listen Harder,'" was the title Jane Mansbridge gave to a recent talk about populism and democratic theory.[63]

---

[59] Marton Dunai, "Hungary's Jobbik Ditches Far-Right Past to Challenge Orbán in 2018," *Reuters*, January 11, 2017, www.reuters.com/article/us-hungary-jobbik/hungarys-jobbik-ditches-far-right-past-to-challenge-Orbán-in-2018-idUSKBN14V1PW (accessed April 14, 2019).

[60] Marc Santora and Benjamin Novak, "Protesting 'Slave Law,' Thousands Take to Streets in Hungary," *The New York Times*, January 6, 2019, www.nytimes.com/2019/01/05/world/europe/hungary-protests-slave-law.html.

[61] DemDigest, "Are Elected Leaders 'Making the World Less Democratic'?," *Democracy Digest* (blog), July 23, 2018, www.demdigest.org/are-elected-leaders-making-the-world-less-democratic/.

[62] Mudde and Kaltwasser, "Exclusionary vs. Inclusionary Populism."

[63] Jane Mansbridge, "Populism is Democracy's Way of Saying 'Listen Harder.'" Presentation, Princeton University, May 11, 2017. See also Jane Mansbridge and Stephen Macedo, "Populism and Democratic Theory," *Annual Review of Law and Social Science* 15 (2019): 59–77.

The reasons I give here for why human rights activists need democratic populism are all variants on this theme of needing to listen. First, human rights law, institutions, and NGOs can sometimes be perceived as elitist and distant from the people they aim to serve.

Lucia Nader, former director of an important human rights NGO in Brazil, told a story about a moment when she and her co-workers looked down from their NGO offices at street protests which they had not helped to organize and which they did not even anticipate. Nader worried that NGOs have had to become too professionalized and "solid." Such solidity may put them at a disadvantage in what Nader refers to as the more "liquid world" of street protests and social media.[64] Building a human rights culture is not only the work of legal tactics or analysis but also the tasks of organizing and mobilizing broader and broader constituencies who demand economic and political systems that meet their needs with dignity. Human rights activists could learn from the democratic populists of the early twentieth century in the United States who were very involved in building movements and constituencies and reflecting the needs and the concerns of the common people. More broadly, populism draws our attention to aspects of the US political system and the political systems in other countries that have a status quo bias.

A *Populism as an Antidote to the Status Quo Bias*

American political arrangements have shaped the nature and need for populism in the United States. Sometimes a social movement targeting elites is necessary to crack through a strongly entrenched and self-reinforcing status quo.

The American political structure is almost uniquely designed to make passage of new laws extremely difficult. Power and authority are dispersed on many levels, not only between States and the Federal levels but at the county, city, and township. At each of these levels, the consideration and passage of legislation are complex. Many rules are inherently undemocratic. Some populations have more voting power than others do, such as in the U.S. Senate, where the half million people of Wyoming have the same influence as the 39 million of California. Senate rules make the matters even less democratic; a tiny number of Senators – even one – can override the will of the majority by claiming the right to filibuster. This creates what Yale political scientist Ted Marmor calls a "status quo bias in American political institutions. America has a constitutional design that reflected the preoccupation of its 18th century citizens – restraining tyranny. It was not designed to accomplish policy ends."[65]

That status quo can become self-reinforcing in many ways. In the United States, for example, the whole system we call "checks and balances" was designed to prevent

---

[64] Lucia Nader, "Solid Organisations in a Liquid World," *Sur International Journal on Human Rights* 11, no. 20 (2014): 482–489.

[65] Telephone interview with the author, March 18, 2018.

either an authoritarian president or the forces of "mob rule" from using the powers of government to contravene rights and act self-interestedly against the common good. The framers designed the system intentionally to make it difficult to pass laws. Today, however, that extreme difficulty frequently produces not only general dysfunction but also the continuation of conditions that benefit existing elites.

As a result, public policy needs can fester and worsen for decades without resolution, and even a crisis will not necessarily resolve them. This status quo bias "serves, but was not intended to serve, the interests of those who are socio-economically powerful."[66] This inertia favors the economic interests of powerful American actors who have an alternative way to make a difference: investing their resources to keep pushing for program attention that, in the absence of their resources, would not move forward. This need to keep a policy proposal on the agenda works best for those whose self-interest is directly served by the policy. The US political system is not the only one with a bias in favor of powerful economic elites. As Charles Lindblom warned years ago in his classic text, *Politics and Markets*, in market systems businesspersons have a privileged role in government that is greater than any leadership group other than government officials themselves.[67]

The status quo bias built into the constitution, which emerges from time to time in deeply dysfunctional ways, creates a permanent need within the American people to find ways to build political power outside of the established system in order to balance the benefits of the political and especially economic system to the needs of all. The tool for doing so often targets the political and economic elites, and so is often called populism. This populism, however, is the arena for doing something counter to the status quo bias. It is popular mobilization on moral grounds. For example, populists like Bernie Sanders are returning to moral language about health care. Moral claims are what keep a social movement attached to a vision. As Marmor puts it, such "social movements are crucial for American reform."[68]

I respect the concerns expressed in these chapters about the renewed strength of authoritarian populism. However, I agree with Mansbridge and with Mounk, who notes,

> These economic populists are right to point out that contemporary democracies are far from flawless. Left to its own devices, capitalist democracy has a tendency to put more power in the hands of the already powerful and more wealth in the hands of the already wealthy. To counterbalance this gradual erosion of economic and

---

[66] Theodore Marmor and Rudolf Klein, *Politics, Health, and Health Care: Selected Essays* (New Haven, CT: Yale University Press, 2012), 1–21.

[67] Charles Lindblom, *Politics and Markets: The World's Political-Economic Systems* (New York: Basic Books, 1980).

[68] Marmor and Klein, *Politics*.

political justice, democracies need occasional eruptions of popular anger. In that sense, left-wing populism can be an important corrective to the self-serving temptations to which any elite is likely to succumb over time.[69]

B *Democratic Populism Is Consonant with Human Rights*

So, is populism antithetical to human rights? Authoritarian populists are "inherently ill-disposed to international regulation or governance and hence to human rights."[70] However, democratic populism is a different matter.

Tom Harkin is one of my political heroes. As a young man serving as a Congressional aide, he uncovered the use of tiger cages to imprison and humiliate accused Viet Cong. Entering Congress as a Democrat from Iowa in 1976, he immediately joined with Minnesota Representative Don Fraser to develop the essential structure of the American human rights policy. Harkin sponsored legislation, pushed for investigative hearings, and hired a dedicated staff to work full-time on human rights protections. From this point forward, every formal and informal group interested in human rights issues worked with his office. Harkin's democratic populism is fully consonant with human rights.

Both American history and today's political scene make it clear that democratic populism and human rights are *not* opposed to one another. Harkin, Warren, Obama, and Sanders believe in US institutions. They also understand the need to mobilize public moral outrage to counterbalance the status quo bias that unduly benefits elites and the powerful. They represent the 99 percent. They are democratic populists who believe in human rights.

They are also populists who believe in inclusion. Cas Mudde and Cristóbal Rovira Kaltwasser note a difference between "exclusive populisms," which focus on shutting out stigmatized groups, such as minorities, immigrants or felons, and "inclusive populisms" that demand that politics be opened up to those stigmatized groups, such as the poor, minorities, and other disenfranchised groups.[71]

In the interests of finding a unifying theory of populism "as exclusionary notion of the people," some scholars equate two very different targets of opprobrium: a racial or ethnic minority or immigrants (exclusionary populism) or corrupt economic elites (inclusionary populism). These are very different kinds of discourse. One is a denial of humanity and rights; the other is a conversation about power. Those who actually call themselves populists are concerned about how those with economic dominance protect and enrich themselves through taking over political power, shaping it in their self-interest. If human rights norms represent the values of fairness

---

[69] Mounk, "Pitchfork Politics," 34.
[70] Personal communication from William Schulz. I am grateful for the feedback and his many suggestions for developing this chapter.
[71] Mudde and Rovira Kaltwasser, "Exclusionary vs. Inclusionary Populism."

to all, of individuals' rights in contrast to their arbitrary abuse, then it must also be a discourse that addresses the misuse of power.

C *The Human Rights Movement Can Learn from Populism*

Only a passion can triumph over a passion.

Helvétius[72]

The headline read "Are Dems Ready for Elizabeth Warren's Angry Populist Message?"[73] Is the populist message one of anger? If so, should it be welcomed or avoided? Much of the literature on populism focuses critically on messages that accentuate fear and anger as mobilizers of the masses. They express implicitly or explicitly discomfort with emotion, especially negative emotions, in political discourse of "populists." Yet emotion is very important not only in political life but in everyday decision-making. Saul Alinsky, the Chicago community organizer and rabble-rouser, used to say that anger was an important motivator to begin social movements. However, he warned that anger burns out quickly and can turn into despair. What sustains a movement is another emotion entirely: hope. Perhaps an important measure of the integrity and sustainability of a populist movement is the hope it engenders and delivers. James M. Jasper notes, "For two thousand years scholars have dismissed protestors as irrational by focusing on two emotions above all, fear and anger. This encouraged a *panic model* of emotions, the dark flip side of the exaggerated *calculating-brain model* of thought and rationality." These emotions are often given as the source and unacceptability of populist discourse. Delving into the new research on emotions, Jasper continues,

> As we come to appreciate the full range of emotions, we will see how distorted these exemplars are, because fear and anger, a subset of reflex emotions, are the emotions most likely to lead to regret and disruption, compared to the dozens of other relevant emotions. They are a misleading paradigm for understanding the impact of emotions on politics (just as the calculating brain is a poor model of how we think, precisely because it excludes our feelings).[74]

The discourse of concern about partisan politics may sometimes dip into sentimentalizing the democracy process, with an emphasis of the need for consensus-building and reconciliations. The Belgian political philosopher Chantal Mouffe, noted earlier regarding her work on a leftist populism, "is known for developing a theory of 'agonistic' democracy – democracy as rooted in conflict rather than consensus."[75] This is a good reminder to the human rights movement that our

[72] James M. Jasper, *The Emotions of Protest* (Chicago: University of Chicago Press, 2018), 1.
[73] Michael A. Cohen, "Are Dems Ready for Elizabeth Warren's Angry Populist Message?," *Boston Globe*, April 12, 2019.
[74] Jasper, *Emotions of Protest*, xi.
[75] Judis, "Rethinking Populism," 118.

current framework, though it involved negotiations and compromises, came about as a result of struggle and demand by social movements allied with government and legal professionals.[76] These struggles will remain important to gain new rights and guarantees, but also to protect what we have thus far achieved.

In the late 1960s and early 1970s, doctors and researchers became alarmed at what they identified as a threat of a new form of malnutrition among infants, marasmus or protein-calorie deficiency. Previously, the nutritional danger of protein malnutrition, or kwashiorkor, would hit toddlers after the move from breastfeeding to solid foods. Both the World Health Assembly and UNICEF began to issue formal reports and resolutions calling, among other things, for the end of aggressive marketing of breastmilk substitutes by multinational corporations. The companies ignored these pleas to tame their marketing practices, and each year resolutions became more urgent and specific. From 1977 to 1984, I led an international grassroots movement to pressure the world's largest food company, Nestlé, to alter its marketing practices for breast-milk substitutes in the developing world in line with the WHO recommendations. Arising from the anti-hunger movements active in North American and European churches, as well as secular movements concerned with the unaccountable power of transnational corporations, the campaign focused pressure on the world's largest food company through an economic boycott that eventually spread to ten nations.[77] A boycott is a hard measure, both by its threat to jobs of innocent workers, but also by the sheer difficulty of keeping momentum. Yet millions of people joined the boycott because of the image of babies dying of diarrhea and marasmus resulting from an aggressive sales strategy. The World Health Organization and UNICEF estimated that the decline of breastfeeding because of aggressive marketing led to about 200,000 infant deaths a year. By making the marketing practices public and controversial, this social movement opened up the political space for WHO and UNICEF to create the UN's first marketing code.[78] The struggles to achieve these gains would be used as lessons for human rights movements working to develop their advocacy campaigns to future human rights treaties.

Yet this success also created a major debility. As the new international standard for the industry, the campaign's message moved from a simple set of four demands to defending a legal document of thirty-nine articles.[79] Nestlé publicly issued a statement that it would fully comply with the new code, backing it up with a

---

[76] See, for example, Kathryn Sikkink, *Evidence for Hope: Making Human Rights Work in the 21st Century* (Princeton, NJ: Princeton University Press, 2017).

[77] In the interests of disclosure, Congressman Tom Harkin was the honorary chair of my organization, INFACT.

[78] The Secretariat of the WHO agreed not to bring forth the code as a treaty to its governing body, the World Health Assembly, to gain the promise of the American government to vote to approve the code. The Reagan administration backed off this promise, and the code was approved at the 1981 WHA with a final vote of 118–1. From the author's experience.

[79] World Health Organization, ed., *International Code of Marketing of Breast-Milk Substitutes* (Geneva: World Health Organization, 1981) (obtainable from WHO Publications Centre).

memorandum to its employees about how they would implement the code. A careful reading showed that these instructions were simply the code the company lobbied to write, not the prohibitions outlined in the official document. We wrote critiques of the management instructions, which were then endorsed by UNICEF as the full meaning of the code. Then followed two years of detailed and technical argument with small changes of company policy. We became adept at these legal analyses and backed up the critique with field data that showed the company in ongoing violation of its word and its obligations. Nestlé became adept at marketing their steps as true signs of corporate responsibility, especially targeting leaders within the endorsing organizations who did not have the time or inclination to study the details. We lost the alliance of a major church before we in the campaign realized: We had lost the emotional momentum. Focusing on the legal text was boring and confusing for our constituency. We had to move outside of the legal discourse and return to emotions, which are the language of values and commitment. Jasper writes: "In addition to their information and communications functions, we sometimes manage our emotions in order to take advantage of their immediacy, their urgency, and their apparent irrationality. We use them to motivate ourselves."[80] Reengaging emotion motivated our base but also the leadership to renew the struggle until the end.

This experience has always made me concerned about the excessive centrality of law and lawyers in the human rights movement. The debate about legal terminologies and methods does not tap into the importance and the power of human emotions. This is what the human rights movement can learn from populists.

First, we must distinguish, as I have stressed in this chapter, between democratic and authoritarian populism. Democratic populism is an ally of the global human rights movement on a moral level. Authoritarian populism is a powerful and often clever opponent of human rights. When human rights practitioners encounter versions of democratic populism, they need to engage with them on a moral level. At the same time, we need to fight authoritarian populism whenever we see the threat to human rights.

Second, we must recognize that we need social movements, especially in countries like the US that have a strong status quo bias. Where authoritarians create constitutional and administrative systems to entrench themselves in power, social movements will be needed to challenge them.

Social movements in turn need clear narratives that encompass both majorities and minorities. Populist narratives can create clear anti-status quo narratives without endangering rights. It is impossible to create such narratives without engaging the emotions, but engaging the emotions is not the same as undermining rights. When movements draw from our communal values, when they make us want to act rather than sit by apathetically, we should welcome this use of the emotions.

---

[80] Jasper, *Emotions of Protest*, 1.

I would actually go further to say that we should *urge* movements to engage in the language of morals, of right and wrong, not just "rights." Health care reform, for example, is a moral issue, not just a technical one. The commitment to the belief that legal procedures are needed to protect the innocent, and all are innocent until proven guilty, is a moral vision. A moral vision and language lie at the core of any social movement but also of human rights. Mobilization requires communication of values; emotion is the language of values.[81] Rather than fear the use of emotion in political discourse, we in the Human Rights movement should embrace it and use our emotions to communicate and build bridges with others. Human Rights law is the structured summary of political agreements between states to the extent possible in that moment to achieve a predictable outcome of ratifications. However, what produced this effect were the powerful beliefs and emotions that were widely shared within and between differing political regimes.

V CONCLUSION

"Populism" has become a popular academic frame, ranging from nuanced to extreme, but uniformly condemnatory. I contend this is not a useful frame because it is used to label those who do not call themselves populists but ignores those who do. Authoritarian populism condemns and excludes minorities; this is the realm of human rights protections we need to reinforce. However, populism that focuses on the contrast between common citizens and elites is a question about power. When casting populism as a negative force and defining it in part as an attack on corrupt elites, the human rights movement should not fall into the belief that there are not powerful elites that are, indeed, corrupt adversaries of the common good.

Democratic populists, of course, can gain power and become increasingly authoritarian as they retrench and reinforce their own power by changing the rules of the game: "Populists can govern as populists. This goes against the conventional wisdom, which holds that populist protest parties cancel themselves out once they win an election, since by definition one cannot protest against oneself in government."[82] Authoritarianism can arrive slowly, in the shadows, and hidden inside the bellies of Trojan horses. Once in power populists may learn from entrenched elites the tactics of gerrymandering, packing the courts or refusing to vote for judges, or extending mandates. When populist movements become in these ways indistinguishable from the forces they intended to supplant, there will be a need for a new

---

[81] I borrow this formulation from colleague and mentor Marshall Ganz who teaches the processes of organizing and mobilizing for social justice. He takes his inspiration from Martha Nussbaum's *Upheavals of Thought: The Intelligence of Emotions* (Cambridge: Cambridge University Press, 2001), especially chapter 1, "Emotions as Judgments of Value." If so, this is an excellent example of the reframing of message that clarifies and motivates, as an organizer must do.

[82] Müller, *What Is Populism?*, 8.

social movement, reaching out to the people, to counteract the new status quo bias inherent to the American system of government. The important focus for the human rights movement, then, is less about the discourse but on the actions undertaken by those in political power.

Democratic populism is a focus on the needs of the common people, both the poor and the middle classes. It involves the notion of building the power of these constituencies to counterbalance and, if necessary, to politically defeat the powerful special interests of the elites, especially the economic elites. While much current work of the human rights movement is about the protection of minorities, in both legal efforts and informational politics, human rights protections are also for majorities. Given that human rights protections are most closely associated with democracies, protecting democracies is critical to implementation of human rights protections (but not sufficient). We need a more conscious framing of human rights that helps construct democratic majorities in elections and governance. This will need not only good legal work but also much more of a focus on the values that motivated generations to struggle for the rights of all.

BIBLIOGRAPHY

"1904 United States Presidential Election."*Wikipedia*, January 8, 2019. https://en.wikipedia
.org/w/index.php?title=1904_United_States_presidential_election&oldid=877442318.
"Are Elected Leaders 'Making the World Less Democratic'?." *Democracy Digest* (blog), July
23, 2018. www.demdigest.org/are-elected-leaders-making-the-world-less-democratic/.
Joint news conference with the Mexican President Peña Nieto and Canadian Prime Minister
Justin Trudeau at the "Three Amigos" summit on June 29, 2016, in Ottawa, Canada.
Transcript by Douglas A. Johnson from the YouTube video: www.youtube.com/watch?
v=QSOWEC1qZRE.
"Populist Caucus,"*Wikipedia*. https://en.wikipedia.org/wiki/Populist_Caucus.
"The Omaha Platform: Launching the Populist Party." http://historymatters.gmu.edu/d/5361/.
"The Omaha Platform: Likely to Serve as a Basis for the St. Louis Declarations." *New York
Times*, July 22, 1896, 2. www.nytimes.com/1896/07/22/archives/the-omaha-platform-likely-
to-serve-as-a-basis-for-the-st-louis.html.
Bonikowski, Bart, and Noam Gidron. "The Populist Style in American Politics: Presidential
Campaign Discourse, 1952–1996." *Social Forces* 94, no. 4 (2016): 1593–1621.
Cohen, Michael A. "Are Dems Ready for Elizabeth Warren's Angry Populist Message?"*Boston Globe*, April 12, 2019.
Darg, Philip L. "The Farmer-Labor Party in Minnesota Politics: 1918–1948." PhD dissertation,
University of North Dakota, 2015. https://search-proquest-com.ezp-prod1.hul.harvard
.edu/docview/1775525061/?pq-origsite=primo.
Dunai, Marton. "Hungary's Jobbik Ditches Far-Right Past to Challenge Orbán in 2018."
Reuters, January 11, 2017. www.reuters.com/article/us-hungary-jobbik/hungarys-jobbik-
ditches-far-right-past-to-challenge-Orbán-in-2018-idUSKBN14V1PW (accessed April 14,
2019).
Friedman, Uri. "Why Conservative Parties Are Central to Democracy." *The Atlantic*, June 14,
2017. www.theatlantic.com/international/archive/2017/06/ziblatt-democracy-conservative-
parties/530118/.

Goodwyn, Lawrence. *Democratic Promise: The Populist Moment in America.* New York: Oxford University Press, 1976.

Haass, Richard. "What the Global Elite Can Learn from the Donald." *Time*, February 5, 2018, 31.

Holbo, Paul S. "The Farmer-Labor Association, Minnesota's Party within a Party." *Minnesota History* 38, no. 7 (1963): 301–309.

Ingelhart, Ronald, and Pippa Norris. "Trump and the Populist Authoritarian Parties: The Silent Revolution in Reverse." *Perspectives on Politics* 15, no. 2 (2017): 443–454. DOI: 10.1017/S1537592717000111.

Jasper, James M. *The Emotions of Protest.* Chicago: University of Chicago Press, 2018.

Jenkins, J. Craig. Review of *Radical Protest and Social Structure: The Southern Farmer's Alliance and Cotton Tenancy, 1880–1890*, by Michael Schwartz, and *Democratic Promise: The Populist Movement in America*, by Lawrence Goodwyn. *Theory and Society* 11, no. 5 (1982): 715–719.

Judis, John. "Rethinking Populism." *Dissent* 63, no. 4 (2016): 116–122. DOI: 10.1353/dss.2016.0082.

Levitsky, Steven, and Lucan Way. "The Rise of Competitive Authoritarianism." *Journal of Democracy* 13, no. 2 (2002): 51–65. DOI: 10.1353/jod.2002.0026.

Lindblom, Charles. *Politics and Markets: The World's Political-Economic Systems.* New York: Basic Books, 1980.

Malone, Julia. "Modern-Day Populist Movement Sprouts among House Democrats." *Christian Science Monitor*, February 28, 1983. www.csmonitor.com/1983/0228/022847.html.

Mansbridge, Jane. "Populism is Democracy's Way of Saying 'Listen Harder.'" Presentation, Princeton University, May 11, 2017.

Mansbridge, Jane, and Stephen Macedo. "Populism and Democratic Theory." *Annual Review of Law and Social Science* 15 (2019): 59–77.

Marmor, Theodore R., and Rudolf Klein. *Politics, Health, and Health Care: Selected Essays.* New Haven, CT: Yale University Press, 2012.

Meltzer, Milton, ed., *Lincoln in His Own Words.* London: Sandpiper, 2009.

Merry, Robert W. "Andy Jackson's Populism." *The American Conservative.* www.theamerican conservative.com/articles/andy-jacksons-populism/ (accessed May 23, 2019).

Minkenberg, Michael. "The Tea Party and American Populism Today: Between Protest, Patriotism and Paranoia." *Der Moderne Staat – DMS: Zeitschrift für Public Policy, Recht und Management* 4, no. 2 (2011): 283–296.

Mounk, Yascha. "Pitchfork Politics: The Populist Threat to Liberal Democracy." *Foreign Affairs* 93, no. 5 (2014): 27–36.

Mudde, Cas. *Populist Radical Right Parties in Europe.* Cambridge: Cambridge University Press, 2007.

Mudde, Cas, and Cristóbal Rovira Kaltwasser. "Exclusionary vs. Inclusionary Populism: Comparing Contemporary Europe and Latin America." *Government and Opposition* 48, no. 2 (2013): 147–174. DOI: 10.1017/gov.2012.11.

Müller, Jan-Werner. *What Is Populism?* Philadelphia, PA: University of Pennsylvania Press, 2016.

Nader, Lucia. "Solid Organisations in a Liquid World." *Sur International Journal on Human Rights* 11, no. 20 (2014): 482–489.

Norris, Pippa, and Ronald Inglehart. *Cultural Backlash: Trump, Brexit and Authoritarian Populism.* Cambridge: Cambridge University Press, 2019.

Nussbaum, Martha. *Upheavals of Thought: The Intelligence of Emotions.* Cambridge: Cambridge University Press, 2001.

Pinker, Steven. "The Moral Instinct," *New York Times*, Magazine, January 13, 2008.

Sandburg, Carl. *Abraham Lincoln: The Prairie Years and The War Years*. New York: Harcourt, Brace and World, 1954.

Santora, Marc, and Benjamin Novak. "Protesting 'Slave Law,' Thousands Take to Streets in Hungary." *The New York Times*, January 6, 2019. www.nytimes.com/2019/01/05/world/europe/hungary-protests-slave-law.html.

Scheppele, Kim Lane. "Autocratic Legalism." *The University of Chicago Law Review* 85, no. 2 (2018): 545–584.

Sikkink, Kathryn. *Evidence for Hope: Making Human Rights Work in the 21st Century*. Princeton, NJ: Princeton University Press, 2017.

Stone, I.F. (Isidor Feinstein). *The Trial of Socrates*. Boston: Little, Brown, 1988.

Taylor, Astra. "Traditions of the Future." *Le Monde diplomatique*, May 9, 2019. https://mondediplo.com/openpage/traditions-of-the-future.

Varol, Ozan O. "Stealth Authoritarianism." *Iowa Law Review* 100, no. 4 (2015): 1673–1742.

Weigant, Chris. "Exclusive Interview with Rep. Bruce Braley, Populist Caucus Founder and Chairman." *Huffington Post*, March 11, 2009. www.huffingtonpost.com/chris-weigant/exclusive-interview-with_b_174033.html.

World Health Organization, ed., *International Code of Marketing of Breast-Milk Substitutes*. Geneva: World Health Organization, 1981.

Zakaria, Fareed. "The Rise of Illiberal Democracy." *Foreign Affairs* 76, no. 6 (1997): 22–43.

10

Populism and International Human Rights Law Institutions

A *Survival Guide*

Laurence R. Helfer[*]

Confronting recalcitrant and even hostile governments is nothing new for international human rights courts, treaty bodies, and monitoring mechanisms. One of the core purposes of these institutions is to provide a venue for holding governments accountable for violations of internationally guaranteed rights and freedoms when domestic legal mechanisms for seeking redress are lacking or inadequate. The early dockets of regional courts and commissions in the Americas or the UN Human Rights Committee, to give just two examples, are replete with decisions documenting systemic abuses and repression by military regimes and autocratic governments, many of which refused to participate in international proceedings, let alone respond favorably to the tribunals' rulings and recommendations.

Yet there is a growing sense that the recent turn to populism[1] in several countries poses a new type of threat, one that international human rights law (IHRL) institutions[2] are ill equipped to meet. This chapter argues that the threat of populism is a product of two convergent phenomena. The first phenomenon is the erosion of several facilitating conditions that have bolstered the creation, activity, and

[*] Thanks to Elizabeth Anderson, Curtis Bradley, Tom Daly, Tom Ginsburg, Jayne Huckerby, and Molly Land for helpful comments and suggestions.

[1] Populism has multiple and often contested meanings. See, e.g., Cas Mudde and Cristóbal Rovira Kaltwasser, "Studying Populism in Comparative Perspective: Reflections on the Contemporary and Future Research Agenda," *Comparative Political Studies* 51, no. 13 (2018): 1667–1693; Gerald L. Neuman, Chapter 1 (in this volume). Most of the examples in this chapter fit within the rubric of "authoritarian populism."

[2] In this chapter, the term "IHRL institutions" encompasses all judicial, quasi-judicial, expert, and political review, monitoring, and fact-finding bodies established by international agreements or international organizations to evaluate the human rights practices of states and, less frequently, non-state actors. These bodies, which operate within the United Nations and at the regional and sub-regional levels, perform a wide range of functions. The challenges that populism poses for these diverse bodies, and how each body responds to those challenges, will necessarily differ from institution to institution. The chapter glosses over some of these details to provide high-level overview of populist threats to IHRL institutions as a whole.

influence of IHRL institutions over the last half century. The decline of these conditions – as reflected, for example, in governments that increasingly criticize specific international rulings or legal doctrines, violate human rights treaties, and openly attack human rights courts or review bodies – cannot be attributed to populist regimes alone. Yet the reduced support and even outright opposition by governments of all political stripes has left IHRL institutions vulnerable to a second phenomenon – the distinctive challenges that populist regimes pose to human rights. These challenges include domestic institutions that maintain a façade of democracy but in practice are beholden to populist leaders and parties, and a political discourse that touts the rights of national, ethnic, and/or racial majorities as both paramount and incompatible with respecting the rights of minority groups.

The remainder of this chapter develops this argument in four sections. Section I identifies the facilitating conditions that, until recently, have supported IHRL institutions and explains why those conditions no longer hold. Section II considers the distinctive challenges that populism poses to those institutions, focusing on the hollowing out of democracy from within and the zero-sum framing of majoritarian rights protections. Section III identifies a range of legal and political mechanisms that might be deployed to counter human rights abuses by populist regimes. Although superficially promising, each of these tools has limited efficacy as well as potential risks. Section IV argues that IHRL institutions should adopt survival strategies for the age of populism, and it offers four suggestions for what those strategies might look like.

I FACILITATING CONDITIONS FOR IHRL INSTITUTIONS

A number of factors have aided the creation and expansion of IHRL institutions since World War II. First, these institutions enjoyed the support of several powerful states – mainly wealthy democracies in western Europe and North America – that pushed to codify IHRL norms and create international bodies to monitor adherence to those norms. To be sure, these efforts were sometimes selective and ignored the proponent states' own spotty human rights records. But as a matter of rhetoric – and often as a matter of concrete action – these states engaged in decades of sustained advocacy that succeeded in making human rights a central pillar of the UN and several regional organizations, and providing mechanisms to expose (if not always remedy) violations.[3]

A second facilitating condition was the progressive evolution, albeit with many fits and starts, toward an improved climate of respect for human rights. This teleology

---

[3] See, e.g., Louis Henkin, *The Age of Rights* (New York: Columbia University Press, 1990), 13–20.

was reflected in the expanding number, subject matter, and membership of international conventions and in decisions to create new IHRL institutions or augment the mandate of existing bodies.[4] Perhaps most important was the widely shared belief, especially in the decade or so following the end of the Cold War, that adherence to human rights norms was improving in many parts of the world as a growing number of democratically elected governments created new domestic institutions, such as constitutional courts and national human rights institutions (NHRIs), charged with protecting individual rights.[5]

A third facilitating circumstance was the extent to which governments were enmeshed by IHRL norms and institutions. States sometimes responded to charges of violations with denials, delays, or hollow promises of reform. But directly challenging the authority an institution or the system as a whole was perceived as out of bounds, notwithstanding the fact that states retain the power unilaterally to withdraw from many human rights treaties and to hobble international courts and review bodies by collectively changing their mandates or starving them of funds.[6]

These facilitating conditions no longer hold. Although some states remain committed to promoting human rights at home and abroad, the tacit consensus in favor of their protection via international institutions has markedly weakened. An isolationist United States, an internally conflicted European Union, deepening authoritarianism in China, Russia, and parts of Latin America, and ongoing armed conflicts in the Middle East have emboldened violators and made violations more pervasive.[7]

In addition, the growth of IHRL norms and institutions has stalled and in some cases is moving backward. Ongoing vociferous debates in the UN Human Rights

---

4 See, e.g., Thomas Buergenthal, "International Human Rights Law and Institutions: Accomplishments and Prospect," *Washington Law Review* 63, no. 1 (1988): 1–20; Thomas Buergenthal, "The Evolving International Human Rights System," *American Journal of International Law* 100, no. 4 (2006): 783–807.

5 See, e.g., Steven Gardbaum, "Human Rights and International Constitutionalism," *in Ruling the World? Constitutionalism, International Law, and Global Governance*, eds. Jeffrey L. Dunoff and Joel P. Trachtman (New York: Cambridge University Press, 2009), 233–257; Linda Camp Keith, "Judicial Independence and Human Rights Protection Around the World," *Judicature* 85, no. 4 (2002): 195–200. For a trenchant critique, see Samuel Moyn, *The Last Utopia: Human Rights in History* (Cambridge, MA: Harvard University Press, 2010).

6 See, e.g., Kathryn Sikkink, *The Justice Cascade: How Human Rights Prosecutions Are Changing World Politics* (New York: W.W. Norton, 2011); Beth A. Simmons, *Mobilizing for Human Rights: International Law in Domestic Politics* (New York: Cambridge University Press, 2009). For an early example of backlash, see Laurence R. Helfer, "Overlegalizing Human Rights: International Relations Theory and the Commonwealth Caribbean Backlash Against Human Rights Regimes," *Columbia Law Review* 102, no. 7 (2002): 1832–1911.

7 See, e.g., Eric A. Posner, "Liberal Internationalism and the Populist Backlash," *Arizona State Law Journal* 49, special issue (2016): 795–819; Eric A. Posner, *The Twilight of Human Rights Law* (New York: Oxford University Press, 2014).

Council over the appointment of a special rapporteur on LGBT rights,[8] concerns that the UN and regional "strengthening" processes are in reality covers to weaken IHRL institutions,[9] dwindling political and financial support for the Inter-American Court of Human Rights (IACtHR) and the Inter-American Commission,[10] and calls by democratic governments and the media to curb judicial activism by the European Court of Human Rights (ECtHR)[11] are just a few examples of this trend.

Lastly, retrenchment of and disengagement from IHRL institutions is no longer unthinkable. Threats by African states and the Philippines to withdraw from the ICC,[12] open defiance of regional human rights court rulings in countries as diverse as the Dominican Republic, Russia, and Tanzania,[13] the United States' withdrawal from the UN Human Rights Council,[14] the Brighton Declaration's not-so-subtle signal to ECtHR judges to give European governments greater deference,[15] Venezuela's denunciation of the American Convention on Human Rights and

---

[8] M. Joel Voss, "Contesting Sexual Orientation and Gender Identity at the UN Human Rights Council," *Human Rights Review* 19, no. 1 (2018): 1–22.

[9] See, e.g., Suzanne Egan, "Strengthening the United Nations Human Rights Treaty Body System," *Human Rights Law Review* 13, no. 2 (2013): 209–243; Doug Cassel, "Regional Human Rights Regimes and State Push Back: The Case of the Inter-American Human Rights System," *Human Rights Law Journal* 33, no. 1-6 (2013): 1–6.

[10] See, e.g., Emilio Álvarez-Icazaa, "The Inter-American System and Challenges for Its Future," *American University International Law Review* 29, no. 5 (2014): 989–1001; René Urueña, "Double or Nothing? The Inter-American Court of Human Rights in an Increasingly Adverse Context," *Wisconsin International Law Journal* 35, no. 2 (2018): 398–425.

[11] See, e.g., Alice Donald, "Backlog, Backlash and Beyond: Debating the Long Term Future of Human Rights Protection in Europe," UK Human Rights Blog, April 14, 2014, https://ukhu manrightsblog.com/2014/04/14/backlog-backlash-and-beyond-debating-the-long-term-future-of-human-rights-protection-in-europe-alice-donald/.

[12] Laurence R. Helfer and Anne E. Showalter, "Opposing International Justice: Kenya's Integrated Backlash Strategy Against the ICC," *International Criminal Law Review* 17, no. 1 (2017): 1–46; Manisuli Ssenyonjo, "State Withdrawal Notifications from the Rome Statute of the International Criminal Court: South Africa, Burundi and The Gambia," *Criminal Law Forum* 29, no. 1 (2018): 63; Press Release: ICC Statement on The Philippines' Notice of Withdrawal (March 20, 2018), www.icc-cpi.int/Pages/item.aspx?name=pr1371.

[13] Tom Gerald Daly and Micha Wiebusch, "The African Court on Human and Peoples' Rights: Mapping Resistance against a Young Court," *International Journal of Law in Context* 14, no. 2 (2018): 294–313; Lauri Mälksoo and Wolfgang Benedek, eds., *Russia and the European Court of Human Rights: The Strasbourg Effect* (New York: Cambridge University Press, 2018); Dinah Shelton and Alexandra Huneeus, "*In re* Direct Action of Unconstitutionality Initiated Against the Declaration of Acceptance of the Jurisdiction of the Inter-American Court of Human Rights," *American Journal of International Law* 109, no. 4 (2015): 869.

[14] Michael Posner, "Why U.S. Withdrawal from the Human Rights Council Is a Dangerous Leadership Mistake," *Forbes*, June 19, 2018.

[15] Oddný Mjöll Arnardóttir, "The Brighton Aftermath and the Changing Role of the European Court of Human Rights," *Journal of International Dispute Settlement* 9, no. 2 (2018): 223–239; Mikael Rask Madsen, "Rebalancing European Human Rights: Has the Brighton Declaration Engendered a New Deal on Human Rights in Europe?," *Journal of International Dispute Settlement* 9, no. 2 (2018): 199–222.

pending withdrawal from the Organization of American States,[16] and Rwanda's abrogation of its declaration giving individuals and NGOs direct access to the African Court on Human and Peoples' Rights (ACtHPR)[17] are among the more significant recent developments.

Considered individually, each of these events is troubling. Viewed collectively, they portend a dark future for IHRL institutions. Just how dark is a matter of debate. Scholars differ as to whether we are merely experiencing "an especially difficult period for international human rights law" or whether, more fundamentally, the "age of human rights is over" and the world is entering a "post-human rights era."[18] For purposes of this chapter, the essential point is that these developments have weakened support structures that might have helped to counter the distinctive challenges that populist regimes pose for IHRL institutions.

II POPULISM'S DISTINCTIVE CHALLENGES FOR IHRL INSTITUTIONS

As noted in the introduction, IHRL institutions have extensive track records of confronting repressive states that engage in a wide array of human rights abuses. Are populist regimes really so different? I suggest several reasons why they might be.[19]

First, populist governments are democratically elected and enjoy widespread public support. Human rights violations by populist regimes are often directed against minorities of different sorts – non-citizens, ethnic or religious groups, and marginalized communities are frequent targets – whose welfare is given pride of place in many IHRL institutions[20] but is of little concern those who vote for populist leaders and support their policies. Moreover, a leitmotif of populist regimes is that

---

[16] Ximena Soley and Silvia Steininger, "Parting Ways or Lashing Back? Withdrawals, Backlash and the Inter-American Court of Human Rights," *International Journal of Law in Context* 14, no. 2 (2018): 252.

[17] *Umuhoza v. Rwanda*, App. 003/2014, ACtHPR (Ruling, June 3, 2016).

[18] Makau Mutua, "Is the Age of Human Rights Over?," in *Routledge Companion to Literature and Human Rights*, eds. Sophia A. McClennen and Alexandra Schultheis Moore (New York: Routledge, 2016), 450–458; Ingrid B. Wuerth, "International Law in the Post-Human Rights Era," *Texas Law Review* 96, no. 2 (2017): 279–349; Stephen Hopgood, *The Endtimes of Human Rights* (Ithaca, NY: Cornell University Press, 2013).

[19] Philip Alston has observed that "the challenges the human rights movement now faces" as a result of populism "are fundamentally different from much of what has gone before." Philip Alston, "The Populist Challenge to Human Rights," *Journal of Human Rights Practice* 9, no. 1 (2017): 2. His prescriptions for addressing those challenges are different from those discussed in this chapter, and include "a renewed focus on social rights and on diminishing inequality." Alston, 6.

[20] See, e.g., Roberto Andorno, "Is Vulnerability the Foundation of Human Rights?," in *Human Dignity of the Vulnerable in the Age of Rights: Interdisciplinary Perspectives,* eds. Aniceto Masferrer and Emilio García-Sánchez ([Cham, Switzerland]: Springer, 2016), 257–272; Marc Bossuyt, "Categorical Rights and Vulnerable Groups: Moving Away from the Universal Human Being," *George Washington International Law Review* 48, no. 4 (2016): 717–742.

the majority's fundamental rights and freedoms are under threat, thereby justifying restrictions on the rights of minorities.[21]

These two facets of populist regimes – their emphasis on the human rights of majorities and their formally democratic pedigree – challenge a foundational premise of IHRL institutions: the need to protect minorities against overreaching by the majority. As the ECtHR has long asserted, "democracy does not simply mean that the views of a majority must always prevail: a balance must be achieved which ensures the fair and proper treatment of minorities and avoids any abuse of a dominant position."[22] This balance is realized not only by international review of rights violations against minorities, but also by urging majorities to temper their own interests and consider the values of "pluralism, tolerance and broadmindedness."[23]

The trumpeting of majority rights by populist regimes reframes this inquiry in important ways. The tension between the "rights" of minorities and the "views" of the majority is recast as a clash between different groups of rights holders, and, more worrisome, as a zero-sum conflict in which a "win" for minority rights is often portrayed, however implausibly, as a "loss" for majority rights. In this fraught environment, IHRL institutions have little room to maneuver. Reconciling opposing human rights claims is challenging for international decision-makers under the best of circumstances.[24] It is all the more so when appeals to pluralist values fall on deaf ears and populist governments and their supporters have little patience for the nuanced, fact-specific balancing that often accompanies international rulings.

A second challenge relates to the legal tools that IHRL institutions have developed to review the decisions of domestic actors. These tools – such as the margin of appreciation doctrine,[25] and the fourth instance review doctrine[26] – give

---

[21] Alston, "Populist Challenge," 6 (arguing that "the majority in society feel that they have no stake in the human rights enterprise, and that human rights groups really are just working for 'asylum seekers', 'felons', 'terrorists', and the like"); Samuel Moyn, "How the Human Rights Movement Failed," *New York Times*, April 23, 2018 (contending that human rights advocates "have ignored how the grievances of newly mobilized majorities have to be addressed if there is to be an opening for better treatment of vulnerable minorities").

[22] *Young, James and Webster v. United Kingdom*, 44 Eur. Ct. H.R. (ser. A) (1981), 25.

[23] *Young, James and Webster*, 25.

[24] See, e.g., Stijn Smet, *Resolving Conflicts between Human Rights: The Judge's Dilemma* (New York: Routledge, 2017).

[25] See, e.g., Dominic McGoldrick, "A Defence of the Margin of Appreciation and an Argument for its Application by the Human Rights Committee," *International and Comparative Law Quarterly* 65, no. 1 (2016): 21–60; Yuval Shany, "Towards a General Margin of Appreciation Doctrine in International Law," *European Journal of International Law* 16, no. 5 (2005): 907–940.

[26] Viljam Engström, "Deference and the Human Rights Committee," *Nordic Journal of Human Rights* 34, no. 2 (2016): 79 (describing the "fourth instance doctrine" as the UN Human Rights Committee's practice of "not substantively scrutiniz[ing] domestic law or decisions of national authorities in accordance with the principle of subsidiarity").

varying degrees of deference to the domestic actors that consider human rights claims. Where a national judge, executive branch official, or agency administrator applies the appropriate legal standards, considers the relevant circumstances, and issues a decision that plausibly reconciles the competing rights and interests at stake, these doctrines counsel against an international body reviewing that decision *de novo*.

IHRL institutions tend to give greater solicitude to domestic actors in democracies. Several structural features of democratic regimes support this practice. The election of politicians, the division of public authority among different branches of government, and the protection of individual rights in constitutions are designed to prevent the concentration of power, enable citizens and interest groups to participate in public debates, and provide multiple avenues for holding governments accountable for their actions. When these structural features function as intended, at least some human rights violations are remedied at home (obviating the need for international review) and decisions reconciling competing rights and interests are made within a system that values the rule of law and individual liberties.[27] In addition, many democracies promote adherence to human rights in other countries as a foreign policy priority.[28]

In many populist regimes, in contrast, the facades of democratic institutions are often retained, but in name only.[29] In reality, these institutions are politically penetrated or hollowed out as populist politicians pack them with cronies, starve them of resources, or create new bodies willing to carry out the government's bidding. If any independent entities remain, they are increasingly sidelined or cowed into silence.[30] Governments that are democratic in name but populist in practice also tend to prioritize domestic over external concerns, which reduces their willingness to challenge the human rights records of even overtly repressive foreign regimes.

These developments have significant adverse consequences for IHRL institutions. In most healthy democracies, national courts, legislatures, administrative agencies, and other sub-state actors serve as compliance partners for international courts and review bodies by implementing their rulings and interpreting individual rights in

---

[27] See, e.g., Shai Dothan, "Special Issue: Margin of Appreciation and Democracy: Human Rights and Deference to Political Bodies," *Journal of International Dispute Settlement* 9, no. 2 (2018): 145–253; Laurence R. Helfer, "Redesigning the European Court of Human Rights: Embeddedness as a Deep Structural Principle of the European Human Rights Regime," *European Journal of International Law* 19, no. 1 (2008): 125–159.

[28] See, e.g., Yukimo Nakanishi, "Mechanisms to Protect Human Rights in the EU's External Relations," in *Contemporary Issues in Human Rights Law: Europe and Asia*, ed. Yumiko Nakanishi (Singapore: Springer Nature, 2017), 3–22.

[29] See, e.g., Patrick Kingsley, "On the Surface, Hungary Is a Democracy. But What Lies Underneath?," *New York Times*, December 25, 2018.

[30] See, e.g., Aziz Huq and Tom Ginsburg, *How to Save a Constitutional Democracy* (Chicago: University of Chicago Press, 2018) (analyzing different pathways of constitutional retrogression and mechanisms for resisting the slide to autocratic rule).

constitutions and statutes in light of those rulings.[31] After populism takes hold, these actors increasingly ignore international law,[32] flout the decisions of IHRL institutions (as in Russia),[33] invalidate declarations recognizing the jurisdiction of international human rights courts (as in the Dominican Republic),[34] and urge governments to denounce human rights conventions (as in Venezuela).[35] Perhaps more insidiously, national courts can twist international law doctrines to reach outcomes favored by populist leaders, as illustrated by a 2018 ruling of the Constitutional Tribunal of Bolivia applying the IACtHR's conventionality control doctrine to invalidate a referendum barring President Evo Morales from seeking a fourth term in office.[36]

One might expect that IHRL institutions would perceive the erosion of democracy and respond by enhancing their scrutiny of human rights abuses by populist regimes. In fact, this shift may be difficult to execute for a number of reasons. It may take time to recognize full extent of democratic retrenchment. In the meanwhile, prior precedents suggest continuing to defer to domestic decision-makers. More troublingly, IHRL institutions may not perceive the true nature of the threat (as in Hungary),[37] the strength of domestic opposition to international

---

[31] See, e.g., Karen J. Alter, *The New Terrain of International Law: Courts, Politics, Rights* (Princeton, NJ: Princeton University Press, 2014); Laurence R. Helfer and Anne-Marie Slaughter, "Toward a Theory of Effective Supranational Adjudication," *Yale Law Journal* 107, no. 2 (1997): 277. However, even longstanding democracies are not immune from leveling attacks on IHRL institutions. See Mikael R. Madsen, "The Challenging Authority of the European Court of Human Rights: From Cold War Legal Diplomacy to the Brighton Declaration and Backlash," *Law and Contemporary Problems* 79, no. 1 (2016): 170 (2016) (describing the United Kingdom's striking *volte face* against the ECtHR).

[32] See Tamar Hostovsky Brandes, "International Law in Domestic Courts in an Era of Populism," *International Journal of Constitutional Law* 17, no. 2 (2019): 577 ("Courts under populist attacks ... are likely to prefer, where possible, to resort to legal sources that enjoy sound domestic legitimacy in order to minimize their exposure to criticism by populist leaders.").

[33] Iryna Marchuk, "Flexing Muscles (Yet Again): The Russian Constitutional Court's Defiance of the Authority of the ECtHR in the Yukos Case," EJIL: Talk! February 13, 2017, www.ejiltalk .org/flexing-muscles-yet-again-the-russian-constitutional-courts-defiance-of-the-authority-of-the-ecthr-in-the-yukos-case/ (analyzing Russian Constitutional Court's refusal to implement large pecuniary damages awarded by the ECtHR).

[34] Alexandra Huneeus and René Urueña, "Treaty Exit and Latin America's Constitutional Courts," *AJIL Unbound* 111 (2017): 458–459 (discussing ruling of the Constitutional Tribunal of the Dominican Republic invalidating the executive's prior acceptance of the jurisdiction of the IACtHR following a judgment rejecting a Tribunal decision that upheld the government's decision to abrogate citizenship of thousands of Dominicans of Haitian descent).

[35] Huneeus and Urueña, "Treaty Exit," 457 (discussing a Venezuelan Supreme Court ruling rejecting an IACtHR judgment that ordered the reinstatement of national judges fired by the government of Hugo Chávez and urging the executive to denounce the American Convention on Human Rights "in light of the clear usurpation of functions" by the Inter-American Court of Human Rights).

[36] Sentencia Constitucional Plurinacional 0084/2017 Sucre, 20960-2017-42-AIA (November 28, 2017).

[37] David Kosař and Katarina Šipulová, "The Strasbourg Court Meets Abusive Constitutionalism: *Baka v. Hungary* and the Rule of Law," *Hague Journal on the Rule of Law* (2017), DOI:10.1007/

monitoring (as in South America),[38] or the ability of populist politicians and candidates for high office to use international human rights rulings as fodder to rally public opposition (as in Costa Rica).[39]

A third challenge of populism stems from the manipulation of social media by populist leaders and their supporters. Such actions implicate multiple human rights guarantees, most notably freedom of expression and association, the right to take part in the conduct of public affairs, the right to vote and to be elected, and the right of privacy.[40] Infringements of these rights can sometimes be easily tied to a government, such as Cambodian Prime Minister Hun Sen's use of Facebook to disseminate false information about political opponents.[41] More often, however, the manipulations of social media by populist leaders are indirect and the resulting rights violations less obvious.[42] Examples include the swarms of Russian bots and trolls created to interfere in the 2016 US presidential election, the "keyboard army" that operates fake social media accounts in support of Philippine President Rodrigo Duterte, and the Turkish ruling party's efforts to enlist thousands of internet users to "manipulate online discussions, drive agendas, and counter opponents."[43]

The indirect uses of social media by populist governments pose multiple challenges for IHRL institutions and for the civil society groups that support them. Deploying private intermediaries enable officials to spread false information, discredit opponents, and create a climate of fear and intimidation while plausibly casting doubt on the existence of rights violations or their connection to them.

---

s40803–017–0065-y (criticizing ECtHR Grand Chamber's analysis of the ouster the Hungarian Supreme Court's president as overlooking the "main structural problem behind the dismissal" – the "broad powers of court presidents" in Central and Eastern European countries).

[38] Alexandra Huneeus, "Courts Resisting Courts: Lessons from the Inter-American Court's Struggle to Enforce Human Rights," *Cornell International Law Journal* 44, no. 3 (2011): 493–534.

[39] Elisabeth Malkin, "In Costa Rica Election, Gay-Marriage Foe Takes First Round," *New York Times*, February 5, 2018 (describing how a little-known presidential candidate in Costa Rica won the first round of voting by labeling an IACtHR advisory opinion on gender identity and same-sex as "a violation of Costa Rica's sovereignty" and "threaten[ing] to pull the country out of the court if he is elected").

[40] UN Human Rights Committee, General Comment 25, UN Doc. CCPR/C/21/Rev.1/Add.7, para. 1 (1996).

[41] Julia Wallace, "Fight over Cambodian Leader's Facebook 'Likes' Reaches a U.S. Court," *New York Times*, February 9, 2018.

[42] Molly K. Land and Jay D. Aronson, "The Promise and Peril of Human Rights Technology," in *New Technologies for Human Rights Law and Practice*, eds. Molly K. Land and Jay D. Aronson (Cambridge: Cambridge University Press, 2018), 4 ("the use of technology by states can obscure and fragment authority and thus disable the mechanisms that human rights advocates use to promote accountability").

[43] Alex Hern, "Thirty Countries Use 'Armies of Opinion Shapers' to Manipulate Democracy – Report," *The Guardian*, November 14, 2017 (describing Freedom House report finding "strong indications that individuals [in 30 countries] are paid to distort the digital information landscape in the government's favour, without acknowledging sponsorship").

International courts and monitoring bodies are ill equipped to conduct the intensive factual inquiries needed to connect the government to these efforts. In addition, existing doctrines of state responsibility are chary about attributing state control over private actors,[44] allowing populist regimes to avoid accountability. Moreover, to the extent that social media companies are themselves to blame for facilitating abuses,[45] the absence of horizontal human rights obligations between private parties makes it all but impossible for victims to hold these firms accountable before IHRL institutions.[46]

III LEGAL AND POLITICAL TOOLS FOR IHRL INSTITUTIONS TO COUNTER POPULIST REGIMES

How should IHRL institutions and their supporters respond to the challenges described above? This section identifies and assesses three potential tools – one doctrinal, one a hybrid of law and politics, and one normative. These responses have some promise, but they are unlikely to be sufficient, either individually or deployed in tandem, to effectively counter the challenges that populism poses for IHRL institutions.[47]

A *Bespoke Legal Doctrines*

The first response involves an IHRL court or review body developing distinctive legal doctrines. Consider Article 18 of the European Convention on Human

---

[44] Danwood Mzikenge Chirwa, "The Doctrine of State Responsibility as a Potential Means of Holding Private Actors Accountable for Human Rights," *Melbourne Journal of International Law* 5, no. 1 (2004): 6, 7 (explaining that "conduct is attributable to the state if it directed or controlled the specific operation and the conduct complained of was an integral part of that operation," and characterizing the "burden of establishing state control" over private actors as "onerous").

[45] IHRL institutions and civil society groups have only recently considered how human rights standards apply in this context. See, e.g., UN Human Rights Council, Report of the Special Rapporteur on the promotion and protection of the right to freedom of opinion and expression (David Kaye), A/HRC/38/35 (April 6, 2018) [Kaye Report], www.ohchr.org/EN/Issues/Freedom Opinion/Pages/ContentRegulation.aspx; Organization for Security and Co-operation in Europe, Joint Declaration on Freedom of Expression and "Fake News," Disinformation and Propaganda (March 3, 2017), www.osce.org/fom/302796?download=true; Rikke Frank Jørgensen, "Human Rights and Private Actors in the Online Domain," in *New Technologies for Human Rights Law and Practice*, eds. Molly K. Land and Jay D. Aronson (Cambridge: Cambridge University Press, 2018), 247.

[46] See, e.g., *Socio-Economic Rights and Accountability Project v. Nigeria*, Case No. ECW/CCJ/ APP/08/09, Ruling of the ECOWAS Community Court of Justice, paras. 69–71 (December 10, 2010) (concluding that corporations have no direct human rights responsibilities under existing international law dismissing human rights claims against them).

[47] For a similarly pessimistic account of the limited capacity of national constitutional courts and regional human rights tribunals to help consolidate the process of democratization, see Tom Gerald Daly, *The Alchemists: Questioning our Faith in Courts as Democracy-Builders* (Cambridge: Cambridge University Press, 2017).

Rights, which prohibits restrictions on the rights protected in the Convention from being "applied for any purpose other than those for which they have been prescribed."[48] Article 18 is intended to prevent government actions that erode the principles or institutions of democracy in the guise of the legitimate restrictions on rights set forth in several articles of the Convention.[49] It thus seems a promising avenue for identifying and condemning human rights violations committed by populist regimes.

For many years, however, the ECtHR narrowly interpreted this provision, imposing a high burden of proof on applicants and refusing to find a violation of Article 18 in mixed motive cases if the government identified a permissible purpose for its actions. In 2017, however, the Court shifted course. In *Merabishvili v. Georgia*, a former Prime Minister and opposition party leader alleged that his pre-trial detention and criminal prosecution for abuse of power impermissibly aimed to prevent his participation in national politics. The ECtHR Grand Chamber held that the existence of multiple purposes for restricting rights does not shield the state from an Article 18 violation. Rather, the appropriate standard is whether a restriction's predominant purpose is illegitimate, taking into account the state's initial actions and the circumstances as they evolve over time.[50] Commentators have criticized various aspects of the Grand Chamber's judgment, but most agree that the decision reflects the ECtHR's increased awareness that Article 18 can be used "as a tool for addressing the suppression of dissent and the silencing of political opposition" and "as a warning bell for when States begin to (back-)slide into undemocratic tendencies."[51]

What are the benefits of bespoke legal doctrines? By providing a distinct basis for human rights violations associated with populism, such doctrines can help to publicize the range of repressive measures deployed by populist regimes. They can lead to enhanced remedies for victims, such as higher awards of damages, non-monetary reparations, and sanctions (discussed further below). And they can signal the opprobrium of IHRL institutions, states, and NGOs for populist governments.

---

[48] European Convention on Human Rights, Article 18. Other human rights agreements contain similar clauses. See, e.g., International Covenant on Civil and Political Rights (ICCPR) Article 5(1) ("Nothing in the present Covenant may be interpreted as implying for any State, group or person any right to engage in any activity or perform any act aimed at the destruction of any of the rights and freedoms recognized herein or at their limitation to a greater extent than is provided for in the present Covenant.").

[49] Helen Keller and Corina Heri, "Selective Criminal Proceedings and Article 18 ECHR: The European Court of Human Rights' Untapped Potential to Protect Democracy," *Human Rights Law Journal* 36, no. 1-6 (2016): 1–10.

[50] *Merabishvili v. Georgia*, Application no. 72508/13 (ECtHR Grand Chamber, November 28, 2017), paras. 305–307.

[51] "Merabishvili, Mammadov and Targeted Criminal Proceedings: Recent Developments under Article 18 ECHR," Strasbourg Observers Blog, December 15, 2017, https://strasbourgobservers .com/2017/12/15/merabishvili-mammadov-and-targeted-criminal-proceedings-recent-developments-under-article-18-echr/.

Weighted against these benefits are the risks of applying different legal standards to some member states but not others.[52] It also uncertain how easily bespoke legal doctrines can be adapted to changing circumstances. This is especially true for Article 18, which is not an autonomous right and can only be violated in conjunction with another provision of the European Convention.[53] Finally, and most significantly, the very act of "naming and shaming" populist governments may add fuel to the fire of public opposition to external institutions that scrutinize and condemn populist leaders and their policies.

B *Infringement Proceedings and Sanctions*

A second approach involves targeting populist regimes through high-profile infringement proceedings. Protocol No. 14 to the European Convention, which entered into force in 2010, for the first time authorizes the Committee of Ministers to file an infringement action against a state that failed to comply with an ECtHR judgment against it.[54] The Protocol's explanatory report states that such proceedings should be reserved for "exceptional circumstances," without identifying what situations meet that high standard.[55] The decision to file an infringement suit requires the support of two-thirds of the Council of Europe's member states, a procedural hurdle that further reduces the likelihood of initiating such proceedings.

The inaugural infringement action filed by the Committee of Ministers involved a prominent Azerbaijani opposition politician detained and later convicted for calling for street protests against the government. In 2014, the ECtHR issued a judgment against Azerbaijan finding numerous violations of the Convention.[56] Included among these was a breach of Article 18, based on a finding that the authorities had detained the politician not "to bring him before a judge to answer for a crime, but to silence or punish him for criticising the government and for attempting to disseminate information that he believed the government were trying to hide."[57] In supervising the execution of the judgment, the Committee of

---

[52] See, e.g., Başak Çalı, "Coping with Crisis: Whither the Variable Geometry in the Jurisprudence of the European Court of Human Rights," *Wisconsin International Law Journal* 35, no. 2 (2018): 237–276; Laurence R. Helfer, "The Benefits and Burdens of Brighton," *ESIL Reflections* 1, no. 1 (2012), http://esil-sedi.eu/node/138.

[53] *Merabishvili v. Georgia*, para. 287.

[54] Protocol No. 14 adds a new paragraph 4 to Article 46 of the European Convention on Human Rights, authorizing the Committee of Ministers to refer to the ECtHR cases in which a state has "refuse[d] to abide by a final judgment in a case to which it is a party."

[55] Explanatory Report to Protocol No. 14 to the Convention for the Protection of Human Rights and Fundamental Freedoms (May 13, 2004), para. 100.

[56] *Mammadov v. Azerbaijan*, Application no. 15172/13 (ECtHR, May 22, 2014).

[57] Lize R. Glas, "The Committee of Ministers Goes Nuclear: Infringement Proceedings against Azerbaijan in the Case of Ilgar Mammadov," Strasbourg Observers Blog, December 20, 2017, https://strasbourgobservers.com/2017/12/20/the-committee-of-ministers-goes-nuclear-infringement-proceedings-against-azerbaijan-in-the-case-of-ilgar-mammadov/.

Ministers ordered Azerbaijan to release the politician from prison, a remedy that the state ignored for more than three years.[58]

In its May 2019 judgment, the ECtHR agreed with the Committee of Ministers that Azerbaijan had not properly executed the Court's prior judgment and that acquittal of the applicant was the only measure capable of remedying the government's violation of the Convention.[59] If Azerbaijan remains recalcitrant, the responses available to the Committee of Ministers are both limited and politically fraught.[60] The Committee could suspend Azerbaijan's voting rights in the Council of Europe (a penalty imposed on Russia in 2000 and 2014 to little effect),[61] invite Azerbaijan to withdraw from the Council, or, in the most extreme case, formally expel the state from the organization.[62]

The sanctions of suspension and expulsion are ultimately political decisions not predicated upon the prior filing of an infringement proceeding or a finding of noncompliance by an international court.[63] The member states of the Council of Europe could thus collectively decide that a country whose populist government repeatedly and flagrantly violates Convention should be encouraged to withdraw or formally expelled from the Council. It is at best uncertain, however, whether the political will exists to threaten, let alone impose, these penalties. Expulsion is especially unlikely when multiple member states in the same treaty system or international organization are controlled by populist regimes. And perhaps most significantly, expulsion may also have serious adverse consequences for civil society groups for which IHRL institutions may be the only meaningful venue for publicizing repressive measures and challenging rights violations.

---

[58] Committee of Ministers, Interim Resolution CM/ResDH(2017)429, Execution of the judgment of the European Court of Human Rights – Ilgar Mammadov against Azerbaijan (Dec. 5, 2017), https://search.coe.int/cm/Pages/result_details.aspx?ObjectID=090000168076fifd.

[59] Kanstantsin Dzehtsiarou, "How Many Judgments Does One Need to Enforce A Judgment? The First Ever Infringement Proceedings at the European Court of Human Rights," Strasbourg Observers Blog, June 4, 2019, https://strasbourgobservers.com/2019/06/04/how-many-judg ments-does-one-need-to-enforce-a-judgment-the-first-ever-infringement-proceedings-at-the-european-court-of-human-rights/.

[60] Fiona de Londras and Kanstantsin Dzehtsiarou, "Mission Impossible? Addressing Non-Execution through Infringement Proceedings in the European Court of Human Rights," *International and Comparative Law Quarterly* 66, no. 2 (2017): 467–490.

[61] Laurence R. Helfer, "Redesigning the European Court of Human Rights: Embeddedness as a Deep Structural Principle of the European Human Rights Regime," *European Journal of International Law* 19, no. 1 (2008): 157.

[62] Statute of the Council of Europe, May 5, 1949, Article 8.

[63] In 2009, for example, the Organization of American States (OAS) suspended Honduras for two years following a military coup that contravened the organization's commitment to upholding democratic governance and human rights. Deborah Charles, "Honduras Readmitted to OAS after Coup," *Reuters*, June 1, 2011, www.reuters.com/article/us-honduras-oas/honduras-readmit ted-to-oas-after-coup-idUSTRE75063P20110601.

C *State Responsibility, Affirmative Obligations, and Social Media*

The development of new legal doctrines by IHRL institutions and the suspension or expulsion of states from international organizations are short- and medium-term responses to populism. They are also premised on a finding that the government and its officials have themselves committed human rights violations. The indirect manipulation of social media by populist regimes requires a longer-term approach, one that involves a more far-reaching revision of existing international rules governing the relationship between the state and private actors.

At least three distinct international legal norms are relevant to this issue. The first involves state responsibility for human rights violations committed by private actors, the second involves the dereliction of a state's affirmative duty to regulate private actors who carry out such violations, and the third involves the imposition of direct human rights responsibilities on business entities.

Existing principles of state responsibility attribute the conduct of private individuals, groups, and business entities to the state if, in the words of the International Law Commission (ILC), the "person or group of persons is in fact acting on the instructions of, or under the direction or control of, that State in carrying out the conduct."[64] According to ILC commentary, the standard for attribution is relatively strict; private conduct "will be attributable to the State only if it directed or controlled the specific operation and the conduct complained of was an integral part of that operation."[65]

As the examples discussed in the previous section reveal, however, populist leaders have been quite skillful in tacitly encouraging supporters to deploy social media campaigns against independent institutions and opposition political parties while publicly maintaining distance from those actions. With enough time and investigatory capacity, it may be possible to link a government to these initiatives. Yet even the exceptionally well-resourced criminal investigation by Special Counsel Robert Mueller of Russia's meddling in the 2016 US presidential election has yielded connections between private actors and the Putin regime that may not satisfy existing international attribution standards.[66]

A different avenue for challenging social media campaigns tacitly encouraged by populist regimes is to bolster the affirmative obligations that international human rights law imposes on states to regulate private actors. This approach focuses on what the government has *not* done – taking proactive steps to prevent, investigate, and punish the individuals, groups, and companies that commit such violations or

---

[64] International Law Commission, Draft Articles on State Responsibility, Article 8.

[65] International Law Commission, Draft Articles on State Responsibility, Commentary on Article 8, para. 3.

[66] See Sarah Grant et al., "Russian Influence Campaign: What's in the Latest Mueller Indictment," Lawfare Blog, February 16, 2018, www.lawfareblog.com/russian-influence-campaign-whats-latest-mueller-indictment.

failing to provide appropriate remedies to victims. The "due diligence" standard, originally developed by the IACtHR and since taken up by many other IHRL institutions, is one promising doctrinal tool.[67] Additional guidance may be gleaned from the "respect, protect, and fulfill" framework first developed by the Committee on Economic, Social and Cultural Rights that requires states to prevent violations by private actors.[68] Imposing an affirmative duty is likely to be somewhat easier to justify for governments that already regulate social media, for example by requiring companies to screen content or localize data.[69]

A third approach involves imposing human rights obligations on social media companies directly. The Guiding Principles on Business and Human Rights, adopted by the UN Human Rights Council in 2011, provided a nonbinding framework that could be used to develop such obligations.[70] IHRL institutions are only beginning to consider how the Guiding Principles apply to the human rights responsibilities of social media companies.[71] The Council's subsequent decision to establish an open-ended intergovernmental working group to develop a binding treaty on the human rights obligations of corporations and other business entities also appears to be focused principally on the offline world.[72]

Revising the three sets of legal standards described above is a long-term and uncertain enterprise. Whether such efforts are worth undertaking depend in part on the efficacy of technological tools for controlling online communications across

---

[67] The obligation of due diligence in this context refers to "the extent of a state's obligations to prevent and respond to infringements of human rights by private actors within its territory or jurisdiction." Jonathan Bonnitcha and Robert McCorquodale, "The Concept of 'Due Diligence' in the UN Guiding Principles on Business and Human Rights," *European Journal of International Law* 28, no. 3 (2017): 904. Confusingly, the same phrase is also used to describe "a process of investigation conducted by a business to identify and manage commercial risks," including risks associated with human rights violations resulting from the business' activities of the business. Bonnitcha and McCorquodale, 901.

[68] Committee on Economic, Social and Cultural Rights, General Comment No. 3, The Nature of States Parties Obligations, U.N. Doc. HRI/GEN/1/Rev. 1 at 45 (1990). For an application of these tripartite framework to the internet, see Gabor Rona and Lauren Aarons, "State Responsibility to Respect, Protect and Fulfill Human Rights Obligations in Cyberspace," *Journal of National Security Law and Policy* 8, no. 3 (2016): 503–530.

[69] The Manila Principles on Intermediary Liability, www.manilaprinciples.org/ (urging governments to follow a variety of practices to limit regulation of social media companies).

[70] Special Representative of the Secretary-General on Human Rights and Transnational Corporations and Other Business Enterprises, "Guiding Principles on Business and Human Rights: Implementing the United Nations' 'Protect, Respect and Remedy' Framework," Human Rights Council, U.N. Doc. A/HRC/17/31, March 21, 2011 (by John Ruggie).

[71] See Kaye Report, para. 70 (asserting that the "Guiding Principles on Business and Human Rights ... provide baseline approaches that all Internet companies should adopt").

[72] Human Rights Council, "Elaboration of an International Legally Binding Instrument on Transnational Corporations and Other Business Enterprises with Respect to Human Rights," U.N. Doc. A/HRC/26/L.22/Rev.1, June 24, 2014. For further discussion, see Pierre Thielbörger and Tobias Ackermann, "A Treaty on Enforcing Human Rights Against Business: Closing the Loophole or Getting Stuck in a Loop?," *Indiana Journal of Global Legal Studies* 24, no. 1 (2017): 43–79.

borders. So long as such controls remain imperfect, human rights-friendly regulations of internet companies in some jurisdictions may limit the ability of populist political leaders to leverage social media platforms to foment repression and stamp out dissent. Social media may also provide an avenue to for human rights groups to mobilize public opposition to populist regimes.[73]

IV FOUR SURVIVAL STRATEGIES FOR AN AGE OF POPULISM

The previous sections have explained why the populist challenges to IHRL institutions are significant and distinctive, and why existing legal and political tools to counter those challenges are likely to be of limited utility or at best uncertain. How, then, should international human rights courts, treaty bodies, and monitoring mechanisms respond to an age of populism?

At a minimum, IHRL institutions must survive so that they can continue to perform their core functions – interpreting international laws, identifying and publicizing violations, and awarding remedies to individuals whose rights have been infringed. The best hope for survival, in turn, is a strategic action – both inside and outside of courtrooms and hearing rooms – that enables the institutions to remain viable forums for those seeking accountability while avoiding, or at least minimizing, opportunities for populist regimes to challenge their authority, narrow their jurisdiction, or withdraw from international monitoring mechanisms altogether.

Four survival strategies in particular are worth pursuing – playing a long game; circumspection in interpretation; publicity and outreach; and creating windows of opportunity for supporters to mobilize. Each of these strategies proceeds from a common premise – that IHRL institutions can increase chances of survival by providing enduring and persuasive justifications for their decisions, publicizing violations, and cultivating a diverse range of compliance constituencies who, in turn, will support the institutions and pressure states to respond to their decisions.[74]

A *Playing a Long Game*

In the short and medium term, international human rights courts, commissions, treaty bodies, and experts may do little to stem the rising tide of populism. These institutions control neither the sword nor the purse, and cannot coerce governments to behave in particular ways.[75] Yet the favorable conditions of the post-Cold War

---

[73] E.g., Enrique Piracés, "The Future of Human Rights Technology: A Practitioner's View," in *New Technologies for Human Rights Law and Practice*, eds. Molly K. Land and Jay D. Aronson (Cambridge: Cambridge University Press, 2018), 289–308.

[74] Alter, *New Terrain*, 20–21 (defining "compliance constituencies" of international courts).

[75] E.g., Karen J. Alter, Laurence R. Helfer, and Mikael Rask Madsen, "How Context Shapes the Authority of International Courts," in *International Court Authority*, eds. Karen J. Alter, Laurence R. Helfer, and Mikael Rask Madsen (Oxford: Oxford University Press, 2018), 28.

era – in which compliance with human rights decisions was quite common – may have obscured the fact that IHRL institutions have often operated in unfavorable political settings. Nascent human rights courts and monitoring bodies survived these fraught environments by playing a long game, laying down institutional and juris-prudential markers for the future, and waiting for more favorable conditions to arise.

The history of Inter-American human rights system provides an apt illustration. From the 1950s through the early 1980s, most Latin American countries were ruled by military regimes or dictatorships that perpetrated or condoned widespread human rights abuses. The Inter-American Commission responded aggressively to these violations, broadly interpreting its open-ended mandate to focus on investigating the actual human rights conditions it found in country visits across the region. The Commission in effect "converted itself into an accusatory agency, a kind of Hemi-spheric Grand Jury, storming around Latin America to vacuum up evidence of high crimes and misdemeanors and marshaling it into bills of indictment in the form of country reports for delivery to the political organs of the OAS and the court of public opinion."[76] These reports were mostly ignored by authoritarian rulers and military leaders, but they created an authoritative record of abuses that would influence the next generation of advocacy groups and governments in the region.

Compliance was also a distant prospect during the IACtHR's first decade of operation. "Very few people believed that the decisions of a court lacking police powers would be implemented in a sovereign state, especially given Latin America's history of coups d'état and rule-in-fact rather than rule of law."[77] Inter-American judges did not, however, squander the opportunities offered by the handful of cases that came before them. Instead, they used the cases to build a productive relation-ship with the Commission and to develop novel legal doctrines that responded to Central and South America's endemic human rights problems, most notably forced disappearances.[78]

By the 1990s and early 2000s, the region had shifted dramatically. Across Latin America, democratically elected governments adopted new constitutions and estab-lished constitutional courts with a mandate to interpret and enforce individual rights, creating natural allies for Inter-American jurists. A new generation of political leaders sought to make amends for the abuses of their authoritarian predecessors, including by implementing the long-delayed remedies indicated by the IACtHR and the Commission. And civil society groups developed sophisticated human rights advocacy

---

[76] Tom Farer, "The Rise of the Inter-American Human Rights Regime: No Longer a Unicorn, Not Yet an Ox," in *The Inter-American Human Rights System*, eds. David J. Harris and Stephen Livingstone (Oxford: Oxford University Press, 1998), 32.

[77] Judge Diego García-Sayán, "The Role of the Inter-American Court of Human Rights in the Americas," *U.C. Davis Journal of International Law and Policy* 19, no. 1 (2012): 105.

[78] Thomas Buergenthal, "New Upload – Remembering the Early Years of the Inter-American Court of Human Rights," *New York University Journal of International Law and Politics* 37, no. 2 (2005): 269–273.

strategies that featured litigating cases before national and regional courts and monitoring bodies. The result of these mutually reinforcing developments was a sharp rise in the case load of the Court and the Commission, which increasingly relied on national executives and legislatures to implement their decisions and on national courts to incorporate Inter-American jurisprudence into domestic judicial rulings.[79]

The evolution of the Inter-American system provides one example of how an IHRL institution can operate with an eye to the future. The long games of other courts, treaty bodies, and monitoring mechanisms are likely to be quite different. Factors such as subject matter mandate, delegated review powers, the nature of violations, and the legal and political systems of member states are all likely to influence how an institution strives to enhance its long-term influence.

Whatever future-oriented strategy an institution adopts does not, however, preclude it from demanding immediate changes in national laws and policies. In addition, the publicity and outreach activities discussed below provide opportunities for IHRL institutions to expand societal awareness of violations, validate and empower domestic rights advocates, and encourage them to mobilize to pressure governments to end violations in the near term. Striking a balance between short- and longer-term approaches may, however, be especially challenging today as compared to earlier eras. This is because, as the next subsection explains, IHRL institutions have developed expansive interpretive methodologies that make them susceptible to resistance and backlash by populist regimes.

B *Circumspection in Interpretation*

International human rights courts and monitoring bodies have, over the last half century, developed a distinctive approach to treaty interpretation. This approach, which varies in its particulars from one IHRL institution to another, shares two overarching features – the elaboration and expansion of individual rights, and the broadening of an institution's delegated authority to determine when states have violated those rights.[80]

The commitment to progressive elaboration proceeds from the premise that international human rights instruments, unlike other multilateral agreements, establish "a legal order in which [States], for the common good, assume various obligations, not in relation to other States, but towards all individuals within their jurisdiction."[81] Since the treaties' object and purpose is "to guarantee rights that

---

[79] See Alexandra Huneeus, "Introduction to Symposium on the Constitutionalization of International Law in Latin America," *AJIL Unbound* 109 (2015): 89–92.

[80] See Başak Çali, "Specialized Rules of Treaty Interpretation: Human Rights," in *The Oxford Guide to Treaties*, ed. Duncan B. Hollis (Oxford: Oxford University Press, 2012), 525.

[81] The Effect of Reservations on the Entry into Force of the American Convention on Human Rights (Arts. 74 and 75), Advisory Opinion OC-2/82, Inter-Am. Ct. H.R. (ser. A) No. 2 (1982), para. 29.

are not theoretical or illusory, but practical and effective," it follows that they should be construed in favor of the individual and against state sovereignty (the *pro homine* principle).[82] A further corollary is that human rights agreements are "living instruments" to be interpreted in light of changing political, social, and economic conditions, as well as global, regional, and national trends that favor wider protection of individual rights.[83] Over time, this distinctive approach has generated an expanding corpus of binding and non-binding legal norms that IHRL institutions apply when carrying out their adjudication and monitoring functions.

In addition to broadening the scope and reach of substantive rights and freedoms, human rights courts and treaty bodies have used these interpretive principles to justify an expansion of their powers and a concomitant narrowing of state discretion. The ECtHR, for example, views itself not merely as the judicial expositor of a regional human rights treaty but as the guardian of a "constitutional instrument of European public order."[84] The UN Human Rights Committee, although lacking the power to issue legally binding interpretations of the ICCPR, has nevertheless asserted that it is the authoritative interpreter of that treaty.[85] And the IACtHR has developed the doctrine of conventionality control, which requires all national actors to apply the American Convention on Human Rights as understood by the regional court.[86]

In the last several years, however, governments of all political stripes have pushed back hard against these developments, characterizing them as flagrant overreaching by IHRL institutions. Recent special issues of journals,[87] edited

[82] Luzius Wildhaber, "The European Convention on Human Rights and International Law," *International and Comparative Law Quarterly* 56, no. 2 (2007): 223; see also Lucas Lixinski, "The European Convention on Human Rights and International Law," *International and Comparative Law Quarterly* 56, no. 2 (2007): 588 (discussing the *pro homine* principle).

[83] See, e.g., Laurence R. Helfer, "Consensus, Coherence and the European Convention on Human Rights," *Cornell International Law Journal* 26, no. 1 (1993): 133–166; Gerald L. Neuman, "Import, Export, and Regional Consent in the Inter-American Court of Human Rights," *European Journal of International Law* 19, no. 1 (2008): 101–123; Birgit Schlütter, "Aspects of Human Rights Interpretation by the UN Treaty Bodies," in *UN Human Rights Treaty Bodies: Law and Legitimacy*, eds. Helen Keller and Geir Ulfstein (Cambridge: Cambridge University Press, 2012), 261–319.

[84] *Loizidou v. Turkey*, 310 Eur. Ct. H.R. (ser. A) at 27 (1995).

[85] General Comment No. 33, UN Doc. CCPR/C/GC/33 (November 5, 2008).

[86] See, e.g., Ariel E. Dultizky, "Conventionality Control: An Inter-American Constitutional Court? The Invention of the Conventionality Control by the Inter-American Court of Human Rights," *Texas International Law Journal* 50, no. 1 (2015): 45–93; Jorge Contesse, "The International Authority of the Inter-American Court of Human Rights: A Critique of the Conventionality Control Doctrine," *International Journal of Human Rights* 22, no. 9 (2018): 1168–1191.

[87] See, e.g., Mikael Rask Madsen et al., "Special Issue – Resistance to International Courts," *International Journal of Law in Context* 14 (2018): 193–313; Par Engstrom and Courtney Hillebrecht, eds., "Special Issue: The Inter-American Human Rights System," *International Journal of Human Rights* 22, no. 9 (2018): 1111–1266; Shai Dothan, ed., "Special Issue: Margin of Appreciation and Democracy: Human Rights and Deference to Political Bodies," *Journal of International Dispute Settlement* 9, no. 2 (2018): 145–253.

volumes,[88] and blog posts[89] are replete with examples, many of them troubling. They include not only actions by one state (such as overt rejections of specific rulings and withdrawals or threats to withdraw from treaties and optional declarations)[90] but also collective criticisms of overreach and efforts to weaken or undermine the institutions. Among the more disconcerting developments in the latter category was the broadside launched by a quartet of populist regimes (Bolivia, Ecuador, Nicaragua, and Venezuela) against the Inter-American Commission on Human Rights that came perilously close to hobbling a review and monitoring system developed and expanded over half a century.[91] A similar crisis is underway in Africa, where African Union member states, spearheaded by Egypt's populist regime, are using a dispute over NGO accreditation to undermine the authority and independence of the African Commission on Human and Peoples' Rights.[92] Meanwhile, five of the six ECtHR judges who are most deferential to governments were appointed since the 2012 Brighton Conference, at which member states strongly indicated a preference for judicial restraint.[93]

In this fraught political environment, IHRL institutions should choose their battles carefully. A continuation of business as usual – by expanding legal norms and institutional competences, or, even more problematically, "doubling down on transnationalism"[94] – creates easy targets for populist backlashes that may undermine decades of hard-won achievements. A comparison of the two oldest regional human rights courts provides a concrete illustration of these risks.

In Europe, the ECtHR has responded to signals of diminished political support by cutting back on expansive interpretations of the European Convention. In several Grand Chamber judgments, dissenting judges have accused the majority of walking back human rights by giving states an excessive margin of appreciation, unduly narrowing the living instrument doctrine, and diverging from or even

---

[88] See, e.g., Alison Brysk and Michael Stohl, *Contracting Human Rights: Crisis, Accountability, and Opportunity* (Cheltenham: Edward Elgar, 2018); Patricia Poperlier, Sarah Lambrecht, and Koen Lemmens, *Criticism of the European Court of Human Rights* (Cambridge: Intersentia, 2016); Spyridon Flogaitis, Tom Zwart, and Julie Frase, eds., *The European Court of Human Rights and its Discontents* (Cheltenham: Edward Elgar, 2013).

[89] See, e.g., Japhet Biegon, "The Rise and Rise of Political Backlash: African Union Executive Council's Decision to Review the Mandate and Working Methods of the African Commission," EJIL: Talk! August 2, 2018; Francisca Pou Giménez, "Quo Vadis, Inter-American Court? Activism, Backlash and Latin American Constitutionalism," International Journal of Constitutional Law Blog, April 11, 2018, www.iconnectblog.com/2018/04/quo-vadis-inter-american-court-activism-backlash-and-latin-american-constitutionalism-i-connect-column/.

[90] See, e.g., Joost Pauwelyn and Rebecca J. Hamilton, "Exit from International Tribunals," *Journal of International Dispute Settlement* 9, no. 4 (2018): 679–690.

[91] Cassel, "Regional Human Rights Regimes," 3–5.

[92] Biegon, "Rise of Political Backlash."

[93] Øyvind Stiansen and Erik Voeten, "Backlash and Judicial Restraint: Evidence from the European Court of Human Rights." Unpublished manuscript, March 30, 2018.

[94] Urueña, "Double or Nothing," 399.

tacitly overruling prior, pro-applicant decisions.[95] Recent empirical studies suggest that ECtHR judges are executing a significant course correction toward a more circumspect interpretation of human rights and concomitantly greater deference to states.[96]

In Latin America, the IACtHR faces similar political signals but seems to be ignoring them. It has relied on unratified treaties, nonbinding norms, and standards from other human rights systems to expand – sometimes dramatically – protected rights and freedoms.[97] And it has declared itself to be the preeminent expositor of regional human rights norms, a move lauded by proponents of a "New Ius Commune" for Latin America,[98] but one that has led some national courts to conclude that certain Inter-American judgments are ultra vires or unenforceable.[99] A recent manifestation of these trends saw the IACtHR pairing the conventionality control doctrine with its advisory jurisdiction, broadly construing the questions presented to issue expansive decisions concerning human rights and the environment,[100] and gender identity and same-sex marriage.[101] These and

[95] See, e.g., *Animal Defenders International* v. *United Kingdom*, App. no. 48876/08 (ECtHR Grand Chamber 2013), Joint Dissenting Opinion, para. 9 (tacit overruling of prior case law); *S.H.* v. *Austria*, App no. 57813/00 (ECtHR Grand Chamber 2011), Joint Dissenting Opinion, para. 8 (excessively narrow European consensus analysis); *Correia de Matos* v. *Portugal*, App. no. 56402/12 (ECtHR Grand Chamber 2018), Dissenting Opinion of Pinto de Albuquerque, paras. 41–42 (improper "proceduralisation of the margin of appreciation" doctrine).

[96] See, e.g., Stiansen and Voeten, "Backlash and Judicial Restraint," 31–33 (finding that recent cases filed by refugees, asylum seekers, and prisoners against consolidated democracies are about half as likely to result in findings of violations by the ECtHR than a decade earlier); Mikael R. Madsen, "Rebalancing European Human Rights: Has the Brighton Declaration Engendered a New Deal on Human Rights in Europe?," *Journal of International Dispute Settlement* 9, no. 2 (2018): 221 (finding greater subsidiarity since 2010 in three areas – the right to privacy, access to court, and torture and inhuman and degrading treatment); see also Clare Ryan, "Europe's Moral Margin: Parental Aspirations and the European Court of Human Rights," *Columbia Journal of Transnational Law* 56, no. 3 (2018): 490 (identifying the risk that "overly progressive Court judgments will galvanize nationalist opposition to the cosmopolitan human rights regime").

[97] See Neuman, "Import, Export," 109–11; see also Simon Zschirntsimon, "Is the Inter-American Human Rights System Biased? A Quantitative Analysis of Regional Human Rights Litigation in the Americas," *International and Comparative Law Review* 17, no. 1 (2017): 51–81.

[98] Armin von Bogdandy et al., eds., *Transformative Constitutionalism in Latin America: The Emergence of a New Ius Commune* (Oxford: Oxford University Press, 2017).

[99] See, e.g., Jorge Contesse, "Judicial Backlash in Inter-American Human Rights Law?," International Journal of Constitutional Law Blog, March 2, 2017, www.iconnectblog.com/2017/03/judicial-backlash-interamerican/; Huneeus, "Courts Resisting Courts," 511–18.

[100] Advisory Opinion OC-23/17, Ser. A No. 23 (November 15, 2017) (concluding that the right to a healthy environment is a justiciable, autonomous right with individual and collective dimensions, and recognizing that the environment has its own legal personality).

[101] Advisory Opinion OC-24/17, Ser. A No. 24 (November 24, 2017) (concluding that states must provide a mechanism for individuals to legally change their name, sex, and photos on identity documents; that this should be done on the basis of self-determination of gender identity, without prohibitive legal or medical preconditions; and that same sex couples should enjoy all patrimonial and family rights without discrimination, including marriage).

other cases have generated unfavorable headlines,[102] charges of judicial activism,[103] and fears that "the Inter-American Human Rights System [is] an easy target for populism and nationalism."[104]

It is too soon to assess the divergent trajectories of the two regional human rights systems. The point of the comparison is not to praise European judges or denigrate their Latin American colleagues, but instead to show that IHRL institutions are not isolated from politics and must make deliberative choices about how to respond to political signals from member states.

C *Publicity and Outreach*

The previous two survival strategies focus on the choices that IHRL institutions make when reviewing complaints, interpreting legal norms, and monitoring state conduct. These strategies are however, insufficient. IHRL institutions must also takes steps to proactively shape the external environment in which their decisions are received. By publicizing their activities, explaining the significance of rulings, and cultivating state and non-state allies, the institutions can increase the likelihood of surviving challenges from populist governments.

Most decisions of international human rights courts and review bodies are public documents. But that fact says little about whether the public is aware of the decisions or understands their significance, let alone whether individuals or groups will support an institution or mobilize in favor of compliance. If IHRL institutions are indeed passive actors with regard to public information about their decisions, their ability to resist pushback from governments is reduced, all other things equal.[105]

A growing number of studies reveal, however, that national and international courts actively engage in publicity and outreach to bolster their legitimacy and expand their influence. The Mexican Supreme Court strategically issues press

[102] See, e.g., Michelle Riestra, "International Court Pushes Gay Marriage on 20 Latin American Nations," *The Daily Signal*, January 17, 2018, available at http://dailysignal.com/2018/01/17/overstepping-its-mandate-inter-american-court-of-human-rights-orders-20-countries-to-recognize-same-sex-marriage/.

[103] See, e.g., Nicolás Carrillo-Santarelli, "The Politics behind the Latest Advisory Opinions of the Inter-American Court of Human Rights," International Journal of Constitutional Law Blog, February 24, 2018, www.iconnectblog.com/2018/02/the-politics-behind-the-latest-advisory-opinions-of-the-inter-american-court-of-human-rights/; Francisca Pou Giménez, "Quo Vadis, Inter-American Court? Activism, Backlash and Latin American Constitutionalism," International Journal of Constitutional Law Blog, April 11, 2018, www.iconnectblog.com/2018/04/quo-vadis-inter-american-court-activism-backlash-and-latin-american-constitutionalism-i-connect-column/.

[104] Urueña, "Double or Nothing," 408.

[105] See Georg Vanberg, *The Politics of Constitutional Review in Germany* (Cambridge: Cambridge University Press, 2005) (developing a public enforcement model for the German Constitutional Court in which public attention is necessary to induce compliance by the government but information about rulings is exogenous to judicial behavior).

releases to push the boundaries of its power.[106] The German Constitutional Court is more likely to hold public hearings when it anticipates government resistance to its judgments.[107] The Court of Justice of the European Union promotes coverage of its cases in the news media.[108] The Supreme Federal Tribunal of Brazil provides access to full hearings on its own YouTube channel.[109] And other international courts use Twitter to disseminate information and attract favorable notice from a wider audience.[110]

IHRL institutions need to develop similar public relations and outreach strategies to counter opposition from populist governments. Such strategies include a wide range of activities – such as inviting supportive civil society groups to attend oral hearings, issuing press briefings, disseminating decisions via social media, and holding press conferences to accompany the release of important rulings. More ambitiously, IHRL institutions might emulate the outreach programs developed by international and hybrid criminal tribunals to interact with key local constituencies.[111] In extreme cases, where the institution's existence is at stake, judges and other decision-makers might even urge supporters to take to the streets in protest.[112]

Publicity and outreach can enhance the survival prospects of IHRL institutions in multiple ways. Such actions can explain legal reasoning in accessible prose, expanding the number and diversity of potential supporters. They can underscore the benefits of international review of human rights treaties, bolstering institutional legitimacy. They can identify the implications of decisions for upholding the rule of law and democracy. And they can help to counter false information

---

[106] Jeffrey K. Staton, *Judicial Power and Strategic Communication in Mexico* (Cambridge: Cambridge University Press, 2010).

[107] Jay N. Krehbiel, "The Politics of Judicial Procedures: The Role of Public Oral Hearings in the German Constitutional Court," *American Journal of Political Science* 60, no. 4 (2016): 990–1005.

[108] Julian Dederke, "Media Attention, Politicization, and the CJEU's Public Relations Toolbox," Paper presented at iCourts: Centre of Excellence for International Courts, University of Copenhagen (September 5, 2018).

[109] STF – YouTube, www.youtube.com/user/STF.

[110] Pablo Barberá, Zuzanna Godzimirska, and Juan A. Mayoral, "Courting the Public? The Strategic Use of Social Media by International Courts," Paper presented at ECPR General Conference, Hamburg, Germany (August 24, 2018).

[111] See, e.g., International Criminal Tribunal for the former Yugoslavia, Outreach Programme, www.icty.org/en/outreach/outreach-programme (describing "an extensive and methodical information campaign" targeted at "communities in the region to reflect on the Tribunal's achievements and carry [its] legacy forward"); Stuart Ford, "How Special Is the Special Court's Outreach Section?," in *The Sierra Leone Special Court and Its Legacy: The Impact for Africa and International Criminal Law*, ed. Charles Chernor Jalloh (New York: Cambridge University Press, 2013), 505–526 (critically evaluating outreach efforts in Sierra Leone).

[112] In Poland, tens of thousands protested after the government carried out a purge of the Supreme Court. Marc Santora, "Poland Purges Supreme Court, and Protesters Take to Streets," *New York Times*, July 3, 2018. The Supreme Court's ousted president rallied protestors on the courthouse steps, defending the rule of law and the constitution. Marc Santora, "Poland's Supreme Court in Disarray after Judges Defy Purge," *New York Times*, July 4, 2018.

circulated by populist leaders. Lastly, publicity and outreach can highlight particular remedies for violations, providing ready-made focal points for domestic or transnational advocacy.

For observers of legal systems in well-functioning democracies, the idea of international courts and quasi-judicial monitoring bodies engaging in public relations may seem incompatible with their primary role as neutral and independent decision-makers.[113] As explained above, however, national courts are already engaging in such activities. For IHRL institutions, which lack the robust enforcement mechanisms and norms of obedience and which depend upon public scrutiny and social mobilization to pressure governments to remedy violations, the need for strategic outreach in an era of populism is that much more urgent.

D *Creating Windows of Opportunity for Supporters to Mobilize*

Most publicity and outreach activities can fairly easily be appended to the regular business of IHRL institutions. But these activities can also help the institutions to survive more momentous challenges, such as campaigns by populist or authoritarian leaders to narrow their jurisdiction and access rules or to shut them down altogether. To be effective, however, such publicity and outreach should seek to create "windows of opportunity" – time and space during which "institutions and political forces can mobilize to mitigate or even undo" the campaigns.[114]

The counter-mobilizations triggered by court-curbing proposals in West, East, and Southern Africa provide telling examples. In each sub-region, states reacted quickly and angrily to politically embarrassing rulings by advancing proposals to hobble the courts or suspend their operations. Faced with potentially existential threats, the judges on these courts gave speeches and issued public statements decrying the interference with their mandates. They also alerted NGOs and international officials about the proposals, triggering coordinated responses that included press releases, emergency lawsuits, calls to adhere to previously agreed decision-making rules, and demands of access to key meetings where backlash proposals were debated.[115] The outcomes of the court-curbing campaigns varied,[116] but a common

---

[113] This concern may be less acute for IHRL institutions, such as the Special Procedures of the UN Human Rights Council, that do not issue judicial rulings or reasoned decisions that resemble such rulings.

[114] Tom Ginsburg and Aziz Huq, "Democracy's Near Misses," *Journal of Democracy* 29, no. 4 (2018): 18.

[115] Karen J. Alter, James T. Gathii, and Laurence R. Helfer, "Backlash against International Courts in West, East and Southern Africa: Causes and Consequences," *European Journal of International Law* 27, no. 2 (2016): 293–328.

[116] Court-curbing campaigns were defeated in the Economic Community of West African States, redirected and modified in East African Community, and ultimately successful in the Southern African Development Community. For further details, see Alter, Gathii, and Helfer, "Backlash," 295–314.

lesson of these examples is the importance of creating time and space for counter-mobilization efforts to bear fruit:

> Delaying and publicizing sanctioning campaigns allows tempers to cool, exposes the ulterior motives of seemingly benign proposals and shames other governments from tacitly supporting court-curbing efforts. In addition, by insisting that states follow [established decision-making] procedures, secretariats, civil society groups and regional parliaments can slow down sanctioning initiatives, enhance transparency and create opportunities to rally against backlash proposals.[117]

This example reveals that successful counter-mobilization in response to populist backlashes against IHRL institutions requires the active support of civil society groups and at least the tacit acquiescence of some governments or international organizations. Although the judges and experts who serve on IHRL institutions can sound the alarm using publicity and outreach, such extra-institutional activities are, on their own, unlikely to thwart backlash proposals. Is there anything that IHRL institutions can do in their adjudicatory and monitoring capacities to create or expand windows of opportunity for counter-mobilization?

International litigation and monitoring are painfully slow and often far too protracted to make a difference in thwarting institution-curbing campaigns. However, most IHRL institutions have expedited procedures for litigants facing imminent or irreparable harm to seek interim, provisional or precautionary measures.[118] Rapidly responding to these requests – by demanding that states respect their international obligations and preserve the status quo – can help catalyze supporters to rally in favor of the institutions. As studies of democratic erosion have recently shown, "a well-timed decision by judges" and other nonmajoritarian actors that "giv[es] political parties and public movements time to regroup and reorganize" in the face of threats to democracy "can make all the difference between a near miss and a fatal blow."[119] At present, however, most IHRL institutions do not publish interim measures orders, nor do they explain the rationales for such decisions.[120] Doing so is essential, both to help create focal points for counter-mobilization and to help diffuse government objections to such orders.[121]

---

[117] Alter, Gathii, and Helfer, "Backlash," 318.
[118] See, e.g., Helen Keller and Cedric Marti, "Interim Relief Compared: Use of Interim Measures by the UN Human Rights Committee and the European Court of Human Rights," *Heidelberg Journal of International Law* 73, no. 3 (2013): 325–372; Jo M. Pasqualucci, "Interim Measures in International Human Rights: Evolution and Harmonization," *Vanderbilt Journal of Transnational Law* 38, no. 1 (2005): 1–49; Eva Rieter, *Preventing Irreparable Harm: Provisional Measures in Human Rights Adjudication* (Oxford: Intersentia, 2010).
[119] Ginsburg and Huq, "Near Misses," 29.
[120] Rieter, *Preventing Irreparable Harm*, 123, 141, 169, 180.
[121] The lack of guidelines and reasoned decisions for provisional measures orders issued by the Inter-American Commission on Human Rights has engendered opposition, in particular from Brazil. See Jorge Contesse, "Resisting Inter-American Human Rights Law," *Yale Journal of International Law* 44 (2019). This has recently led to reforms that bolstered the Commission's authority to issue such orders. Ibid.

V CONCLUSION

International human rights law institutions face new and distinctive challenges from the rise of populist regimes in a growing number of countries. The (admittedly uneven) progress that these institutions have made over the last half century is under significant threat of retrenchment. Effectively responding to these challenges and threats is unlikely to be achieved – at least in the short and medium term – by developing legal doctrines tailored to human rights abuses by populist states, by threats of sanctions against their governments, or by extending international law to address the manipulation of social media by populist leaders. What is instead required is the adoption of integrated survival strategies by IHRL institutions, strategies that recognize that legal battles against repression are often won not only in courtrooms and hearing rooms but in response to social and political mobilization that pressures recalcitrant governments to respond to the decisions of those institutions rather than undermine their authority.

BIBLIOGRAPHY

Alston, Philip. "The Populist Challenge to Human Rights." *Journal of Human Rights Practice* 9, no. 1 (2017): 1–15.
Alter, Karen J. *The New Terrain of International Law: Courts, Politics, Rights.* Princeton, NJ: Princeton University Press, 2014.
Alter, Karen J., James T. Gathii, and Laurence R. Helfer. "Backlash against International Courts in West, East and Southern Africa: Causes and Consequences." *European Journal of International Law* 27, no. 2 (2016): 293–328.
Alter, Karen J., Laurence R. Helfer, and Mikael Rask Madsen. "How Context Shapes the Authority of International Courts." In *International Court Authority*, edited by Karen J. Alter, Laurence R. Helfer, and Mikael Rask Madsen, 24–58. Oxford: Oxford University Press, 2018.
Álvarez-Icazaa, Emilio. "The Inter-American System and Challenges for its Future." *American University International Law Review* 29, no. 5 (2014): 989–1001.
Andorno, Roberto. "Is Vulnerability the Foundation of Human Rights?" In *Human Dignity of the Vulnerable in the Age of Rights: Interdisciplinary Perspectives*, edited by Aniceto Masferrer and Emilio García-Sánchez, 257–272. Cham, Switzerland: Springer, 2016.
Arnardóttir, Oddný Mjöll. "The Brighton Aftermath and the Changing Role of the European Court of Human Rights." *Journal of International Dispute Settlement* 9, no. 2 (2018): 223–239.
Barberá, Pablo, Zuzanna Godzimirska, and Juan A. Mayoral. "Courting the Public? The Strategic Use of Social Media by International Courts." Paper presented at ECPR General Conference, Hamburg, Germany, August 24, 2018.
Biegon, Japhet. "The Rise and Rise of Political Backlash: African Union Executive Council's Decision to Review the Mandate and Working Methods of the African Commission." EJIL: Talk! August 2, 2018.
Bonnitcha, Jonathan, and Robert McCorquodale. "The Concept of 'Due Diligence' in the UN Guiding Principles on Business and Human Rights." *European Journal of International Law* 28, no. 3 (2017): 899–919.

Bossuyt, Marc. "Categorical Rights and Vulnerable Groups: Moving Away from the Universal Human Being." *George Washington International Law Review* 48, no. 4 (2016): 717–742.

Brandes, Tamar Hostovsky. "International Law in Domestic Courts in an Era of Populism." *International Journal of Constitutional Law* 17, no. 2 (2019): 576–596.

Brysk, Alison, and Michael Stohl, ed. *Contracting Human Rights: Crisis, Accountability, and Opportunity.* Cheltenham: Edward Elgar, 2018.

Buergenthal, Thomas. "International Human Rights Law and Institutions: Accomplishments and Prospects." *Washington Law Review* 63, no. 1 (1988): 1–20.

"New Upload – Remembering the Early Years of the Inter-American Court of Human Rights." *New York University Journal of International Law and Politics* 37, no. 2 (2005): 259–280.

"The Evolving International Human Rights System." *American Journal of International Law* 100, no. 4 (2006): 783–807.

Çali, Başak. "Specialized Rules of Treaty Interpretation: Human Rights." In *The Oxford Guide to Treaties*, edited by Duncan B. Hollis, 525–550. Oxford: Oxford University Press, 2012.

"Coping with Crisis: Whither the Variable Geometry in the Jurisprudence of the European Court of Human Rights." *Wisconsin International Law Journal* 35, no. 2 (2018): 237–276.

Carrillo-Santarelli, Nicolás. "The Politics behind the Latest Advisory Opinions of the Inter-American Court of Human Rights." International Journal of Constitutional Law Blog, February 24, 2018. www.iconnectblog.com/2018/02/the-politics-behind-the-latest-advisory-opinions-of-the-inter-american-court-of-human-rights/

Cassel, Doug. "Regional Human Rights Regimes and State Push Back: The Case of the Inter-American Human Rights System." *Human Rights Law Journal* 33, no. 1–6 (2013): 1–10.

Charles, Deborah. "Honduras Readmitted to OAS after Coup." *Reuters*, June 1, 2011. www.reuters.com/article/us-honduras-oas/honduras-readmitted-to-oas-after-coup-idUSTRE75063P20110601.

Chirwa, Danwood Mzikenge. "The Doctrine of State Responsibility as a Potential Means of Holding Private Actors Accountable for Human Rights." *Melbourne Journal of International Law* 5, no. 1 (2004): 1–36.

Contesse, Jorge. "Judicial Backlash in Inter-American Human Rights Law?" International Journal of Constitutional Law Blog, March 2, 2017. www.iconnectblog.com/2017/03/judicial-backlash-interamerican/

"The International Authority of the Inter-American Court of Human Rights: A Critique of the Conventionality Control Doctrine." *International Journal of Human Rights* 22, no. 9 (2018): 1168–1191.

"Resisting Inter-American Human Rights Law." *Yale Journal of International Law* 44 (2019): 179–237.

Daly, Tom Gerald. *The Alchemists: Questioning our Faith in Courts as Democracy-Builders.* Cambridge: Cambridge University Press, 2017.

Daly, Tom Gerald, and Micha Wiebusch. "The African Court on Human and Peoples' Rights: Mapping Resistance against a Young Court." *International Journal of Law in Context* 14, no. 2 (2018): 294–313.

Dederke, Julian. "Media Attention, Politicization, and the CJEU's Public Relations Toolbox." Paper presented at iCourts: Centre of Excellence for International Courts, University of Copenhagen, September 5, 2018.

de Londras, Fiona, and Kanstantsin Dzehtsiarou. "Mission Impossible? Addressing Non-Execution through Infringement Proceedings in the European Court of Human Rights." *International and Comparative Law Quarterly* 66, no. 2 (2017): 467–490.

Donald, Alice. "Backlog, Backlash and Beyond: Debating the Long Term Future of Human Rights Protection in Europe." UK Human Rights Blog, April 14, 2014. https://ukhuman rightsblog.com/2014/04/14/backlog-backlash-and-beyond-debating-the-long-term-future-of-human-rights-protection-in-europe-alice-donald/.

Dothan, Shai, ed. "Special Issue: Margin of Appreciation and Democracy: Human Rights and Deference to Political Bodies." *Journal of International Dispute Settlement* 9, no. 2 (2018): 145–253.

Dulitzky, Ariel E. "Conventionality Control: An Inter-American Constitutional Court? The Invention of the Conventionality Control by the Inter-American Court of Human Rights." *Texas International Law Journal* 50, no. 1 (2015): 45–93.

Dzehtsiarou, Kanstantsin. "How Many Judgments Does One Need to Enforce A Judgment? The First Ever Infringement Proceedings at the European Court of Human Rights." Strasbourg Observers Blog, June 4, 2019. https://strasbourgobservers.com/2019/06/04/how-many-judgments-does-one-need-to-enforce-a-judgment-the-first-ever-infringement-proceedings-at-the-european-court-of-human-rights/.

Egan, Suzanne. "Strengthening the United Nations Human Rights Treaty Body System." *Human Rights Law Review* 13, no. 2 (2013): 209–243.

Engstrom, Par, and Courtney Hillebrecht, eds. "Special Issue: The Inter-American Human Rights System." *International Journal of Human Rights* 22, no. 9 (2018): 1111–1266.

Engström, Viljam. "Deference and the Human Rights Committee." *Nordic Journal of Human Rights* 34, no. 2 (2016): 73–88.

Farer, Tom. "The Rise of the Inter-American Human Rights Regime: No Longer a Unicorn, Not Yet an Ox." In *The Inter-American Human Rights System*, edited by David J. Harris and Stephen Livingstone, 31–64. Oxford: Oxford University Press, 1998.

Flogaitis, Spyridon, Tom Zwart, and Julie Frase, eds. *The European Court of Human Rights and its Discontents*. Cheltenham: Edward Elgar, 2013.

Ford, Stuart. "How Special is the Special Court's Outreach Section?" In *The Sierra Leone Special Court and Its Legacy: The Impact for Africa and International Criminal Law*, edited by Charles Chernor Jalloh, 505–526. New York: Cambridge University Press, 2013.

García-Sayán, Diego. "The Role of the Inter-American Court of Human Rights in the Americas." *U.C. Davis Journal of International Law and Policy* 19, no. 1 (2012): 103–112.

Gardbaum, Steven. "Human Rights and International Constitutionalism." In *Ruling the World? Constitutionalism, International Law, and Global Governance*, edited by Jeffrey L. Dunoff and Joel P. Trachtman, 233–257. New York: Cambridge University Press, 2009.

Giménez, Francisca Pou. "Quo Vadis, Inter-American Court? Activism, Backlash and Latin American Constitutionalism." International Journal of Constitutional Law Blog, April 11, 2018. www.iconnectblog.com/2018/04/quo-vadis-inter-american-court-activism-backlash-and-latin-american-constitutionalism-i-connect-column/.

Ginsburg, Tom, and Aziz Huq. "Democracy's Near Misses." *Journal of Democracy* 29, no. 4 (2018): 16–30.

Glas, Lize R. "The Committee of Ministers Goes Nuclear: Infringement Proceedings against Azerbaijan in the Case of Ilgar Mammadov." Strasbourg Observers Blog, December 20, 2017. https://strasbourgobservers.com/2017/12/20/the-committee-of-ministers-goes-nuclear-infringement-proceedings-against-azerbaijan-in-the-case-of-ilgar-mammadov/.

Grant, Sarah, Quinta Jurecic, Matthew Kahn, Matt Tait, and Benjamin Wittes. "Russian Influence Campaign: What's in the Latest Mueller Indictment." *Lawfare* Blog, February 16, 2018. www.lawfareblog.com/russian-influence-campaign-whats-latest-mueller-indictment.

Helfer, Laurence R. "Consensus, Coherence and the European Convention on Human Rights." *Cornell International Law Journal* 26, no. 1 (1993): 133–166.

"Overlegalizing Human Rights: International Relations Theory and the Commonwealth Caribbean Backlash Against Human Rights Regimes." *Columbia Law Review* 102, no. 7 (2002): 1832–1911.

"Redesigning the European Court of Human Rights: Embeddedness as a Deep Structural Principle of the European Human Rights Regime." *European Journal of International Law* 19, no. 1 (2008): 125–159.

"The Benefits and Burdens of Brighton." *ESIL Reflections* 1, no. 1 (2012), http://esil-sedi.eu/node/138.

Helfer, Laurence R., and Anne-Marie Slaughter "Toward a Theory of Effective Supranational Adjudication." *Yale Law Journal* 107, no. 2 (1997): 273–391.

Helfer, Laurence R., and Anne E. Showalter, "Opposing International Justice: Kenya's Integrated Backlash Strategy Against the ICC." *International Criminal Law Review* 17, no. 1 (2017): 1–46.

Henkin, Louis. *The Age of Rights*. New York: Columbia University Press, 1990.

Heri, Corina. "Merabishvili, Mammadov and Targeted Criminal Proceedings: Recent Developments under Article 18 ECHR." Strasbourg Observers Blog, December 15, 2017. https://strasbourgobservers.com/2017/12/15/merabishvili-mammadov-and-targeted-criminal-proceedings-recent-developments-under-article-18-echr/.

Hern, Alex. "Thirty Countries Use 'Armies of Opinion Shapers' to Manipulate Democracy – Report." *The Guardian*, November 14, 2017.

Hopgood, Stephen. *The Endtimes of Human Rights*. Ithaca, NY: Cornell University Press, 2013.

Human Rights Council, "Elaboration of an International Legally Binding Instrument on Transnational Corporations and Other Business Enterprises with Respect to Human Rights." U.N. Doc. A/HRC/26/L.22/Rev.1, June 24, 2014.

Huneeus, Alexandra. "Courts Resisting Courts: Lessons from the Inter-American Court's Struggle to Enforce Human Rights." *Cornell International Law Journal* 44, no. 3 (2011): 493–534.

"Introduction to Symposium on the Constitutionalization of International Law in Latin America." *AJIL Unbound* 109 (2015): 89–92.

Huneeus, Alexandra, and René Urueña. "Treaty Exit and Latin America's Constitutional Courts." *AJIL Unbound* 111 (2017): 456–460.

Huq, Aziz, and Tom Ginsburg. *How to Save a Constitutional Democracy*. Chicago: University of Chicago Press, 2018.

Jørgensen, Rikke Frank. "Human Rights and Private Actors in the Online Domain." In *New Technologies for Human Rights Law and Practice*, edited by Molly K. Land and Jay D. Aronson, 243–269. Cambridge: Cambridge University Press, 2018.

Keith, Linda Camp. "Judicial Independence and Human Rights Protection Around the World." *Judicature* 85, no. 4 (2002): 195–200.

Keller, Helen, and Corina Heri. "Selective Criminal Proceedings and Article 18 ECHR: The European Court of Human Rights' Untapped Potential to Protect Democracy." *Human Rights Law Journal* 36, no. 1-6 (2016): 1–10.

Keller, Helen, and Cedric Marti. "Interim Relief Compared: Use of Interim Measures by the UN Human Rights Committee and the European Court of Human Rights." *Heidelberg Journal of International Law* 73, no. 3 (2013): 325–372.

Kingsley, Patrick. "On the Surface, Hungary Is a Democracy. But What Lies Underneath?" *New York Times*, December 25, 2018.

Kosař, David, and Katarina Šipulová. "The Strasbourg Court Meets Abusive Constitutionalism: *Baka v. Hungary* and the Rule of Law." *Hague Journal on the Rule of Law* (2017). DOI:10.1007/s40803-017-0065-y.

Krehbiel, Jay N. "The Politics of Judicial Procedures: The Role of Public Oral Hearings in the German Constitutional Court." *American Journal of Political Science* 60, no. 4 (2016): 990–1005.

Land, Molly K., and Jay D. Aronson, "The Promise and Peril of Human Rights Technology." In *New Technologies for Human Rights Law and Practice*, edited by Molly K. Land and Jay D. Aronson, 1–10. Cambridge: Cambridge University Press, 2018.

Lixinski, Lucas. "The European Convention on Human Rights and International Law." *International and Comparative Law Quarterly* 56, no. 2 (2007): 585–604.

Madsen, Mikael R. "The Challenging Authority of the European Court of Human Rights: From Cold War Legal Diplomacy to the Brighton Declaration and Backlash." *Law and Contemporary Problems* 79, no. 1 (2016): 141–178.

"Rebalancing European Human Rights: Has the Brighton Declaration Engendered a New Deal on Human Rights in Europe?" *Journal of International Dispute Settlement* 9, no. 2 (2018): 199–222.

Madsen, Mikael Rask, Pola Cebulak, and Micha Wiebusch. "Special Issue – Resistance to International Courts." *International Journal of Law in Context* 14 (2018): 193–313.

Malkin, Elisabeth. "In Costa Rica Election, Gay-Marriage Foe Takes First Round." *New York Times*, February 5, 2018.

Mälksoo, Lauri, and Wolfgang Benedek. *Russia and the European Court of Human Rights: The Strasbourg Effect*. New York: Cambridge University Press, 2018.

Marchuk, Iryna. "Flexing Muscles (Yet Again): The Russian Constitutional Court's Defiance of the Authority of the ECtHR in the Yukos Case." EJIL: Talk! February 13, 2017. www .ejiltalk.org/flexing-muscles-yet-again-the-russian-constitutional-courts-defiance-of-the-authority-of-the-ecthr-in-the-yukos-case/.

McGoldrick, Dominic. "A Defence of the Margin of Appreciation and an Argument for its Application by the Human Rights Committee." *International and Comparative Law Quarterly* 65, no. 1 (2016): 21–60.

Moyn, Samuel. *The Last Utopia: Human Rights in History*. Cambridge, MA: Harvard University Press, 2010.

Moyn, Samuel. "How the Human Rights Movement Failed." *New York Times*, April 23, 2018.

Mudde, Cas, and Cristóbal Rovira Kaltwasser. "Studying Populism in Comparative Perspective: Reflections on the Contemporary and Future Research Agenda." *Comparative Political Studies* 51, no. 13 (2018): 1667–1693.

Mutua, Makau. "Is the Age of Human Rights Over?" In *Routledge Companion to Literature and Human Rights*, edited by Sophia A. McClennen and Alexandra Schultheis Moore, 450–458. New York: Routledge, 2016.

Nakanishi, Yumiko. "Mechanisms to Protect Human Rights in the EU's External Relations." In *Contemporary Issues in Human Rights Law: Europe and Asia*, edited by Yumiko Nakanishi, 3–22. Singapore: Springer Nature, 2017.

Neuman, Gerald L. "Import, Export, and Regional Consent in the Inter-American Court of Human Rights." *European Journal of International Law* 19, no. 1 (2008): 101–123.

Pasqualucci, Jo M. "Interim Measures in International Human Rights: Evolution and Harmonization." *Vanderbilt Journal of Transnational Law* 38, no. 1 (2005): 1–49.

Pauwelyn, Joost, and Rebecca J. Hamilton. "Exit from International Tribunals." *Journal of International Dispute Settlement* 9, no. 4 (2018): 679–690.

Piracés, Enrique. "The Future of Human Rights Technology: A Practitioner's View." In *New Technologies for Human Rights Law and Practice*, edited by Molly K. Land and Jay D. Aronson, 289–308. Cambridge: Cambridge University Press, 2018.

Poperlier, Patricia Sarah Lambrecht, and Koen Lemmens. *Criticism of the European Court of Human Rights*. Cambridge: Intersentia, 2016.

Posner, Eric A. *The Twilight of Human Rights Law*. New York: Oxford University Press, 2014.
"Liberal Internationalism and the Populist Backlash." *Arizona State Law Journal* 49, special issue (2016): 795–819.

Posner, Michael. "Why U.S. Withdrawal from the Human Rights Council Is a Dangerous Leadership Mistake." *Forbes*, June 19, 2018.

Riestra, Michelle. "International Court Pushes Gay Marriage on 20 Latin American Nations." *The Daily Signal*, January 17, 2018, available at http://dailysignal.com/2018/01/17/overstep ping-its-mandate-inter-american-court-of-human-rights-orders-20-countries-to-recognize-same-sex-marriage/.

Rieter, Eva. *Preventing Irreparable Harm: Provisional Measures in Human Rights Adjudication*. Oxford: Intersentia, 2010.

Rona, Gabor, and Lauren Aarons. "State Responsibility to Respect, Protect and Fulfill Human Rights Obligations in Cyberspace." *Journal of National Security Law and Policy* 8, no. 3 (2016): 503–530.

[Ruggie, John.] Special Representative of the Secretary-General on Human Rights and Transnational Corporations and Other Business Enterprises, "Guiding Principles on Business and Human Rights: Implementing the United Nations 'Protect, Respect and Remedy' Framework." Human Rights Council, U.N. Doc. A/HRC/17/31, March 21, 2011.

Ryan, Clare. "Europe's Moral Margin: Parental Aspirations and the European Court of Human Rights." *Columbia Journal of Transnational Law* 56, no. 3 (2018): 467–530.

Santora, Marc. "Poland Purges Supreme Court, and Protesters Take to Streets." *New York Times*, July 3, 2018.
"Poland's Supreme Court in Disarray after Judges Defy Purge." *New York Times*, July 4, 2018.

Schlütter, Birgit. "Aspects of Human Rights Interpretation by the UN Treaty Bodies." In *UN Human Rights Treaty Bodies: Law and Legitimacy*, edited by Helen Keller and Geir Ulfstein, 261–319. Cambridge: Cambridge University Press, 2012.

Shany, Yuval. "Towards a General Margin of Appreciation Doctrine in International Law." *European Journal of International Law* 16, no. 5 (2005): 907–940.

Shelton, Dinah, and Alexandra Huneeus. "*In re* Direct Action of Unconstitutionality Initiated Against the Declaration of Acceptance of the Jurisdiction of the Inter-American Court of Human Rights." *American Journal of International Law* 109, no. 4 (2015): 866–872.

Sikkink, Kathryn. *The Justice Cascade: How Human Rights Prosecutions Are Changing World Politics*. New York: W.W. Norton, 2011.

Simmons, Beth A. *Mobilizing for Human Rights: International Law in Domestic Politics*. New York: Cambridge University Press, 2009.

Smet, Stijn. *Resolving Conflicts between Human Rights: The Judge's Dilemma*. New York: Routledge, 2017.

Soley, Ximena, and Silvia Steininger. "Parting Ways or Lashing Back? Withdrawals, Backlash and the Inter-American Court of Human Rights." *International Journal of Law in Context* 14, no. 2 (2018): 237–257.

Ssenyonjo, Manisuli. "State Withdrawal Notifications from the Rome Statute of the International Criminal Court: South Africa, Burundi and The Gambia." *Criminal Law Forum* 29, no. 1 (2018): 63–119.

Staton, Jeffrey K. *Judicial Power and Strategic Communication in Mexico*. Cambridge: Cambridge University Press, 2010.

Stiansen, Øyvind, and Erik Voeten. "Backlash and Judicial Restraint: Evidence from the European Court of Human Rights." Unpublished manuscript, March 30, 2018. PDF file.

Thielbörger, Pierre, and Tobias Ackermann, "A Treaty on Enforcing Human Rights Against Business: Closing the Loophole or Getting Stuck in a Loop?" *Indiana Journal of Global Legal Studies* 24, no. 1 (2017): 43–79.

Urueña, René. "Double or Nothing? The Inter-American Court of Human Rights in an Increasingly Adverse Context." *Wisconsin International Law Journal* 35, no. 2 (2018): 398–425.

Vanberg, Georg. *The Politics of Constitutional Review in Germany.* Cambridge: Cambridge University Press 2005.

von Bogdandy, Armin, Eduardo Ferrer Mac-Gregor, Mariela Morales Antoniazzi, and Flavia Piovesan. *Transformative Constitutionalism in Latin America: The Emergence of a New Ius Commune.* Oxford: Oxford University Press, 2017.

Voss, M. Joel. "Contesting Sexual Orientation and Gender Identity at the UN Human Rights Council." *Human Rights Review* 19, no. 1 (2018): 1–22.

Wallace, Julia. "Fight over Cambodian Leader's Facebook 'Likes' Reaches a U.S. Court." *New York Times,* February 9, 2018.

Wildhaber, Luzius. "The European Convention on Human Rights and International Law." *International and Comparative Law Quarterly* 56, no. 2 (2007): 217–231.

Wuerth, Ingrid B. "International Law in the Post-Human Rights Era." *Texas Law Review* 96, no. 2 (2017): 279–349.

Zschirntsimon, Simon. "Is the Inter-American Human Rights System Biased? A Quantitative Analysis of Regional Human Rights Litigation in the Americas." *International and Comparative Law Review* 17, no. 1 (2017): 51–81.

11

Human Rights Responses to the Populist Challenge

Gerald L. Neuman

I INTRODUCTION

The current wave of exclusionary populism – particularly as defined by the ideational approach – poses threats to human rights within the national borders, human rights outside them, and to the international human rights system. How should the system respond?

Human rights courts and other international human rights monitoring bodies do not have the ability to "solve" the problem posed by the rise in populism. They can aid in addressing underlying social causes of populism; they can help to preserve the rule of law and democratic alternatives to populism; they can identify human rights violations committed by populist governments and seek to provide remedies. They can also change behavior of their own that may have contributed to populism, and avoid making things worse. And, as Laurence Helfer emphasizes, they can try to preserve their own capacity to make greater progress once the populist wave has passed.

The limited power of the human rights institutions in this context is not unusual – it is typical of their situation. Human rights courts and monitoring bodies normally depend for success on the cooperation of actors with other powers and roles. Other international bodies, governments of other countries, international NGOs, and local civil society are potential allies in motivating branches of a national government to change rules and practices.

In this chapter, I will focus on human rights courts and monitoring bodies that are tasked with making impartial evaluations of whether a state complies with its existing international obligations.[1] Examples include the regional human rights courts and

---

[1] Thus, the chapter will not analyze the degree to which similar considerations apply to the work of human rights NGOs making claims about existing obligations, or various actors proposing new international obligations that would not take effect without the future consent of governments.

commissions, the global human rights treaty bodies, and the International Court of Justice, among others. For brevity, I will refer to them all as "monitoring bodies." Even within this category, the situations of different human rights bodies will vary, as will the types of populist challenges they face. Appropriate responses may depend on the nature of their mandates, the options and procedures available to them, and the kinds of support they receive. Accordingly, some of the recommendations made here appear to have general application, while others are more relevant to particular environments.

The chapter first discusses the manner in which monitoring bodies should address exclusionary populism, by its substance rather than by its name. It then examines how monitoring bodies should share with local actors the task of opposing populist discourse. In the third section, the chapter asks what monitoring bodies can learn from populist attacks on their work, which may indeed identify occasions when their conclusions or their explanations need improvement.

II DIRECT AND INDIRECT APPROACHES TO EXCLUSIONARY POPULISM

Human rights experts with international legal mandates have important contributions to make in resisting populist abuses. Nonetheless, I suggest, they should concentrate on the abuses rather than on populism as such. They should seek to protect and support the advocacy of local actors, who are often better situated to persuade the domestic audience about the threats that populist leaders pose.

A *Confronting Populism as Such*

Should international human rights monitoring bodies directly address populism as an operative legal category? In particular, should they determine whether a specific politician, party or government qualifies as "populist," and attach legal consequences to that characterization? I believe for several reasons that they should not.

First, "populism" is not a legal term recognized in international law, and it has no universally accepted definition. The disputes among scholars regarding the proper understanding of the term have been sufficiently illustrated in Chapter 1 to show the difficulty, while explaining my own preference for the ideational approach. Despite agreement on some core examples, social scientists disagree not only on how to conceptualize populism but also on which politicians or parties should count as populist.[2] The empirical bases for evaluation employed by academics would not

---

[2] E.g., Jan-Werner Müller, *What Is Populism?* (Philadelphia, PA: University of Pennsylvania Press, 2016), 93 (denying that Senator Bernie Sanders was a populist); Wayne Steger, "Populist Waves in the 2016 Presidential Nominations: Another Limit to the Party Decides Thesis," in *The State of the Parties, 2018*, ed. John C. Green, Daniel J. Coffey, and David B. Cohen (2018) (Lanham, MD: Rowman & Littlefield), 150 (characterizing both Sanders and Trump as

necessarily be appropriate for legal institutions.[3] Monitoring bodies would open themselves to charges of bias and political selectivity if they relied on such a concept as a reason for finding violations or condemning states.

Instead, monitoring bodies can focus on the actions of populists without explicitly categorizing them as such, especially in dealing with the policies of populist governments.[4] Abuses emphasized in previous chapters, such as discriminatory laws, assaults on the independence of the judiciary, suppression of political competition, police violence, and similar outcomes of populism are already human rights violations that come within the jurisdiction of various human rights bodies. Some of these bodies have limited subject matter mandates that would restrict their authority to a particular subset of the violations – those affecting women, for example, or racial minorities – and others have fuller oversight responsibilities. The retail nature of the adjudicatory procedures of human rights courts may narrow their field of vision, but other bodies have more flexible oversight mechanisms that enable them to analyze broad patterns of violations.

The particular threats posed by populism vary depending on its targets at a specific time. Some forms of populism involve racist or xenophobic incitement that is already regulated by human rights treaties before it produces discriminatory action.[5] For those forms of populism, monitoring bodies can address specific populist rhetoric for its content, rather than make the label "populist" the key.

Other forms of populism target groups that lack specific protection in human rights law, such as groups identified as "criminals," "drug criminals," or "globalized elites." In comparison with racial and religious incitement, there is greater need for caution here. Monitoring bodies can remind politicians that individuals suspected or convicted of crimes have rights, and they can condemn actual violations of the rights of those individuals. But there would be less legitimacy in efforts to censor the

---

populists); Benjamin De Cleen, "Populism, Exclusion, Post-truth. Some Conceptual Caveats," *International Journal of Health Policy and Management* 7, no. 3 (2018): 269 (characterizing Evo Morales of Bolivia, Sanders, and Spain's PODEMOS party as populist).

3   See, e.g., Teun Pauwels, "Measuring Populism: A Review of Current Approaches," in *Political Populism: A Handbook*, ed. Reinhard C. Heinisch, Christina Holtz-Bacha, and Oscar Mazzoleni (Baden-Baden: Nomos, 2017), 123–136 (describing computerized content analysis, holistic grading, and expert surveys as possible methods for measuring populism).

4   See, e.g., Human Rights Committee, Concluding observations on the sixth periodic report of Hungary, UN Doc. CCPR/C/HUN/CO/6 (2018); Human Rights Committee, Concluding observations on the seventh periodic report of Poland, UN Doc. CCPR/C/POL/CO/7 (2016). But see *Erdel* v. *Germany*, App. no. 30067/04, ECHR (2007) (dec.), 7 (holding that the state acted within its margin of appreciation in limiting the opportunities of a reserve officer on account of his active membership in *Die Republikaner*, "a party which is considered right-wing and populist and which has been under scrutiny by the offices for the protection of the Constitution").

5   See International Convention on the Elimination of All Forms of Racial Discrimination, art. 4; International Covenant on Civil and Political Rights (ICCPR), art. 20; American Convention on Human Rights (ACHR), art. 13(5); see also *R.B.* v. *Hungary*, App. no. 64602/12, ECHR (2016); Chapter 8 (in this volume).

rhetoric of moralistic condemnation against these groups, and more danger that such efforts would strengthen public resentment against external intervention.

I am not saying that human rights monitoring bodies should take no notice of the phenomenon of populism, or should never mention it. On the contrary, they should be alert to the risks that it creates for human rights, and to the special challenges of interacting with populist governments. International bodies should not, however, try to make populism as such an element of a human rights violation. And they should be alert to the ambiguity of the term.

Human rights bodies differ in the flexibility of their mandates and procedures – some operate primarily as neutral receivers of complaints or reports that establish their dockets, while others exercise more initiative in choosing issues or countries on which to focus their limited capacity. Some treaty bodies maintain inquiry procedures for addressing severe ongoing situations within their jurisdiction *sua sponte*, or issue ad hoc statements in response to pressing current events. Bodies that exercise such discretion face pressures to justify their impartiality against the charge of "selectivity," understood as the biased targeting of certain countries or certain rights.

There should be room for monitoring bodies to keep a wary eye on populist governments among others in accordance with their mandates. They should be prepared to defend their resulting activities as responses to worse problems rather than worse governments. In the present environment, they should allocate attention to characteristic issues that intensify human rights violations and prevent reforms, such as manipulation of electoral systems, undermining of checks and balances, and attacks on civil society – at least, to the extent that these issues lie within the body's jurisdiction.

For some treaty bodies, such as the Human Rights Committee, a favorably timed state report from a populist government may present the best opportunity to address relevant issues.[6]

Political rights, expression and association are squarely within the Human Rights Committee's mandate – more so than for other global treaty bodies. These topics should be given adequate space and time in the list of issues sent to the state and the public dialogue with the state's delegation. In the past, those rights have often

---

[6]   The ICCPR requires all states-parties to submit periodic reports on their compliance with the treaty, and the Human Rights Committee holds a public dialogue with each reporting state, structured primarily by a list of issues drafted by the committee. The committee is free to include any issues within its mandate, and after the dialogue the committee publishes concluding observations on the matters that were discussed. The committee also maintains an additional case-based procedure by which individual victims can submit communications, but only against those states-parties that have accepted this optional procedure, and the committee's response is limited by the subject matter of the communication. See Gerald L. Neuman, "Giving Meaning and Effect to Human Rights: The Contributions of Human Rights Committee Members," in *The Human Rights Covenants at 50: Their Past, Present, and Future*, ed. Daniel Moeckli, Helen Keller, and Corina Heri (Oxford: Oxford University Press, 2018), 32–34.

received hurried attention toward the end of the proceedings, merely because the relevant articles 19, 22 and 25 appear late in the enumeration in the ICCPR. The committee should be more willing to ensure sufficient opportunity for discussion, and enable fuller treatment of these issues in the committee's concluding observations on the report.

One significant contribution that the Human Rights Committee and other monitoring bodies could make involves specifying something that human rights to political participation do *not* require. As other chapters in the book have pointed out, populist leaders have sought to extend their power by eliminating rules that prevent their reelection.[7] At times, subservient courts have invalidated such rules by finding that they are unconstitutional or that they violate human rights – either the rights of the leader or the rights of the voters.[8] I agree with Laurence Helfer's characterization of these holdings as insidiously twisting human rights law. Currently human rights treaties do not include an explicit prohibition against indefinite reelection, but they permit restrictions on candidacy that are necessary for the functioning of democracy and the protection of human rights.[9] Monitoring bodies should explain unequivocally that the human rights argument for indefinite reelection of presidents is specious. Recently, the Venice Commission of the Council of Europe issued a useful report analyzing the issues relating to term limits for presidents, at the request of the OAS. The report concludes that nondiscriminatory term limits for presidents may be necessary for the preservation of democracy, and do not violate human rights of candidates or voters.[10] It did not go so far as to maintain that the absence of a term limit would violate the human rights of voters or of competing candidates; indeed, that would be harder to demonstrate, especially given uncertainty about the appropriate maximum period of service. Admittedly,

---

[7] See Chapters 5 and 10 (in this volume); see also Tom Ginsburg, James Melton, and Zachary Elkins, "On the Evasion of Executive Term Limits," *William and Mary Law Review* 52, no. 6 (2011): 1807–1872.

[8] See David Landau, "Presidential Term Limits in Latin America: A Critical Analysis of the Migration of the Unconstitutional Constitutional Amendment Doctrine," *Law and Ethics of Human Rights* 12, no. 2 (2018): 225–249 (discussing decisions in Costa Rica, Nicaragua, Honduras, and Bolivia).

[9] The lack of such a prohibition is clearer in the texts of the ICCPR and the European and African regional treaties than in the text of the ACHR, but the Inter-American Court of Human Rights has made clear that the wording of Article 23 ACHR contemplates the creation of rules that structure the electoral system in order to enable the free exercise of the rights to vote and to be elected. See *Castañeda Gutman v. Mexico*, 184 Inter-Am. Ct. H.R. (ser. C) (2008) (upholding a requirement that candidates be nominated by a party).

[10] European Commission for Democracy Through Law, Report on Term-Limits: Part I – Presidents, CDL-AD(2018)010 (2018). A subsequent report on term limits for legislators and local officials found less urgent need for regulation, but also concluded that restricting indefinite reelection does not violate human rights. European Commission for Democracy Through Law, Report on Term-Limits: Part II – Members of Parliament; Part III – Representatives Elected at Sub-National and Local Level and Executive Officials Elected at Sub-National and Local Level, CDL-AD(2019)007 (2019).

term limits for a particular office would not prevent populist leaders from guiding their governing parties from alternative posts or unofficial positions,[11] but they do at least restrict de jure concentration of power over long periods of time, and create opportunities for rivalries within a populist party to weaken its threat to competitive democracy. The Human Rights Committee, which has at times been unduly receptive to the claims of candidates,[12] and the regional courts should clarify their positions on this issue when the occasion arises.

Despite the monitoring bodies' care to exercise impartiality and objectivity, populist governments may seek to reduce their activity, perhaps in partnership with fully authoritarian governments in the related international organization. Human rights bodies can survive lean years when their budgets shrink, maintaining continuity while awaiting more adequate funds. The financing of human rights institutions often depends on a combination of regular budgetary support from their associated international organization and voluntary contributions from member states, outside states, and other public or private entities. Decreases in funding have resulted from economic setbacks, competing priorities, or conscious attempts to manipulate or punish the human rights body.[13] Short-term reductions in funding, whatever their cause, threaten lessened activity, longer backlogs, and decline in effectiveness.[14] Nonetheless, if the cuts are not too deep and the human rights body retains control of its spending choices within the lower amount, it can manage the situation and rebuild later when member states and donors are more willing and able to provide funding. Preserving the quality and objectivity of the body's outputs should be high priorities, and in my opinion they should not be sacrificed to achieving volume.

The more serious threats involve interference with the body's independence, and restraint of its functions. States may seek to impose direct control on the body's members, as in the Russia-led effort to adopt a "code of conduct" subjecting treaty bodies to the Human Rights Council.[15] They may seek procedural revisions to make the body's actions ineffectual in particular types of cases or in general.

---

[11] Cf. Chapter 4 (in this volume).

[12] See *Paksas v. Lithuania*, HRC Communication No. 2155/2012 (March 25, 2014), UN Doc. CCPR/C/110/D/2155/2012; *Arias Leiva v. Colombia*, HRC Communication No. 2537/2015 (July 27, 2018), UN Doc. CCPR/C/123/D/2537/2015.

[13] See, e.g., Raísa Cetra and Jefferson Nascimento, "Counting Coins: Funding the Inter-American Human Rights System," in Camila Barretto Maia et al., *The Inter-American Human Rights System: Changing Times, Ongoing Challenges* (Washington, DC: Due Process of Law Foundation, 2016), 53–94.

[14] See, e.g., Markus Schmidt, "Servicing and Financing Human Rights Supervisory Bodies," in *The Future of UN Human Rights Treaty Monitoring*, ed. Philip Alston and James Crawford (Cambridge: Cambridge University Press, 2000), 482–484.

[15] Suzanne Egan, "Strengthening the United Nations Treaty Body System," *Human Rights Law Review* 13, no. 2 (2013): 233, 242; cf. Philip Alston, "Hobbling the Monitors: Should U.N. Human Rights Monitors be Accountable?," *Harvard International Law Journal* 52, no. 2 (2011): 561–649 (critiquing the earlier code of conduct for mandate holders appointed by the Human Rights Council).

Proposals of this kind portend longer-term impairment of the institution's mandate, and human rights bodies should oppose them as persuasively as they can, enlisting allies where possible.

B *Counterframing against Populist Politics*

Without explicitly condemning populism as such, monitoring bodies can contribute to the struggle against populism by defending the contrasting ideology of universal human rights and by facilitating open political contestation at the national level, where the conflict of ideas must ultimately be won. In the context of discontent with the status quo, populism and human rights provide incompatible perspectives on where the problem lies and how to go about improving it.

Sociologists have emphasized the role of framing in the efforts of social and political movements to persuade citizens to accept their proposals. "[M]ovement adherents negotiate a shared understanding of some problematic condition or situation they define as in need of change, make attributions regarding who or what is to blame, articulate an alternative set of arrangements, and urge others to act in concert to affect change."[16] Populists promote an account in which corrupt elites are to blame for numerous ills, and reassertion of the unconstrained popular will through the leadership of the populists will correct them.[17] Human rights advocates offer competing accounts whose common theme is that unconstrained government power leads to invasion or neglect of universal rights of individuals.

As often in the system of human rights protection, different roles are appropriate for different actors. The monitoring bodies at the universal or regional levels have more generic justifications for the obligations that they enforce. Advocates closer to the ground can particularize their arguments with culturally based references and locally held values that international bodies do not, or even should not, rely on.

For the monitoring bodies, their usual framing of human rights issues addresses the foundations and some of the standard risks of ideational populism. The basic orientation of the human rights system asserts that universal individual rights should constrain the exercise of popular sovereignty, and that the positive law of human rights provides standards by which government action should be judged. More specifically, human rights are possessed by all, and should protect the social groups that populists denigrate and exclude. Democratic governance requires rights constraints and judicial independence, not unlimited pursuit of majority will. Governments must accept criticism and political competition.

The messages of monitoring bodies aim at varied audiences – the populist government itself; its population, including critics and supporters of the government,

---

[16] Robert D. Benford and David A. Snow, "Framing Processes and Social Movements: An Overview and Assessment," *Annual Review of Sociology* 26 (2000): 615.

[17] See, e.g., Paris Aslandis, "Populism and Social Movements," in *The Oxford Handbook of Populism*, ed. Cristóbal Rovira Kaltwasser et al. (Oxford: Oxford University Press, 2017), 309.

and the undecided; and other governments that may be in a stronger position to influence the country in question. However, international bodies often have limited power to persuade the domestic audience. First, most people have little or no knowledge of the texts issued by the monitoring bodies, which may be ignored, filtered, or distorted by local media. Second, populists often condemn international bodies as illegitimate foreign intruders upon the sovereignty of the people, and thus impede the ability of the bodies to communicate effectively.

When a monitoring body's message does reach the domestic audience, its influence may depend on how it aligns with local values. For example, in a context where populists hijack an established democratic culture, defending the right to criticize the government against suppression and retaliation may resonate with the voters, and alert people to risks to their own rights as well.

Most of the work to resist ideational populism, however, must be performed by local actors – human rights defenders, journalists, political opponents, and social movements. Monitoring bodies can support their efforts, and their right to undertake these efforts, but should not expect their advocacy to follow international models. First of all, local advocates are not bound by norms of neutrality and expertise that monitoring bodies profess; they are free to engage politically and to make openly emotional appeals.[18] Second, societies differ in their receptivity to a discourse of internationally protected human rights. In some countries, the very notion of individual rights lacks currency among most of the population. In other countries, prior mobilization for rights against authoritarian governments has resulted in broader awareness and the embedding of the international treaties in the domestic legal regime. For yet others, rights discourse is familiar but it focuses on a national canon of rights that only partly reflects the international regime.

In fact, even where international obligations are fully reflected in domestic law, the national versions of universal norms may be more relevant in domestic political debate. The subsidiarity of the human rights regime normally allows states to comply with treaty obligations by respecting adequate constitutional or statutory equivalents, and requires them to elaborate more detailed implementation measures, rather than merely copy treaty provisions verbatim into domestic law.

For these and other reasons, local critics of populist governments will have local discourses that they can employ instead of or alongside the international rights discourse. National rights and national values may supply framings that are more persuasive to a wider audience in periods of populist rule.[19] Monitoring bodies that lack fluency in these local dialects have little standing to contest a government's

---

[18] See Chapter 9 (in this volume); César Rodríguez-Garavito and Krizna Gomez, "Responding to the Populist Challenge: A New Playbook for the Human Rights Field," in César Rodríguez-Garavito and Krizna Gomez, *Rising to the Populist Challenge: A New Playbook for Human Rights Actors* (Bogotá: Dejusticia, 2018), 39.

[19] See Rodríguez-Garavito and Gomez, "Populist Challenge," 36–38.

understanding of its own culture, and local actors are better positioned to mount such challenges.

Populists have one inherent vulnerability, which has led some authors to hope that populism may be self-limiting.[20] Once populists have governed for a while, they are no longer outsiders defending the people against entrenched elites. They are insiders who present their own dangers. Then both monitoring bodies and local critics can call attention to abuses, and broader risks, each using their own criteria.

Ultimately, successful opposition to populist governments requires locally credible political alternatives. Ideally the alternative will be respectful of universal rights, but rights compliance should be coupled with a particular affirmative vision that attracts voters.

III LEARNING FROM POPULIST CRITIQUES

There may also be important lessons for the human rights system to learn from the current wave of populism. Populist rhetoric often includes explicit attacks on international human rights bodies. These bodies are seen as part of the global elite, or the world government that threatens the nation; their decisions are said to favor the rights of criminals, terrorists, migrants, prisoners, and other enemies over the rights of the people. I do not want to make claims of causation regarding the importance of human rights backlash for the success of populists. Multiple factors contribute to the performance of populists in elections and referenda. Nonetheless, there is value in examining some of the prominent objections, to see what lessons could be learned from them, to reduce the appeal of populists or simply to improve the performance of the human rights system.

A *Rule by Outsiders*

Populists often object that human rights treaties result in the people's being ruled by foreign judges.[21] This objection is to a limited degree true, and inevitable. Ambiguous treaty provisions need to be interpreted, and treaties that provide for binding adjudication give a mixed panel of international judges the responsibility to construe the provisions and thus to specify more fully the obligations of states. Sometimes the judges' decisions require the state to change laws or practices that enjoy popular support. Sometimes even welcome changes are resented when outsiders seem to dictate them.

Monitoring bodies should contradict this narrative of foreign imposition, and human rights advocates should assist them in doing so. Countries ought to take

---

[20] E.g., Paul Taggart, "Populism and Representative Politics in Contemporary Europe," *Journal of Political Ideologies* 9, no. 3 (2004): 284.

[21] See, e.g., Chapter 3 (in this volume).

ownership of their human rights obligations, and to recognize them as principles they have agreed to be guided by, for their own protection. The principles should be defended on their own terms, but also as the products of consent. In agreeing to transnational adjudication, states are accepting the authority of external institutions to enforce obligations that a current majority may no longer want – that is the purpose of a human rights treaty. It protects current minorities against present harm, and members of current majorities against future harm. Transnational decisionmaking inherently involves sharing authority with foreign actors – that is a mutual benefit that should be defended. It protects the stability of the system of rights against local reversals, and it gives the state a reciprocal opportunity to protect rights in its neighbors.

The theme of consented obligation faces further challenge, however, when populists not only attack foreign judges but condemn as corrupt the prior governments that accepted them. Moreover, the strength of the consent argument may depend on how far the monitoring body has strayed from the text it is construing, supplemented by later articulations of its meaning. The more normative creativity a monitoring body exercises, the more it leaves itself vulnerable to the critique of lack of consent, and the more it needs to be prepared to defend its normative choices convincingly.

It should also be emphasized that the intervention of foreign judges relates only to a limited set of constraints on government policy. For some audiences, any interference by outsiders with a substantial public decision threatens popular sovereignty. But others will be more sensitive to the breadth of authority that foreign judges exercise. Just as the European Union's expanding regulatory authority has been perceived as crowding out domestic politics in member states,[22] the scope of jurisdiction claimed by monitoring bodies – individually, and by the human rights regime as a whole – is relevant to their defense.

Particularly at a time when attacks on well-established human rights principles are increasing, some monitoring bodies need to consider whether they should be more cautious about discovering new ones. The continual recognition of new rights and obligations in more fields of public and private activity may represent progress for human rights, but not if they merely widen the gap between rights in theory and rights in reality.

B *Neglect of Economic and Social Rights*

One relevant failing of the human rights system may lie in its inadequate enforcement of economic and social rights. Analysts have identified economic hardship and inequality as a contributing factor in the rise of populism – both on the left and on

---

[22] See, e.g., Gareth Davies, "Democracy and Legitimacy in the Shadow of Purposive Competence," *European Law Journal* 21, no. 1 (2015): 2–22.

the right – in various countries (though not all).[23] Philip Alston argues that economic and social rights have been marginalized, with "deeply negative consequences for the potential of the human rights movement to gain the widespread support that it needs in order to establish its credibility in the eyes of the literally billions of people whose fundamental needs continue to be of only minor relevance to the core human rights agenda."[24] Could that failing be corrected?

Three different sources of that failing should be distinguished here.[25] First, some human rights treaties explicitly disfavor economic and social rights, by making them progressively realizable, by subjecting them to resource constraints, or by assigning them weaker mechanisms of enforcement. Second, some softening of economic and social rights enforcement arises from treaty interpretation rather than explicit treaty language. Third, given the wide variation in wealth among states in the international system, treaties that focus on the obligations of states to their own populations do not ensure the availability of funds needed for adequate implementation.

These defects of the regime could be addressed by changes to the treaties or by changes to the interpretation and application of the treaties. The former requires the joint action of states, for which many political barriers need to be overcome; the latter may be attempted by monitoring bodies within their present frameworks. Monitoring bodies may articulate cross-border obligations to pay for the realization of economic and social rights in other states, as the Committee on Economic, Social and Cultural Rights has long done, but no monitoring body has been entrusted with the power to make such global redistribution happen.

Recent developments in the Inter-American human rights system may illustrate the upgrading of economic and social rights within existing treaties. Apparently in response to the criticisms made by left-populist states, the Inter-American Commission on Human Rights created the position of a special rapporteurship on economic and social rights in 2014.[26] That new mandate may also be seen as a counterpoint to the U.S.-funded special rapporteurship on freedom of expression, to which those countries had strongly objected.[27] Then in 2017, the Inter-American Court

---

[23] See Chapter 1 (in this volume).

[24] [Philip Alston], Report of the Special Rapporteur on extreme poverty and human rights, UN Doc. A/HRC/32/31 (2016), 9. Ruth Okediji made this point eloquently as a panelist at the conference that preceded the writing of this volume. See also Philip Alston, "The Populist Challenge to Human Rights," *Journal of Human Rights Practice* 9, no. 1 (2017): 6 ("[A] renewed focus on social rights and on diminishing inequality must be part of a new human rights agenda which promises to take into account the concerns ... of those who feel badly done by as a result of what we loosely call globalization-driven economic change.").

[25] I leave aside for present purposes a fourth factor discussed by Alston, the priorities of certain international NGOs.

[26] See Annual Report of the Special Rapporteur on Economic, Social, Cultural and Environmental Rights (SRESCER), OEA/Ser.L/V/II. Doc. 10 (2017), 5. The Commission finally dedicated the necessary funds and filled the position in 2017. Annual Report, 5–7.

[27] See Katya Salazar, "Between Reality and Appearances," *Aportes DPLf* 19 (April 2014): 17–18. Since 2017, economic and political crises in Venezuela have weakened the regional influence of left populism, at least for the present, while some other countries have shifted to the right.

of Human Rights reversed its prior interpretation of the American Convention on Human Rights, greatly expanding the justiciability of economic and social rights (by means of the generally worded article 26 ACHR).[28] These initiatives are too recent to evaluate their consequences. The Commission's soft-law rapporteurship is unlikely to appease left-populists, but a rebalancing of the Commission's activities may lessen the persuasiveness of their arguments to others in the OAS. It remains to be seen how the Inter-American Court will define the hard-law obligations of states to implement economic and social rights under the American Convention, and how much compliance its orders will receive if they require expensive changes in policy. The results will also test the limits of a human rights court's ability to champion economic and social rights by redefining its own mandate, in a region that includes both left-populist and right-populist governments.

It also bears recalling that the two wealthiest states in the region, the United States and Canada, are not subject to the Inter-American Court's jurisdiction. Even if the United States were not undergoing its own right-populist crisis, under the banner of "America First," the Court would not be in a position to order North-to-South transfers. Ultimately, within the Americas as in the larger world, the effects of unequal national wealth on economic and social rights will need to be addressed by the joint action of states.

C Overprotecting Criminals

Particular claims that human rights bodies overprotect unpopular groups may merely be hateful rhetoric, but examination sometimes reveals elements of valid concern within them.[29] Human rights institutions should not disregard such objections to their rulings without reflection.

The fundamental principle of international human rights law is that every human being has rights, and populist movements that seek to deny that principle are essentially rejecting the system. They should not be followed. Not all populist critiques, however, depend on denying a right altogether.

While protection of minorities is one major rationale for human rights law, protecting the rights of everyone means protecting the rights of non-minority

---

[28] See *Lagos del Campo v. Peru*, 340 Inter-Am. Ct. H.R. (ser. C) (2017); Isaac de Paz González, *The Social Rights Jurisprudence in the Inter-American Court of Human Rights: Shadow and Light in International Human Rights* (Cheltenham: Edward Elgar, 2018), chapter 6. Article 26 ACHR provides: "The States Parties undertake to adopt measures, both internally and through international cooperation, especially those of an economic and technical nature, with a view to achieving progressively, by legislation or other appropriate means, the full realization of the rights implicit in the economic, social, educational, scientific and cultural standards set forth in the Charter of the Organization of American States as amended by the Protocol of Buenos Aires."

[29] See Chapter 3 (in this volume).

individuals as well. Most human rights are subject to justified limitation for the purpose of directly protecting the rights of others, and also for certain more general purposes that are indirectly related to the rights of others (such as "national security"). Both the rights and the limitations are important.

A common populist objection to the human rights system maintains that human rights bodies give too much weight to the rights of criminals. Once more, claims that people identified as criminals do not deserve to have human rights at all should be repudiated. Yet claims of excessive weight, or excessive attention, need not take that form.

Some populists complain that monitoring bodies focus exclusively on the rights of criminals. Thus, "the only people who benefit are self-serving lawyers and the criminal classes."[30] Taken literally, this objection badly mischaracterizes contemporary human rights law.

For example, human rights law places great emphasis on the rights of victims, including victims of private crime, and some authors have argued that human rights law goes too far in the opposite direction of encouraging criminal sanctions for a wide range of harms.[31]

Although monitoring bodies rarely lose sight altogether of victims of crime, the greater risk may be that in particular decisions adjudicators will strike the wrong balance between competing interests. That concern requires a differentiated response. First, the structure of human rights litigation often presents a monitoring body with a bilateral dispute between a complainant alleging to be the victim of a human rights violation and the state alleged to have violated the victim's right. In the broader factual context, the complainant may be both a victim and a perpetrator, and the complainant's victim or victims may not be represented in the litigation; indeed there may be no procedural opportunity for the complainant's victim to learn about the litigation.

Some complainants are only suspected perpetrators, or were convicted in trials of dubious fairness, while other complainants are concededly perpetrators. Even a conceded perpetrator can still be a victim of a human rights violation. A few human rights are, and should be, absolute. Torture is the primary example here: the decision to outlaw torture absolutely as a method of investigation is a basic commitment of human rights conventions, and it should not be regarded as treating anyone else's rights as unimportant.

Other methods of law enforcement, however, either for investigation or for prevention, may involve rights that are protected in qualified terms, or explicitly

---

[30] Leo McKinstry, "Human Right's Act [sic] Has Become the Villain's Charter," *Express*, October 3, 2011, www.express.co.uk/comment/columnists/leo-mckinstry/275220/Human-right-s-act-has-become-the-villain-s-charter.

[31] See, e.g., *Anti-Impunity and the Human Rights Agenda*, ed. Karen Engle, Zinaida Miller, and D.M. Davis (Cambridge: Cambridge University Press, 2016).

subject to limitation.[32] In determining violations of those rights, monitoring bodies should make clear that they are not disproportionately restricting the government's response to criminal activity, and in particular that they recognize the need to protect the rights of others. As a matter of substance, this recognition should inform the reasoning that leads to a finding of violation. As a matter of exposition – and especially when faced with this type of critique – there would be value in making explicit for readers the decision's attention to the rights of nonparticipating victims.

D *Migration*

Issues of migration law provide another common populist focus, in Europe and elsewhere,[33] given the xenophobic character of many populist movements. Populists incite hostility to immigrants who are already present in their societies, but also raise fear of uncontrolled migration. They object to human rights decisions that limit the expulsion of noncitizens who have violated the law, and decisions that they see as increasing the arrivals of unwanted migrants.[34] There may be important lessons for some monitoring bodies to learn in this area.

The human rights treaties recognize the legitimate authority of states, within certain limits, to regulate migration. Monitoring bodies have confirmed this principle as a general matter.[35] The treaties do not require states to open their labor markets to the world, and they do not require small states to submerge their identity in their larger neighbors. At the same time, migrants are human beings with rights, and the treaties restrict how states treat people within their jurisdiction. A few treaty

---

[32] See, e.g., ICCPR art. 17(1) (prohibiting arbitrary or unlawful interference with privacy, family, home, and correspondence); European Convention on Human Rights and Fundamental Freedoms, art. 8(2) (permitting interference with private and family life, home, and correspondence where necessary for enumerated purposes).

[33] See, e.g., Carlo Ruzza, "Populism, Migration and Xenophobia in Europe," in *Routledge Handbook of Global Populism*, ed. Carlos de la Torre (Abingdon: Routledge, 2019), 201–215; Dani Filc, "Populism in the Middle East," in *Routledge Handbook*, 393–398 (discussing Israel); Benjamin Moffitt, "Populism in Australia and New Zealand," in *Oxford Handbook of Populism*, 121–139.

[34] See, e.g., Siobhán Lloyd, "Deportation and the Human Rights Act 1998: Debunking the Myths," in *Critically Examining the Case Against the 1998 Human Rights Act*, ed. Frederick Cowell (Abingdon: Routledge, 2018), 136–150; David Mead, "'You Couldn't Make it Up': Some Narratives of the Media's Coverage of Human Rights," in *The UK and European Human Rights: A Strained Relationship?*, ed. Katja Ziegler, Elizabeth Wicks, and Loveday Hodson (Oxford: Hart, 2015), 453–472.

[35] See, e.g., *Paposhvili v. Belgium*, App. no. 41738/10, ECHR (2016) [GC], para. 172; *Vélez-Loor v. Panama*, 218 Inter-Am. Ct. H.R. (ser. C) (2010), para. 97; Communication 292/04, *Institute for Human Rights and Development in Africa v. Angola*, African Commission on Human and Peoples' Rights (2008), para 84; Human Rights Committee, General comment No. 15 (The position of aliens under the Covenant) (1986), in Compilation of General Comments and General Recommendations Adopted by Human Rights Treaty Bodies, UN Doc. HRI/GEN/1/Rev.9 (Vol. I) (2008), para. 5.

norms, like the prohibition against torture, are absolute, but most norms elaborate rights as subject to proportionate limitation.

Populist criticisms of human rights decisions take a variety of forms. Some argue that control of migration is a fundamental power of state sovereignty not subject to human rights limitations; some complain that certain human rights doctrines do not allow due consideration of the interests of states and their citizens in border control; and some make case-specific challenges that an individual decision has struck the wrong balance between the interests of a migrant, typically one convicted of crime or accused of terrorism, and the interests of others.

The sweeping argument that sovereignty precludes all limitations on migration control misconceives human rights principles in general and the various human rights treaties. Monitoring bodies should be aware that such arguments exist but should firmly refute them. As for the case-specific claims, it is harder to generalize. Some criticisms may indeed have merit, and others bring to light the body's failure to adequately explain its reasoning. Yet others are mistaken, biased, or deliberately distorted. Sometimes hard cases make bad journalism.

The critiques of doctrines deserve closer attention here. The Convention Against Torture contains an explicit provision against returning migrants to states where they risk being tortured, which is absolute and exceptionless; monitoring bodies under other human rights treaties have construed prohibitions of torture and comparable ill-treatment as including a similar ban.[36] The European Court of Human Rights has expressly rejected states' arguments to qualify or dilute this ban in cases involving terrorism, emphasizing the centrality of the prohibition of torture.[37] The court also applies this absolute ban to risks of violation of the right to life, in view of its particularly fundamental nature,[38] and in certain exceptional cases to the risk of "flagrant" violations of the core of the rights to fair trial and against arbitrary detention.[39]

Going beyond these narrow rules, human rights advocates make some very broad arguments about state obligations to receive migrants, including arguments for absolute rules that prevent return of irregular migrants to their own country, and absolute rules that preclude traditional methods of migration enforcement. Some monitoring bodies have taken positions favorable to such arguments,

---

[36] See, e.g., *Soering* v. *United Kingdom*, 161 Eur. Ct. H.R. (ser. A) (1989); Human Rights Committee, General Comment No. 31 (The Nature of the General Legal Obligation Imposed on States Parties to the Covenant), para. 12 (2004); Advisory Opinion OC-21/14, Rights and guarantees of children in the context of migration and/or in need of international protection, 21 Inter-Am. Ct. H.R. (ser. A) (2014), paras. 225–226.

[37] See, e.g., *Saadi* v. *United Kingdom*, App. no. 37201/06, ECHR (2008) [GC], paras. 127, 137–141.

[38] See, e.g., *Al-Saadoon and Mufdhi* v. *United Kingdom*, App. no. 61498/08, ECHR (2010), para. 138.

[39] See *El-Masri* v. *"Former Yugoslav Republic of Macedonia,"* App. no. 39630/09, ECHR (2012) [GC]; *Harkins* v. *United Kingdom*, App. no. 71537/14, ECHR (2017) (dec.) [GC], paras. 62–67 (explaining limits of doctrine).

occasionally with reasoning that disparages the importance of state authority to enforce migration controls.

For example, some monitoring bodies have characterized criminal punishment of irregular migration as prohibited arbitrary detention, on the ground that the state's interest in controlling migration is never sufficient to justify imprisonment. The Inter-American Court of Human Rights,[40] the Committee on Migrant Workers (a treaty body at the global level),[41] and the UN Working Group on Arbitrary Detention (which arguably counts as a monitoring body),[42] have taken this position. The Inter-American Court has further held that a state's interest in enforcing migration rules, which the Court regards as merely of an administrative nature, can never justify expelling an irregular migrant if the migrant has a child who is entitled to the state's nationality or to lawful permanent residence.[43]

These absolute rules are derived from non-absolute rights by means of evaluations of proportionality that categorically deprecate states' interest in controlling migration. The bodies that adopt them do not explore the states' alternative methods for achieving their goals, or examine case-by-case the competing considerations in particular situations, but rather dismiss the state goal as insufficiently important. This

---

[40] *Vélez-Loor v. Panama*, para. 169.

[41] See Committee on the Protection of the Rights of All Migrant Workers and Members of Their Families, General comment No. 2 on the rights of migrant workers in an irregular situation and members of their families, UN Doc. CMW/C/GC/2 (2013), para. 24 (interpreting article 16(4) of the convention, which prohibits arbitrary detention). The Convention on the Protection of the Rights of All Migrant Workers and Members of Their Families, though adopted at the global level in 1990, has fewer than sixty parties.

[42] See, e.g., Working Group on Arbitrary Detention, Basic Principles and Guidelines on the right of anyone deprived of their liberty to bring proceedings before a court, UN Doc. WGAD/CRP.1/2015 (2015), para. 63 ("The deprivation of liberty as a penalty or punitive sanction in the area of immigration control is prohibited."). The WGAD is a body of five independent experts appointed by the UN Human Rights Council as one of its thematic special procedures, for the purpose of promoting the right to be free of arbitrary detention; unusually, it issues formal (though non-binding) opinions on claims of arbitrary detention. See Jared M. Genser, "The Intersection of Politics and International Law: The United Nations Working Group on Arbitrary Detention in Theory and in Practice," *Columbia Human Rights Law Review* 39, no. 3 (2008): 687–755.

[43] Advisory Opinion OC-21/14, para. 280. The child's entitlement to nationality would often result from a *jus soli* law that grants nationality to children born within the state's territory, even when both parents are irregular migrants.

The Committee on the Rights of the Child has taken a comparable stand, though with more ambiguous scope, in a joint general comment with the Committee on Migrant Workers. See Joint general comment no. 4 (2017) of the Committee on the Protection of the Rights of All Migrant Workers and Members of Their Families and No. 23 (2017) of the Committee on the Rights of the Child on State obligations regarding the human rights of children in the context of international migration in countries of origin, transit, destination and return, UN Doc. CMW/C/GC/4-CRC/GC/23 (2017), para. 29.

The European Court of Human Rights, in contrast, gives greater respect to migration rules in comparable situations, even when it finds that the balance between public and private interests should be struck on an exceptional basis in favor of the family. See, e.g., *Jeunesse v. The Netherlands*, App. no. 12737/10, ECHR (2014) [GC].

form of reasoning not only proscribes particular enforcement policies but signals to states that their enforcement efforts will carry similarly little weight in the future.

Monitoring bodies that seek to offer impartial and authoritative analysis should not be dismissive of the countervailing interests in cases of this kind. The limited scope of freedom of movement in the human rights treaties reflects basic rules of international law and the structure of the international system as it currently exists, rather than an imagined borderless world. As in the situation of criminal law, a state's general interest in regulating migration indirectly serves the aggregated human rights of its population.

In the context of populism, minimizing the state interest in migration control may be counterproductive as well as unjustified. International bodies risk reinforcing populist opposition when they openly deny valid reasons their proper role in evaluating politically salient policies. In saying this, I do not mean to overestimate the priority that populists give to legal methodology, or to claim that populists will pay more attention to reasoning than to results. Nonetheless, a monitoring body will face enough populist agitation over results that it can defend, and over case-specific errors. It should not hand populists the target of explicit disregard of important national interests.

E *Extraterritoriality of Rights*

Another subject of accusations in UK polemics in particular involves the extraterritorial application of human rights treaties, especially in situations of armed conflict.[44] Critics have objected that European human rights rulings on that subject have obstructed necessary military operations.[45] Here there genuinely are serious questions that can be raised, regarding who has which rights against which states under the relevant treaties. Over the past two decades, various monitoring bodies

---

[44] See, e.g., Francesca Gillett, "Theresa May Attacks 'Left-Wing Human Rights Lawyers Harassing UK Troops,'" *Evening Standard*, October 5, 2016, www.standard.co.uk/news/uk/theresa-may-attacks-leftwing-human-rights-lawyers-harassing-uk-troops-a3361716.html.

    The problem of extraterritoriality is also relevant to populist agitation over migration law, when monitoring bodies interpret treaties as limiting states' efforts to extend border control beyond their borders, notably by high seas operations in the Mediterranean. See *Hirsi Jamaa v. Italy*, App. no. 27765/09, ECHR (2012) [GC]; when *Hirsi Jamaa* was decided, Matteo Salvini of the Lega Nord condemned the judgment as "crazy." See "European Court Verdict Prompts Italy Immigration 'Re-think,'" *Agence France Press*, February 23, 2012, Nexis Uni; see also John Finnis, "Judicial Power: Past, Present and Future," in *Judicial Power and the Balance of Our Constitution: Two Lectures by John Finnis*, ed. Richard Ekins (London: Policy Exchange, 2018), 56–58 (denying the legitimacy of the judgment). The Inter-American Court of Human Rights also construes its regional convention as applying extraterritorially to migration control. See Advisory Opinion OC-21/14, paras. 219–220; Advisory Opinion OC-25/18, The institution of asylum, and its recognition as a human right under the Inter-American System of Protection (interpretation and scope of Articles 5, 22(7) and 22(8) in relation to Article 1(1) of the American Convention on Human Rights), 25 Inter-Am. Ct. H.R. (ser. A) (2018), paras. 171–177.

[45] See, e.g., Richard Ekins, "Lawfare against the Armed Forces Must Be on the Next Government's Agenda," May 15, 2017, https://policyexchange.org.uk/lawfare-against-the-armed-forces-must-be-on-the-next-governments-agenda/.

have been redefining the circumstances under which human rights treaties restrict extraterritorial interference with the asserted rights of foreign nationals. In part, the monitoring bodies have been broadening their interpretations of the concept of "jurisdiction," which some treaties make a precondition for applying a right as between a state and an individual. In part, the disputes concern the relationship between a state's obligations under a human rights treaty and its obligation under other fields of international law, such as the international humanitarian law that applies in armed conflicts.

The European Court of Human Rights famously avoided a challenge to the NATO bombing of Belgrade during the Kosovo intervention in its *Banković* decision of 2001.[46] The Court held that the air strikes did not bring Serbian victims within the "jurisdiction" of the NATO states, and therefore they were not protected by the set of rights in the European Convention. The decision produced controversy, and some critics argued that all individuals affected by a state's extraterritorial action should be protected by all human rights. Not surprisingly, governments engaged in military action abroad, including for humanitarian purposes, have favored narrower interpretations of the reach of human rights treaties.

The European Court revised its approach a decade later, applying some rights to British actions during the occupation of Iraq. Notably, the court abandoned the assumption in *Banković* that extraterritorial application presented a binary choice, and concluded instead that the set of Convention rights can be "divided and tailored" as relevant to the situation of a particular extraterritorial exercise of jurisdiction.[47] Nonetheless, in *Al-Jedda* v. *United Kingdom*, the Court rigidly applied the unusual structure of Article 5 of the Convention to British detention in occupied Iraq. Unlike other major treaties on civil and political rights, which prohibit arbitrary detention in general terms,[48] Article 5 contains a short list of the permissible grounds for deprivation of liberty of person, which the European Court has interpreted as exclusive. That list does not include the detention of prisoners of war or other categories traditional in armed conflict. The court held in *Al-Jedda* that detention for security purposes violated Article 5, and would be consistent with the Convention only if the United Kingdom had made a formal derogation from Article 5 under the emergency clause of the Convention.[49]

---

[46] *Banković* v. *Belgium et al.*, 2001-XI Eur. Ct. H.R., App. no. 52207/99 (dec.) [GC].

[47] *Al-Skeini* v. *United Kingdom*, App. no. 55721/07, ECHR (2011) [GC], para. 137.

[48] Compare ICCPR art. 9(1); African Charter of Human and Peoples' Rights, art. 6; ACHR art. 7(3).

[49] *Al-Jedda* v. *United Kingdom*, App. no. 27021/08, ECHR (2011) [GC], para. 99. The Court also found that the European Convention obligation had not been displaced by an order from the Security Council, which did not explicitly order the United Kingdom to detain individuals without regard to Article 5. *Al-Jedda* v. *UK*, paras. 102–109. For criticism of the *Al-Jedda* decision from the perspective of international humanitarian law, see Jelena Pejic, "The European Court of Human Rights' *Al-Jedda* Judgment: The Oversight of International Humanitarian Law," *International Red Cross Review* 93 (2011): 837–851.

Meanwhile advocates and some monitoring bodies have pursued more expansive interpretations of extraterritorial rights, seemingly on the assumption that if a right is universal then all individuals worldwide must be able to assert the right against any state that is in a position to affect its enjoyment. These interpretations extend far beyond individuals subject to a state's governance or in its custody; they impose duties to protect the rights of people over whom the state exercises no authority, not only against the state itself but against interference by third parties that the state can influence.[50]

The UK government has repeatedly argued in Strasbourg that extraterritorial application of European human rights law to situations of armed conflict is both impracticable and legally inappropriate. These arguments achieved partial success in *Hassan v. United Kingdom*, where the Grand Chamber modified its interpretation of Article 5. The majority held that during international armed conflict, where the Third and Fourth Geneva Conventions applied, states did not need to lodge derogations in order to engage in detention contemplated by those Conventions.[51] The dissenting judges protested that the court was retreating from its prior approach, in a manner that could not be reconciled with the wording of Article 5.[52] Indeed, the *Hassan* judgment pays greater attention to consistency with international humanitarian law and the realities of extraterritorial operations, and less to textual literalism and the internal consistency of the court's own constructions. As the UK Supreme Court subsequently observed, the European Court had broadened the scope of the Convention by an evolutive interpretation of "jurisdiction," and then recognized the necessity of adapting the interpretation of Article 5 to the resulting dilemma.[53] One UK judge added that the European Convention's "very credibility was at stake" in determining whether it could accommodate the exigencies of an armed conflict.[54] The wavering

---

[50] See, e.g., Committee on Economic, Social and Cultural Rights, General Comment No. 24 (2017) on State obligations under the International Covenant on Economic, Social and Cultural Rights in the context of business activities, UN Doc. E/C.12/GC/24 (2017), paras. 25–37; Committee on the Rights of the Child, General comment No. 16 (2013) on State obligations regarding the impact of the business sector on children's rights, UN Doc. CRC/C/GC/16 (2013), paras. 43–46. Advisory Opinion OC-23/17, The Environment and Human Rights (State obligations in relation to the environment in the context of the protection and guarantee of the rights to life and to personal integrity – interpretation and scope of Articles 4(1) and 5(1) of the American Convention on Human Rights), 23 Inter-Am. Ct. H.R. (ser. A) (2017), paras. 95–104; Human Rights Committee, General Comment No. 36 (2018), on article 6 of the International Covenant on Civil and Political Rights, on the right to life, UN Doc. CCPR/C/GC/36 (2018) (advance unedited version), para. 22.

[51] *Hassan v. United Kingdom*, App. no. 29750/09 (2014) [GC], paras. 101–104.

[52] *Hassan v. UK* (partly dissenting opinion of Judge Spano joined by Judges Nicolaou, Bianku, and Kalaydjieva).

[53] *Al-Waheed v. Ministry of Defence*, [2017] UKSC 2 (2017) (extending *Hassan* to non-international armed conflicts in Iraq and Afghanistan).

[54] *Al-Waheed v. Ministry of Defence*, para. 143 (judgment of Lord Wilson). On the political context, see also Fionnuala Ní Aoláin, "To Detain Lawfully or Not to Detain: Reflections on UK Supreme Court Decision in Serdar Mohammed," *Just Security*, February 2, 2017, www.justsecurity.org/37013/detain-lawfully-detain-question-reflection-uk-supreme-court-decision-serdar-mohammed/.

course of adjudication in this line of cases may point toward the need for greater caution and closer analysis in the extraterritorial expansion of human rights. Quick and simple answers may not provide viable solutions for complex problems that combine attenuated state authority and multiple fields of international law.

F No Panacea

What follows if monitoring bodies conclude that some populist objections to particular decisions or doctrines may have some accuracy? Perhaps less than we might hope. There may be lessons that would help the monitoring bodies avoid similar errors in the future, and not supply new fuel to populist fires.

I do not claim that changing erroneous interpretations would, as a byproduct, eliminate populists' concerns and undermine public support for populists. Once populist attacks have been unleashed, their rhetoric often operates at a level that can gloss over changes in factual reality. Moreover, monitoring bodies are unlikely to agree with all of the populists' criticisms, and the disputes that continue will provide targets for polemics.

Furthermore, once exclusionary populists come to power, they are likely to acquire new reasons for quarreling with monitoring bodies. As candidates they may have appreciated an open political system and their own freedom of expression, but as rulers they may seek to entrench their power and to deny those opportunities to others.

Still, monitoring bodies should not complacently attribute all criticism of their work to bias and distortion. They should be prepared to justify their conclusions, and they should be open to reconsideration of their interpretations when strong reasons appear, while having regard to the stability of the system

The preceding discussion seeks to make certain that human rights bodies can conscientiously deny the populists' accusations. That assurance would be valuable even if it would not be sufficient to defeat unscrupulous opponents in public debate.

IV CONCLUSION

Human rights monitoring bodies play a crucial role in the international human rights system, articulating the content of states' legal obligations and evaluating the actual conduct of states in relation to those obligations. These evaluations may be formulated as definite findings of fact and conclusions of law, or as advisory expressions of concern and recommendations. To achieve effect, monitoring bodies need responsive partners, within the government, within civil society, or within the governments of other states, and preferably all three.

The current wave of exclusionary populism poses great challenges to this process, and at a time when the human rights system faces other challenges from the increasing influence of fully authoritarian states such as China and Russia. Populist governments seek to deflect external criticism and delegitimate internal opposition. The simultaneous advance of populism in the governments of states that had traditionally been key supporters of the human rights system undermines the mechanisms of intergovernmental pressure and assistance. It may also portend inroads on their budgets and their activities.

Monitoring bodies cannot solve the problem of exclusionary populism, but they can contribute to the solutions, which will vary with local circumstances. One common factor that monitoring bodies provide is their engagement in truth-telling. They complicate the simple narrative that populists try to convey, and bring to bear internationally recognized values. The impartial and expert determinations of independent institutions address both domestic and foreign audiences. The bodies need to maintain their objectivity and expertise for that purpose.

To that end, the monitoring bodies should focus on the harms that accompany populism, and not the characterization of populism as such. They should defend human rights principles, including the expressive and political rights that enable internal critics to mount legitimate opposition. Those domestic activists can supplement universal principles with culturally specific advocacy that has greater local resonance.

At the same time, monitoring bodies and the human rights system more generally should listen to the grievances of populists, and should not assume their own infallibility. Some objections are flatly inconsistent with human rights principles, but others may point to failures of reasoning or of explanation that monitoring bodies should correct. Certain failings may be beyond the power of monitoring bodies to change, such as global economic inequality, and require the attention of states.

The rise of populism, especially in the United States and Europe, raises serious concerns about the future of democracy, human rights, and the character of international cooperation. The trend needs to be opposed on multiple fronts, in multiple ways. Human rights monitoring bodies and their allies should be alert to the challenges, and attentive to their complexity.

BIBLIOGRAPHY

Alston, Philip. "Hobbling the Monitors: Should U.N. Human Rights Monitors be Accountable?" *Harvard International Law Journal* 52, no. 2 (2011): 561–649.
   Report of the Special Rapporteur on extreme poverty and human rights. UN Doc. A/HRC/ 32/31 (2016).
   "The Populist Challenge to Human Rights." *Journal of Human Rights Practice* 9, no. 1 (2017): 1–15.
Annual Report of the Special Rapporteur on Economic, Social, Cultural and Environmental Rights (SRESCER). OEA/Ser.L/V/II. Doc. 10 (2017).
Aoláin, Fionnuala Ní. "To Detain Lawfully or Not to Detain: Reflections on UK Supreme Court Decision in Serdar Mohammed." *Just Security*, February 2, 2017. www.justsecurity .org/37013/detain-lawfully-detain-question-reflection-uk-supreme-court-decision-serdar- mohammed/.

Aslandis, Paris. "Populism and Social Movements." In *The Oxford Handbook of Populism*, ed. Cristóbal Rovira Kaltwasser et al., 305–325. Oxford: Oxford University Press, 2017.

Benford, Robert D., and David A. Snow. "Framing Processes and Social Movements: An Overview and Assessment." *Annual Review of Sociology* 26 (2000): 611–639.

Cetra, Raísa, and Jefferson Nascimento, "Counting Coins: Funding the Inter-American Human Rights System." In Camila Barretto Maia et al., *The Inter-American Human Rights System: Changing Times, Ongoing Challenges*, 53–94. Washington, DC: Due Process of Law Foundation, 2016.

Davies, Gareth. "Democracy and Legitimacy in the Shadow of Purposive Competence." *European Law Journal* 21, no. 1 (2015): 2–22.

De Cleen, Benjamin. "Populism, Exclusion, Post-truth. Some Conceptual Caveats." *International Journal of Health Policy and Management* 7, no. 3 (2018): 268–271.

de Paz González, Isaac. *The Social Rights Jurisprudence in the Inter-American Court of Human Rights: Shadow and Light in International Human Rights*. Cheltenham: Edward Elgar, 2018.

Egan, Suzanne. "Strengthening the United Nations Treaty Body System." *Human Rights Law Review* 13, no. 2 (2013): 209–243.

Ekins, Richard. "Lawfare Against the Armed Forces Must Be on the Next Government's Agenda," May 15, 2017. https://policyexchange.org.uk/lawfare-against-the-armed-forces-must-be-on-the-next-governments-agenda/.

Engle, Karen, Zinaida Miller, and D.M. Davis, eds. *Anti-Impunity and the Human Rights Agenda*. Cambridge: Cambridge University Press, 2016.

European Commission for Democracy Through Law. Report on Term-Limits: Part I – Presidents, CDL-AD (2018)010 (2018).

Report on Term-Limits: Part II – Members of Parliament; Part III – Representatives Elected at Sub-National and Local Level and Executive Officials Elected at Sub-National and Local Level, CDL-AD (2019)007 (2019).

European Court Verdict Prompts Italy Immigration "Re-think." Agence France Press, February 23, 2012, Nexis Uni.

Filc, Dani. "Populism in the Middle East." In *Routledge Handbook of Global Populism*, ed. Carlos de la Torre, 385–401. Abingdon: Routledge, 2019.

Finnis, John. "Judicial Power: Past, Present and Future." In *Judicial Power and the Balance of Our Constitution: Two Lectures by John Finnis*, ed. Richard Ekins, 26–61. London: Policy Exchange, 2018.

Genser, Jared M. "The Intersection of Politics and International Law: The United Nations Working Group on Arbitrary Detention in Theory and in Practice." *Columbia Human Rights Law Review* 39, no. 3 (2008): 687–755.

Gillett, Francesca. Theresa May Attacks 'Left-Wing Human Rights Lawyers Harassing UK Troops.' *Evening Standard*, October 5, 2016. www.standard.co.uk/news/uk/theresa-may-attacks-leftwing-human-rights-lawyers-harassing-uk-troops-a3361716.html.

Ginsburg, Tom, James Melton, and Zachary Elkins. "On the Evasion of Executive Term Limits." *William and Mary Law Review* 52, no. 6 (2011), 1807–1872.

Landau, David. "Presidential Term Limits in Latin America: A Critical Analysis of the Migration of the Unconstitutional Constitutional Amendment Doctrine." *Law and Ethics of Human Rights* 12, no. 2 (2018): 225–249.

Lloyd, Siobhán. "Deportation and the Human Rights Act 1998: Debunking the Myths." In *Critically Examining the Case Against the 1998 Human Rights Act*, ed. Frederick Cowell, 136–150. Abingdon: Routledge, 2018.

McKinstry, Leo. Human Right's Act [sic] Has Become the Villain's Charter. *Express*, October 23, 2011.

Mead, David. "'You Couldn't Make it Up': Some Narratives of the Media's Coverage of Human Rights." In *The UK and European Human Rights: A Strained Relationship?*, ed. Katja Ziegler, Elizabeth Wicks, and Loveday Hodson, 453–472. Oxford: Hart, 2015.

Moffitt, Benjamin. "Populism in Australia and New Zealand." In *The Oxford Handbook of Populism*, ed. Cristóbal Rovira Kaltwasser et al., 121–139. Oxford: Oxford University Press, 2017.

Müller, Jan-Werner. *What Is Populism?* Philadelphia, PA: University of Pennsylvania Press, 2016.

Neuman, Gerald L. "Giving Meaning and Effect to Human Rights: The Contributions of Human Rights Committee Members." In *The Human Rights Covenants at 50: Their Past, Present, and Future*, ed. Daniel Moeckli, Helen Keller, and Corina Heri. Oxford: Oxford University Press, 2018.

Pauwels, Teun. "Measuring Populism: A Review of Current Approaches." In *Political Populism: A Handbook*, ed. Reinhard C. Heinisch, Christina Holtz-Bacha, and Oscar Mazzoleni, 123–136. Baden-Baden: Nomos, 2017.

Pejic, Jelena. "The European Court of Human Rights' *Al-Jedda* Judgment: The Oversight of International Humanitarian Law." *International Red Cross Review* 93 (2011): 837–851.

Rodríguez-Garavito, César, and Krizna Gomez. "Responding to the Populist Challenge: A New Playbook for the Human Rights Field." In *A New Playbook for Human Rights Actors*, ed. César Rodríguez-Garavito and Krizna Gomez, 11–53. Bogotá: Dejusticia, 2018, 39.

Ruzza, Carlo. "Populism, Migration and Xenophobia in Europa." In *Routledge Handbook of Global Populism*, ed. Carlos de la Torre, 201–215. Abingdon: Routledge, 2019.

Salazar, Katya. "Between Reality and Appearances." *Aportes DPLf* 19 (April 2014): 16–19.

Schmidt, Markus. "Servicing and Financing Human Rights Supervisory Bodies." In *The Future of UN Human Rights Treaty Monitoring*, ed. Philip Alston and James Crawford, 482–484. Cambridge: Cambridge University Press, 2000.

Steger, Wayne. "Populist Waves in the 2016 Presidential Nominations: Another Limit to the Party Decides Thesis." In *The State of the Parties, 2018*, ed. John C. Green, Daniel J. Coffey, and David B. Cohen. Lanham, MD: Rowman & Littlefield, 2018.

Taggart, Paul. "Populism and Representative Politics in Contemporary Europe." *Journal of Political Ideologies* 9, no. 3 (2004): 269–288.

Index